THE

Genealogist's Virtual Library

THE

Genealogist's Virtual Library

FULL-TEXT BOOKS ON THE WORLD WIDE WEB

THOMAS JAY KEMP

SR *Scholarly Resources Inc.*
Wilmington, Delaware

© 2000 by Scholarly Resources Inc.
All rights reserved
First published 2000
Printed and bound in the United States of America

Scholarly Resources Inc.
104 Greenhill Avenue
Wilmington, DE 19805-1897
www.scholarly.com

Library of Congress Cataloging-in-Publication Data

Kemp, Thomas Jay.
    The genealogist's virtual library : full-text books on the World Wide Web /
Thomas Jay Kemp.
       p.   cm.
    Includes bibliographical references.
    ISBN 0-8420-2864-1 (cloth : alk. paper) — ISBN 0-8420-2865-X (pbk. : alk. paper)
    1. Genealogy—Bibliography. 2. Genealogy—Computer network resources. I. Title.
Z5311.K46   2000
[CS9]
025.06'9291'072—dc21   99-088351

∞ The paper used in this publication meets the minimum requirements of the American
National Standard for permanence of paper for printed library materials, Z39.48, 1984.

To my wife, Vi, our children

Andrew and Sarah,

and to my parents,

all lifelong readers in print and on the web

About the Author

THOMAS JAY KEMP, a well-known librarian and archivist, is the chair of the Genealogy Committee of the American Library Association and a past chair of the ALA History Section. He is a member of the board of directors of the Federation of Genealogical Societies and has served as the chair of the Council of National Library and Information Associations and as president of the American Society of Indexers. He is also a life member of the Association for the Bibliography of History, the New York Genealogical and Biographical Society, the New England Archivists, and the New Hampshire Library Association.

He is the author of numerous books and articles including *Virtual Roots: A Guide to Genealogy and Local History on the World Wide Web* (1997), the *International Vital Records Handbook* (4th ed., 2000), and the *Connecticut Researcher's Handbook* (1981). His articles have appeared in *Library Journal, School Library Journal, NAGARA Clearinghouse,* and the Society of American Archivists' *Archival Outlook*.

Contents

Introduction

With the publication of *The Genealogist's Virtual Library: Full-Text Books on the World Wide Web*, researchers have a comprehensive list of books that they can read on the web. The promise of the web has been instant access; its problem has been that search engines bring back too many "matches." Often these partial match web sites contain the terms being researched but have nothing to do with our research interest, or else they are a complete match but the content is shallow and unreliable. This book helps researchers to solve these problems.

The *Genealogist's Virtual Library* is a guide to entire books and materials that have been digitized and made available for free on the Internet. Book chapters, excerpts, and sites that charge to read books online are not included. Researchers can now reliably read, consult, and study thousands of local histories, genealogies, and personal histories that have been published over the past two hundred years. Users of this book may simply point, click, and begin reading the complete text of thousands of family genealogies, biographies, and local histories. The library of tomorrow is here today.

There are now three core tools for keeping current in genealogical and historical research in print and on the web. The *Genealogy Annual: A Bibliography of Published Sources*, published since 1995, is the annual bibliography of genealogical and local history books, serials, and videos. *Virtual Roots: A Guide to Genealogy and Local History on the World Wide Web* provides clear directions to the 1,000+ practical web sites that researchers find most useful. *The Genealogist's Virtual Library* takes the researcher one step further by identifying full-text books that have been digitized and placed on the Internet. It is divided into three sections: FAMILY HISTORIES, LOCAL HISTORIES, and GENERAL SUBJECTS. The section on FAMILY HISTORIES is arranged alphabetically by the major surnames covered in each book; LOCAL HISTORIES is arranged by state and then by locality, while GENERAL SUBJECTS lists digitized books on a wide variety of topics from "African Americans" to "Women" and includes a selection of foreign countries.

Librarians today are focused on providing more and more service online, at no cost to the public. Hundreds of libraries, genealogical and historical societies, and other groups are mounting various levels of research content on their web sites. The Library of Congress launched its enormous *American Memory* project, with a goal of listing millions of records and images by the end of 2000. The University of Michigan began its *Making of America* project in the fall of 1995 and has mounted over 1,600 books and serials and has plans to add 7,500 more titles within the next two years. *Project Gutenberg*, the University of North

Carolina's *Documenting the American South*, and dozens of similar projects are adding to our online research capabilities. These important national sites are dedicated to keeping permanent web addresses—URLs. This commitment underscores the reliability and value of placing these historic books and materials online for researchers to use now and in the future. All URLs cited in this work were accurate and operational as of March 2000. In 1999 the Family History Library launched its online presence, *FamilySearch.Org*™, bringing hundreds of guidebooks and millions of records to the web. Commercial sites such as Ancestry.Com, Broderbund's *GenealogyLibrary.Com*, and Primary Source Media's *City Directories Online* are offering reasonably priced opportunities to access original materials.

Clearly these public and commercial projects have been a success. Scarce documents are now easily located and used by students, historians, and genealogists. The next decades will see a nearly comprehensive digitization of published secondary sources. In many cases, only one copy of these documents has survived. We will see the opening up of items that have seldom been included in the standard bibliographies and available previously to only a few researchers. Moreover, new research genres of detailed sources that have long been hidden in libraries and repositories will become more readily available. For example, in our nation's libraries there are hundreds of thousands of published funeral orations from the eighteenth and nineteenth centuries. These funeral orations contain detailed biographical and genealogical information that have been overlooked by historians and genealogists because they are uncataloged or undercataloged, often grouped under the general terms "sermons" or "pamphlets." The next decades will also see the completion of international digitization projects by medieval, agricultural, and economic historians that will make available a broad range of documents extending genealogical sources well beyond the general barrier of the year 1525 and the beginning of ecclesiastical parish registers.

The nation's first Centennial in 1876 was celebrated at a time of a strong economy and a generation united by winning an intense civil war—a generation with the keen memory of brothers, fathers, and friends lost in battle. It was President Ulysses Grant who encouraged the nation to document our history and launched a surge in genealogy and local history that lasted until the Great Depression of the 1930s. Our Bicentennial in 1976, the publication of Alex Haley's *Roots*, which captured the imagination of the press, coupled with the roaring economy of the 1980s, the rise of the personal computer, and now the popularity of the Internet, has established family history research as one of the universal pursuits in the world today. We are beginning to see the push from both directions as researchers in the old and new worlds tie together genealogies and trace family history through the chain of records across the globe. Having the ability to read thousands of full-text biographies, local histories, and genealogies online is making the world a little smaller and genealogical work much easier.

TJK

Further Suggested Readings

Key Websites

American Memory, Historical Collections for the National Digital Library
http://lcweb2.loc.gov/ammem/ammemhome.html
Library of Congress mega-offering of books, photographs, and other documents

Avalon Project
http://www.yale.edu/lawweb/avalon/avalon.htm
Yale's online book project

Documenting the American South
http://metalab.unc.edu/docsouth/
University of North Carolina's offering, the model for other sites to follow

Electronic Text Center
http://etext.lib.virginia.edu/uvaonline.html
University of Virginia's ambitious project, mounting books in more than ten languages

FamilySearch™
http://www.familysearch.org
The Church of Jesus Christ of Latter-day Saints portal website for genealogical research

Making of America
http://www.umdl.umich.edu/moa/index.html
University of Michigan's project with 1,600 titles projected to grow to 10,000 titles

Project Bartleby
http://www.cc.columbia.edu/acis/bartleby/index.html
Columbia University's offering of full-text online books

Project Gutenberg
http://www.promo.net/pg/
The granddaddy of full-text online book projects

Journals

American Libraries http://www.ala.org/alonline/index.html
Computers in Libraries http://www.infotoday.com/cilmag/ciltop.htm
D-Lib Magazine http://www.dlib.org/dlib.html
Information Today http://www.infotoday.com/it/itnew.htm
The Journal of Electronic Publishing http://www.press.umich.edu/jep
Library Journal http://www.bookwire.com/ljdigital/
LinkUp: The Newsmagazine for Users of Online Services, CD-ROM and the Internet
    http://www.infotoday.com/lu/lunew.htm

Books and Articles

Atkinson, Ross. "Library Functions, Scholarly Communication, and the Foundation of the Digital Library: Laying Claim to the Control Zone." *Library Quarterly* 66, no. 3 (July 1996): 239–65.

Bates, Mary Ellen. *The Online Deskbook, Online Magazine's Essential Desk Reference for Online and Internet Searchers*. Wilton, CT: Pemberton Press, 1996.

Bruce, Harry. "User Satisfaction with Information Seeking on the Internet." *Journal of the American Society for Information Science* 49, no. 6 (May 1998): 541–56.

Demas, Samuel G. "Collection Development for the Electronic Library, a Conceptual and Organizational Model." *Library Hi Tech* 12, no. 3 (1994): 71–80.

Doran, Kirk. "The Internot: Helping Library Patrons Understand What the Internet Is Not (Yet)." *Computers in Libraries* 15, no. 6 (June 1995): 22–26.

Kemp, Thomas Jay. "Full-text Books Online: A Growing Resource." *FGS Forum* 11, no. 4 (Winter 1999): 14–16.

Koutnik, Chuck. "The World Wide Web Is Here, Is the End of Printed Reference Sources Near?" *RQ* 36, no. 3 (Spring 1997): 422–29.

Pitkin, Gary M., ed. *The National Electronic Library: A Guide to the Future for Library Managers*. Westport, CT: Greenwood Press, 1996.

Rioux, M. A. "Hunting and Gathering in Cyberspace: Finding and Selecting Web Resources for the Library's Virtual Collection." *Serials Librarian* 30, nos. 3–4 (1997): 129–36.

Smith, Natalia, and Helen R. Tibbo. "Libraries and the Creation of Electronic Texts for the Humanities." *College and Research Libraries* (November 1996): 535–53.

Veatch, James R. "Insourcing the Web." *American Libraries* (January 1999): 64–67.

FAMILY HISTORIES

–A

Abbey

Abbey, James. *California. A Trip across the Plains in the Spring of 1850, being a Daily Record of Incidents of the Trip and Containing Valuable Information to Emigrants.* New Albany, IN: Kent & Norman, 1850. 63p.
http://memory.loc.gov/cgi-bin/query/r?ammem/calbkbib:@field(AUTHOR+@band(Abbey,+James.+))

Abbott

Abbot, Abiel and Ephraim Abbot. *Genealogical Register of the Descendants of George Abbot of Andover, George Abbot of Rowley, Thomas Abbot of Andover, Arthur Abbot of Ipswich, Robert Abbot of Branford, CT and George Abbot, of Norwalk, CT.* Boston, MA: James Munroe, 1847. 197p.
http://genweb.net/~books/ma/abbot1847/

Abbott, John S. C. *South and North, or Impressions Received during a Trip to Cuba and the South.* New York, NY: Abbey & Abbot, 1860. 352p.
http://moa.umdl.umich.edu/cgi-bin/moa/sgml/moa-idx?notisid=AAW0177

Adams

Adams, Emma Hildreth. *To and Fro in Southern California.* Cincinnati, OH: W.M.B.C. Press, 1887. 288p.
http://memory.loc.gov/cgi-bin/query/r?ammem/calbkbib:@field(AUTHOR+@band(Adams,+Emma+H.+Emma+Hildreth++))

Albertson

Bunker, Mary Powell. *Long Island Genealogies, Families of Albertson, Andrews, Bedell, Birdsall, Bowne, Carman, Carr, Clowes, Cock, Cornelius, Covert, Dean, Doughty, Duryea, Feke, Frost, Haff, Hallock, Haydock, Hicks, Hopkins, Jackson, Jones, Keese, Ketcham, Kirby, Liones, Marvin, Merritt, Moore, Mott, Oakley, Onderdonck, Pearsall, Post, Powell, Prior, Robbins, Rodman, Rowland, Rushmore, Sands, Scudder, Seaman, Searing, Smith, Strickland, Titus, Townsend, Underhill, Valentine, Vanderdonk, Weeks, Whitman, Whitson, Willets, Williams, Willis, Wright, and other Families. Being Kindred Descendants of Thomas Powell of Bethpage, L.I., 1688.* Albany, NY: Munsell's, 1895. 350p.
http://moa.cit.cornell.edu/dienst/moabrowse.fly/MOA-JOURNALS2:BUNK-0101/5/1:TIFF2GIF:100

Allen

Palmer, John M. *Was Richard Allen Great?* Philadelphia, PA: Weekly Astonisher Print, 1898. 9p.
http://memory.loc.gov/cgi-bin/query/r?ammem/aap:@field(SUBJ+@band(Allen,+Richard,-1760-1831.+))

Andrews

Andrews, Christopher Columbus. *Minnesota and Dacotah, in Letters Descriptive of a Tour through the Northwest, in the Autumn of 1856.* Washington, DC: Farnham, 1857. 215p.
http://memory.loc.gov/cgi-bin/query/r?ammem/lhbumbib:@field(SUBJ+@band(Andrews,+Christopher+Columbus,-1829-1922.+))

Andrews, Eliza Frances. *The Wartime Journal of a Georgia Girl, 1864-1865.* New York, NY: Appleton, 1908. 387p.
http://metalab.unc.edu/docsouth/andrews/menu.html

Bunker, Mary Powell. *Long Island Genealogies, Families of Albertson, Andrews, Bedell, Birdsall, Bowne, Carman, Carr, Clowes, Cock, Cornelius, Covert, Dean, Doughty, Duryea, Feke, Frost, Haff, Hallock, Haydock, Hicks, Hopkins, Jackson, Jones, Keese, Ketcham, Kirby, Liones, Marvin, Merritt, Moore, Mott, Oakley, Onderdonck, Pearsall, Post, Powell, Prior, Robbins, Rodman, Rowland, Rushmore, Sands, Scudder, Seaman, Searing, Smith, Strickland, Titus, Townsend, Underhill, Valentine, Vanderdonk, Weeks, Whitman, Whitson, Willets, Williams, Willis, Wright, and other Families. Being Kindred Descendants of Thomas Powell of Bethpage, L.I., 1688.* Albany, NY: Munsell's, 1895. 350p.
http://moa.cit.cornell.edu/dienst/moabrowse.fly/MOA-JOURNALS2:BUNK-0101/5/1:TIFF2GIF:100

Ashby

Ashby, Thomas Almond. *The Valley Campaigns, being the Reminiscences of a Non-Combatant while between the Lines in the Shenandoah Valley during the War of the States.* New York, NY: Neale, 1914. 327p.
http://metalab.unc.edu/docsouth/ashby/menu.html

Aughey

Aughey, John Hill. *Tupelo.* Chicago, IL: Rhodes & McLure Publishing, 1905. Unpgd.
http://metalab.unc.edu/docsouth/aughey/menu.html

Austin

Austin, Mary Hunter. *The Land of Little Rain.* Boston, MA: Houghton, Mifflin, 1903. 280p.
http://memory.loc.gov/cgi-bin/query/r?ammem/calbkbib:@field(AUTHOR+@band(Austin,+Mary+Hunter,1868-1934.+))

Avary

Avary, Myrta Lockett. *A Virginia Girl in the Civil War, 1861-1865. Being a Record of the Actual Experiences of the Wife of a Confederate Officer.* New York, NY: Appleton, 1903. 384p.
http://metalab.unc.edu/docsouth/avary/menu.html

Avirett

Avirett, James Battle. *The Old Plantation: How We Lived in the Great House and Cabin before the War.* New York, NY: Tennyson Neely, 1901. 202p.
http://metalab.unc.edu/docsouth/avirett/menu.html

Ayers

Ayers, James J. *Gold and Sunshine, Reminiscences of Early California.* Boston, MA: Badger, 1922. 359p.
http://memory.loc.gov/cgi-bin/query/r?ammem/calbkbib:@field(AUTHOR+@band(Ayers,+James+J.+))

Bacon

Bacon, Edward. *Among the Cotton Thieves.* Detroit, MI: Free Press Steam Book, 1867. 300p.
http://moa.umdl.umich.edu/cgi-bin/moa/sgml/moa-idx?notisid=ACK4755

Bagby

Bagby, George William. *Canal Reminiscences, Recollections of Travel in the Old Days on the James River and Kanawha Canal.* Richmond, VA: West, Johnston & Co., Publishers, 1879. 37p.
http://metalab.unc.edu/docsouth/bagby/menu.html

Bagg

Bagg, Lyman Hotchkiss. *Four Years at Yale.* New Haven, CT: Chatfield, 1871. 728p.
http://moa.umdl.umich.edu/cgi-bin/moa/sgml/moa-idx?notisid=AGE3953

Baker

Baker, Samuel White. *Eight Years Wandering in Ceylon.* New York, NY: Lovell Co., 1883. 323p.
http://tom.cs.cmu.edu/cgi-bin/book/lookup?num=2036

Balch

Balch, Thomas Bloomer. *My Manse during the War, a Decade of Letters to the Rev. J. (Joshua) Thomas Murray, Editor of the Methodist Protestant.* Baltimore, MD: Sherwood, 1866. 42p.
http://metalab.unc.edu/docsouth/balch/menu.html

Baldwin

Baldwin, Joseph Glover. *Flush Times of Alabama and Mississippi, a Series of Sketches.* New York, NY: Appleton, 1854. 366p.
http://metalab.unc.edu/docsouth/baldwin/menu.html
http://moa.umdl.umich.edu/cgi-bin/moa/sgml/moa-idx?notisid=ADS9517

Ball

Ball, Charles. *Fifty Years in Chains, or the Life of an American Slave.* New York, NY: Dayton, 1859. 430p.
http://metalab.unc.edu/docsouth/ball/menu.html

Bancroft

Bancroft, Hubert Howe. *Literary Industries, a Memoir*. San Francisco, CA: History Company, 1891. 808p.
http://memory.loc.gov/cgi-bin/query/r?ammem/calbkbib:@field(AUTHOR+@band(Bancroft,+Hubert+Howe,1832-1918.+))

Barber

Parkinson, John Barber. *Memories of Early Wisconsin and the Gold Mines*. Author, 1921. 25p.
http://memory.loc.gov/cgi-bin/query/r?ammem/lhbum:@field(DOCID+@lit(M456542))

Barker

Bryan, George J. *Biographies of Attorney General George P. Barker, John C. Lord, D.D., Mrs. John C. Lord and William G. Bryan, Esq. Also Lecture on Journalism*. Buffalo, NY: Courier Co., 1886. 232p.
http://moa.cit.cornell.edu/dienst/moabrowse.fly/MOA-JOURNALS2:BRYN-0003/5/1:TIFF2GIF:100

Barry

Barry, Theodore Augustus and Benjamin Ada Patten. *Men and Memories of San Francisco, in the Spring of '50*. San Francisco, CA: Bancroft, 1873. 296p.
http://memory.loc.gov/cgi-bin/query/r?ammem/calbkbib:@field(AUTHOR+@band(Barry,+Theodore+Augustus,1825-1881.+))

Bass

Bass, Charissa Taylor and Emma Lee Walton. *Descendants of Deacon Samuel and Ann Bass*. Freeport, IL: Author, 1940. 223p.
http://genweb.net/~blackwell/ma/bass1940/

Batchelder

Boston Slave Riot, and Trial of Anthony Burns, Containing the Report of the Faneuil Hall Meeting, the Murder of Batchelder, Theodore Parker's Lesson for the Day, Speeches of Counsel on Both Sides, Corrected by Themselves, a Verbatim Report of Judge Loring's Decision and Detailed Account of the Embarkation. Boston, MA: Fetridge and Co., 1854. 98p.
http://moa.umdl.umich.edu/cgi-bin/moa/sgml/moa-idx?notisid=ABT7939

Bates

Bates, D. B. *Incidents on Land and Water, or Four Years on the Pacific Coast. Being a Narrative of the Burning of the Ships Nonantum, Humayoon and Fanchon, together with Many Startling and Interesting Adventures on Sea and Land*. Boston, MA: Author, 1861. 344p.
http://moa.umdl.umich.edu/cgi-bin/moa/sgml/moa-idx?notisid=AJL3457

Baxley

Baxley, Henry Willis. *What I Saw on the West Coast of South and North America and at the Hawaiian Islands*. New York, NY: Appleton, 1865. 646p.
http://moa.umdl.umich.edu/cgi/sgml/moa-idx?notisid=ABF7940

Beard

Beard, Ida May. *My Own Life, or a Deserted Woman*. NC: Author, 1898. 212p.
http://metalab.unc.edu/docsouth/beard/menu.html

Bedell

Bunker, Mary Powell. *Long Island Genealogies, Families of Albertson, Andrews, Bedell, Birdsall, Bowne, Carman, Carr, Clowes, Cock, Cornelius, Covert, Dean, Doughty, Duryea, Feke, Frost, Haff, Hallock, Haydock, Hicks, Hopkins, Jackson, Jones, Keese, Ketcham, Kirby, Liones, Marvin, Merritt, Moore, Mott, Oakley, Onderdonck, Pearsall, Post, Powell, Prior, Robbins, Rodman, Rowland, Rushmore, Sands, Scudder, Seaman, Searing, Smith, Strickland, Titus, Townsend, Underhill, Valentine, Vanderdonk, Weeks, Whitman, Whitson, Willets, Williams, Willis, Wright, and other Families. Being Kindred Descendants of Thomas Powell of Bethpage, L.I., 1688.* Albany, NY: Munsell's, 1895. 350p.
http://moa.cit.cornell.edu/dienst/moabrowse.fly/MOA-JOURNALS2:BUNK-0101/5/1:TIFF2GIF:100

Beech

Ward, David. *The Autobiography of David Ward.* New York, NY: Author, 1912. 194p.
http://memory.loc.gov/cgi-bin/query/r?ammem/lhbumbib:@field(SUBJ+@band(Michigan-Social+life+and+customs.+))

Belden

Belden, George P. *Belden, the White Chief, or Twelve Years among the Wild Indians of the Plains, from the Diaries and Manuscripts of George P. Belden.* New York, NY: Vent, 1870. 522p.
http://moa.umdl.umich.edu/cgi-bin/moa/sgml/moa-idx?notisid=ABJ1451

Bell

Bell, Horace. *Reminiscences of a Ranger or Early Times in Southern California.* Los Angeles, CA: Yarnell, Caystile & Mathes, 1881. 457p.
http://memory.loc.gov/cgi-bin/query/r?ammem/calbkbib:@field(AUTHOR+@band(Bell,+Horace,1830-1918.+))

Bemis

Bemis, Stephen Allen. *Recollections of a Long and Somewhat Uneventful Life.* St. Louis, MO: Author, 1932. 92p.
http://memory.loc.gov/cgi-bin/query/r?ammem/calbkbib:@field(AUTHOR+@band(Bemis,+Stephen+Allen,1828-1919.+))

Berry

Smith, Amanda. *An Autobiography, the Story of the Lord's Dealings with Mrs. Amanda Smith, the Colored Evangelist, Containing an Account of Her Life Work of Faith, and Her Travels in America, England, Ireland, Scotland, India and Africa, as an Independent Missionary.* Chicago, IL: Meyer and Brother, 1893. 506p.
http://digilib.nypl.org/dynaweb/digs/wwm97264/

Bethune

The Marvelous Musical Prodigy, Blind Tom, the Negro Boy Pianist, Whose Performances at the Great St. James and Egyptian Halls, London and Salle Hertz, Paris, Have Created Such a Profound Sensation. Anecdotes, Songs, Sketches of the Life, Testimonials of Musicians and Savans, and Opinions of the American and English Press of Blind Tom (Thomas Greene Bethune). New York, NY: French & Wheat, 1868. 30p.
http://memory.loc.gov/cgi-bin/query/r?ammem/aap:@field(SUBJ+@band(Bethune,+Thomas+Greene,--1849-1908.+))

Betts

Betts, Alexander Davis. *Experience of a Confederate Chaplain, 1861-1864*. Greenville, SC: Author, Date Unknown. 104p.
http://metalab.unc.edu/docsouth/betts/menu.html

Bidwell

Bidwell, John. *Echoes of the Past about California*. Published with *In Camp and Cabin*, by Rev. John Steele. Chicago, IL: Donnelley, 1928. 377p.
http://memory.loc.gov/cgi-bin/query/r?ammem/calbkbib:@field(AUTHOR+@band(Bidwell,+John,1819-1900.+))

Royce, Charles C. *Addresses, Reminiscences, etc. of General John Bidwell*. Chico, CA: Charles C. Royce, 1906. 221p.
http://memory.loc.gov/cgi-bin/query/r?ammem/calbkbib:@field(AUTHOR+@band(Bidwell,+John,1819-1900.+))

Bigelow

Bigelow, Timothy. *Journal of a Tour to Niagara Falls in the Year 1805*. Boston, MA: John Wilson and Son, 1876. 144p.
http://moa.cit.cornell.edu/dienst/moabrowse.fly/MOA-JOURNALS2:BIGE-0075/3/1:TIFF2GIF:100

Biggs

Biggs, Asa. *Autobiography of Asa Biggs, including a Journal of a Trip from North Carolina to New York in 1832*. Raleigh, NC: Edwards and Broughton Printing Co., 1915. 51p.
http://metalab.unc.edu/docsouth/biggs/menu.html

Bird

Bird, Isabella L. *The Hawaiian Archipelago, Six Months among the Palm Groves, Coral Reefs and Volcanoes of the Sandwich Islands*. London: Murray, 1875. 473p.
http://www.indiana.edu/~letrs/vwwp/bird/hawaii.html

————. *Life in the Rocky Mountains*. New York, NY: Putnam's, 1881. 296p.
http://www.indiana.edu/~letrs/vwwp/bird/rocky.html

Birdsall

Bunker, Mary Powell. *Long Island Genealogies, Families of Albertson, Andrews, Bedell, Birdsall, Bowne, Carman, Carr, Clowes, Cock, Cornelius, Covert, Dean, Doughty, Duryea, Feke, Frost, Haff, Hallock, Haydock, Hicks, Hopkins, Jackson, Jones, Keese, Ketcham, Kirby, Liones, Marvin, Merritt, Moore, Mott, Oakley, Onderdonck, Pearsall, Post, Powell, Prior, Robbins, Rodman, Rowland, Rushmore, Sands, Scudder, Seaman, Searing, Smith, Strickland, Titus, Townsend, Underhill, Valentine, Vanderdonk, Weeks, Whitman, Whitson, Willets, Williams, Willis, Wright, and other Families. Being Kindred Descendants of Thomas Powell of Bethpage, L.I., 1688*. Albany, NY: Munsell's, 1895. 350p.
http://moa.cit.cornell.edu/dienst/moabrowse.fly/MOA-JOURNALS2:BUNK-0101/5/1:TIFF2GIF:100

Bixby

Smith, Sarah Hathaway Bixby. *Adobe Days, Being the Truthful Narrative of the Events in the Life of a California Girl on a Sheep Ranch and in El Pueblo de Nuestra Senora de Los Angeles while It Was Yet a Small and Humble Town, together with an Account of How Three Young Men from Maine in Eighteen Hundred and Fifty-three Drove Sheep and Cattle across*

the Plains, Mountains and Deserts from Illinois to the Pacific Coast, and the Strange Prophecy of Admiral Thatcher about San Pedro Harbor. Cedar Rapids, IA: Torch Press, 1925. 208p.
http://memory.loc.gov/cgi-bin/query/r?ammem/calbkbib:@field(AUTHOR+@band(Smith,+Sarah+Hathaway+Bixby,1871-1935.+))

Blackford
Green, Fletcher M. *Ferry Hill Plantation Journal, January 4, 1838-January 15, 1839 (by John Blackford, 1771-1839).* Chapel Hill, NC: University of North Carolina Press, 1961. 139p.
http://metalab.unc.edu/docsouth/blackford/menu.html

Boggs
Boggs, William Robertson. *Military Reminiscences of General Wm. R. Boggs, C.S.A.* Durham, NC: Seeman Printery, 1913. 115p.
http://metalab.unc.edu/docsouth/boggs/menu.html

Bokum
Bokum, Hermann. *The Testimony of a Refugee from East Tennessee by Hermann Bokum, Chaplain, U.S.A.* Philadelphia, PA: Author, 1863. 24p.
http://metalab.unc.edu/docsouth/bokum/menu.html

Booth
Booth, Edmund. *Edmund Booth (1810-1905), Forty-niner, the Life Story of a Deaf Pioneer, including Portions of His Autobiographical Notes and Gold Rush Diary, and Selections from Family Letters and Reminiscences.* Stockton, CA: San Joaquin Pioneer and Historical Society, 1953. 72p.
http://memory.loc.gov/cgi-bin/query/r?ammem/calbkbib:@field(AUTHOR+@band(Booth,+Edmund,1810-1905.+))

Borthwick
Borthwick, John David. *Three Years in California.* Edinburgh: Blackwood, 1857. 384p.
http://memory.loc.gov/cgi-bin/query/r?ammem/calbkbib:@field(AUTHOR+@band(Borthwick,+J.+D.+))

Gaer, Joseph. *Index, Three Years in California.* Author, 1935. 16p.
http://memory.loc.gov/cgi-bin/query/r?ammem/calbkbib:@field(AUTHOR+@band(Gaer,+Joseph,1897-ed.+))

Boston
Boston, Thomas. *Memoirs of the Life and Times and Writings of the Reverend and Learned Thomas Boston, M.A.*
http://www.iclnet.org/pub/resources/text/ipb-e/epl-10/web/boston-memoirs-00.html

Botta
Botta, Anne C. Lynch. *Memoirs of Anne C. L. Botta, Written by Her Friends. With Selections from Her Correspondence and from Her Writings in Prose and Poetry.* New York, NY: J. S. Tait & Sons, 1894. 480p.
http://moa.umdl.umich.edu/cgi-bin/moa/sgml/moa-idx?notisid=ABX9247

Bowden

Carroll, Mary Bowden. *Ten Years in Paradise. Leaves from a Society Reporter's Notebook.* San Jose, CA: Popp & Hogan, 1903. 212p.
hhttp://memory.loc.gov/cgi-bin/query/r?ammem/calbkbib:@field(AUTHOR+@band(Carroll,+Mary+Bowden.+))

Bowne

Bunker, Mary Powell. *Long Island Genealogies, Families of Albertson, Andrews, Bedell, Birdsall, Bowne, Carman, Carr, Clowes, Cock, Cornelius, Covert, Dean, Doughty, Duryea, Feke, Frost, Haff, Hallock, Haydock, Hicks, Hopkins, Jackson, Jones, Keese, Ketcham, Kirby, Liones, Marvin, Merritt, Moore, Mott, Oakley, Onderdonck, Pearsall, Post, Powell, Prior, Robbins, Rodman, Rowland, Rushmore, Sands, Scudder, Seaman, Searing, Smith, Strickland, Titus, Townsend, Underhill, Valentine, Vanderdonk, Weeks, Whitman, Whitson, Willets, Williams, Willis, Wright, and other Families. Being Kindred Descendants of Thomas Powell of Bethpage, L.I., 1688.* Albany, NY: Munsell's, 1895. 350p.
http://moa.cit.cornell.edu/dienst/moabrowse.fly/MOA-JOURNALS2:BUNK-0101/5/1:TIFF2GIF:100

Bradbury

Bradbury, John. *Travels in the Interior of America in the Years 1809, 1810, and 1811.* London: Sherwood, Neely and Jones, 1819.
http://www.xmission.com/~drudy/mtman/html/bradbury.html

Bradford

Bradford, Mary Davison. *Memoirs of Mary D. Bradford, Autobiographical and Historical Reminiscences of Education in Wisconsin, through Progressive Service from Rural School Teaching to City Superintendent.* Evansville, WI: Antes Press, 1932. 542p.
http://memory.loc.gov/cgi-bin/query/r?ammem/lhbumbib:@field(SUBJ+@band(Education--Wisconsin--History.+))

Eppes, Susan Bradford. *Through Some Eventful Years.* Macon, GA: Burke, 1926. 382p.
http://moa.umdl.umich.edu/cgi-bin/moa/sgml/moa-idx?notisid=AFJ8883

Branch

Branch, Mary Jones Polk. *Memoirs of a Southern Woman, "Within the Lines," and a Genealogical Table.* Chicago, IL: Joseph G. Branch Publishing, 1912. 107p.
http://metalab.unc.edu/docsouth/branch/menu.html

Brandt

Felton, Rebecca Latimer. *County Life in Georgia in the Days of My Youth.* Atlanta, GA: Index Printing Co., 1919. 303p.
http://metalab.unc.edu/docsouth/felton/menu.html

Branham

Branham, Levi. *My Life and Travels.* Dalton, GA: Showalter, 1929. 64p.
http://metalab.unc.edu/docsouth/branham/menu.html

Brewer

Brewer, William Henry. *Up and Down California in 1860-1864, the Journal of William H. Brewer.* New Haven, CT: Yale, 1930. 601p.
http://memory.loc.gov/cgi-bin/query/r?ammem/calbkbib:@field(AUTHOR+@band(Brewer,+William+Henry,1828-1910.+))

Briggs

Briggs, Lloyd Vernon. *California and the West, 1881 and later*. Boston, MA: Wright & Potter, 1931. 214p.
http://memory.loc.gov/cgi-bin/query/r?ammem/calbkbib:@field(AUTHOR+@band(Briggs,+Lloyd+Vernon,1863-1941.+))

Brooks

Albert, Octavia V. Rogers, Mrs. *The House of Bondage, or Charlotte Brooks and Other Slaves Original and Life-like, as They Appeared in Their Old Plantation and City Slave Life, together with Pen Pictures of the Peculiar Institution, with Sights and Insights into Their Relations as Freedmen, Freemen and Citizens*. New York, NY: Hunt & Eaton, 1890. 161p.
http://digilib.nypl.org/dynaweb/digs/wwm972/

Broughton

Broughton, V. W. *Twenty Years Experience of a Missionary*. Chicago, IL: Pony Press, 1907. 140p.
http://digilib.nypl.org/dynaweb/digs/wwm974/

Brown

Brown, John Henry. *Reminiscences and Incidents of the Early Days of San Francisco*. San Francisco, CA: Mission Journal Publishing, 1886. 106p.
http://memory.loc.gov/cgi-bin/query/r?ammem/calbkbib:@field(AUTHOR+@band(Brown,+John+Henry, 1810-1905.+))

Brown, Josephine. *Biography of an American Bondsman, Written by His Daughter*. Boston, MA: Wallcut, 1856. 104p.
http://digilib.nypl.org/dynaweb/digs/wwm975/

Brown, William Wells. *Narrative of William W. Brown, an American Slave*. 3rd ed. London: Charles Gilpin, 1849. 168p.
http://metalab.unc.edu/docsouth/brownw/menu.html

Browne, John Ross. *Crusoe's Island*. New York, NY: Harper, 1864. 436p.
http://memory.loc.gov/cgi-bin/query/r?ammem/calbkbib:@field(AUTHOR+@band(Browne,+John+Ross, 1821-1875.+))

Bruce

Bruce, Henry Clay. *The New Man, Twenty-nine Years a Slave, Twenty-nine Years a Free Man, Recollections of H. C. Bruce*. York, PA: Anstadt & Sons, 1895. 176p.
http://metalab.unc.edu/docsouth/bruce/menu.html

Bryan

Bryan, George J. *Biographies of Attorney General George P. Barker, John C. Lord, D.D., Mrs. John C. Lord and William G. Bryan, Esq. Also Lecture on Jounalism*. Buffalo, NY: Courier Co., 1886. 232p.
http://moa.cit.cornell.edu/dienst/moabrowse.fly/MOA-JOURNALS2:BRYN-0003/5/1:TIFF2GIF:100

Bryan, Mary Norcott. *A Grandmother's Recollection of Dixie*. New Bern, NC: Dunn, 1912. 43p.
http://metalab.unc.edu/docsouth/bryan/menu.html

Buck

Buck, Franklin Agustus. *A Yankee Trader in the Gold Rush, the Letters of Franklin A. Buck.* Boston, MA: Houghton, Mifflin, 1930. 294p.
http://memory.loc.gov/cgi-bin/query/r?ammem/calbkbib:@field(AUTHOR+@band(Buck,+Franklin+Agustus,1826-1909.+))

Buffum

Buffum, Edward Gould. *Six Months in the Gold Mines from a Journal of Three Years' Residence in Upper and Lower California, 1847-8-9.* Philadelphia, PA: Lea & Blanchard, 1850. 172p.
http://memory.loc.gov/cgi-bin/query/r?ammem/calbkbib:@field(AUTHOR+@band(Buffum,+Edward+Gould,1820-1867.+))

Buford

Worthington, C. J. *The Woman in Battle, a Narrative of the Exploits, Adventures, and Travels of Madame Loreta Janeta Velazquez, otherwise Known as Lieutenant Harry T. Buford, Confederate States Army in which is Given Full Descriptions of the Numerous Battles in which She Participated as a Confederate Officer.* Richmond, VA: Dustin, Gilman, 1876. 606p.
http://metalab.unc.edu/docsouth/velazquez/menu.html

Bundy

Bundy, Charles Smith. *Early Days in the Chippewa Valley.* Menominie, WI: Flint Douglas Printing, 1916. 16p.
http://memory.loc.gov/cgi-bin/query/r?ammem/lhbum:@field(DOCID+@lit(16807T000)):@@@REF

Bunnell

Bunnell, Lafayette Houghton. *Discovery of the Yosemite and the Indian War of 1851, which Led to That Event.* New York, NY: Revell, 1892. 359p.
http://memory.loc.gov/cgi-bin/query/r?ammem/calbkbib:@field(AUTHOR+@band(Bunnell,+Lafayette+Houghton,1824-1903.+))

Burge

Burge, Dolly Sumner Lunt. *A Woman's Wartime Journal, an Account of the Passage over Georgia's Plantation of Sherman's Army on the March to the Sea, as Recorded in the Diary of Dolly Sumner Lunt (Mrs. Thomas Burge).* New York, NY: Century Co., 1918. 54p.
http://metalab.unc.edu/docsouth/burge/menu.html

Burnett

Burnett, Peter Hardeman. *Recollections and Opinions of an Old Pioneer.* New York, NY: Appleton, 1880. 448p.
http://memory.loc.gov/cgi-bin/query/r?ammem/calbkbib:@field(AUTHOR+@band(Burnett,+Peter+H[ardeman],1807-1895.+))

Burns

Boston Slave Riot, and Trial of Anthony Burns, Containing the Report of the Faneuil Hall Meeting, the Murder of Batchelder, Theodore Parker's Lesson for the Day, Speeches of Counsel on Both Sides, Corrected by Themselves, a Verbatim Report of Judge Loring's Decision and Detailed Account of the Embarkation. Boston, MA: Fetridge and Co., 1854. 98p.
http://moa.umdl.umich.edu/cgi-bin/moa/sgml/moa-idx?notisid=ABT7939

Burr

Thompson, George. *Prison Life and Reflections or a Narrative of the Arrest, Trial, Conviction, Imprisonment, Treatment, Observations, Reflections and Deliverance of Work, Burr and Thompson Who Suffered an Unjust and Cruel Imprisonment in Missouri Penitentiary for Attempting to Aid Some Slaves to Liberty.* Hartford, CT: Alanson Work, 1850. 376p.
http://moa.umdl.umich.edu/cgi-bin/moa/sgml/moa-idx?notisid=ACK4077

Burton

Burton, Annie L. *Memories of Childhood's Slavery Days.* Boston, MA: Ross Publishing, 1909. 97p.
http://digilib.nypl.org/dynaweb/digs/wwm97252/
http://metalab.unc.edu/docsouth/burton/menu.html

Burton, Thomas William. *What Experience Has Taught Me, an Autobiography of Thomas William Burton, Doctor of Medicine, Springfield, Ohio.* Cincinnati, OH: Jennings and Graham, 1910, 126p.
http://metalab.unc.edu/docsouth/burtont/menu.html

Burwell

Burwell, Letitia M. *A Girl's Life in Virginia before the War.* New York, NY: Stokes, 1895. 209p.
http://metalab.unc.edu/docsouth/burwell/menu.html

Butler

Andrews, Eliza Frances. *The Wartime Journal of a Georgia Girl, 1864-1865.* New York, NY: Appleton, 1908. 387p.
http://metalab.unc.edu/docsouth/andrews/menu.html

Butler, Benjamin Clapp. *From New York to Montreal.* New York, NY: American News Co., 1873. 194p.
http://moa.cit.cornell.edu/dienst/moabrowse.fly/MOA-JOURNALS2:BUTL-0014/3/1:TIFF2GIF:100

Cabot

Harrisse, Henry. *John Cabot, the Discoverer of North America and Sebastian, His Son, a Chapter of the Maritime History of England under the Tudors, 1496-1557.* London: Stevens, 1896. 557p.
http://www.canadiana.org/cgi-bin/ECO/mtq?id=04ee01375f&display=05393+0001

Hodges, Elizabeth. *The Cabots and the Discovery of America, with a Description and History of Brandon Hill, the Site of the Cabot Memorial Tower.* London: Mack, 1897. 41p.
http://www.canadiana.org/cgi-bin/ECO/mtq?id=04ee01375f&doc=06796

Caldwell

Autobiography and Biography of Rev. Joseph Caldwell, D.D. Chapel Hill, NC: J. B. Neathery, 1860. 68p.
http://metalab.unc.edu/docsouth/caldwell/menu.html

Cannon

Swisshelm, Jane Grey Cannon. *Half a Century*. Chicago, IL: Author, 1880. 263p.
http://memory.loc.gov/cgi-bin/query/r?ammem/lhbumbib:@field(SUBJ+@band(Slavery+in+the+United+
States--Anti-slavery+movements.+))

Carey

Smith, George. *The Life of William Carey, Shoemaker and Missionary*. N.p., n.d.
http://www.datacanyon.com/mirrors/gutenberg/etext00/wmcry10.txt

Carman

Bunker, Mary Powell. *Long Island Genealogies, Families of Albertson, Andrews, Bedell, Birdsall,
Bowne, Carman, Carr, Clowes, Cock, Cornelius, Covert, Dean, Doughty, Duryea, Feke,
Frost, Haff, Hallock, Haydock, Hicks, Hopkins, Jackson, Jones, Keese, Ketcham, Kirby,
Liones, Marvin, Merritt, Moore, Mott, Oakley, Onderdonck, Pearsall, Post, Powell, Prior,
Robbins, Rodman, Rowland, Rushmore, Sands, Scudder, Seaman, Searing, Smith, Strickland,
Titus, Townsend, Underhill, Valentine, Vanderdonk, Weeks, Whitman, Whitson, Willets, Wil-
liams, Willis, Wright, and other Families. Being Kindred Descendants of Thomas Powell of
Bethpage, L.I., 1688*. Albany, NY: Munsell's, 1895. 350p.
http://moa.cit.cornell.edu/dienst/moabrowse.fly/MOA-JOURNALS2:BUNK-0101/5/1:TIFF2GIF:100

Carrigan

Carriagan, Wilhelmina Bruce. *Captured by the Indians, Reminiscences of Pioneer Life in Minnesota*. Buffalo Lake, MN: News Print, 1912. 68p.
http://memory.loc.gov/cgi-bin/query/r?ammem/lhbumbib:@field(SUBJ+@band(Carrigan,+Wilhelmina+
Buce.+))

Carroll

Carroll, John William. *Autobiography and Reminiscences of John W. Carroll, Henderson, Tenn*.
Henderson, TN: Author, 1898. 66p.
http://metalab.unc.edu/docsouth/carroll/menu.html

Carroll, Mary Bowden. *Ten Years in Paradise. Leaves from a Society Reporter's Notebook*. San
Jose, CA: Popp & Hogan, 1903. 212p.
http://memory.loc.gov/cgi-bin/query/r?ammem/calbkbib:@field(AUTHOR+@band(Carroll,+Mary+
Bowden.+))

Carson

Abbott, John S. C. *Christopher Carson, Familiarly Known as Kit Carson*. New York, NY:
Dodd, Mead, 1874. 362p.
http://moa.umdl.umich.edu/cgi-bin/moa/sgml/moa-idx?notisid=ABE2513

Carson, James H. *Early Recollections of the Mines and a Description of the Great Tulare
Valley*. Tarrytown, NY: Abbatt, 1931. 82p.
http://memory.loc.gov/cgi-bin/query/r?ammem/calbkbib:@field(AUTHOR+@band(Carson,+James+H.,d.+
1853.+))

Cary

Harrison, Mrs. Burton. *Recollections Grave and Gay*. New York, NY: Scribners, 1911. 386p.
http://metalab.unc.edu/docsouth/harrison/menu.html

Chamberlain

Manley, John. *Cattaraugus County, Embracing Its Agricultural Society, Newspapers, Civil List, from the Organization of the County to 1857, Biographies of the Old Pioneers, with Portraits, Benjamin Chamberlain, Peter Ten Broeck, Frederick S. Martin, Chauncey J. Fox, Alson Leavenworth, Stanley N. Clarke, and of Congressmen Francis S. Edwards and Reuben E. Fenton, Colonial and State Governors of New York, Names of Towns and Post Offices with the Statistics of Each Town*. Little Valley, NY: Author, 1857. 140p.
http://moa.cit.cornell.edu/dienst/moabrowse.fly/MOA-JOURNALS2:MANL-0089/3/1:TIFF2GIF:100

Chambliss

Chambliss, William H. Chambliss. *Diary of Society as It Really Is*. New York, NY: Chambliss & Co., 1895. 408p.
http://memory.loc.gov/cgi-bin/query/r?ammem/calbkbib:@field(AUTHOR+@band(Chambliss,+William+H.,+1865++))

Chase

Chase, John Carroll and George Walter Chamberlain. *Seven Generations of the Descendants of Aquila and Thomas Chase*. Derry, NH: Authors, 1928. 621p.
http://genweb.net/~blackwell/ma/Chase1928/

Chestnut

Chestnut, Mary Boykin Miller. *A Diary from Dixie, as Written by Mary Boykin Chestnut, Wife of James Chestnut, Jr., United States Senator from South Carolina, 1859-1861, and afterward an Aide to Jefferson Davis and a Brigadier General in the Confederate Army*. New York, NY: Appleton, 1905. 424p.
http://metalab.unc.edu/docsouth/chesnut/menu.html

Childs

Childs, B. F. *Marquette, Mackinac Island and the Soo*. New York, NY: Albertype, 1889. 12p.
http://memory.loc.gov/cgi-bin/query/r?ammem/lhbumbib:@field(SUBJ+@band(Marquette+co.,+Mich.--Description+and+travel--Views.+))

Christman

Christman, Enos. *One Man's Gold, the Letters & Journal of a Forty-niner, Enos Christman*. New York, NY: Whittlesey House, 1930. 278p.
http://memory.loc.gov/cgi-bin/query/r?ammem/calbkbib:@field(AUTHOR+@band(Christman,+Enos, 1828-1912.+))

Church

Bundy, Charles Smith. *Early Days in the Chippewa Valley*. Menominie, WI: Flint Douglas Printing, 1916. 16p.
http://memory.loc.gov/cgi-bin/query/r?ammem/lhbum:@field(DOCID+@lit(16807T000)):@@@REF

Churchill

Churchill, Caroline M. Nichols. *Little Sheaves Gathered while Gleaning after Reapers. Being Letters of Travel Commencing in 1870 and Ending in 1873*. San Francisco, CA: Author, 1874. 110p.
http://memory.loc.gov/cgi-bin/query/r?ammem/calbk:@field(DOCID+@lit(C091T00)):@@@REF

————. *Over the Purple Hills, or Sketches of Travel in California, Embracing all the Important Points Usually Visited by Tourists.* Denver, CO: Author, 1881. 252p.
http://memory.loc.gov/cgi-bin/query/r?ammem/calbk:@field(DOCID+@lit(C092T00)):@@@REF

Clappe

Clappe, Louise Amelia Knapp Smith. *The Shirley Letters from California Mines in 1851-52.* San Francisco, CA: Russell, 1922. 350p.
http://memory.loc.gov/cgi-bin/query/r?ammem/calbkbib:@field(AUTHOR+@band(Clappe,+Louise+Amelia+Knapp+Smith,1819-1906.+))

Clark

Bacon, Edward. *Among the Cotton Thieves.* Detroit, MI: Free Press Steam Book, 1867. 300p.
http://moa.umdl.umich.edu/cgi-bin/moa/sgml/moa-idx?notisid=ACK4755

Clark, Susie Champney. *The Round Trip from the Hub to the Golden Gate.* Boston, MA: Lee & Shepard, 1890. 193p.
http://memory.loc.gov/cgi-bin/query/r?ammem/calbkbib:@field(AUTHOR+@band(Clark,+Susie+Champney,1856-+))

Manley, John. *Cattaraugus County, Embracing Its Agricultural Society, Newspapers, Civil List, from the Organization of the County to 1857, Biographies of the Old Pioneers, with Portraits, Benjamin Chamberlain, Peter Ten Broeck, Frederick S. Martin, Chauncey J. Fox, Alson Leavenworth, Stanley N. Clarke, and of Congressmen Francis S. Edwards and Reuben E. Fenton, Colonial and State Governors of New York, Names of Towns and Post Offices with the Statistics of Each Town.* Little Valley, NY: Author, 1857. 140p.
http://moa.cit.cornell.edu/dienst/moabrowse.fly/MOA-JOURNALS2:MANL-0089/3/1:TIFF2GIF:100

Salisbury, John Edwin and George Castor Martin. *The American Ancestors of Oratio Dyer Clark and of His Wife Laura Ann King, together with the Ancestry of Anne Marbury Hutchinson, Ancestress of Oratio Dyer Clark.* Asbury Park, NJ: Martin, 1917. 387p.
http://genweb.net/~blackwell/blql/cka1917.htm

Van Cleve, Charlotte Ouisconsin Clark. *Three Score Years and Ten, Life-long Memories of Fort Snelling, Minnesota and Other Parts of the West.* Minneapolis, MN: Harrison & Smith, 1888. 176p.
http://memory.loc.gov/cgi-bin/query/r?ammem/lhbumbib:@field(SUBJ+@band(Fort+Snelling,+Minn.+))

Clay

Clay Clopton, Virginia. *A Belle of the Fifties, Memoirs of Mrs. Clay of Alabama.* New York, NY: Doubleday, 1905. 386p.
http://metalab.unc.edu/docsouth/clay/menu.html

Clinkscales

Clinkscales, John George. *On the Old Plantation, Reminiscences of His Childhood.* Spartanburg, SC: Band & White, 1916. 142p.
http://metalab.unc.edu/docsouth/clinkscales/menu.html

Clopton

Clay Clopton, Virginia. *A Belle of the Fifties, Memoirs of Mrs. Clay of Alabama.* New York, NY: Doubleday, 1905. 386p.
http://metalab.unc.edu/docsouth/clay/menu.html

Clough

Lenroot, Clara Clough. *Long, Long Ago*. Appleton, WI: Badger Printing, 1929. 68p.
http://memory.loc.gov/cgi-bin/query/r?ammem/lhbum:@field(DOCID+@lit(09423T000)):@@@REF

Clowes

Bunker, Mary Powell. *Long Island Genealogies, Families of Albertson, Andrews, Bedell, Birdsall, Bowne, Carman, Carr, Clowes, Cock, Cornelius, Covert, Dean, Doughty, Duryea, Feke, Frost, Haff, Hallock, Haydock, Hicks, Hopkins, Jackson, Jones, Keese, Ketcham, Kirby, Liones, Marvin, Merritt, Moore, Mott, Oakley, Onderdonck, Pearsall, Post, Powell, Prior, Robbins, Rodman, Rowland, Rushmore, Sands, Scudder, Seaman, Searing, Smith, Strickland, Titus, Townsend, Underhill, Valentine, Vanderdonk, Weeks, Whitman, Whitson, Willets, Williams, Willis, Wright, and other Families. Being Kindred Descendants of Thomas Powell of Bethpage, L.I., 1688*. Albany, NY: Munsell's, 1895. 350p.
http://moa.cit.cornell.edu/dienst/moabrowse.fly/MOA-JOURNALS2:BUNK-0101/5/1:TIFF2GIF:100

Cochrane

Barber, Edward W. *The Vermontville Colony, Its Genesis and History, with Personal Sketches of the Colonists*. Lansing, MI: Smith, 1897. 93p.
http://memory.loc.gov/cgi-bin/query/r?ammem/lhbumbib:@field(SUBJ+@band(Vermontville,+Mich.+))

Cock

Bunker, Mary Powell. *Long Island Genealogies, Families of Albertson, Andrews, Bedell, Birdsall, Bowne, Carman, Carr, Clowes, Cock, Cornelius, Covert, Dean, Doughty, Duryea, Feke, Frost, Haff, Hallock, Haydock, Hicks, Hopkins, Jackson, Jones, Keese, Ketcham, Kirby, Liones, Marvin, Merritt, Moore, Mott, Oakley, Onderdonck, Pearsall, Post, Powell, Prior, Robbins, Rodman, Rowland, Rushmore, Sands, Scudder, Seaman, Searing, Smith, Strickland, Titus, Townsend, Underhill, Valentine, Vanderdonk, Weeks, Whitman, Whitson, Willets, Williams, Willis, Wright, and other Families. Being Kindred Descendants of Thomas Powell of Bethpage, L.I., 1688*. Albany, NY: Munsell's, 1895. 350p.
http://moa.cit.cornell.edu/dienst/moabrowse.fly/MOA-JOURNALS2:BUNK-0101/5/1:TIFF2GIF:100

Cody

Wetmore, Helen Cody. *Last of the Great Scouts, the Life Story of Col. William F. Cody, Buffalo Bill, as Told by His Sister*. Chicago, IL: Duluth Press, 1899. 296p.
http://www.ukans.edu/carrie/kancoll/books/cody/index.html

Coffin

Coffin, Charles Carleton. *The Seat of Empire*. Boston, MA: Fields, Osgood & Co., 1870. 262p.
http://moa.umdl.umich.edu/cgi-bin/moa/sgml/moa-idx?notisid=AFK4419

Collis

Collis, Septima Maria Levy. *A Woman's War Record, 1861-1865*. New York, NY: Putnam, 1889. 78p.
http://metalab.unc.edu/docsouth/collis/menu.html

Colt

Colt, Miriam Davis. *Went to Kansas, Being a Thrilling Account of an Ill Fated Expedition to That Fairy Land and Its Sad Result, together with a Sketch of the Life of the Author and How the World Goes with Her*. Watertown, NY: Ingalls & Co., 1862. 294p.
http://www.ukans.edu/carrie/kancoll/books/colt/

Colton

Colton, Walter. *Three Years in California*. New York, NY: A. S. Barnes, 1850. 480p.
http://moa.umdl.umich.edu/cgi-bin/moa/sgml/moa-idx?notisid=ABE2329

Compton

Compton, Lucius Bunyan. *Life of Lucius B. Compton, the Mountain Evangelist, or from the Depths of Sin to the Heights of Holiness*. Cincinnati, OH: Author, 1903. 102p.
http://metalab.unc.edu/docsouth/compton/menu.html

Cone

Cone, Mary. *Two Years in California*. Chicago, IL: Griggs, 1876. 238p.
http://memory.loc.gov/cgi-bin/query/r?ammem/calbkbib:@field(AUTHOR+@band(Cone,+Mary.+))

Cook

Vandergon, Gertrude Braat. *Our Pioneer Days in Minnesota*. Author, 1949. 138p.
http://memory.loc.gov/cgi-bin/query/r?ammem/lhbum:@field(DOCID+@lit(03667T000)):@@@REF

Cooper

Shaw, S. M. *A Centennial Offering, Being a Brief History of Cooperstown, with a Biographical Sketch of James Fenimore Cooper by Hon. Isaac H. Arnold*. Cooperstown, NY: Freeman's Journal Office, 1886. 240p.
http://moa.cit.cornell.edu/dienst/moabrowse.fly/MOA-JOURNALS2:SHAW-0108/3/1:TIFF2GIF:100

Copley

Copley, John M. *A Sketch of the Battle of Franklin, Tennessee with Reminiscences of Camp Douglas*. Austin, TX: Eugene von Boeckmann, 1893. 206p.
http://metalab.unc.edu/docsouth/copley/menu.html

Cornelius

Bunker, Mary Powell. *Long Island Genealogies, Families of Albertson, Andrews, Bedell, Birdsall, Bowne, Carman, Carr, Clowes, Cock, Cornelius, Covert, Dean, Doughty, Duryea, Feke, Frost, Haff, Hallock, Haydock, Hicks, Hopkins, Jackson, Jones, Keese, Ketcham, Kirby, Liones, Marvin, Merritt, Moore, Mott, Oakley, Onderdonck, Pearsall, Post, Powell, Prior, Robbins, Rodman, Rowland, Rushmore, Sands, Scudder, Seaman, Searing, Smith, Strickland, Titus, Townsend, Underhill, Valentine, Vanderdonk, Weeks, Whitman, Whitson, Willets, Williams, Willis, Wright, and other Families. Being Kindred Descendants of Thomas Powell of Bethpage, L.I., 1688*. Albany, NY: Munsell's, 1895. 350p.
http://moa.cit.cornell.edu/dienst/moabrowse.fly/MOA-JOURNALS2:BUNK-0101/5/1:TIFF2GIF:100

Cornell

Cornell, John. *Genealogy of the Cornell Family: Being an Account of the Descendants of Thomas Cornell of Portsmouth, R.I.* New York, NY: T. A. Wright, 1902. 468p.
http://moa.cit.cornell.edu/dienst/moabrowse.ez/MOA-JOURNALS2:GENE-0001/1/20:GIF89:10

Covert

Bunker, Mary Powell. *Long Island Genealogies, Families of Albertson, Andrews, Bedell, Birdsall, Bowne, Carman, Carr, Clowes, Cock, Cornelius, Covert, Dean, Doughty, Duryea, Feke, Frost, Haff, Hallock, Haydock, Hicks, Hopkins, Jackson, Jones, Keese, Ketcham, Kirby,*

Liones, Marvin, Merritt, Moore, Mott, Oakley, Onderdonck, Pearsall, Post, Powell, Prior, Robbins, Rodman, Rowland, Rushmore, Sands, Scudder, Seaman, Searing, Smith, Strickland, Titus, Townsend, Underhill, Valentine, Vanderdonk, Weeks, Whitman, Whitson, Willets, Williams, Willis, Wright, and other Families. Being Kindred Descendants of Thomas Powell of Bethpage, L.I., 1688. Albany, NY: Munsell's, 1895. 350p.
http://moa.cit.cornell.edu/dienst/moabrowse.fly/MOA-JOURNALS2:BUNK-0101/5/1:TIFF2GIF:100

Cowley

Spratt, Thomas. *An Account of the Life and Writings of Mr. Abraham Cowley.* Unknown.
http://library.utoronto.ca/www/utel/rp/criticism/cowle_il.html

Crosby

Crosby, Elisha Oscar. *Memoirs of Elisha Oscar Crosby, Reminiscences of California and Guatemala from 1849 to 1864.* San Marino, CA: Huntington Library, 1945. 119p.
http://memory.loc.gov/cgi-bin/query/r?ammem/calbkbib:@field(AUTHOR+@band(Crosby,+Elisha+Oscar, 1818-1895.+))

Cross

Cross, Jonathan. *Five Years in the Alleghanies.* New York, NY: American Tract Society, 1863. 208p.
http://moa.umdl.umich.edu/cgi-bin/moa/sgml/moa-idx?notisid=ANY9680

Cross, Lilian A. *Appreciation of Loved Ones Who Made Life Rich for Many. My Father, John Francis Cross, My Mother, Sarah Jane Cross.* Oakland, CA: Tribune Press, 1933. 101p.
http://memory.loc.gov/cgi-bin/query/r?ammem/calbkbib:@field(AUTHOR+@band(Cross,+Lilian+A.+))

Crummell

Crummell, Alexander. *1844-1894, the Shades and the Lights of a Fifty Years' Ministry, Juilate, a Sermon.* Washington, DC: St. Luke's Church, 1894. 31p.
http://memory.loc.gov/cgi-bin/query/r?ammem/aap:@field(SUBJ+@band(Afro-American+clergy--Biography.+))

Phillips, Henry L. *In Memoriam of the Late Rev. Alex Crummell, D.D. of Washington, D.C., an Address Delivered before the American Negro Historical Society of Philadelphia.* Philadelphia, PA: Coleman Printery, 1899. 21p.
http://memory.loc.gov/cgi-bin/query/r?ammem/murray:@field(FLD001+91898532+):@@@REF

Crumper

Beard, Ida May. *My Own Life, or a Deserted Woman.* NC: Author, 1898. 212p.
http://metalab.unc.edu/docsouth/beard/menu.html

Crumpton

Crumpton, Hezekiah John and Washington Bryan Crumpton. *The Adventure of Two Alabama Boys (California Gold Rush).* Montgomery, AL: Paragon Press, 1912. 238p.
http://metalab.unc.edu/docsouth/crumpton/menu.html

Curtiss

Curtiss, Daniel S. *Western Portraiture, and Emigrants' Guide, a Description of Wisconsin, Illinois, and Iowa with Remarks on Minnesota and Other Territories.* New York, NY: Colton, 1852. 370p.
http://moa.umdl.umich.edu/cgi-bin/moa/sgml/moa-idx?notisid=AJA3436

Curwen

Vinton, John Adams. *The Giles Memorial. Genealogical Memoirs of the Families Bearing the Names of Giles, Gould, Holmes, Jennison, Leonard, Lindall, Curwen, Marshall, Robinson, Sampson and Webb, also Genealogical Sketches of the Pool, Very, Tarr and other Families, with a History of Pemaquid, Ancient and Modern, Some Accounts of Early Settlements in Maine and Some Details of Indian Warfare.* Boston, MA: Dutton, 1864. 600p.
http://genweb.net/~blackwell/ma/Gyles1864/

Custer

Custer, George Armstrong. *My Life on the Plains.* New York, NY: Sheldon and Co., 1874. 256p.
http://www.ukans.edu/carrie/kancoll/books/custerg/

Dabney

Maury, Dabney Herndon. *Recollections of a Virginian in the Mexican, Indian and Civil Wars.* New York, NY: Scribners, 1894. 279p.
http://metalab.unc.edu/docsouth/maury/menu.html

Smedes, Susan Dabney. *Memorials of a Southern Planter.* Baltimore, MD: Cushings & Bailey, 1888. 348p.
http://moa.umdl.umich.edu/cgi-bin/moa/sgml/moa-idx?notisid=AFK4047

Dally

Dally, Nathan. *Track and Trails, or Incidents in the Life of a Minnesota Territorial Pioneer.* Walker, MN: Cass County Pioneer, 1931. 138p.
http://memory.loc.gov/cgi-bin/query/r?ammem/lhbum:@field(DOCID+@lit(07519T000)):@@@REF

Darby

Darby, William. *A Tour from the City of New York to Detroit in the Michigan Territory Made between the 22d of September 1818. The Tour is Accompanied with a Map upon Which the Route Will be Designated, a Particular Map of the Falls and River of Niagra, and the Environs of the City of Detroit.* New York, NY: Kirk & Mercein, 1819. 300p.
http://memory.loc.gov/cgi-bin/query/r?ammem/lhbumbib:@field(SUBJ+@band(New+York++State+--Description+and+travel.+))

Davis

Colt, Miriam Davis. *Went to Kansas, Being a Thrilling Account of an Ill Fated Expedition to That Fairy Land and Its Sad Result, together with a Sketch of the Life of the Author and How the World Goes with Her.* Watertown, NY: Ingalls & Co., 1862. 294p.
http://www.ukans.edu/carrie/kancoll/books/colt/

Davis, Stephen Chapin. *California Gold Rush Merchant, the Journal of Stephen Chapin Davis.* San Marino, CA: Huntington Library, 1956. 124p.
http://memory.loc.gov/cgi-bin/query/r?ammem/calbkbib:@field(AUTHOR+@band(Davis,+Stephen+Chapin,1833-1856.+))

Davis, William Heath. *Seventy-five Years in California, a History of Events and Life in California, Personal, Political and Military, under the Mexican Regime, during the Quasi-military Government of the Territory by the United States and after the Admission of the State to the Union.* San Francisco, CA: Howell, 1929. 422p.
http://memory.loc.gov/cgi-bin/query/r?ammem/calbkbib:@field(AUTHOR+@band(Davis,+William+Heath,1822-1909.+))

Dawson
Dawson, Sarah Morgan. *A Confederate Girl's Diary.* Boston, MA: Houghton, Mifflin, 1913. 441p.
http://metalab.unc.edu/docsouth/dawson/menu.html

Day
Arms, Mary L. *Incidents in the Life of a Blind Girl, Mary L. Day, a Graduate of the Maryland Institution for the Blind.* Baltimore, MD: Young, 1859. 208p.
http://moa.umdl.umich.edu/cgi-bin/moa/sgml/moa-idx?notisid=AEU2592

Dean
Bunker, Mary Powell. *Long Island Genealogies, Families of Albertson, Andrews, Bedell, Birdsall, Bowne, Carman, Carr, Clowes, Cock, Cornelius, Covert, Dean, Doughty, Duryea, Feke, Frost, Haff, Hallock, Haydock, Hicks, Hopkins, Jackson, Jones, Keese, Ketcham, Kirby, Liones, Marvin, Merritt, Moore, Mott, Oakley, Onderdonck, Pearsall, Post, Powell, Prior, Robbins, Rodman, Rowland, Rushmore, Sands, Scudder, Seaman, Searing, Smith, Strickland, Titus, Townsend, Underhill, Valentine, Vanderdonk, Weeks, Whitman, Whitson, Willets, Williams, Willis, Wright, and other Families. Being Kindred Descendants of Thomas Powell of Bethpage, L.I., 1688.* Albany, NY: Munsell's, 1895. 350p.
http://moa.cit.cornell.edu/dienst/moabrowse.fly/MOA-JOURNALS2:BUNK-0101/5/1:TIFF2GIF:100

Delano
Delano, Alonzo. *Alonzo Delano's California Correspondence, being Letters Hitherto Uncollected from the Ottawa (Illinois) Free Trader and the New Orleans True Delta, 1849-1952.* Sacramento, CA: Sacramento Book Collector's Club, 1952. 155p.
http://memory.loc.gov/cgi-bin/query/r?ammem/calbk:@field(DOCID+@lit(C073T00)):@@@REF

————. *Life on the Plains and among the Diggings, Being Scenes and Adventures of an Overland Journey to California, with Particular Incidents of the Route, Mistakes and Sufferings of the Emigrants, the Indian Tribes, the Present and Future of the Great West.* New York, NY: Miller, Orton & Co., 1857. 384p.
http://memory.loc.gov/cgi-bin/query/r?ammem/calbk:@field(DOCID+@lit(C171T00)):@@@REF

Delany
Delany, Lucy A. *From the Darkness Cometh the Light, or Struggles for Freedom.* St. Louis, MO: J. T. Smith, unknown. 64p.
http://digilib.nypl.org/dynaweb/digs/wwm97254/

Rollin, Frank A. *Life and Public Services of Martin R. Delany, Sub-Assistant Commissioner Bureau Relief of Refugees, Freedmen and of Abandoned Lands, and Late Major 104th U.S. Colored Troops.* Boston, MA: Lee and Shepard, 1883. 367p.
http://digilib.nypl.org/dynaweb/digs/wwm9720/

Depew

Depew, Chauncey Mitchell. *My Memories of Eighty Years*. New York, NY: Scribner's Sons, 1922. 417p.
http://tom.cs.cmu.edu/cgi-bin/book/lookup?num=2045

De Saussure

De Saussure, Nancy Bostick. *Old Plantation Days, Being Recollections of Southern Life before the Civil War*. New York, NY: Duffield & Co., 1909. 123p.
http://metalab.unc.edu/docsouth/desaussure/menu.html

Den

McGowan, Edward. *Narrative of Edward McGowan, including a Full Account of the Author's Adventures and Perils while Persecuted by the San Francisco Vigilance Committee of 1856, together with a Report of His Trial, which Resulted in His Acquittal*. San Francisco, CA: Russell, 1917. 240p.
http://memory.loc.gov/cgi-bin/query/r?ammem/calbkbib:@field(AUTHOR+@band(McGowan,+Edward, 1813-1893.+))

Donner

Houghton, Eliza Poor Donner. *The Expedition of the Donner Party and Its Tragic Fate*. Chicago, IL: McClurg, 1911. 374p.
http://memory.loc.gov/cgi-bin/query/r?ammem/calbkbib:@field(AUTHOR+@band(Houghton,+Eliza+Poor+Donner,1843-1922.+))

Douglass

Douglass, Frederick. *Life and Times of Frederick Douglass, His Early Life as a Slave, His Escape from Bondage and His Complete History to the Present Time*. Hartford, CT: Park, 1881. 516p.
http://metalab.unc.edu/docsouth/douglasslife/menu.html

Dowsett

Dowsett, Charles Finch. *A Start in Life. A Journey across America, Fruit Farming in California*. London: Dowsett & Co., 1891. 112p.
http://memory.loc.gov/cgi-bin/query/r?ammem/calbkbib:@field(AUTHOR+@band(Dowsett,+Charles+Finch,1835+or+6-1915.+))

Doy

Doy, John. *The Narrative of John Doy, of Lawrence, Kansas*. New York, NY: Holman, 1860. 136p.
http://moa.umdl.umich.edu/cgi-bin/moa/sgml/moa-idx?notisid=ABJ5091

Doughty

Bunker, Mary Powell. *Long Island Genealogies, Families of Albertson, Andrews, Bedell, Birdsall, Bowne, Carman, Carr, Clowes, Cock, Cornelius, Covert, Dean, Doughty, Duryea, Feke, Frost, Haff, Hallock, Haydock, Hicks, Hopkins, Jackson, Jones, Keese, Ketcham, Kirby, Liones, Marvin, Merritt, Moore, Mott, Oakley, Onderdonck, Pearsall, Post, Powell, Prior, Robbins, Rodman, Rowland, Rushmore, Sands, Scudder, Seaman, Searing, Smith, Strickland,*

Titus, Townsend, Underhill, Valentine, Vanderdonk, Weeks, Whitman, Whitson, Willets, Williams, Willis, Wright, and other Families. Being Kindred Descendants of Thomas Powell of Bethpage, L.I., 1688. Albany, NY: Munsell's, 1895. 350p.
http://moa.cit.cornell.edu/dienst/moabrowse.fly/MOA-JOURNALS2:BUNK-0101/5/1:TIFF2GIF:100

Dudley

Jones, Augustine. *The Life and Work of Thomas Dudley, the Second Governor of Massachusetts.* Boston, MA: Houghton, Mifflin, 1899. 486p.
http://moa.cit.cornell.edu/dienst/moabrowse.fly/MOA-JOURNALS2:JONE-0212/5/1:TIFF2GIF:100

Duffield

Duffield, Samuel Willoughby. *A Farewell Sermon Delivered in the First Presbyterian Church, Ann Arbor, Michigan.* Ann Arbor, MI: Courier Steam Printing, 1874. 20p.
http://moa.umdl.umich.edu/cgi-bin/moa/sgml/moa-idx?notisid=AAM7378

Duryea

Bunker, Mary Powell. *Long Island Genealogies, Families of Albertson, Andrews, Bedell, Birdsall, Bowne, Carman, Carr, Clowes, Cock, Cornelius, Covert, Dean, Doughty, Duryea, Feke, Frost, Haff, Hallock, Haydock, Hicks, Hopkins, Jackson, Jones, Keese, Ketcham, Kirby, Liones, Marvin, Merritt, Moore, Mott, Oakley, Onderdonck, Pearsall, Post, Powell, Prior, Robbins, Rodman, Rowland, Rushmore, Sands, Scudder, Seaman, Searing, Smith, Strickland, Titus, Townsend, Underhill, Valentine, Vanderdonk, Weeks, Whitman, Whitson, Willets, Williams, Willis, Wright, and other Families. Being Kindred Descendants of Thomas Powell of Bethpage, L.I., 1688.* Albany, NY: Munsell's, 1895. 350p.
http://moa.cit.cornell.edu/dienst/moabrowse.fly/MOA-JOURNALS2:BUNK-0101/5/1:TIFF2GIF:100

Dwight

Bacon, Edward. *Among the Cotton Thieves.* Detroit, MI: Free Press Steam Book, 1867. 300p.
http://moa.umdl.umich.edu/cgi-bin/moa/sgml/moa-idx?notisid=ACK4755

Dyer

Rogers, Horatio, *Mary Dyer of Rhode Island, the Quaker Martyr That Was Hanged on Boston Common, June 1, 1660.* Providence, RI: Preston and Rounds, 1896. 115p.
http://moa.cit.cornell.edu/dienst/moabrowse.fly/MOA-JOURNALS2:ROGE-0035/5/1:TIFF2GIF:100

-E

Early

Early, R. H. *Lieutenant General Jubal Anderson Early, C.S.A. Autobiographical Sketch and Narrative of the War between the States.* Philadelphia, PA: Lippincott, 1912. 496p.
http://metalab.unc.edu/docsouth/early/menu.html

Eastman

Eastman, Edwin. *Seven and Nine Years among the Comanches and Apaches, an Autobiography.* Jersey City, NJ: Johnson, 1874. 326p.
http://moa.umdl.umich.edu/cgi-bin/moa/sgml/moa-idx?notisid=ABB5201

Edwards

Edwards, William James. *Twenty-five Years in the Black Belt.* Boston, MA: Cornhill Co., 1918. 143p.
http://metalab.unc.edu/docsouth/edwards/menu.html

Manley, John. *Cattaraugus County, Embracing Its Agricultural Society, Newspapers, Civil List, from the Organization of the County to 1857, Biographies of the Old Pioneers, with Portraits, Benjamin Chamberlain, Peter Ten Broeck, Frederick S. Martin, Chauncey J. Fox, Alson Leavenworth, Stanley N. Clarke, and of Congressmen Francis S. Edwards and Reuben E. Fenton, Colonial and State Governors of New York, Names of Towns and Post Offices with the Statistics of Each Town.* Little Valley, NY: Author, 1857. 140p.
http://moa.cit.cornell.edu/dienst/moabrowse.fly/MOA-JOURNALS2:MANL-0089/3/1:TIFF2GIF:100

Eggleston

Eggleston, George Cary. *A Rebel's Recollections.* New York, NY: Hurd and Houghton, 1875. 260p.
http://metalab.unc.edu/docsouth/eggleston/menu.html

Ellis

Ellis, Henry Hiram. *From the Kennebec to California, Reminiscences of a California Pioneer.* Los Angeles, CA: Lewis, 1959. 88p.
http://memory.loc.gov/cgi-bin/query/r?ammem/calbkbib:@field(AUTHOR+@band(Ellis,+Henry+Hiram, 1829-1909.+))

Ellis, William Turner. *Memories, My Seventy-two Years in the Romantic County of Yuba, California.* Eugene, OR: University of Oregon, 1939. 308p.
http://memory.loc.gov/cgi-bin/query/r?ammem/calbkbib:@field(AUTHOR+@band(Ellis,+William+Turner,1866-+))

Embree

Hoss, Elijah Embree. *Elihu Embree, Abolitionist.* Nashville, TN: University Press Co., 1897. 28p.
http://memory.loc.gov/cgi-bin/query/r?ammem/aap:@field(SUBJ+@band(Embree,+Elihu,--1782-1820.+))

Eppes

Eppes, Susan Bradford. *Through Some Eventful Years.* Macon, GA: Burke, 1926. 382p.
http://moa.umdl.umich.edu/cgi-bin/moa/sgml/moa-idx?notisid=AFJ8883

Erwin

Biography of James Patton. Asheville, NC: Patton Family, 1850. 34p.
http://metalab.unc.edu/docsouth/patton/menu.html

Evans

Evans, Albert S. *A la California, Sketch of Life in the Golden State.* San Francisco, CA: Bancroft, 1873. 379p.
http://memory.loc.gov/cgi-bin/query/r?ammem/calbkbib:@field(AUTHOR+@band(Evans,+Albert+S.+))

-F

Fairchild

Fairchild, Lucius. *California Letters of Lucius Fairchild*. Madison, WI: State Historical Society of Wisconsin, 1931. 212p.
http://memory.loc.gov/cgi-bin/query/r?ammem/calbkbib:@field(AUTHOR+@band(Fairchild,+Lucius,1831-1896.+))

Faribault

Casgrain, Henri Raymond. *G. B. Faribault*. Quebec, Canada: Brousseau, 1867. 130p.
http://www.canadiana.org/cgi-bin/ECO/mtq?id=04ee01375f&doc=00522

Farnham

Farnham, Eliza Woodson Burhans. *California, Indoors and Out, or How We Farm, Mine and Live Generally in the Golden State*. New York, NY: Dix, Edwards, 1856. 508p.
http://memory.loc.gov/cgi-bin/query/r?ammem/calbkbib:@field(AUTHOR+@band(Farnham,+Eliza+Woodson+Burhans,1815-1864.+))

Farrar

Farrar, J. Maurice. *Five Years in Minnesota. Sketches of Life in a Western State*. London: Low, Marston, Searle & Rivington, 1880. 269p.
http://memory.loc.gov/cgi-bin/query/r?ammem/lhbum:@field(DOCID+@lit(05676T000)):@@@REF

Fearn

Fearn, Frances Hewitt. *Diary of a Refugee*. New York, NY: Moffat, Yard and Co. 1910. 149p.
http://metalab.unc.edu/docsouth/fearn/menu.html

Fee

Fee, John Gregg. *Autobiography of John G. Fee, Berea, Kentucky*. Chicago, IL: National Christian Association, 1891. 211p.
http://metalab.unc.edu/docsouth/fee/menu.html

Feke

Bunker, Mary Powell. *Long Island Genealogies, Families of Albertson, Andrews, Bedell, Birdsall, Bowne, Carman, Carr, Clowes, Cock, Cornelius, Covert, Dean, Doughty, Duryea, Feke, Frost, Haff, Hallock, Haydock, Hicks, Hopkins, Jackson, Jones, Keese, Ketcham, Kirby, Liones, Marvin, Merritt, Moore, Mott, Oakley, Onderdonck, Pearsall, Post, Powell, Prior, Robbins, Rodman, Rowland, Rushmore, Sands, Scudder, Seaman, Searing, Smith, Strickland, Titus, Townsend, Underhill, Valentine, Vanderdonk, Weeks, Whitman, Whitson, Willets, Williams, Willis, Wright, and other Families. Being Kindred Descendants of Thomas Powell of Bethpage, L.I., 1688*. Albany, NY: Munsell's, 1895. 350p.
http://moa.cit.cornell.edu/dienst/moabrowse.fly/MOA-JOURNALS2:BUNK-0101/5/1:TIFF2GIF:100

Felton

Felton, Rebecca Latimer. *County Life in Georgia in the Days of My Youth*. Atlanta, GA: Index Printing Co., 1919. 303p.
http://metalab.unc.edu/docsouth/felton/menu.html

Fenton

Manley, John. *Cattaraugus County, Embracing Its Agricultural Society, Newspapers, Civil List, from the Organization of the County to 1857, Biographies of the Old Pioneers, with Portraits, Benjamin Chamberlain, Peter Ten Broeck, Frederick S. Martin, Chauncey J. Fox, Alson Leavenworth, Stanley N. Clarke, and of Congressmen Francis S. Edwards and Reuben E. Fenton, Colonial and State Governors of New York, Names of Towns and Post Offices with the Statistics of Each Town.* Little Valley, NY: Author, 1857. 140p.
http://moa.cit.cornell.edu/dienst/moabrowse.fly/MOA-JOURNALS2:MANL-0089/3/1:TIFF2GIF:100

Ferebee

Ferebee, London R. *A Brief History of the Slave Life of Rev. L. R. Ferebee, and the Battles of Life and Four Years of His Ministerial Life.* Raleigh, NC: Edwards, Broughton & Co., Steam Printers, Publishers and Binders, 1882. 24p.
http://metalab.unc.edu/docsouth/ferebee/menu.html

Field

Field, Stephen Johnson. *Personal Reminiscences of Early Days in California, with Other Sketches.* San Francisco, CA: Author, 1880. 248p.
http://memory.loc.gov/cgi-bin/query/r?ammem/calbkbib:@field(AUTHOR+@band(Field,+Stephen+Johnson,1816-1899.+))

Fisher

Fisher, Walter Mulrea. *The Californians.* London: Macmillan, 1876. 236p.
http://memory.loc.gov/cgi-bin/query/r?ammem/calbkbib:@field(AUTHOR+@band(Fisher,+Walter+Mulrea,1849-1919.+))

Fitzgerald

Fitzgerald, Oscar Penn. *California Sketches.* Nashville, TN: Southern Methodist Publishing House, 1880. 208p.
http://memory.loc.gov/cgi-bin/query/r?ammem/calbk:@field(DOCID+@lit(C059T00)):@@@REF

————. *California Sketches, New Series.* Nashville, TN: Southern Methodist Publishing House, 1881. 288p.
http://memory.loc.gov/cgi-bin/query/r?ammem/calbk:@field(DOCID+@lit(C060T00)):@@@REF

Fleetwood

Fleetwood, Christian Abraham. *The Negro as a Soldier.* Washington, DC: Howard University Press, 1895. 19p.
http://memory.loc.gov/cgi-bin/query/r?ammem/murray:@field(FLD001+12000751+):@@@REF

Flipper

United States. Congress. House Committee on Military Affairs. *Second Lieut. Henry Ossian Flipper.* Washington, DC: Government Printing Office, 1901. 5p.
http://memory.loc.gov/cgi-bin/query/r?ammem/aap:@field(SUBJ+@band(Flipper,+Henry+Ossian,--1856-1940--Trials,+litigation,+etc.+))

Folsom

Folsom, William Henry Carman. *Fifty Years in the Northwest.* St. Paul, MN: Pioneer Press Co., 1888. 763p.
http://memory.loc.gov/cgi-bin/query/r?ammem/lhbum:@field(DOCID+@lit(01070T000)):@@@REF

Foot

Foot, Samuel A. *Autobiography, Collateral Reminiscences, Arguments in Important Causes, Speeches, Addresses, Lectures and Other Writings.* New York, NY: Smith & McDougall, 1873. 2 vols.
http://moa.cit.cornell.edu/dienst/moabrowse.fly/MOA-JOURNALS2:FOOT-0012/3/1:TIFF2GIF:100

Foote

Foote, Julia A. J. *A Brand Plucked from the Fire, an Autobiographical Sketch.* Cleveland, OH: Lauer & Yost, 1879. 124p.
http://digilib.nypl.org/dynaweb/digs/wwm978/

Force

Special Report of the Librarian of Congress to the Joint Committee on the Library Concerning the Historical Library of Peter Force, Esq. Washington, DC: Library of Congress, 1867. 8p.
http://memory.loc.gov/cgi-bin/query/r?ammem/aap:@field(SUBJ+@band(Force,+Peter,--1790-1868.+))

Ford

Ford, Arthur Peronneau. *Life in the Confederate Army, Being Personal Experiences of a Private Soldier in the Confederate Army and Some Experiences and Sketches of Southern Life and Marion Johnstone Ford.* New York, NY: Neale, 1905. 136p.
http://metalab.unc.edu/docsouth/ford/menu.html

Foster

Byron Curtiss, Arthur Lester Byron. *The Life and Adventures of Nat Foster, Trapper and Hunter of the Adirondacks.* Utica, NY: Griffiths, 1897. 286p.
http://moa.cit.cornell.edu/dienst/moabrowse.fly/MOA-JOURNALS2:CURT-0015/5/1:TIFF2GIF:100

Simms, Jeptha Root. *Trappers of New York or a Biography of Nicholas Stoner and Nathaniel Foster, together with Anecdotes of other Celebrated Hunters and Some Account of Sir William Johnson.* Albany, NY: Munsell, 1850. 280p.
http://moa.cit.cornell.edu/dienst/moabrowse.fly/MOA-JOURNALS2:SIMM-0023/5/1:TIFF2GIF:100

Fox

Manley, John. *Cattaraugus County, Embracing Its Agricultural Society, Newspapers, Civil List, from the Organization of the County to 1857, Biographies of the Old Pioneers, with Portraits, Benjamin Chamberlain, Peter Ten Broeck, Frederick S. Martin, Chauncey J. Fox, Alson Leavenworth, Stanley N. Clarke, and of Congressmen Francis S. Edwards and Reuben E. Fenton, Colonial and State Governors of New York, Names of Towns and Post Offices with the Statistics of Each Town.* Little Valley, NY: Author, 1857. 140p.
http://moa.cit.cornell.edu/dienst/moabrowse.fly/MOA-JOURNALS2:MANL-0089/3/1:TIFF2GIF:100

Francis

Francis, John W. *Old New York or Reminiscences of the Past Sixty Years.* New York, NY: Roe, 1858. 384p.
http://moa.cit.cornell.edu/dienst/moabrowse.fly/MOA-JOURNALS2:FRAN-0061/5/1:TIFF2GIF:100

Fremont

Fremont, Jessie Benton. *Far West Sketches.* Boston, MA: Lothrop, 1890. 206p.
http://memory.loc.gov/cgi-bin/query/r?ammem/calbk:@field(DOCID+@lit(C192T00)):@@@REF

————. *A Year of American Travel*. New York, NY: Harper, 1878. 190p.
http://memory.loc.gov/cgi-bin/query/r?ammem/calbk:@field(DOCID+@lit(C188T00)):@@@REF

Fremont, John Charles. *The Life of Col. John Charles Fremont and His Narrative of Explorations and Adventures in Kansas, Nebraska, Oregon and California*. New York, NY: Auburn, Miller, Orton & Mulligan, 1856. 514p.
http://moa.umdl.umich.edu/cgi-bin/moa/sgml/moa-idx?notisid=AAZ9580

Frost
Bunker, Mary Powell. *Long Island Genealogies, Families of Albertson, Andrews, Bedell, Birdsall, Bowne, Carman, Carr, Clowes, Cock, Cornelius, Covert, Dean, Doughty, Duryea, Feke, Frost, Haff, Hallock, Haydock, Hicks, Hopkins, Jackson, Jones, Keese, Ketcham, Kirby, Liones, Marvin, Merritt, Moore, Mott, Oakley, Onderdonck, Pearsall, Post, Powell, Prior, Robbins, Rodman, Rowland, Rushmore, Sands, Scudder, Seaman, Searing, Smith, Strickland, Titus, Townsend, Underhill, Valentine, Vanderdonk, Weeks, Whitman, Whitson, Willets, Williams, Willis, Wright, and other Families. Being Kindred Descendants of Thomas Powell of Bethpage, L.I., 1688*. Albany, NY: Munsell's, 1895. 350p.
http://moa.cit.cornell.edu/dienst/moabrowse.fly/MOA-JOURNALS2:BUNK-0101/5/1:TIFF2GIF:100

Fuller
Ossoli, Sarah Margaret Fuller. *Summer on the Lakes in 1843*. Boston, MA: Little & Brown, 1844. 256p.
http://memory.loc.gov/cgi-bin/query/r?ammem/lhbum:@field(DOCID+@lit(01714T000)):@@@REF

–G

Galpin
Galpin, Charles Josiah. *My Drift into Rural Sociology, Memoirs of Charles Josiah Galpin*. University, LA: Louisiana State University Press, 1938. 166p.
http://chla.mannlib.cornell.edu/cgi-bin/chla/viewer.cgi?docid=title2c.chla.mannlib.cornell/0049galp&format=1:75-GIF&section=Title+Page

Garcelon
Garcelon, Pierre. *Mon Adieu à Mes Chers Enfans, Rev. Pierre Garcelon, Rector of St. Pierre du Bois, Island of Guernsey, 1739-1772*. Unknown.
http://www.lib.usf.edu/spccoll/guide/g/garcelon/page1.html

Geary
Gihon, John H. *Geary and Kansas. Governor Geary's Administration in Kansas, with a Complete History of the Territory until July 1857, Embracing a Full Account of Its Discovery, Geography, Soil, Rivers, Climate, Products, Its Organization as a Territory*. Philadelphia, PA: Rhodes, 1857. 348p.
http://moa.umdl.umich.edu/cgi-bin/moa/sgml/moa-idx?notisid=ABA0699

Gent

Gent, Thomas. *The Life of Thomas Gent, Printer of York, 1693-1778*. London, England: T. Thorpe, 1832. 208p.
http://www.eclipse.co.uk/exeshul/thomasgent/thomasgent.html

George

George, Alice Mendenhall. *The Story of My Childhood, Written for My Children*. Whittier, CA: Smith, 1923. 87p.
http://memory.loc.gov/cgi-bin/query/r?ammem/lhbum:@field(DOCID+@lit(04681T000)):@@@REF

Gerstacker

Gerstacker, Friedrich Wilhelm Christian. *Gerstacker's Travels*. London: Nelson, 1854. 290p.
http://memory.loc.gov/cgi-bin/query/r?ammem/calbk:@field(DOCID+@lit(C110T00)):@@@REF

————. *Scenes of Life in California*. San Francisco, CA: Howell, 1942. 188p.
http://memory.loc.gov/cgi-bin/query/r?ammem/calbk:@field(DOCID+@lit(C017T00)):@@@REF

Gilbert

Douthit, Davis. *Nobody Owns Us, the Story of Joe Gilbert, Midwestern Rebel*. Chicago, IL: Cooperative League of the USA, 1948. 240p.
http://memory.loc.gov/cgi-bin/query/r?ammem/lhbumbib:@field(SUBJ+@band(Gilbert,+Joseph,--1865-+))

Rowlandson, Mary. *Narrative of the Captivity and Restoration of Mrs. Mary Rowlandson*. Unknown. 1862. 316p.
ftp://uiarchive.cso.uiuc.edu/pub/etext/gutenberg/etext97/crmmr10.txt
http://tom.cs.cmu.edu/cgi-bin/book/lookup?num=851

Giles

Vinton, John Adams. *The Giles Memorial. Genealogical Memoirs of the Families Bearing the Names of Giles, Gould, Holmes, Jennison, Leonard, Lindall, Curwen, Marshall, Robinson, Sampson and Webb, also Genealogical Sketches of the Pool, Very, Tarr and other Families, with a History of Pemaquid, Ancient and Modern, Some Account of Early Settlements in Maine and Some Details of Indian Warfare*. Boston, MA: Dutton, 1864. 600p.
http://genweb.net/~blackwell/ma/Gyles1864/

Glisan

Glisan, Rodney. *Journal of Army Life*. San Francisco, CA: Bancroft, 1874. 568p.
http://moa.umdl.umich.edu/cgi-bin/moa/sgml/moa-idx?notisid=AFK1071

Gordon

Gordon, John Brown. *Reminiscences of the Civil War*. New York, NY: Scribners, 1904. 474p.
http://metalab.unc.edu/docsouth/gordon/menu.html

Gordon Cumming, Constance Frederica. *Granite Crags*. Edinburgh: Blackwood, 1884. 384p.
http://memory.loc.gov/cgi-bin/query/r?ammem/calbkbib:@field(AUTHOR+@band(Gordon-Cumming,+C[onstance]+F[rederica],1837-1924.+))

Gould

Vinton, John Adams. *The Giles Memorial. Genealogical Memoirs of the Families Bearing the Names of Giles, Gould, Holmes, Jennison, Leonard, Lindall, Curwen, Marshall, Robinson,*

Sampson and Webb, also Genealogical Sketches of the Pool, Very, Tarr and other Families, with a History of Pemaquid, Ancient and Modern, Some Account of Early Settlements in Maine and Some Details of Indian Warfare. Boston, MA: Dutton, 1864. 600p.
http://genweb.net/~blackwell/ma/Gyles1864/

Grandy
Grandy, Moses. *Narrative of the Life of Moses Grandy, Late a Slave in the United States of America.* London: Gilpin, 1843. 72p.
http://metalab.unc.edu/docsouth/grandy/menu.html

Graves
Graves, Jackson Alpheus. *My Seventy Years in California, 1857-1927.* Los Angeles, CA: Times Mirror Press, 1927. 478p.
http://memory.loc.gov/cgi-bin/query/r?ammem/calbkbib:@field(AUTHOR+@band(Graves,+Jackson+Alpheus,1852-1933.+))

Green
Green, Wharton Jackson. *Recollections and Reflections, an Auto of Half a Century and More.* Raleigh, NC: Edwards & Broughton Printing, 1906. 349p.
http://metalab.unc.edu/docsouth/green/menu.html

Greenhow
Greenhow, Rose O'Neal. *My Imprisonment and the First Year of Abolition Rule at Washington.* London: Bentley, 1863. 352p.
http://metalab.unc.edu/docsouth/greenhow/menu.html

Gregson
Gregson, Eliza Marshall. *The Gregson Memoirs, Containing Mrs. Eliza Gregson's Memory and the Statement of James Gregson.* San Francisco, CA: Kennedy, 1940. 31p.
http://memory.loc.gov/cgi-bin/query/r?ammem/calbkbib:@field(AUTHOR+@band(Gregson,+Eliza+Marshall,1824-+))

Grimes
Grimes, Bryan. *Extracts of Letters of Major General Bryan Grimes to His Wife, Written while in Active Service in the Army of Northern Virginia, together with Some Personal Recollections of the War, Written by Him after Its Close.* Raleigh, NC: Broughton, 1883. 137p.
http://metalab.unc.edu/docsouth/grimes/menu.html

Gronniosaw
Gronniosaw, James Albert Ukawsaw. *A Narrative of the Most Remarkable Particulars in the Life of James Albert Ukawsaw Gronniosaw, an African Prince, Written by Himself.* Newport, RI: Solomon Southwick, 1774. 48p.
http://www.lib.virginia.edu/etext/readex/13311.html

Gunn
Gunn, Lewis Carstairs. *Records of a California Family, Journals and Letters of Lewis C. Gunn and Elizabeth Le Breton Gunn.* San Diego, CA: Johnck and Seeger, 1928. 279p.
http://memory.loc.gov/cgi-bin/query/r?ammem/calbkbib:@field(AUTHOR+@band(Gunn,+Lewis+Carstairs,1813-1892.+))

Guyon

Guyon, Jean Marie Bouvier de la Motte. *Autobiography of Madame Guyon*. New York, NY: Jones, 1880. 346p.
http://ccel.wheaton.edu/guyon/auto/autobi.htm

 –H

Haff

Bunker, Mary Powell. *Long Island Genealogies, Families of Albertson, Andrews, Bedell, Birdsall, Bowne, Carman, Carr, Clowes, Cock, Cornelius, Covert, Dean, Doughty, Duryea, Feke, Frost, Haff, Hallock, Haydock, Hicks, Hopkins, Jackson, Jones, Keese, Ketcham, Kirby, Liones, Marvin, Merritt, Moore, Mott, Oakley, Onderdonck, Pearsall, Post, Powell, Prior, Robbins, Rodman, Rowland, Rushmore, Sands, Scudder, Seaman, Searing, Smith, Strickland, Titus, Townsend, Underhill, Valentine, Vanderdonk, Weeks, Whitman, Whitson, Willets, Williams, Willis, Wright, and other Families. Being Kindred Descendants of Thomas Powell of Bethpage, L.I., 1688*. Albany, NY: Munsell's, 1895. 350p.
http://moa.cit.cornell.edu/dienst/moabrowse.fly/MOA-JOURNALS2:BUNK-0101/5/1:TIFF2GIF:100

Hall

Hall, Harlan Page. *H.P. Hall's Observations, Being More or Less a History of Political Contests in Minnesota from 1849 to 1904*. St. Paul, MN: Author, 1904. 384p.
http://memory.loc.gov/cgi-bin/query/r?ammem/lhbumbib:@field(SUBJ+@band(Minnesota--Politics+and+government--1858-1950.+))

Hall, Linville John and George Gideon Webster. *Around the Horn in '49, Journal of the Hartford Union Mining and Trading Company. Containing the Name, Residence and Occupation of Each Member, with Incidents of the Voyage*. Wethersfield, CT: L. J. Hall, 1898. 252p.
http://memory.loc.gov/cgi-bin/query/r?ammem/calbkbib:@field(AUTHOR+@band(Hartford+Union+Mining+and+Trading+Company.+))

Hallock

Bunker, Mary Powell. *Long Island Genealogies, Families of Albertson, Andrews, Bedell, Birdsall, Bowne, Carman, Carr, Clowes, Cock, Cornelius, Covert, Dean, Doughty, Duryea, Feke, Frost, Haff, Hallock, Haydock, Hicks, Hopkins, Jackson, Jones, Keese, Ketcham, Kirby, Liones, Marvin, Merritt, Moore, Mott, Oakley, Onderdonck, Pearsall, Post, Powell, Prior, Robbins, Rodman, Rowland, Rushmore, Sands, Scudder, Seaman, Searing, Smith, Strickland, Titus, Townsend, Underhill, Valentine, Vanderdonk, Weeks, Whitman, Whitson, Willets, Williams, Willis, Wright, and other Families. Being Kindred Descendants of Thomas Powell of Bethpage, L.I., 1688*. Albany, NY: Munsell's, 1895. 350p.
http://moa.cit.cornell.edu/dienst/moabrowse.fly/MOA-JOURNALS2:BUNK-0101/5/1:TIFF2GIF:100

Hamill

Hamill, Howard Melancthon. *The Old South, a Monograph*. Nashville, TN: Smith & Lamar, 1904. 79p.
http://metalab.unc.edu/docsouth/hamill/menu.html

Hamilton

Hamilton, James Gillespie. *Notebooks of James Gillespie Hamilton, a Merchant of Old Westport, Missouri (1844-1858)*. Fresno, CA: Katharine Jones Moore, 1953. 301p.
http://memory.loc.gov/cgi-bin/query/r?ammem/calbkbib:@field(AUTHOR+@band(Hamilton,+James+Gillespie,1816-1869.+))

Hammon

Hammon, Jupiter. *An Address to the Negroes in the State of New York, by Jupiter Hammon, Servant of John Lloyd, Jun., Esq. of the Manor of Queen's Village, Long Island*. New York, NY: Carroll and Patterson, 1787. 20p.
http://www.lib.virginia.edu/etext/readex/20400.html

Hammond

Hammond, Samuel H. *Hunting Adventures in the Northern Wilds, or a Tramp in the Chateaugay, over Hills, Lakes and Forest Streams*. Philadelphia, PA: Keystone Publishing Co., 1890. 340p.
http://moa.cit.cornell.edu/dienst/moabrowse.fly/MOA-JOURNALS2:HAMM-0076/5/1:TIFF2GIF:100

———, and L. W. Mansfield. *Country Margins and Rambles of a Journalist*. New York, NY: Derby, 1855. 356p.
http://moa.cit.cornell.edu/dienst/moabrowse.fly/MOA-JOURNALS2:HAMM-0022/5/1:TIFF2GIF:100

Hardeman

Burnett, Peter Hardeman. *Recollections and Opinions of an Old Pioneer*. New York, NY: Appleton, 1880. 448p.
http://memory.loc.gov/cgi-bin/query/r?ammem/calbkbib:@field(AUTHOR+@band(Burnett,+Peter+H[ardeman],1807-1895.+))

Harland

Harland, Marion. *Marion Harland's Autobiography, the Story of a Long Life*. New York, NY: Harper, 1910. 498p.
http://metalab.unc.edu/docsouth/harland/menu.html

Harper

Harper, Harriet. *Letters from California*. Portland, ME: Thurston, 1888. 104p.
http://memory.loc.gov/cgi-bin/query/r?ammem/calbkbib:@field(AUTHOR+@band(Harper,+Harriet.+))

Harper, I. I. *An Artic Boat Journey in the Autumn of 1854*. Boston, MA: Osgood, 1871. 436p.
http://moa.umdl.umich.edu/cgi-bin/moa/sgml/moa-idx?notisid=AFK7247

Harrison

Harrison, Mrs. Burton. *Recollections Grave and Gay*. New York, NY: Scribners, 1911. 386p.
http://metalab.unc.edu/docsouth/harrison/menu.html

Hatheway

Grimke, Francis J. *Anne M. Purvis*. Washington, DC: Colored Orphans Home, 1899. 18p.
http://memory.loc.gov/cgi-bin/query/r?ammem/aap:@field(SUBJ+@band(Funeral+addresses--Washington++D.C.+--1899.+))

Haugen

Haugen, Nils Pederson. *Pioneer and Political Reminiscences*. Evansville, WI: Antes Press, 1930. 109p.
http://memory.loc.gov/cgi-bin/query/r?ammem/lhbumbib:@field(SUBJ+@band(Frontier+and+pioneer+ life--Wisconsin--Pierce+Co.+))

Haviland

Haviland, Laura Smith. *A Woman's Life-work, Labors and Experiences of Laura S. Haviland*. Cincinnati, OH: Walden & Stowe, 1882. 531p.
http://memory.loc.gov/cgi-bin/query/r?ammem/lhbumbib:@field(SUBJ+@band(Freedmen.+))

Hawes

Harland, Marion. *Marion Harland's Autobiography, the Story of a Long Life*. New York, NY: Harper, 1910. 498p.
http://metalab.unc.edu/docsouth/harland/menu.html

Haycock

Bunker, Mary Powell. *Long Island Genealogies, Families of Albertson, Andrews, Bedell, Birdsall, Bowne, Carman, Carr, Clowes, Cock, Cornelius, Covert, Dean, Doughty, Duryea, Feke, Frost, Haff, Hallock, Haydock, Hicks, Hopkins, Jackson, Jones, Keese, Ketcham, Kirby, Liones, Marvin, Merritt, Moore, Mott, Oakley, Onderdonck, Pearsall, Post, Powell, Prior, Robbins, Rodman, Rowland, Rushmore, Sands, Scudder, Seaman, Searing, Smith, Strickland, Titus, Townsend, Underhill, Valentine, Vanderdonk, Weeks, Whitman, Whitson, Willets, Williams, Willis, Wright, and other Families. Being Kindred Descendants of Thomas Powell of Bethpage, L.I., 1688*. Albany, NY: Munsell's, 1895. 350p.
http://moa.cit.cornell.edu/dienst/moabrowse.fly/MOA-JOURNALS2:BUNK-0101/5/1:TIFF2GIF:100

Hayes

Hayes, Benjamin Ignatius. *Pioneer Notes from the Diaries of Judge Benjamin Hayes, 1849-1875*. Los Angeles, CA: Author, 1929. 307p.
http://memory.loc.gov/cgi-bin/query/r?ammem/calbkbib:@field(AUTHOR+@band(Hayes,+Benjamin+ Ignatius,1815-1877.+))

Headley

Headley, Joel Tyler. *The Adirondack, or, Life in the Woods*. New York, NY: Baker & Scribner, 1853. 316p.
http://moa.umdl.umich.edu/cgi-bin/moa/sgml/moa-idx?notisid=AAS0215

Heco

Heco, Joseph. *The Narrative of a Japanese, What He Has Seen and the People He Has Met in the Course of the Last Forty Years*. Tokyo, Japan: Maruzen, 1895. 2 vols.
http://memory.loc.gov/cgi-bin/query/r?ammem/calbkbib:@field(AUTHOR+@band(Heco,+Joseph,1837-1897.+))

Helper

Helper, Hinton Rowan. *The Land of Gold, Reality Versus Fiction*. Baltimore, MD: Taylor, 1855. 300p.
http://memory.loc.gov/cgi-bin/query/r?ammem/calbkbib:@field(AUTHOR+@band(Helper,+Hinton+ Rowan,1829-1909.+))

Henagan

Jervey, Susan Ravenel and Charlotte St. J. Ravenel. *Two Diaries from Middle St. John's, Berkeley, South Carolina, February-May, 1865. Journals Kept by Miss Susan R. Jervey and Miss Charlotte St. J. Ravenel at Northampton and Pooshee Plantations, and Reminiscences of Mrs. (Waring) Henagan with Two Contemporary Reports from Federal Officials.* St. John's Hunting Club, 1921. 56p.
http://metalab.unc.edu/docsouth/jervey/menu.html

Henry

Wirt, William. *Sketches of the Life and Character of Patrick Henry.* Philadelphia, PA: James Webster, 1817. 427p.
http://metalab.unc.edu/docsouth/wirt/menu.html

Hewitt

Fearn, Frances Hewitt. *Diary of a Refugee.* New York, NY: Moffat, Yard and Co. 1910. 149p.
http://metalab.unc.edu/docsouth/fearn/menu.html

Hicks

Bunker, Mary Powell. *Long Island Genealogies, Families of Albertson, Andrews, Bedell, Birdsall, Bowne, Carman, Carr, Clowes, Cock, Cornelius, Covert, Dean, Doughty, Duryea, Feke, Frost, Haff, Hallock, Haydock, Hicks, Hopkins, Jackson, Jones, Keese, Ketcham, Kirby, Liones, Marvin, Merritt, Moore, Mott, Oakley, Onderdonck, Pearsall, Post, Powell, Prior, Robbins, Rodman, Rowland, Rushmore, Sands, Scudder, Seaman, Searing, Smith, Strickland, Titus, Townsend, Underhill, Valentine, Vanderdonk, Weeks, Whitman, Whitson, Willets, Williams, Willis, Wright, and other Families. Being Kindred Descendants of Thomas Powell of Bethpage, L.I., 1688.* Albany, NY: Munsell's, 1895. 350p.
http://moa.cit.cornell.edu/dienst/moabrowse.fly/MOA-JOURNALS2:BUNK-0101/5/1:TIFF2GIF:100

Wright, Marcus J. *Diary of Brigadier General Marcus J. Wright, C.S.A., April 23, 1861-February 26, 1863.* Author, Date Unknown. 8p.
http://metalab.unc.edu/docsouth/wrightmarcus/menu.html

Higginson

Higginson, Thomas Wentworth. *Cheerful Yesterdays.* Boston, MA: Houghton Mifflin, 1898. 376p.
http://moa.cit.cornell.edu/dienst/moabrowse.fly/MOA-JOURNALS2:HIGG-0042/5/1:TIFF2GIF:100

————. *Life of Francis Higginson, First Minister in the Massachusetts Bay Colony and Author of New England's Plantation (1630).* New York, NY: Dodd, Mead and Co., 1891.
http://moa.cit.cornell.edu/dienst/moabrowse.fly/MOA-JOURNALS2:HIGG-0038/3/1:TIFF2GIF:100

Hines

Hines, Gustavus. *A Voyage Round the World, with a History of the Oregon Mission, to which Is Appended a Full Description of Oregon Territory, Its Geography, History and Religion, Designed for the Benefit of Emigrants to That Rising Country.* Buffalo, NY: Derby, 1850. 436p.
http://moa.umdl.umich.edu/cgi-bin/moa/sgml/moa-idx?notisid=ABE0943

Hines, Joseph Wilkinson. *Touching Incidents in the Life and Labors of a Pioneer on the Pacific Coast since 1853.* San Jose, CA: Eaton & Co., 1911. 198p.
http://memory.loc.gov/cgi-bin/query/r?ammem/calbkbib:@field(AUTHOR+@band(Hines,+Joseph+Wilkinson+))

Hoag

Hoag, Joseph. *The Transformation of Joseph Hoag.* Philadelphia, PA: Tract Association of Friends. N.p., n.d.
http://people.delphi.com/pdsippel/hoag.htm

Hoar

Rowlandson, Mary. *Narrative of the Captivity and Restoration of Mrs. Mary Rowlandson.* Unknown. 1862. 316p.
ftp://uiarchive.cso.uiuc.edu/pub/etext/gutenberg/etext97/crmmr10.txt
http://tom.cs.cmu.edu/cgi-bin/book/lookup?num=851

Hodge

Hodge, William. *A Memoir of the Late William Hodge, Sen.* Buffalo, NY: Bigelow Brothers, 1885. 160p.
http://moa.cit.cornell.edu/dienst/moabrowse.fly/MOA-JOURNALS2:HODG-0068/5/1:TIFF2GIF:100

Holbrook

Holbrook, James. *Ten Years among the Mail Bags, or Notes from the Diary of a Special Agent of the Post Office Department.* Philadelphia, PA: H. Cowperthwait & Co., 1855. 454p.
http://moa.umdl.umich.edu/cgi-bin/moa/sgml/moa-idx?notisid=AEC9697

Holder

Holder, Charles Frederick. *Life in the Open, Sport with Rod, Gun Horse, and Hound in Southern California.* New York, NY: Putnam's, 1906. 401p.
http://memory.loc.gov/cgi-bin/query/r?ammem/calbkbib:@field(AUTHOR+@band(Holder,+Charles+Frederick,1851-1915.+))

Holmes

Vinton, John Adams. *The Giles Memorial. Genealogical Memoirs of the Families Bearing the Names of Giles, Gould, Holmes, Jennison, Leonard, Lindall, Curwen, Marshall, Robinson, Sampson and Webb, also Genealogical Sketches of the Pool, Very, Tarr and other Families, with a History of Pemaquid, Ancient and Modern, Some Account of Early Settlements in Maine and Some Details of Indian Warfare.* Boston, MA: Dutton, 1864. 600p.
http://genweb.net/~blackwell/ma/Gyles1864/

Holton

Holton, Edward Dwight. *Travels with Jottings. From Midland to the Pacific.* Milwaukee, WI: Trayser Brothers, 1880. 94p.
http://memory.loc.gov/cgi-bin/query/r?ammem/calbkbib:@field(AUTHOR+@band(Holton,+Edward+D.+))

Homans

Inventory of the Homans Family Papers, 1850-1938. New York, NY: New York Public Library, Manuscripts and Archives Division, 1997. Unpgd.
http://digilib.nypl.org/dynaweb/ead/human/homans/@Generic__BookView

Hone

Hone, Philip. *The Diary of Philip Hone, 1828-1851.* New York, NY: Dodd, Mead and Co., 1889. 2 Vols.
http://moa.cit.cornell.edu/dienst/moabrowse.fly/MOA-JOURNALS2:HONE-0024/5/1:TIFF2GIF:100

Hopkins

Bunker, Mary Powell. *Long Island Genealogies, Families of Albertson, Andrews, Bedell, Birdsall, Bowne, Carman, Carr, Clowes, Cock, Cornelius, Covert, Dean, Doughty, Duryea, Feke, Frost, Haff, Hallock, Haydock, Hicks, Hopkins, Jackson, Jones, Keese, Ketcham, Kirby, Liones, Marvin, Merritt, Moore, Mott, Oakley, Onderdonck, Pearsall, Post, Powell, Prior, Robbins, Rodman, Rowland, Rushmore, Sands, Scudder, Seaman, Searing, Smith, Strickland, Titus, Townsend, Underhill, Valentine, Vanderdonk, Weeks, Whitman, Whitson, Willets, Williams, Willis, Wright, and other Families. Being Kindred Descendants of Thomas Powell of Bethpage, L.I., 1688.* Albany, NY: Munsell's, 1895. 350p.
http://moa.cit.cornell.edu/dienst/moabrowse.fly/MOA-JOURNALS2:BUNK-0101/5/1:TIFF2GIF:100

Horden

Buckland, Augustus Robert. *John Horden, Missionary Bishop, a Life on the Shores of Hudson's Bay.* Toronto, Ontario: Mission Book, 1890. 153p.
http://www.canadiana.org/cgi-bin/ECO/mtq?id=04ee01375f&browse=1220:title

Horton

Horton, George Moses. *Life of George M. Horton, the Colored Bard of North Carolina.* Hillsborough, NC: Heartt, 1845. 20p.
http://metalab.unc.edu/docsouth/hortonlife/menu.html

Houghton

Houghton, Eliza Poor Donner. *The Expedition of the Donner Party and Its Tragic Fate.* Chicago, IL: McClurg, 1911. 374p.
http://memory.loc.gov/cgi-bin/query/r?ammem/calbkbib:@field(AUTHOR+@band(Houghton,+Eliza+Poor+Donner,1843-1922.+))

Houghton, William Robert. *Two Boys in the Civil War and after.* Montgomery, AL: Paragon Press, 1912. 242p.
http://metalab.unc.edu/docsouth/houghton/menu.html

Howard

Howard, John Harris. *A History of Herring Lake, with an Introductory Legend, the Bride of Mystery by the Bard of Benzie.* Boston, MA: Christopher Publishing House, 1929. 84p.
http://memory.loc.gov/cgi-bin/query/r?ammem/lhbumbib:@field(SUBJ+@band(Benzie+Co.,+Mich.--Biography.+))

Howard, Wiley C. *Sketch of Cobb Legion Cavalry and Some Incidents and Scenes Remembered.* Author, 1901. 20p.
http://metalab.unc.edu/docsouth/howard/menu.html

Hubbard

Hubbard, Bela. *Memorials of a Half Century.* New York, NY: Putnam's, 1887. 581p.
http://memory.loc.gov/cgi-bin/query/r?ammem/lhbumbib:@field(SUBJ+@band(Michigan--History--1837-+))

Hubbard, Nathaniel Tuthill. *Autobiography of N. T. Hubbard, with Personal Reminiscences of New York City.* New York, NY: Trow, 1875. 246p.
http://moa.cit.cornell.edu/dienst/moabrowse.fly/MOA-JOURNALS2:HUBB-0026/5/1:TIFF2GIF:100

Huggins

In Memoriam William S. Huggins, Three Sermons to Young Men, Preached by Rev. William S. Huggins of Kalamazoo, Michigan, and a Funeral Discourse by Rev. Samuel Haskell, with an Account of the Funeral and Memorial Meeting. Philadelphia, PA: Presbyterian Publication Committee, 1862. 150p.
http://moa.umdl.umich.edu/cgi-bin/moa/sgml/moa-idx?notisid=AJK3161

Hughes

Hughes, Louis. *Thirty Years a Slave, from Bondage to Freedom, the Institution of Slavery as Seen on the Plantation and in the Home of the Planter.* Milwaukee, WI: South Side Printing Co., 1897. 210p.
http://metalab.unc.edu/docsouth/hughes/menu.html

Hughes, Thomas. *A Boy's Experience in the Civil War, 1860-1865.* Baltimore, MD: Daily Record Co., 1904. 55p.
http://metalab.unc.edu/docsouth/hughest/menu.html

Huntington

Ellis, William Turner. *Memories, My Seventy-two Years in the Romantic County of Yuba, California.* Eugene, OR: University of Oregon, 1939. 308p.
http://memory.loc.gov/cgi-bin/query/r?ammem/calbkbib:@field(AUTHOR+@band(Ellis,+William+Turner,1866-+))

Huntley

Huntly, Henry Veel. *California, Its Gold and Its Inhabitants.* London: Newby, 1856. 2 vols.
http://memory.loc.gov/cgi-bin/query/r?ammem/calbkbib:@field(AUTHOR+@band(Huntley,+Henry+Veel,Sir,1795-1864.+))

Hussey

Greeno, Follet Lamberton. *Obed Hussey, Who, of All Inventors, Made Bread Cheap, Being a True Record of His Life and Struggles to Introduce His Greatest Invention, the Reaper, and Its Success, as Gathered from Pamphlets Published heretofore by Some of His Friends and Associates and Reprinted in This Volume, together with Some Additional Facts and Testimonials from Other Sources.* Rochester, NY: Rochester Herald Publishing, 1912. 262p.
http://chla.mannlib.cornell.edu/cgi-bin/chla/viewer.cgi?docid=title2c.chla.mannlib.cornell/0214gree&format=1:75-GIF&section=Title+Page

Hutchinson

Hosmer, James Kendall. *The Life of Thomas Hutchinson, Royal Governor of the Province of Massachusetts Bay.* Boston, MA: Houghton Mifflin, 1896. 454p.
http://moa.cit.cornell.edu/dienst/moabrowse.fly/MOA-JOURNALS2:HOSM-0221/5/1:TIFF2GIF:100

Salisbury, John Edwin and George Castor Martin. *The American Ancestors of Oratio Dyer Clark and of His Wife Laura Ann King, together with the Ancestry of Anne Marbury Hutchinson, Ancestress of Oratio Dyer Clark.* Asbury Park, NJ: Martin, 1917. 387p.
http://genweb.net/~blackwell/blql/cka1917.htm

Hutton

Hutton, William Rich. *Glances at California, 1847-1853, Diaries and Letters of William Rich Hutton, with a Brief Memoir and Notes.* San Marino, CA: Huntington, 1942. 86p.
http://memory.loc.gov/cgi-bin/query/r?ammem/calbkbib:@field(AUTHOR+@band(Hutton,+William+Rich,1826-1901.+))

-I

Immen

Immen, Looraine Pratt. *Letters of Travel in California in the Winter and Spring of 1896*. Grand Rapids, MI: Author, 1896. 53p.
http://memory.loc.gov/cgi-bin/query/r?ammem/calbkbib:@field(AUTHOR+@band(Immen,+Loraine+[Pratt],1840-+))

-J

Jackson

Bunker, Mary Powell. *Long Island Genealogies, Families of Albertson, Andrews, Bedell, Birdsall, Bowne, Carman, Carr, Clowes, Cock, Cornelius, Covert, Dean, Doughty, Duryea, Feke, Frost, Haff, Hallock, Haydock, Hicks, Hopkins, Jackson, Jones, Keese, Ketcham, Kirby, Liones, Marvin, Merritt, Moore, Mott, Oakley, Onderdonck, Pearsall, Post, Powell, Prior, Robbins, Rodman, Rowland, Rushmore, Sands, Scudder, Seaman, Searing, Smith, Strickland, Titus, Townsend, Underhill, Valentine, Vanderdonk, Weeks, Whitman, Whitson, Willets, Williams, Willis, Wright, and other Families. Being Kindred Descendants of Thomas Powell of Bethpage, L.I., 1688*. Albany, NY: Munsell's, 1895. 350p.
http://moa.cit.cornell.edu/dienst/moabrowse.fly/MOA-JOURNALS2:BUNK-0101/5/1:TIFF2GIF:100

Garrison, William Lloyd. *In Memoriam. Testimonials to the Life and Character of the Late Francis Jackson (1789-1861)*. Boston, MA: R. F. Wallcut, 1861. 36p.
http://moa.umdl.umich.edu/cgi-bin/moa/sgml/moa-idx?notisid=ABT7275

Inventory of the William Henry Jackson Papers. New York, NY: New York Public Library, Manuscripts and Archives Division, 1998. Unpgd.
http://digilib.nypl.org/dynaweb/ead/human/jacksonw/@Generic__BookView

Jackson, Helen Maria Fiske Hunt. *Glimpses of California and the Mission*. Boston, MA: Little, Brown & Co., 1902. 292p.
http://memory.loc.gov/cgi-bin/query/r?ammem/calbkbib:@field(AUTHOR+@band(Jackson,+Helen+[Maria+Fiske]+Hunt,1831-1885.+))

Jackson, John Andrew. *The Experience of a Slave in South Carolina*. London: Passmore & Alabaster, 1862. 48p.
http://metalab.unc.edu/docsouth/jackson/menu.html

Jacobs

Jacobs, Harriet A. *Incidents in the Life of a Slave Girl*. Boston, MA: Author, 1861. 306p.
http://digilib.nypl.org/dynaweb/digs/wwm97255/

James

James, Thomas. *Wonderful Eventful Life of Rev. Thomas James.* Rochester, NY: Post Express Printing Co., 1887. 24p.
http://memory.loc.gov/cgi-bin/query/r?ammem/aap:@field(SUBJ+@band(Autobiographies--New+York++State+--1887.+))

Janney

Janney, Samuel M. *Memoirs of Samuel M. Janney, Late of Lincoln, Loudon County, Virginia. A Minister in the Religious Society of Friends.* Philadelphia, PA: Friends' Book Association, 1881. 309p.
http://metalab.unc.edu/docsouth/janney/menu.html

Jefferson

Shuffelton, Frank. *Thomas Jefferson, a Comprehensive Annotated Bibliography of Writings about Him (1826-1980).* New York, NY: Garland, 1983. 486p.
http://etext.lib.virginia.edu/jefferson/bibliog/shuf1/index.html

————. *Thomas Jefferson, 1981-1990.* New York, NY: Garland, 1992. 238p.
http://etext.lib.virginia.edu/jefferson/bibliog/shuf2/index.html

Jennison

Vinton, John Adams. *The Giles Memorial. Genealogical Memoirs of the Families Bearing the Names of Giles, Gould, Holmes, Jennison, Leonard, Lindall, Curwen, Marshall, Robinson, Sampson and Webb, also Genealogical Sketches of the Pool, Very, Tarr and other Families, with a History of Pemaquid, Ancient and Modern, Some Account of Early Settlements in Maine and Some Details of Indian Warfare.* Boston, MA: Dutton, 1864. 600p.
http://genweb.net/~blackwell/ma/Gyles1864/

Johnson

Johnson, Theodore Taylor. *Sights in the Gold Region and Scenes by the Way.* New York, NY: Baker & Scribner, 1849. 278p.
http://memory.loc.gov/cgi-bin/query/r?ammem/calbkbib:@field(AUTHOR+@band(Johnson,+Theodore+Taylor,b.+1818.+))

Narrative of Facts in the Case of Passmore Williamson. Philadelphia, PA: Pennsylvania Anti-Slavery Society, 1855. 24p.
http://moa.umdl.umich.edu/cgi-bin/moa/sgml/moa-idx?notisid=ABJ1564

Simms, Jeptha Root. *Trappers of New York or a Biography of Nicholas Stoner and Nathaniel Foster, together with Anecdotes of other Celebrated Hunters and Some Account of Sir. William Johnson.* Albany, NY: Munsell, 1850. 280p.
http://moa.cit.cornell.edu/dienst/moabrowse.fly/MOA-JOURNALS2:SIMM-0023/5/1:TIFF2GIF:100

Johnston

Johnston, David Emmons. *The Story of a Confederate Boy in the Civil War.* Portland, OR: Glass & Prudhomme, 1914. 379p.
http://metalab.unc.edu/docsouth/johnstond/menu.html

Johnston, Richard Malcolm. *Autobiography of Col. Richard Malcolm Johnston.* Washington, DC: Neale Co., 1900. 190p.
http://metalab.unc.edu/docsouth/johnstonr/menu.html

Jones

Bunker, Mary Powell. *Long Island Genealogies, Families of Albertson, Andrews, Bedell, Birdsall, Bowne, Carman, Carr, Clowes, Cock, Cornelius, Covert, Dean, Doughty, Duryea, Feke, Frost, Haff, Hallock, Haydock, Hicks, Hopkins, Jackson, Jones, Keese, Ketcham, Kirby, Liones, Marvin, Merritt, Moore, Mott, Oakley, Onderdonck, Pearsall, Post, Powell, Prior, Robbins, Rodman, Rowland, Rushmore, Sands, Scudder, Seaman, Searing, Smith, Strickland, Titus, Townsend, Underhill, Valentine, Vanderdonk, Weeks, Whitman, Whitson, Willets, Williams, Willis, Wright, and other Families. Being Kindred Descendants of Thomas Powell of Bethpage, L.I., 1688.* Albany, NY: Munsell's, 1895. 350p.
http://moa.cit.cornell.edu/dienst/moabrowse.fly/MOA-JOURNALS2:BUNK-0101/5/1:TIFF2GIF:100

Jones, Charles Colcock. *The Siege of Savannah in December, 1864, and the Confederate Operations in Georgia, and the Third Military District of South Carolina during General Sherman's March from Atlanta to the Sea.* Albany, NY: Munsell's, 1874. 184p.
http://metalab.unc.edu/docsouth/jonescharles/menu.html

Jones, Thomas H. *The Experience of Thomas H. Jones, Who Was a Slave for Forty-Three Years.* Boston, MA: Bazin & Chandler, 1862. 48p.
http://metalab.unc.edu/docsouth/jones/menu.html

Kane

Kane, Paul. *Wanderings of an Artist among the Indians of North America from Canada to Vancouver's Island and Oregon through the Hudson's Bay Company's Territory and Back Again.* London: Longman, Brown, Green, Longmans and Roberts, 1859. 515p.
http://www.canadiana.org/cgi-bin/ECO/mtq?id=985701065f&doc=35931

Kearney

Kearney, Belle. *A Slaveholder's Daughter.* New York, NY: Abbey Press, 1900. 269p.
http://metalab.unc.edu/docsouth/kearney/menu.html

Keating

Keating, William Hypolitus. *Narrative of an Expedition to the Source of St. Peter's River, Lake Winnepeck, Lake of the Woods, Performed in the Year 1823, by Order of the Hon. J. C. Calhoun, Secretary of War, under the Command of Stephen H. Long, Major, USTE.* Philadelphia, PA: Carey & Lea, 1824. 2 vols.
http://memory.loc.gov/cgi-bin/query/r?ammem/lhbum:@field(DOCID+@lit(1607aT000)):@@@REF

Keckley

Keckley, Elizabeth. *Behind the Scenes, by Elizabeth Keckley, formerly a Slave, but More Recently Modiste, and Friend to Mrs. Abraham Lincoln or Thirty Years a Slave, and Four Years in the White House.* New York, NY: G. W. Carleton & Co., 1868. 371p.
http://metalab.unc.edu/docsouth/keckley/menu.html
http://digilib.nypl.org/dynaweb/digs/wwm9713/

Kell, John McIntosh. *Recollections of a Naval Life, Including the Cruises of the Confederate States Steamers, Sumter and Alabama.* Washington, DC: Neale, 1900. 307p.
http://metalab.unc.edu/docsouth/kell/menu.html

Keese

Bunker, Mary Powell. *Long Island Genealogies, Families of Albertson, Andrews, Bedell, Birdsall, Bowne, Carman, Carr, Clowes, Cock, Cornelius, Covert, Dean, Doughty, Duryea, Feke, Frost, Haff, Hallock, Haydock, Hicks, Hopkins, Jackson, Jones, Keese, Ketcham, Kirby, Liones, Marvin, Merritt, Moore, Mott, Oakley, Onderdonck, Pearsall, Post, Powell, Prior, Robbins, Rodman, Rowland, Rushmore, Sands, Scudder, Seaman, Searing, Smith, Strickland, Titus, Townsend, Underhill, Valentine, Vanderdonk, Weeks, Whitman, Whitson, Willets, Williams, Willis, Wright, and other Families. Being Kindred Descendants of Thomas Powell of Bethpage, L.I., 1688.* Albany, NY: Munsell's, 1895. 350p.
http://moa.cit.cornell.edu/dienst/moabrowse.fly/MOA-JOURNALS2:BUNK-0101/5/1:TIFF2GIF:100

Kelly

Kelly, Fanny Wiggins. *Narrative of My Captivity among the Sioux Indians, with a Brief Account of General Sully's Indian Expedition in 1864, Bearing upon Events Occuring in My Captivity.* Hartford, CT: Mutual Publishing Co., 1871. 310p.
http://moa.umdl.umich.edu/cgi-bin/moa/sgml/moa-idx?notisid=ABB5283

Kelly, William. *An Excursion to California over the Prairie, Rocky Mountains and Great Sierra Nevada, with a Stroll through the Diggings and Ranches of That Country.* London: Chapman & Hall, 1851. 2 vols.
http://memory.loc.gov/cgi-bin/query/r?ammem/calbk:@field(DOCID+@lit(C054T00)):@@@REF

Kenderdine

Kenderdine, Thaddeus S. *California Revisited, 1858-1897.* Doylestown, PA: Doylestown Publishing, 1898. 310p.
http://memory.loc.gov/cgi-bin/query/r?ammem/calbk:@field(DOCID+@lit(C164T00)):@@@REF

————. *A California Tramp and Later Footprints, or Life on the Plains and in the Golden State Thirty Years Ago, with Miscellaneous Sketches in Prose and Verse.* Philadelphia, PA: Globe Printing, 1888. 415p.
http://memory.loc.gov/cgi-bin/query/r?ammem/calbk:@field(DOCID+@lit(C005T00)):@@@REF

Kenworthy

George, Alice Mendenhall. *The Story of My Childhood, Written for My Children.* Whittier, CA: Smith, 1923. 87p.
http://memory.loc.gov/cgi-bin/query/r?ammem/lhbum:@field(DOCID+@lit(04681T000)):@@@REF

Ketchum

Bunker, Mary Powell. *Long Island Genealogies, Families of Albertson, Andrews, Bedell, Birdsall, Bowne, Carman, Carr, Clowes, Cock, Cornelius, Covert, Dean, Doughty, Duryea, Feke, Frost, Haff, Hallock, Haydock, Hicks, Hopkins, Jackson, Jones, Keese, Ketcham, Kirby, Liones, Marvin, Merritt, Moore, Mott, Oakley, Onderdonck, Pearsall, Post, Powell, Prior, Robbins, Rodman, Rowland, Rushmore, Sands, Scudder, Seaman, Searing, Smith, Strickland, Titus, Townsend, Underhill, Valentine, Vanderdonk, Weeks, Whitman, Whitson, Willets, Williams, Willis, Wright, and other Families. Being Kindred Descendants of Thomas Powell of Bethpage, L.I., 1688.* Albany, NY: Munsell's, 1895. 350p.
http://moa.cit.cornell.edu/dienst/moabrowse.fly/MOA-JOURNALS2:BUNK-0101/5/1:TIFF2GIF:100

King

King, Clarence. *Mountaineering in the Sierra Nevada.* New York, NY: Scribners, 1902. 378p.
http://memory.loc.gov/cgi-bin/query/r?ammem/calbkbib:@field(AUTHOR+@band(King,+Clarence,1842-1901.+))

King, John Lyle. *Trouting on the Brule River, or Lawyers' Summer-wayfaring in the Northern Wilderness.* Chicago, IL: Chicago Legal News Co., 1879. 272p.
http://memory.loc.gov/cgi-bin/query/r?ammem/lhbumbib:@field(SUBJ+@band(Trout+fishing--Michigan.+))

McGowan, Edward. *Narrative of Edward McGowan, Including a Full Account of the Author's Adventures and Perils while Persecuted by the San Francisco Vigilance Committee of 1856, together with a Report of His Trial, which Resulted in His Acquittal.* San Francisco, CA: Russell, 1917. 240p.
http://memory.loc.gov/cgi-bin/query/r?ammem/calbkbib:@field(AUTHOR+@band(McGowan,+Edward, 1813-1893.+))

Morrison, George Austin, Jr. *King Genealogy, Clement King of Marshfield, Mass., 1668 and His Descendants.* Albany, NY: Munsell's, 1898. 65p.
http://genweb.net/~blackwell/ma/King1898/

Salisbury, John Edwin and George Castor Martin. *The American Ancestors of Oratio Dyer Clark and of His Wife Laura Ann King, together with the Ancestry of Anne Marbury Hutchinson, Ancestress of Oratio Dyer Clark.* Asbury Park, NJ: Martin, 1917. 387p.
http://genweb.net/~blackwell/blql/cka1917.htm

Kinzie

Kinzie, Juliette Augusta Magill. *Wau-bun, the Early Day in the Northwest.* Philadelphia, PA: Lippincott, 1873. 390p.
http://memory.loc.gov/cgi-bin/query/r?ammem/lhbum:@field(DOCID+@lit(16762T000)):@@@REF

Kip

Kip, Leonard. *California Sketches, with Recollections of the Gold Mines.* Los Angeles, CA: Kovach, 1946. 58p.
http://memory.loc.gov/cgi-bin/query/r?ammem/calbkbib:@field(AUTHOR+@band(Kip,+Leonard,1826-1906.+))

Kip, William Ingraham. *The Early Days of My Episcopate.* New York, NY: Whittaker, 1892. 263p.
http://memory.loc.gov/cgi-bin/query/r?ammem/calbkbib:@field(AUTHOR+@band(Kip,+William+Ingraham,bp.,1811-1893.+))

Kirby

Bunker, Mary Powell. *Long Island Genealogies, Families of Albertson, Andrews, Bedell, Birdsall, Bowne, Carman, Carr, Clowes, Cock, Cornelius, Covert, Dean, Doughty, Duryea, Feke, Frost, Haff, Hallock, Haydock, Hicks, Hopkins, Jackson, Jones, Keese, Ketcham, Kirby, Liones, Marvin, Merritt, Moore, Mott, Oakley, Onderdonck, Pearsall, Post, Powell, Prior, Robbins, Rodman, Rowland, Rushmore, Sands, Scudder, Seaman, Searing, Smith, Strickland, Titus, Townsend, Underhill, Valentine, Vanderdonk, Weeks, Whitman, Whitson, Willets, Williams, Willis, Wright, and other Families. Being Kindred Descendants of Thomas Powell of Bethpage, L.I., 1688.* Albany, NY: Munsell's, 1895. 350p.
http://moa.cit.cornell.edu/dienst/moabrowse.fly/MOA-JOURNALS2:BUNK-0101/5/1:TIFF2GIF:100

Knapp

Knapp, Shepherd. *Gideon Lee Knapp and Augusta Murray Spring, His Wife, Extracts from Letter and Journal, ed. by One of Their Grandsons.* Author, 1909. 66p.
http://memory.loc.gov/cgi-bin/query/r?ammem/calbkbib:@field(AUTHOR+@band(Knapp,+Gideon+Lee, 1822?-1875.+))

Knower

Knower, Daniel. *The Adventures of a Forty-niner. An Historic Description of California, with Events and Ideas of San Francisco and Its People in Those Early Days.* Albany, NY: Weed Parsons, 1894. 200p.
http://memory.loc.gov/cgi-bin/query/r?ammem/calbkbib:@field(AUTHOR+@band(Knower,+Daniel.+))

Kraft

Howard, John Harris. *A History of Herring Lake, with an Introductory Legend, the Bride of Mystery by the Bard of Benzie.* Boston, MA: Christopher Publishing House, 1929. 84p.
http://memory.loc.gov/cgi-bin/query/r?ammem/lhbumbib:@field(SUBJ+@band(Benzie+Co.,+Mich.-- Biography.+))

– L

La Follette

La Follette, Robert Marion. *La Follette's Autobiography, a Personal Narrative of Political Experiences.* Madison, WI: La Follette Co., 1913. 807p.
http://memory.loc.gov/cgi-bin/query/r?ammem/lhbumbib:@field(SUBJ+@band(Presidents--United+States --Election--1912.+))

Lane

Lane, Isaac. *Autobiography of Bishop Isaac Lane, LL.D. with a Short History of the C.M.E. Church in America and of Methodism.* Nashville, TN: Publishing House of the M.E. Church, South, 1916. 192p.
http://metalab.unc.edu/docsouth/lane/menu.html

Lane, Lunsford. *The Narrative of Lunsford Lane, formerly of Raleigh, NC. Embracing an Account of His Early Life, the Redemption by Purchase of Himself and Family from Slavery, and His Banishment from the Place of His Birth for the Crime of Wearing a Colored Skin.* 2nd ed. Boston, MA: Torrey,1842. 56p.
http://metalab.unc.edu/docsouth/lanelunsford/menu.html

Lapham

Lapham, Macy Harvey. *Crisscross Trails, Narrative of a Soil Surveyor.* Berkeley, CA: Berg, 1949. 258p.
http://chla.mannlib.cornell.edu/cgi-bin/chla/viewer.cgi?docid=title2c.chla.mannlib.cornell/0219laph& format=1:75-GIF&section=Title+Page

Latham

Austin, John Osborne. *Ancestry of Thirty-three Rhode Islanders, Born in the Eighteenth Century, Also Twenty-seven Charts of Roger Williams' Descendants to the Fifth Generation and an Account of Lewis Latham, Falconer to King Charles I, with a Chart of His American Descendants to the Fourth Generation and a List of 180 Existing Portraits of Rhode Island Governors, Chief Justices, Senators, etc. and of Certain Military Officers, Divines, Physicians, Authors, Lawyers, Merchants etc.* Albany, NY: Munsell's, 1889. 127p.
http://genweb.net/~blackwell/ri/33ri1889/

Latimer

Felton, Rebecca Latimer. *County Life in Georgia in the Days of My Youth*. Atlanta, GA: Index Printing Co., 1919. 303p.
http://metalab.unc.edu/docsouth/felton/menu.html

Lawrence

Lawrence, Amos. *Extracts from the Diary and Correspondence of the Late Amos Lawrence, with a Brief Account of Some Incidents in His Life*. Boston, MA: Gould & Lincoln, 1855. 370p.
http://moa.cit.cornell.edu/dienst/moabrowse.fly/MOA-JOURNALS2:LAWR-0043/7/1:TIFF2GIF:100

Leach

Leach, Frank Aleamon. *Recollections of a Newspaperman, a Record of Life and Events in California*. San Francisco, CA: Levinson,1917. 416p.
http://memory.loc.gov/cgi-bin/query/r?ammem/calbkbib:@field(AUTHOR+@band(Leach,+Frank+Aleamon,1846-+))

Leavenworth

Manley, John. *Cattaraugus County, Embracing Its Agricultural Society, Newspapers, Civil List, from the Organization of the County to 1857, Biographies of the Old Pioneers, with Portraits, Benjamin Chamberlain, Peter Ten Broeck, Frederick S. Martin, Chauncey J. Fox, Alson Leavenworth, Stanley N. Clarke, and of Congressmen Francis S. Edwards and Reuben E. Fenton, Colonial and State Governors of New York, Names of Towns and Post Offices with the Statistics of Each Town*. Little Valley, NY: Author, 1857. 140p.
http://moa.cit.cornell.edu/dienst/moabrowse.fly/MOA-JOURNALS2:MANL-0089/3/1:TIFF2GIF:100

Le Conte

Le Conte, Joseph. *The Autobiography of Joseph Le Conte*. New York, NY: Appleton, 1903. 337p.
http://metalab.unc.edu/docsouth/leconte/menu.html

Lecouvreur

Lecouvreur, Frank. *From East Prussia to the Golden Gate. Letters and Diary of the California Pioneer*. New York, NY: Angelina Book, 1906. 355p.
http://memory.loc.gov/cgi-bin/query/r?ammem/calbkbib:@field(AUTHOR+@band(Lecouvreur,+Frank,1829-1901.+))

Lee

Lee, Jarena. *Religious Life and Experience and Journal of Mrs. Jarena Lee, Giving an Account of Her Call to Preach the Gospel*. Philadelphia, PA: Author, 1849. 97p.
http://digilib.nypl.org/dynaweb/digs/wwm9716/

Lee, William Mack. *History of the Life of Rev. William Mack Lee, Body Servant of General Robert E. Lee through the Civil War, Cook from 1861 to 1865*. Norfolk, VA: Smith Printing, 1908. 10p.
http://metalab.unc.edu/docsouth/leewilliam/menu.html

Leeper

Leeper, David Rohrer. *The Argonauts of 'Forty-nine, Some Recollections of the Plains and the Diggings*. South Bend, IN: Stoll, 1894. 146p.
http://memory.loc.gov/cgi-bin/query/r?ammem/calbkbib:@field(AUTHOR+@band(Leeper,+David+Rohrer,1832-1900.+))

Leigh

Leigh, Frances Butler. *Ten Years on a Georgia Plantation since the War*. London: Richard Bentley & Son, 1883. 347p.
http://metalab.unc.edu/docsouth/leigh/menu.html

Lenroot

Lenroot, Clara Clough. *Long, Long Ago*. Appleton, WI: Badger Printing, 1929. 68p.
http://memory.loc.gov/cgi-bin/query/r?ammem/lhbum:@field(DOCID+@lit(09423T000)):@@@REF

Leon

Leon, Louis. *Diary of a Tar Heel Confederate Soldier*. Charlotte, NC: Stone Publishing Co., 1913. 87p.
http://metalab.unc.edu/docsouth/leon/menu.html

Leonard

Vinton, John Adams. *The Giles Memorial. Genealogical Memoirs of the Families Bearing the Names of Giles, Gould, Holmes, Jennison, Leonard, Lindall, Curwen, Marshall, Robinson, Sampson and Webb, also Genealogical Sketches of the Pool, Very, Tarr and other Families, with a History of Pemaquid, Ancient and Modern, Some Account of Early Settlements in Maine and Some Details of Indian Warfare*. Boston, MA: Dutton, 1864. 600p.
http://genweb.net/~blackwell/ma/Gyles1864/

Le Sueur

Le Sueur, Meridel. *Crusaders*. New York, NY: Blue Heron Press, 1955. 94p.
http://memory.loc.gov/cgi-bin/query/r?ammem/lhbumbib:@field(SUBJ+@band(Le+Sueur,+Arthur,--1867-1950.+))

Letts

Letts, John M. *California Illustrated, Including a Description of the Panama and Nicaragua Routes*. New York, NY: Young, 1853. 224p.
http://memory.loc.gov/cgi-bin/query/r?ammem/calbkbib:@field(AUTHOR+@band(Letts,+John+M.+))

Lienhard

Lienhard, Heinrich. *A Pioneer at Sutter's Fort, 1846-1850, the Adventures of Heinrich Lienhard, Translated, Edited and Annotated by Marguerite Eyer Wilbur from the Original German Script*. Los Angeles, CA: Calafia Society, 1941. 291p.
hhttp://memory.loc.gov/cgi-bin/query/r?ammem/calbkbib:@field(AUTHOR+@band(Lienhard,+Heinrich,1822-1903.+))

Likins

Likins, James W., Mrs. *Six Year's Experience as a Book Agent in California, Including My Trip from New York to San Francisco via Nicaragua.* San Francisco, CA: Women's Union Book and Job Printing Office, 1874. 168p.

http://memory.loc.gov/cgi-bin/query/r?ammem/calbkbib:@field(AUTHOR+@band(Likins,+J.+W.,Mrs.+))

Lindall

Vinton, John Adams. *The Giles Memorial. Genealogical Memoirs of the Families Bearing the Names of Giles, Gould, Holmes, Jennison, Leonard, Lindall, Curwen, Marshall, Robinson, Sampson and Webb, also Genealogical Sketches of the Pool, Very, Tarr and other Families, with a History of Pemaquid, Ancient and Modern, Some Account of Early Settlements in Maine and Some Details of Indian Warfare.* Boston, MA: Dutton, 1864. 600p.

http://genweb.net/~blackwell/ma/Gyles1864/

Liones

Bunker, Mary Powell. *Long Island Genealogies, Families of Albertson, Andrews, Bedell, Birdsall, Bowne, Carman, Carr, Clowes, Cock, Cornelius, Covert, Dean, Doughty, Duryea, Feke, Frost, Haff, Hallock, Haydock, Hicks, Hopkins, Jackson, Jones, Keese, Ketcham, Kirby, Liones, Marvin, Merritt, Moore, Mott, Oakley, Onderdonck, Pearsall, Post, Powell, Prior, Robbins, Rodman, Rowland, Rushmore, Sands, Scudder, Seaman, Searing, Smith, Strickland, Titus, Townsend, Underhill, Valentine, Vanderdonk, Weeks, Whitman, Whitson, Willets, Williams, Willis, Wright, and other Families. Being Kindred Descendants of Thomas Powell of Bethpage, L.I., 1688.* Albany, NY: Munsell's, 1895. 350p.

http://moa.cit.cornell.edu/dienst/moabrowse.fly/MOA-JOURNALS2:BUNK-0101/5/1:TIFF2GIF:100

Loguen

Loguen, Jermain Wesley. *The Rev. J. W. Loguen, as a Slave and as a Freeman, a Narrative of Real Life.* Syracuse, NY: Truair, 1859. 454p.

http://moa.umdl.umich.edu/cgi-bin/moa/sgml/moa-idx?notisid=ABT6752

Lomax

Lomax, Virginia. *The Old Capitol (Prison) and Its Inmates. By a Lady Who Enjoyed the Hospitalities of the Government for a Season.* New York, NY: Hale, 1867. 226p.

http://metalab.unc.edu/docsouth/lomax/menu.html

Long

Branch, Mary Jones Polk. *Memoirs of a Southern Woman, "Within the Lines," and a Genealogical Table.* Chicago, IL: Joseph G. Branch Publishing, 1912. 107p.

http://metalab.unc.edu/docsouth/branch/menu.html

Lord

Bryan, George J. *Biographies of Attorney General George P. Barker, John C. Lord, D.D., Mrs. John C. Lord and William G. Bryan, Esq. Also Lecture on Jounalism.* Buffalo, NY: Courier Co., 1886. 232p.

http://moa.cit.cornell.edu/dienst/moabrowse.fly/MOA-JOURNALS2:BRYN-0003/5/1:TIFF2GIF:100

Love

Love, Emanuel K. *Introductory Sermon of Rev. Emanuel K. Love, on Entering the Pastorate of the First African Baptist Church, Savannah, Georgia.* Augusta, GA: Sentinel Print, 1885. 11p.
http://memory.loc.gov/cgi-bin/query/r?ammem/aap:@field(SUBJ+@band(Installation+sermons--Georgia--Savannah--1885.+))

Low

Plato, Ann. *Essays, Including Biographies and Miscellaneous Pieces in Prose and Poetry.* Hartford, CT: Author, 1841. 122p.
http://digilib.nypl.org/dynaweb/digs/wwm97251/

Lowther

Jacobs, Harriet A. *Incidents in the Life of a Slave Girl.* Boston, MA: Author, 1861. 306p.
http://digilib.nypl.org/dynaweb/digs/wwm97255/

Ludlow

Ludlow, William. *Report of a Reconnaissance from Carroll, Montana Territory, on the Upper Missouri to the Yellowstone National Park and Return Made in the Summer of 1875.* Washington, DC: Governement Printing Office, 1876. 160p.
http://moa.umdl.umich.edu/cgi-bin/moa/sgml/moa-idx?notisid=ADQ3957

Lurting

Lurting, Thomas. *The Fighting Sailor Turn'd Peaceable Christian, Manifested in the Convincement and Conversion of Thomas Lurting with a Short Relation of Many Great Dangers and Wonderful Deliverances He Met withal.* London: Sowle, 1711.
http://www.voicenet.com/~kuenning/qhp/lurting.html

Lykins

Likins, James W., Mrs. *Six Years' Experience as a Book Agent in California, Including My Trip from New York to San Francisco via Nicaragua.* San Francisco, CA: Women's Union Book and Job Printing Office, 1874. 168p.
http://memory.loc.gov/cgi-bin/query/r?ammem/calbkbib:@field(AUTHOR+@band(Likins,+J.+W.,Mrs.+))

– M

Mackie

Mackie, J. Milton. *From Cape Cod to Dixie and the Tropics.* New York, NY: Putnam, 1864. 446p.
http://moa.umdl.umich.edu/cgi-bin/moa/sgml/moa-idx?notisid=AFJ8891

Mackinnon

Mackinnon, Lauchlan Bellingham. *Atlantic and Transatlantic Sketches Afloat and Ashore*. New York, NY: Harper, 1852. 332p.
http://moa.umdl.umich.edu/cgi-bin/moa/sgml/moa-idx?notisid=ABF8697

Maclay

Maclay, William. *The Journal of William Maclay, United States Senator from Pennsylvania, 1789-1791*. New York, NY: Appleton, 1890. 438p.
http://memory.loc.gov/ammem/amlaw/lwmj.html

Macon

Macon, Thomas Joseph. *Life Gleanings*. Richmond, VA: Author, 1913. 101p.
http://metalab.unc.edu/docsouth/macon/menu.html

Mallard

Mallard, Robert Q. *Plantation Life before Emancipation*. Richmond, VA: Whittet & Shepperson, 1892. 237p.
http://metalab.unc.edu/docsouth/mallard/menu.html

Malone

Malone, Bartlett Yancey. *The Diary of Bartlett Yancey Malone*. Vol. 16, No. 2 , James Sprunt Historical Publications, North Carolina Historical Society. 58p.
http://metalab.unc.edu/docsouth/malone/menu.html

Manahan

Manahan, James. *Trials of a Lawyer, Autobiography*. Minneapolis, MN: Farnaham Printing, 1933. 248p.
http://memory.loc.gov/cgi-bin/query/r?ammem/lhbumbib:@field(SUBJ+@band(Lawyers--Minnesota--Correspondence,+reminiscences,+etc.+))

Manly

Manly, William Lewis. *Death Valley in '49. Important Chapter of California Pioneer History. The Autobiography of a Pioneer, Detailing His Life from a Humble Home in the Green Mountains to the Gold Mines of California and Particularly Reciting the Sufferings of the Band of Men, Women and Children Who Gave "Death Valley" Its Name*. San Jose, CA: Pacific Tree and Vine Co., 1894. 498p.
http://memory.loc.gov/cgi-bin/query/r?ammem/calbkbib:@field(AUTHOR+@band(Manly,+William+Lewis,b.+1820.+))

Manship

Manship, Andrew. *Thirteen Years' Experience in the Itinerancy*. Philadelphia, PA: Higgins and Perkinpine, 1856. 412p.
http://moa.umdl.umich.edu/cgi-bin/moa/sgml/moa-idx?notisid=AJK2747

Marcy

Marcy, Randolph Barnes. *Exploration of the Red River of Louisiana in the Year 1852*. Washington, DC: Tucker, 1854. 390p.
http://moa.umdl.umich.edu/cgi-bin/moa/sgml/moa-idx?notisid=ABB2532

———. *Thirty Years of Army Life on the Border, Comprising Descriptions of the Indians Nomads of the Plains, Explorations of New Territory, a Trip Across the Rocky Mountains in the Winter, Descriptions of the Habits of Different Animals Found in the West, and the Methods of Hunting Them, with Incidents in the Life of Different Frontier Men*. New York, NY: Harper, 1866. 444p.
http://moa.umdl.umich.edu/cgi-bin/moa/sgml/moa-idx?notisid=AAZ9581

Marryat

Marryat, Francis Samuel. *Mountains and Molehills or Recollections of a Burnt Journal*. New York, NY: Harper, 1855. 393p.
http://memory.loc.gov/cgi-bin/query/r?ammem/calbkbib:@field(AUTHOR+@band(Marryat,+Francis+Samuel,1826-1855.+))

Marshall

Felton, Rebecca Latimer. *County Life in Georgia in the Days of My Youth*. Atlanta, GA: Index Printing Co., 1919. 303p.
http://metalab.unc.edu/docsouth/felton/menu.html

Gregson, Eliza Marshall. *The Gregson Memoirs, Containing Mrs. Eliza Gregson's Memory and the Statement of James Gregson*. San Francisco, CA: Kennedy, 1940. 31p.
http://memory.loc.gov/cgi-bin/query/r?ammem/calbkbib:@field(AUTHOR+@band(Gregson,+Eliza+Marshall,1824-+))

Vinton, John Adams. *The Giles Memorial. Genealogical Memoirs of the Families Bearing the Names of Giles, Gould, Holmes, Jennison, Leonard, Lindall, Curwen, Marshall, Robinson, Sampson and Webb, also Genealogical Sketches of the Pool, Very, Tarr and other Families, with a History of Pemaquid, Ancient and Modern, Some Account of Early Settlements in Maine and Some Details of Indian Warfare*. Boston, MA: Dutton, 1864. 600p.
http://genweb.net/~blackwell/ma/Gyles1864/

Marston

Gunn, Lewis Carstairs. *Records of a California Family, Journals and Letters of Lewis C. Gunn and Elizabeth Le Breton Gunn*. San Diego, CA: Johnck and Seeger, 1928. 279p.
http://memory.loc.gov/cgi-bin/query/r?ammem/calbkbib:@field(AUTHOR+@band(Gunn,+Lewis+Carstairs,1813-1892.+))

Marston, Benjamin. *Diaries of Benjamin Marston, 1776-1787*. 20 vols. Unknown.
http://ultratext.hil.unb.ca/Texts/Marston/Marston.html

Martin

Manley, John. *Cattaraugus County, Embracing Its Agricultural Society, Newspapers, Civil List, from the Organization of the County to 1857, Biographies of the Old Pioneers, with Portraits, Benjamin Chamberlain, Peter Ten Broeck, Frederick S. Martin, Chauncey J. Fox, Alson Leavenworth, Stanley N. Clarke, and of Congressmen Francis S. Edwards and Reuben E. Fenton, Colonial and State Governors of New York, Names of Towns and Post Offices with the Statistics of Each Town*. Little Valley, NY: Author, 1857. 140p.
http://moa.cit.cornell.edu/dienst/moabrowse.fly/MOA-JOURNALS2:MANL-0089/3/1:TIFF2GIF:100

Marvin

Bunker, Mary Powell. *Long Island Genealogies, Families of Albertson, Andrews, Bedell, Birdsall, Bowne, Carman, Carr, Clowes, Cock, Cornelius, Covert, Dean, Doughty, Duryea, Feke,*

Frost, Haff, Hallock, Haydock, Hicks, Hopkins, Jackson, Jones, Keese, Ketcham, Kirby, Liones, Marvin, Merritt, Moore, Mott, Oakley, Onderdonck, Pearsall, Post, Powell, Prior, Robbins, Rodman, Rowland, Rushmore, Sands, Scudder, Seaman, Searing, Smith, Strickland, Titus, Townsend, Underhill, Valentine, Vanderdonk, Weeks, Whitman, Whitson, Willets, Williams, Willis, Wright, and other Families. Being Kindred Descendants of Thomas Powell of Bethpage, L.I., 1688. Albany, NY: Munsell's, 1895. 350p.
http://moa.cit.cornell.edu/dienst/moabrowse.fly/MOA-JOURNALS2:BUNK-0101/5/1:TIFF2GIF:100

Mason

Mason, Isaac. *Life of Isaac Mason as a Slave.* Worcester, MA: Author, 1893. 74p.
http://metalab.unc.edu/docsouth/mason/menu.html

Matthews

Smith, Amanda. *An Autobiography, the Story of the Lord's Dealings with Mrs. Amanda Smith, the Colored Evangelist, Containing an Account of Her Life Work of Faith, and Her Travels in America, England, Ireland, Scotland, India and Africa, as an Independent Missionary.* Chicago, IL: Meyer and Brother, 1893. 506p.
http://digilib.nypl.org/dynaweb/digs/wwm97264/

Maury

Maury, Dabney Herndon. *Recollections of a Virginian in the Mexican, Indian and Civil Wars.* New York, NY: Scribners, 1894. 279p.
http://metalab.unc.edu/docsouth/maury/menu.html

Mayer

Mayer, Francis Blackwell. *With Pen and Pencil on the Frontier in 1851, the Diary and Sketches of Frank Blackwell Mayer.* Saint Paul, MN: Minnesota Historical Society, 1932. 214p.
http://memory.loc.gov/cgi-bin/query/r?ammem/lhbum:@field(DOCID+@lit(17122T000)):@@@REF

Mazzuchelli

Mazzuchelli, Samuel Charles. *Memoirs, Historical and Edifying of a Missionary Apostolic of the Order of Saint Dominic among Various Indian Tribes and among the Catholics and Protestants in the United States of America.* Chicago, IL: Hall Printing Co., 1915. 375p.
http://memory.loc.gov/cgi-bin/query/r?ammem/lhbumbib:@field(SUBJ+@band(Catholic+church+in+the+United+States.+))

McCollum

McCollum, William S. *California as I Saw It. Pencillings by the Way of Its Gold and Gold Diggers and Incidents of Travel by Land and Water. With Five Letters from the Isthmus.* Los Gatos, CA: Talisman Press, 1960. 219p.
http://memory.loc.gov/cgi-bin/query/r?ammem/calbkbib:@field(AUTHOR+@band(M'Collum,+William+S.+))

McCormick

Hutchinson, William T. *Cyrus Hall McCormick.* New York, NY: Appleton, 1935. 2 vols.
http://chla.mannlib.cornell.edu/cgi-bin/chla/viewer.cgi?docid=title2c.chla.mannlib.cornell/0992hutc&format=1:75-GIF&section=Title+Page

McCoy

McCoy, Joseph Geiting. *Historic Sketches of the Cattle Trade of the West and Southwest.* Kansas City, MO: Ramsey, Millett & Hudson, 1874. 427p.
http://www.ukans.edu/carrie/kancoll/books/mccoy/

McCray

McCray, S. J. *Life of Mary F. McCray, Born and Raised a Slave in the State of Kentucky, By Her Husband and Son.* Lima, OH: Author, 1898. 115p.
http://metalab.unc.edu/docsouth/mccray/menu.html

McGowan

McGowan, Edward. *Narrative of Edward McGowan, Including a Full Account of the Author's Adventures and Perils while Persecuted by the San Francisco Vigilance Committee of 1856, together with a Report of His Trial, which Resulted in His Acquittal.* San Francisco, CA: Russell, 1917. 240p.
http://memory.loc.gov/cgi-bin/query/r?ammem/calbkbib:@field(AUTHOR+@band(McGowan,+Edward, 1813-1893.+))

McIlhany

McIlhany, Edward Washington. *Recollections of a '49er, a Quaint and Thrilling Narrative of a Trip across the Plains, and Life in the California Gold Fields during the Stirring Days following the Discovery of Gold in the far West.* Kansas City, MO: Hailman Printing, 1908. 212p.
http://memory.loc.gov/cgi-bin/query/r?ammem/calbkbib:@field(AUTHOR+@band(McIlhany,+Edward+ Washington,b.+1828.+))

McKin

McKin, Randolph Harrison. *A Soldier's Recollections, Leaves from the Diary of a Young Confederate, with an Oration on the Motives and Aims of the Soldiers of the South.* New York, NY: Longmans, Green & Co., 1910. 362p.
http://metalab.unc.edu/docsouth/mckim/menu.html

McNair

Swisshelm, Jane Grey Cannon. *Half a Century.* Chicago, IL: Author, 1880. 263p.
http://memory.loc.gov/cgi-bin/query/r?ammem/lhbumbib:@field(SUBJ+@band(Slavery+in+the+United+ States--Anti-slavery+movements.+))

McNeil

McNeil, Samuel. *McNeil's Travels in 1849, to, through and from the Gold Regions in California.* Columbus, OH: Scott & Sascom, 1850. 40p.
http://memory.loc.gov/cgi-bin/query/r?ammem/calbkbib:@field(AUTHOR+@band(McNeil,+Samuel.+))

Mead

Mead, Solomon. *Notes of Two Trips to California and Return, Taken in 1883 and 1886-7.* Greenwich, CT: Author, 1890. 144p.
http://memory.loc.gov/cgi-bin/query/r?ammem/calbkbib:@field(AUTHOR+@band(Mead,+Solomon,1808- 1897.+))

Mendenhall

George, Alice Mendenhall. *The Story of My Childhood, Written for My Children*. Whittier, CA: Smith, 1923. 87p.

http://memory.loc.gov/cgi-bin/query/r?ammem/lhbum:@field(DOCID+@lit(04681T000)):@@@REF

Merrick

Merrick, Caroline Elizabeth Thomas. *Old Times in Dixie Land, a Southern Matron's Memories*. New York, NY: Grafton, 1901. 241p.

http://metalab.unc.edu/docsouth/merrick/menu.html

Merritt

Bunker, Mary Powell. *Long Island Genealogies, Families of Albertson, Andrews, Bedell, Birdsall, Bowne, Carman, Carr, Clowes, Cock, Cornelius, Covert, Dean, Doughty, Duryea, Feke, Frost, Haff, Hallock, Haydock, Hicks, Hopkins, Jackson, Jones, Keese, Ketcham, Kirby, Liones, Marvin, Merritt, Moore, Mott, Oakley, Onderdonck, Pearsall, Post, Powell, Prior, Robbins, Rodman, Rowland, Rushmore, Sands, Scudder, Seaman, Searing, Smith, Strickland, Titus, Townsend, Underhill, Valentine, Vanderdonk, Weeks, Whitman, Whitson, Willets, Williams, Willis, Wright, and other Families. Being Kindred Descendants of Thomas Powell of Bethpage, L.I., 1688*. Albany, NY: Munsell's, 1895. 350p.

http://moa.cit.cornell.edu/dienst/moabrowse.fly/MOA-JOURNALS2:BUNK-0101/5/1:TIFF2GIF:100

Mevis

Mevis, Daniel Stafford. *Pioneer Recollections, Semi-historic Side Lights on the Early Days of Lansing*. Lansing, MI: Robert Smith Printing, 1911. 129p.

http://memory.loc.gov/cgi-bin/query/r?ammem/lhbum:@field(DOCID+@lit(10313T000)):@@@REF

Meyer

Meyer, Carl. *Bound for Sacramento, Travel Pictures of a Returned Wanderer, Translated from the German by Ruth Frey Axe*. Claremont, CA: Saunders Studio Press, 1938. 282p.

http://memory.loc.gov/cgi-bin/query/r?ammem/calbkbib:@field(AUTHOR+@band(Meyer,+Carl,of+Basel.+))

Miller

Miller, Wesson Gage. *Thirty Years in the Itinerancy*. Milwaukee, WI: Hauser, 1875. 304p.

http://memory.loc.gov/cgi-bin/query/r?ammem/lhbum:@field(DOCID+@lit(27351T000)):@@@REF

Mitchel

Mitchel, Cora. *Reminiscences of the Civil War*. Providence, RI: Snow & Farnham, 1916. 43p.

http://metalab.unc.edu/docsouth/mitchel/menu.html

Moak

Moak, Sim. *The Last of the Mill Creeks and Early Life in Northern California*. Chico, CA: Author, 1923. 47p.

http://memory.loc.gov/cgi-bin/query/r?ammem/calbkbib:@field(AUTHOR+@band(Moak,+Sim,1845-+))

Montgomery

Montgomery, Frank Alexander. *Reminiscences of a Mississippian in Peace and War*. Cincinnati, OH: Robert Clarke Press, 1901. 305p.

http://metalab.unc.edu/docsouth/montgomery/menu.html

Moore

Bunker, Mary Powell. *Long Island Genealogies, Families of Albertson, Andrews, Bedell, Birdsall, Bowne, Carman, Carr, Clowes, Cock, Cornelius, Covert, Dean, Doughty, Duryea, Feke, Frost, Haff, Hallock, Haydock, Hicks, Hopkins, Jackson, Jones, Keese, Ketcham, Kirby, Liones, Marvin, Merritt, Moore, Mott, Oakley, Onderdonck, Pearsall, Post, Powell, Prior, Robbins, Rodman, Rowland, Rushmore, Sands, Scudder, Seaman, Searing, Smith, Strickland, Titus, Townsend, Underhill, Valentine, Vanderdonk, Weeks, Whitman, Whitson, Willets, Williams, Willis, Wright, and other Families. Being Kindred Descendants of Thomas Powell of Bethpage, L.I., 1688.* Albany, NY: Munsell's, 1895. 350p.
http://moa.cit.cornell.edu/dienst/moabrowse.fly/MOA-JOURNALS2:BUNK-0101/5/1:TIFF2GIF:100

Moore, Frank. *Reminiscences of Pioneer Days in St. Paul.* St. Paul, MN: Author, 1908. 134p.
http://memory.loc.gov/cgi-bin/query/r?ammem/lhbum:@field(DOCID+@lit(00866T000)):@@@REF

Morgan

Dawson, Sarah Morgan. *A Confederate Girl's Diary.* Boston, MA: Houghton, Mifflin, 1913. 441p.
http://metalab.unc.edu/docsouth/dawson/menu.html

Morgan, Mrs. Irby. *How It Was, Four Years among the Rebels.* Nashville, TN: Methodist Episcopal Church, South, 1892. 204p.
http://metalab.unc.edu/docsouth/morgan/menu.html

Morgan, James Morris. *Recollections of a Rebel Reefer.* Boston, MA: Houghton, Mifflin, 1917. 492p.
http://metalab.unc.edu/docsouth/morganjames/menu.html

Mortenson

Howard, John Harris. *A History of Herring Lake, with an Introductory Legend, the Birde of Mystery by the Bard of Benzie.* Boston, MA: Christopher Publishing House, 1929. 84p.
http://memory.loc.gov/cgi-bin/query/r?ammem/lhbumbib:@field(SUBJ+@band(Benzie+Co.,+Mich.--Biography.+))

Mosby

Mosby, John Singleton. *The Memoirs of Colonel John S. Mosby.* Boston, MA: Little, Brown & Co., 1917. 414p.
http://metalab.unc.edu/docsouth/mosby/menu.html

Moton

Moton, Robert Russa. *Finding a Way Out, an Autobiography.* Garden City, NY: Doubleday, 1921. 296p.
http://metalab.unc.edu/docsouth/moton/menu.html

Mott

Bunker, Mary Powell. *Long Island Genealogies, Families of Albertson, Andrews, Bedell, Birdsall, Bowne, Carman, Carr, Clowes, Cock, Cornelius, Covert, Dean, Doughty, Duryea, Feke, Frost, Haff, Hallock, Haydock, Hicks, Hopkins, Jackson, Jones, Keese, Ketcham, Kirby, Liones, Marvin, Merritt, Moore, Mott, Oakley, Onderdonck, Pearsall, Post, Powell, Prior, Robbins, Rodman, Rowland, Rushmore, Sands, Scudder, Seaman, Searing, Smith, Strickland, Titus, Townsend, Underhill, Valentine, Vanderdonk, Weeks, Whitman, Whitson, Willets,*

Williams, Willis, Wright, and other Families. Being Kindred Descendants of Thomas Powell of Bethpage, L.I., 1688. Albany, NY: Munsell's, 1895. 350p.
http://moa.cit.cornell.edu/dienst/moabrowse.fly/MOA-JOURNALS2:BUNK-0101/5/1:TIFF2GIF:100

Mowry

Mowry, William Augustus. *The Descendants of Nathaniel Mowry of Rhode Island.* Providence, RI: Rider, 1878. Supplement and Monument. 343p.
http://whipple.dyndns.com/~books/mowry/mowry.html

Muir

Muir, John. *The Story of My Boyhood and Youth.* Boston, MA: Houghton Mifflin, 1913. 294p.
http://memory.loc.gov/cgi-bin/query/r?ammem/lhbum:@field(DOCID+@lit(05573T000)):@@@REF

Mulford

Mulford, Prentice. *Life by Land and Sea.* New York, NY: Needham, 1889. 299p.
http://memory.loc.gov/cgi-bin/query/r?ammem/calbkbib:@field(AUTHOR+@band(Mulford,+Prentice, 1834-1891.+))

Murdock

Murdock, Charles Albert. *A Backward Glance at Eighty, Recollections and Comments by Charles A. Murdock, Massachusetts 1841, Humboldt Bay 1855, San Francisco, 1864.* San Francisco, CA: Elder, 1921. 275p.
http://memory.loc.gov/cgi-bin/query/r?ammem/calbkbib:@field(AUTHOR+@band(Murdock,+Charles+ Albert,1841-+))

Murray

Murray, Amelia Matilda. *Letters from the United States, Cuba and Canada.* New York, NY: Putnam, 1856. 410p.
http://moa.umdl.umich.edu/cgi-bin/moa/sgml/moa-idx?notisid=ABE5962

Mylar

Mylar, Isaac L. *Early Days at the Mission San Juan Bautista.* Watsonville, CA: Evening Pajarorian, 1929. 195p.
http://memory.loc.gov/cgi-bin/query/r?ammem/calbkbib:@field(AUTHOR+@band(Mylar,+Isaac+L.+))

-N

Newell

Moor, John. *The Heads of a Sermon, Spoken at the Funeral of Mr. Thomas Newell in Newfoundland, Trinity on the 30th Day of June in 1724.* Gosport, England: Printed for F. Moor's, 1724. Unpgd.
http://www.mun.ca/rels/ang/texts/moor.html

Newmark

Newmark, Harris. *Sixty Years in Southern California, 1853-1913, Containing the Reminiscences of Harris Newmark.* New York, NY: Knickerbocker Press, 1916. 732p.
http://memory.loc.gov/cgi-bin/query/r?ammem/calbkbib:@field(AUTHOR+@band(Newmark,+Harris, 1834-1916.+))

Nichols

Churchill, Caroline M. Nichols. *Little Sheaves Gathered while Gleaning after Reapers. Being Letters of Travel Commencing in 1870 and Ending in 1873.* San Francisco, CA: Author, 1874. 110p.
http://memory.loc.gov/ammem/mdbquery.html

————. *Over the Purple Hills, or Sketches of Travel in California, Embracing All the Important Points Usually Visited by Tourists.* Denver, CO: Author, 1881. 252p.
http://memory.loc.gov/ammem/mdbquery.html

Noble

Bundy, Charles Smith. *Early Days in the Chippewa Valley.* Menominie, WI: Flint Douglas Printing, 1916. 16p.
http://memory.loc.gov/ammem/mdbquery.html

Nolan

Nowlin, William. *The Bark Covered House, or Back in the Woods again, Being a Graphic and Thrilling Description of Real Pioneer Life in the Wilderness of Michigan.* Detroit, MI: Author, 1876. 253p.
http://memory.loc.gov/cgi-bin/query/r?ammem/lhbumbib:@field(SUBJ+@band(Dearborn,+Mich.--History.+))

Nordhoff

Nordhoff, Charles. *California for Health, Pleasure and Residence. A Book for Travelers and Settlers.* New York, NY: Harper, 1873. 255p.
http://memory.loc.gov/cgi-bin/query/r?ammem/calbkbib:@field(AUTHOR+@band(Nordhoff,+Charles, 1830-1901.+))

————. *Northern California, Oregon, and the Sandwich Islands.* New York, NY: Harper, 1875. 256p.
http://moa.umdl.umich.edu/cgi-bin/moa/sgml/moa-idx?notisid=AJL3484

Northrop

Northup, Solomon. *Narrative of Solomon Northup, a Citizen of New York, Kidnapped in Washington City in 1841, Rescued in 1853, from a Cotton Plantation near the Red River, in Louisiana.* Auburn, NY: Derby and Miller, 1853. 336p.
http://metalab.unc.edu/docsouth/northup/menu.html

Norton

Norton, Lewis Adelbert. *Life and Adventures of Col. L. A. Norton.* Oakland, CA: Pacific Press, 1887. 492p.
http://memory.loc.gov/cgi-bin/query/r?ammem/calbkbib:@field(AUTHOR+@band(Norton,+Lewis+Adelbert,b.+1819.+))

Nowlin

Nowlin, William. *The Bark Covered House, or Back in the Woods again, Being a Graphic and Thrilling Description of Real Pioneer Life in the Wilderness of Michigan.* Detroit, MI: Author, 1876. 253p.
http://memory.loc.gov/cgi-bin/query/r?ammem/lhbumbib:@field(SUBJ+@band(Dearborn,+Mich.--History.+))

Oakley

Bunker, Mary Powell. *Long Island Genealogies, Families of Albertson, Andrews, Bedell, Birdsall, Bowne, Carman, Carr, Clowes, Cock, Cornelius, Covert, Dean, Doughty, Duryea, Feke, Frost, Haff, Hallock, Haydock, Hicks, Hopkins, Jackson, Jones, Keese, Ketcham, Kirby, Liones, Marvin, Merritt, Moore, Mott, Oakley, Onderdonck, Pearsall, Post, Powell, Prior, Robbins, Rodman, Rowland, Rushmore, Sands, Scudder, Seaman, Searing, Smith, Strickland, Titus, Townsend, Underhill, Valentine, Vanderdonk, Weeks, Whitman, Whitson, Willets, Williams, Willis, Wright, and other Families. Being Kindred Descendants of Thomas Powell of Bethpage, L.I., 1688.* Albany, NY: Munsell's, 1895. 350p.
http://moa.cit.cornell.edu/dienst/moabrowse.fly/MOA-JOURNALS2:BUNK-0101/5/1:TIFF2GIF:100

Oatman

Stratton, Royal B. *Captivity of the Oatman Girls, Being an Interesting Narrative of Life among the Apache and Mohave Indians, Containing an Interesting Account of the Massacre of the Oatman Family by the Apache Indians in 1851, the Narrow Escape of Lorenze D. Oatman, the Capture of Olive A. and Mary A. Oatman, as Given by Lorenzo D. and Olive A. Oatman.* New York, NY: Carlton & Porter, 1858. 312p.
http://moa.umdl.umich.edu/cgi-bin/moa/sgml/moa-idx?notisid=ABB5623

Older

Older, Fremont. *My Own Story.* San Francisco, CA: Call Publishing, 1919. 197p.
http://memory.loc.gov/cgi-bin/query/r?ammem/calbkbib:@field(AUTHOR+@band(Older,+Fremont,1856-1935+))

Olive

Olive, Johnson. *One of the Wonders of the Age or the Life and Times of Rev. Johnson Olive, Wake County, North Carolina, Written by Himself, at the Solicitation of Friends and for the Benefit of All Who Read It, with Supplement by His Son, H. C. Olive.* Raleigh, NC: Edwards, Broughton, 1886. 314p.
http://metalab.unc.edu/docsouth/olive/menu.html

Olivier

Roy, Paul Eugene. *L. A. Olivier.* Levis, Quebec: Author, 1891. 32p.
http://www.canadiana.org/cgi-bin/ECO/mtq?id=985701065f&doc=12728

Onderdonk

Bunker, Mary Powell. *Long Island Genealogies, Families of Albertson, Andrews, Bedell, Birdsall, Bowne, Carman, Carr, Clowes, Cock, Cornelius, Covert, Dean, Doughty, Duryea, Feke, Frost, Haff, Hallock, Haydock, Hicks, Hopkins, Jackson, Jones, Keese, Ketcham, Kirby, Liones, Marvin, Merritt, Moore, Mott, Oakley, Onderdonck, Pearsall, Post, Powell, Prior, Robbins, Rodman, Rowland, Rushmore, Sands, Scudder, Seaman, Searing, Smith, Strickland, Titus, Townsend, Underhill, Valentine, Vanderdonk, Weeks, Whitman, Whitson, Willets, Williams, Willis, Wright, and other Families. Being Kindred Descendants of Thomas Powell of Bethpage, L.I., 1688.* Albany, NY: Munsell's, 1895. 350p.
http://moa.cit.cornell.edu/dienst/moabrowse.fly/MOA-JOURNALS2:BUNK-0101/5/1:TIFF2GIF:100

Ossoli

Ossoli, Sarah Margaret Fuller. *Summer on the Lakes in 1843.* Boston, MA: Little & Brown, 1844. 256p.
http://memory.loc.gov/ammem/mdbquery.html

–P

Painter

Painter, Charles Cornelius Coffin. *The Condition of Affairs in Indian Territory and California.* Philadelphia, PA: Indian Rights Association, 1888. 114p.
http://memory.loc.gov/cgi-bin/query/r?ammem/calbkbib:@field(AUTHOR+@band(Painter,+Charles+Cornelius+Coffin.+))

Palmer

Palmer, John Williamson. *The New and the Old, or California and India in Romantic Aspects.* New York, NY: Rudd & Carleton, 1859. 433p.
http://memory.loc.gov/cgi-bin/query/r?ammem/calbkbib:@field(AUTHOR+@band(Palmer,+J[ohn]+W[illiamson],1825-1906.+))

Parker

Parker, Theodore. *The Trial of Theodore Parker for the Misdemeanor of a Speech in Faneuil Hall against Kidnapping before the Circuit Court of the United States at Boston, April 3, 1855, with the Defence by Theodore Parker.* Boston, MA: Author, 1855. 244p.
http://moa.umdl.umich.edu/cgi-bin/moa/sgml/moa-idx?notisid=ACK4839

Parkinson

Parkinson, Edward S. *Wonderland or Twelve Weeks In and Out of the United States. Brief Account of a Trip across the Continent, Short Run in Mexico, Ride to the Yosemite Valley, Steamer Voyage to Alaska, the Land of Glaciers, Visit to the Great Shoshone Falls and a Stage Ride through the Yellowstone National Park.* Trenton, NJ: MacCrellish & Quigley, 1894. 259p.
http://memory.loc.gov/cgi-bin/query/r?ammem/calbkbib:@field(AUTHOR+@band(Parkinson,+Edward+S.+))

Parkinson, John Barber. *Memories of Early Wisconsin and the Gold Mines*. N.p.: Author, 1921. 25p.
http://memory.loc.gov/ammem/mdbquery.html

Patoo

Memoir of Thomas Hamitah Patoo, a Native of the Marqueas Islands, Who Died June 19, 1823, while a Member of the Foreign Mission School in Cornwall, Connecticut. New York, NY: New York Religious Tract Society, 1823. 48p.
http://memory.loc.gov/cgi-bin/query/r?ammem/aap:@field(SUBJ+@band(Biographies--New+York++N.Y.+--1825.+))

Patton

Barry, Theodore Augustus and Benjamin Ada Patten. *Men and Memories of San Francisco, in the Spring of '50*. San Francisco, CA: Bancroft, 1873. 296p.
http://memory.loc.gov/cgi-bin/query/r?ammem/calbkbib:@field(AUTHOR+@band(Barry,+Theodore+Augustus,1825-1881.+))

Biography of James Patton. Asheville, NC: Patton Family, 1850. 34p.
http://metalab.unc.edu/docsouth/patton/menu.html

Paxton

Paxton, Elisha Franklin. *Memoir and Memorials, Composed of His Letters from Camp and Field while an Officer in the Confederate Army, with an Introductory and Connecting Narrative Collected and Arranged by His Son, John Gallatin Paxton*. New York, NY: Neale, 1907. 114p.
http://metalab.unc.edu/docsouth/paxton/menu.html

Pearsall

Bunker, Mary Powell. *Long Island Genealogies, Families of Albertson, Andrews, Bedell, Birdsall, Bowne, Carman, Carr, Clowes, Cock, Cornelius, Covert, Dean, Doughty, Duryea, Feke, Frost, Haff, Hallock, Haydock, Hicks, Hopkins, Jackson, Jones, Keese, Ketcham, Kirby, Liones, Marvin, Merritt, Moore, Mott, Oakley, Onderdonck, Pearsall, Post, Powell, Prior, Robbins, Rodman, Rowland, Rushmore, Sands, Scudder, Seaman, Searing, Smith, Strickland, Titus, Townsend, Underhill, Valentine, Vanderdonk, Weeks, Whitman, Whitson, Willets, Williams, Willis, Wright, and other Families. Being Kindred Descendants of Thomas Powell of Bethpage, L.I., 1688*. Albany, NY: Munsell's, 1895. 350p.
http://moa.cit.cornell.edu/dienst/moabrowse.fly/MOA-JOURNALS2:BUNK-0101/5/1:TIFF2GIF:100

Peters

Peters, Charles. *The Autobiography of Charles Peters in 1915 the Oldest Pioneer Living in California, Who Mined in the Days of '49. Also Historical Happenings, Interesting Incidents and Illustrations of the Old Mining Towns in the Good Luck Era, the Placer Mining Days of the '50s*. Sacramento, CA: LaGrave, 1915. 231p.
http://memory.loc.gov/cgi-bin/query/r?ammem/calbkbib:@field(AUTHOR+@band(Peters,+Charles,b.+1825.+))

Phillips

Grimke, Archibald Henry. *A Eulogy on Wendell Phillips*. Boston, MA: Rockwell & Churchill, 1884. 40p.
http://memory.loc.gov/cgi-bin/query/r?ammem/aap:@field(SUBJ+@band(Eulogies--Massachusetts--Boston--1884.+))

Phillips, David L. *Letters from California, Its Mountains, Valleys, Plains, Lakes, Rivers, Climate and Productions. Also Its Railroads, Cities, Towns and People, as Seen in 1876.* Springfield, IL: Illinois State Journal, 1877. 171p.
http://memory.loc.gov/cgi-bin/query/r?ammem/calbkbib:@field(AUTHOR+@band(Phillips,+David+L., 1823-1880.+))

Pickard

Pickard, Samuel. *Autobiography of a Pioneer or the Nativity, Experience, Travels and Ministerial Laborer of Rev. Samuel Pickard.* Chicago, IL: Church & Goodman, 1866. 406p.
http://moa.umdl.umich.edu/cgi-bin/moa/sgml/moa-idx?notisid=AGU8807

Pickens

Pickens, William. *The Heir of Slaves, an Autobiography.* Boston, MA: Pilgrim Press, 1911. 138p.
http://metalab.unc.edu/docsouth/pickens/menu.html

Pickett

Pickett, George Edward. *The Heart of a Soldier as Revealed in the Intimate Letters of General George E. Pickett, C.S.A.* New York, NY: Moyle, 1913. 215p.
http://metalab.unc.edu/docsouth/pickett/menu.html

Pierce

Harland, Marion. *Marion Harland's Autobiography, the Story of a Long Life.* New York, NY: Harper, 1910. 498p.
http://metalab.unc.edu/docsouth/harland/menu.html

Pierce, Hiram Dwight. *A Forty-niner Speaks, a Chronological Record of a New Yorker and His Adventures in Various Mining Localities in California, His Return Trip across Nicaragua, Including Several Descriptions of the Changes in San Francisco and other Mining Centers from March 1849 to January 1851.* Oakland, CA: Keystone Inglett Printing, 1930. 74p.
http://memory.loc.gov/cgi-bin/query/r?ammem/calbkbib:@field(AUTHOR+@band(Pierce,+Hiram+Dwight,b.+1810.+))

Pike

Sanders, Sue A. Pike. *A Journey to, on and from the Golden Shore.* Delavan, IL: Times Printing Office, 1887. 118p.
http://memory.loc.gov/cgi-bin/query/r?ammem/calbkbib:@field(AUTHOR+@band(Sanders,+Sue+A.+Pike,1842-1931.+))

Piquet

Mattison, Hiram. *Louisa Picquet, the Octoroon, a Tale of Southern Slave Life.* New York, NY: Author, 1861. 60p.
http://digilib.nypl.org/dynaweb/digs/wwm97258/

Player

Player Frowd, J. G. *Six Months in California.* London: Longmans, Green and Co., 1872. 162p.
http://memory.loc.gov/cgi-bin/query/r?ammem/calbkbib:@field(AUTHOR+@band(Player-Frowd,+J.+G.+))

Pond

Harris, Edward Doubleday. *A Genealogical Record of Daniel Pond and His Descendants.* Saratoga Springs, NY: Judson, 1873. 210p.
http://genweb.net/~blackwell/ma/Pond1873/Pond1873.htm

Pond, William Chauncey. *Gospel Pioneering, Reminiscences of Early Congregationalism in California, 1833-1920.* Oberlin, OH: New Printing Co., 1921. 191p.
http://memory.loc.gov/cgi-bin/query/r?ammem/calbkbib:@field(AUTHOR+@band(Pond,+William+Chauncey,1830-1925.+))

Port

Sevareid, Arnold Eric. *Canoeing with the Cree.* New York, NY: Macmillan, 1935. 201p.
http://memory.loc.gov/cgi-bin/query/r?ammem/lhbumbib:@field(SUBJ+@band(Canoes+and+canoeing.+))

Post

Bunker, Mary Powell. *Long Island Genealogies, Families of Albertson, Andrews, Bedell, Birdsall, Bowne, Carman, Carr, Clowes, Cock, Cornelius, Covert, Dean, Doughty, Duryea, Feke, Frost, Haff, Hallock, Haydock, Hicks, Hopkins, Jackson, Jones, Keese, Ketcham, Kirby, Liones, Marvin, Merritt, Moore, Mott, Oakley, Onderdonck, Pearsall, Post, Powell, Prior, Robbins, Rodman, Rowland, Rushmore, Sands, Scudder, Seaman, Searing, Smith, Strickland, Titus, Townsend, Underhill, Valentine, Vanderdonk, Weeks, Whitman, Whitson, Willets, Williams, Willis, Wright, and other Families. Being Kindred Descendants of Thomas Powell of Bethpage, L.I., 1688.* Albany, NY: Munsell's, 1895. 350p.
http://moa.cit.cornell.edu/dienst/moabrowse.fly/MOA-JOURNALS2:BUNK-0101/5/1:TIFF2GIF:100

Powell

Bunker, Mary Powell. *Long Island Genealogies, Families of Albertson, Andrews, Bedell, Birdsall, Bowne, Carman, Care, Clowes, Cock, Cornelius, Covert, Dean, Doughty, Duryea, Feke, Frost, Haff, Hallock, Haydock, Hicks, Hopkins, Jackson, Jones, Keese, Ketcham, Kirby, Liones, Marvin, Merritt, Moore, Mott, Oakley, Onderdonck, Pearsall, Post, Powell, Prior, Robbins, Rodman, Rowland, Rushmore, Sands, Scudder, Seaman, Searing, Smith, Strickland, Titus, Townsend, Underhill, Valentine, Vanderdonk, Weeks, Whitman, Whitson, Willets, Williams, Willis, Wright, and other Families. Being Kindred Descendants of Thomas Powell of Bethpage, L.I., 1688.* Albany, NY: Munsell's, 1895. 350p.
http://moa.cit.cornell.edu/dienst/moabrowse.fly/MOA-JOURNALS2:BUNK-0101/5/1:TIFF2GIF:100

Prince

Prince, Mary. *The History of Mary Prince, a West Indian Slave, Related by Herself with a Supplement by the Editor to which is Added the Narrative of Asa Asa, a Captured African.* London: Westley and Davis, 1831. 44p.
http://digilib.nypl.org/dynaweb/digs/wwm97262/

Prince, Nancy. *A Narrative of the Life and Travels of Mrs. Nancy Prince.* 2nd ed. Boston, MA: Author, 1853. 89p.
http://digilib.nypl.org/dynaweb/digs/wwm97263/

Pryor

Bunker, Mary Powell. *Long Island Genealogies, Families of Albertson, Andrews, Bedell, Birdsall, Bowne, Carman, Carr, Clowes, Cock, Cornelius, Covert, Dean, Doughty, Duryea, Feke, Frost, Haff, Hallock, Haydock, Hicks, Hopkins, Jackson, Jones, Keese, Ketcham, Kirby,*

Liones, Marvin, Merritt, Moore, Mott, Oakley, Onderdonck, Pearsall, Post, Powell, Prior, Robbins, Rodman, Rowland, Rushmore, Sands, Scudder, Seaman, Searing, Smith, Strickland, Titus, Townsend, Underhill, Valentine, Vanderdonk, Weeks, Whitman, Whitson, Willets, Williams, Willis, Wright, and other Families. Being Kindred Descendants of Thomas Powell of Bethpage, L.I., 1688. Albany, NY: Munsell's, 1895. 350p.
http://moa.cit.cornell.edu/dienst/moabrowse.fly/MOA-JOURNALS2:BUNK-0101/5/1:TIFF2GIF:100

Pryor, Sara Agnes Rice. *My Day, Reminiscences of a Long Life.* New York, NY: Macmillan, 1909. 454p.
http://metalab.unc.edu/docsouth/pryor/menu.html

Purvis

Grimke, Francis J. *Anne M. Purvis.* Washington, DC: Colored Orphans Home, 1899. 18p.
http://memory.loc.gov/cgi-bin/query/r?ammem/aap:@field(SUBJ+@band(Funeral+addresses--Washington++D.C.+--1899.+))

Quinn

Funeral Services in Respect to the Memory of Rev. William Paul Quinn, Late Senior Bishop of the African M.E. Church, Held at Warren Chapel, Toledo, Ohio, March 9th, 1873. Toledo, OH: Warren Chapel, 1873. 52p.
http://memory.loc.gov/cgi-bin/query/r?ammem/aap:@field(SUBJ+@band(Quinn,+William+Paul,--1799-1873.+))

Rankin

Rankin, George C. *The Story of My Life or More than a Half Century as I Have Lived It and Seen It Lived.* Nashville, TN: Smith & Lamar, 1912. 356p.
http://metalab.unc.edu/docsouth/rankin/menu.html

Ravenel

Jervey, Susan Ravenel and Charlotte St. J. Ravenel. *Two Diaries from Middle St. John's, Berkeley, South Carolina, February-May, 1865. Journals Kept by Miss Susan R. Jervey and Miss Charlotte St. J. Ravenel at Northampton and Pooshee Plantations, and Reminiscences of Mrs. (Waring) Henagan with Two Contemporary Reports from Federal Officials.* Berkeley, SC: St. John's Hunting Club, 1921. 56p.
http://metalab.unc.edu/docsouth/jervey/menu.html

Reid

Reid, Hugo. *The Indians of Los Angeles County, Hugh Reid's Letters of 1852*. Los Angeles, CA: Southwest Museum, 1968. 142p.
http://memory.loc.gov/cgi-bin/query/r?ammem/calbkbib:@field(AUTHOR+@band(Reid,+Hugo,1811?-1853.+))

Reimann

Reimann, Lewis Charles. *Between the Iron and the Pine, a Biography of a Pioneer Family and a Pioneer Town*. Ann Arbor, MI: Edwards Brothers, 1951. 225p.
http://memory.loc.gov/cgi-bin/query/r?ammem/lhbumbib:@field(SUBJ+@band(Frontier+and+pioneer+life--Michigan,+Upper+Peninsula.+))

Reynolds

Reynolds, John N. *The Twin Hells, A Thrilling Narrative of Life in the Kansas and Missouri Penitentiaries*. Chicago, IL: Donohue, 1890. 331p.
http://www.ukans.edu/carrie/kancoll/books/twnhells/

Rice

Pryor, Sara Agnes Rice. *My Day, Reminiscences of a Long Life*. New York, NY: Macmillan, 1909. 454p.
http://metalab.unc.edu/docsouth/pryor/menu.html

Rice, Harvey. *Letters from the Pacific Slope or First Impressions*. New York, NY: Appleton, 1870. 135p.
http://memory.loc.gov/cgi-bin/query/r?ammem/calbkbib:@field(AUTHOR+@band(Rice,+Harvey,1800-1891.+))

Richardson

Vinton, John Adams. *Richardson Memorial*. Portland, ME: B. Thurston, 1876. 944p.
http://genweb.net/~blackwell/ma/Richardson1876/

Rideout

Rideout, Jacob Barzilla, Mrs. *Camping Out in California*. San Francisco, CA: Patterson, 1889. 237p.
http://memory.loc.gov/cgi-bin/query/r?ammem/calbkbib:@field(AUTHOR+@band(Rideout,+Jacob+Barzilla,Mrs.+))

Rindge

Rindge, Frederick Hastings. *Happy Days in Southern California*. Cambridge, MA: Author, 1898. 199p.
http://memory.loc.gov/cgi-bin/query/r?ammem/calbkbib:@field(AUTHOR+@band(Rindge,+Frederick+Hastings,1857-1905.+))

Ripley

Ripley, Eliza Moore Chinn McHatton. *From Flag to Flag, a Woman's Adventures and Experiences in the South during the War, in Mexico and in Cuba*. New York, NY: Appleton, 1889. 296p.
http://metalab.unc.edu/docsouth/ripleyflag/menu.html

————. *Social Life in Old New Orleans, being Recollections of My Girlhood*. New York, NY: Appleton, 1912. 332p.
http://metalab.unc.edu/docsouth/ripley/menu.html

Robbins
Bunker, Mary Powell. *Long Island Genealogies, Families of Albertson, Andrews, Bedell, Birdsall, Bowne, Carman, Carr, Clowes, Cock, Cornelius, Covert, Dean, Doughty, Duryea, Feke, Frost, Haff, Hallock, Haydock, Hicks, Hopkins, Jackson, Jones, Keese, Ketcham, Kirby, Liones, Marvin, Merritt, Moore, Mott, Oakley, Onderdonck, Pearsall, Post, Powell, Prior, Robbins, Rodman, Rowland, Rushmore, Sands, Scudder, Seaman, Searing, Smith, Strickland, Titus, Townsend, Underhill, Valentine, Vanderdonk, Weeks, Whitman, Whitson, Willets, Williams, Willis, Wright, and other Families. Being Kindred Descendants of Thomas Powell of Bethpage, L.I., 1688*. Albany, NY: Munsell's, 1895. 350p.
http://moa.cit.cornell.edu/dienst/moabrowse.fly/MOA-JOURNALS2:BUNK-0101/5/1:TIFF2GIF:100

Roberts
Roberts, Edwards. *Santa Barbara and around There*. Boston, MA: Roberts Brothers, 1886. 191p.
http://memory.loc.gov/cgi-bin/query/r?ammem/calbkbib:@field(AUTHOR+@band(Roberts,+Edwards.+))

Robinson
Robinson, Mary. *Memoirs of Mary Robinson*. Philadelphia, PA: Lippincott, 1895. 251p.
http://www.cs.cmu.edu/~mmbt/women/robinson/memoirs/memoirs.html

Robinson, William H. *From Log Cabin to Pulpit, or Fifteen Years in Slavery*. 3rd ed. Eau Claire, WI: Tifft, 1913. 200p.
http://metalab.unc.edu/docsouth/robinson/menu.html

Vinton, John Adams. *The Giles Memorial. Genealogical Memoirs of the Families Bearing the Names of Giles, Gould, Holmes, Jennison, Leonard, Lindall, Curwen, Marshall, Robinson, Sampson and Webb, also Genealogical Sketches of the Pool, Very, Tarr and other Families, with a History of Pemaquid, Ancient and Modern, Some Account of Early Settlements in Maine and Some Details of Indian Warfare*. Boston, MA: Dutton, 1864. 600p.
http://genweb.net/~blackwell/ma/Gyles1864/

Robson
Robson, John S. *How a One Legged Rebel Lives, Reminiscences of the Civil War. The Story of the Campaigns of Stonewall Jackson, as Told by a High Private in the "Foot Cavalry" from Alleghany Mountain to Chancellorsville, with the Complete Regimental Rosters of both the Great Armies at Gettysburg, by John S. Robson, Late of the 52d Regiment Virginia Infantry*. Durham, NC: Author, 1898. 186p.
http://metalab.unc.edu/docsouth/robson/menu.html

Rodman
Bunker, Mary Powell. *Long Island Genealogies, Families of Albertson, Andrews, Bedell, Birdsall, Bowne, Carman, Carr, Clowes, Cock, Cornelius, Covert, Dean, Doughty, Duryea, Feke, Frost, Haff, Hallock, Haydock, Hicks, Hopkins, Jackson, Jones, Keese, Ketcham, Kirby, Liones, Marvin, Merritt, Moore, Mott, Oakley, Onderdonck, Pearsall, Post, Powell, Prior, Robbins, Rodman, Rowland, Rushmore, Sands, Scudder, Seaman, Searing, Smith, Strickland,*

Titus, Townsend, Underhill, Valentine, Vanderdonk, Weeks, Whitman, Whitson, Willets, Williams, Willis, Wright, and other Families. Being Kindred Descendants of Thomas Powell of Bethpage, L.I., 1688. Albany, NY: Munsell's, 1895. 350p.
http://moa.cit.cornell.edu/dienst/moabrowse.fly/MOA-JOURNALS2:BUNK-0101/5/1:TIFF2GIF:100

Ronning

Ronning, Nils Nilsen. *Fifty Years in America.* Minneapolis, MN: Friend Publishing Co., 1938. 243p.
http://memory.loc.gov/cgi-bin/query/r?ammem/lhbum:@field(DOCID+@lit(08330T000)):@@@REF

Roper

Roper, Moses. *A Narrative of the Adventures and Escape of Moses Roper, from American Slavery.* Philadelphia, PA: Merrihew & Gunn, 1838. 89p.
http://metalab.unc.edu/docsouth/roper/menu.html

Ropes

Ropes, Hannah Anderson. *Six Months in Kansas.* Boston, MA: Jewett, 1856. 231p.
http://www.ukans.edu/carrie/kancoll/books/ropes/index.html

Round

Hines, Joseph Wilkinson. *Touching Incidents in the Life and Labors of a Pioneer on the Pacific Coast since 1853.* San Jose, CA: Eaton & Co., 1911. 198p.
http://memory.loc.gov/cgi-bin/query/r?ammem/calbkbib:@field(AUTHOR+@band(Hines,+Joseph+Wilkinson+))

Rowland

Bunker, Mary Powell. *Long Island Genealogies, Families of Albertson, Andrews, Bedell, Birdsall, Bowne, Carman, Carr, Clowes, Cock, Cornelius, Covert, Dean, Doughty, Duryea, Feke, Frost, Haff, Hallock, Haydock, Hicks, Hopkins, Jackson, Jones, Keese, Ketcham, Kirby, Liones, Marvin, Merritt, Moore, Mott, Oakley, Onderdonck, Pearsall, Post, Powell, Prior, Robbins, Rodman, Rowland, Rushmore, Sands, Scudder, Seaman, Searing, Smith, Strickland, Titus, Townsend, Underhill, Valentine, Vanderdonk, Weeks, Whitman, Whitson, Willets, Williams, Willis, Wright, and other Families. Being Kindred Descendants of Thomas Powell of Bethpage, L.I., 1688.* Albany, NY: Munsell's, 1895. 350p.
http://moa.cit.cornell.edu/dienst/moabrowse.fly/MOA-JOURNALS2:BUNK-0101/5/1:TIFF2GIF:100

Rowlandson

Rowlandson, Mary. *Narrative of the Captivity and Restoration of Mrs. Mary Rowlandson.* 1862.
ftp://uiarchive.cso.uiuc.edu/pub/etext/gutenberg/etext97/crmmr10.txt
http://tom.cs.cmu.edu/cgi-bin/book/lookup?num=851

Royall

Royall, William L. *Some Reminiscences.* New York, NY: Neale Publishing Co., 1909. 210p.
http://metalab.unc.edu/docsouth/royall/royall.html

Rushmore

Bunker, Mary Powell. *Long Island Genealogies, Families of Albertson, Andrews, Bedell, Birdsall, Bowne, Carman, Carr, Clowes, Cock, Cornelius, Covert, Dean, Doughty, Duryea, Feke,*

Frost, Haff, Hallock, Haydock, Hicks, Hopkins, Jackson, Jones, Keese, Ketcham, Kirby, Liones, Marvin, Merritt, Moore, Mott, Oakley, Onderdonck, Pearsall, Post, Powell, Prior, Robbins, Rodman, Rowland, Rushmore, Sands, Scudder, Seaman, Searing, Smith, Strickland, Titus, Townsend, Underhill, Valentine, Vanderdonk, Weeks, Whitman, Whitson, Willets, Williams, Willis, Wright, and other Families. Being Kindred Descendants of Thomas Powell of Bethpage, L.I., 1688. Albany, NY: Munsell's, 1895. 350p.
http://moa.cit.cornell.edu/dienst/moabrowse.fly/MOA-JOURNALS2:BUNK-0101/5/1:TIFF2GIF:100

Ryan

Ryan, William Redmond. *Personal Adventures in Upper and Lower California in 1848-9, with the Author's Experience at the Mines.* London: Shoberl, 1850. 2 vols.
http://memory.loc.gov/cgi-bin/query/r?ammem/calbkbib:@field(AUTHOR+@band(Ryan,+William+Redmond,1791-1855.+))

-S

Saint John

Whiting, William. *Memoir of Rev. Samuel Whiting, D.D. and of His Wife Elizabeth St. John, with References to Some of Their English Ancestors and American Descendants.* Boston, MA: Rand, Avery and Co., 1873. 334p.
http://genweb.net/~books/ma/whiting1873/

Sampson

Vinton, John Adams. *The Giles Memorial. Genealogical Memoirs of the Families Bearing the Names of Giles, Gould, Holmes, Jennison, Leonard, Lindall, Curwen, Marshall, Robinson, Sampson and Webb, also Genealogical Sketches of the Pool, Very, Tarr and other Families, with a History of Pemaquid, Ancient and Modern, Some Account of Early Settlements in Maine and Some Details of Indian Warfare.* Boston, MA: Dutton, 1864. 600p.
http://genweb.net/~blackwell/ma/Gyles1864/

Sanders

Sanders, Sue A. Pike. *A Journey to, on and from the Golden Shore.* Delavan, IL: Times Printing Office, 1887. 118p.
http://memory.loc.gov/cgi-bin/query/r?ammem/calbkbib:@field(AUTHOR+@band(Sanders,+Sue+A.+Pike,1842-1931.+))

Sands

Bunker, Mary Powell. *Long Island Genealogies, Families of Albertson, Andrews, Bedell, Birdsall, Bowne, Carman, Carr, Clowes, Cock, Cornelius, Covert, Dean, Doughty, Duryea, Feke, Frost, Haff, Hallock, Haydock, Hicks, Hopkins, Jackson, Jones, Keese, Ketcham, Kirby, Liones, Marvin, Merritt, Moore, Mott, Oakley, Onderdonck, Pearsall, Post, Powell, Prior, Robbins, Rodman, Rowland, Rushmore, Sands, Scudder, Seaman, Searing, Smith, Strickland, Titus, Townsend, Underhill, Valentine, Vanderdonk, Weeks, Whitman, Whitson, Willets,*

Williams, Willis, Wright, and other Families. Being Kindred Descendants of Thomas Powell of Bethpage, L.I., 1688. Albany, NY: Munsell's, 1895. 350p.
http://moa.cit.cornell.edu/dienst/moabrowse.fly/MOA-JOURNALS2:BUNK-0101/5/1:TIFF2GIF:100

Sawyer

Sawyer, Lemuel. *Auto-biography of Lemuel Sawyer, formerly Member of Congress from North Carolina.* New York, NY: Author, 1844. 48p.
http://metalab.unc.edu/docsouth/sawyer/menu.html

Saxon

Saxon, Elizabeth Lyle. *A Southern Woman's War Time Reminiscences.* Memphis, TN: Pilcher Printing, Co., 1905. 72p.
http://metalab.unc.edu/docsouth/saxon/menu.html

Schaeffer

Schaeffer, Luther Melanchthon. *Sketches of Travels in South America, Mexico and California.* New York, NY: Egbert, 1860. 247p.
http://memory.loc.gov/cgi-bin/query/r?ammem/calbkbib:@field(AUTHOR+@band(Schaeffer,+Luther+Melanchthon.+))

Scharmann

Scharmann, Hermann B. *Scharmann's Journey to California, from the Pages of a Pioneer's Diary from the German of H. B. Scharmann by Margaret Hoff Zimmermann, A.B. and Erich W. Zimmermann, Ph.D.* New York, NY: New Yorker Stats Zeitung, 1852, 1918. 114p.
http://memory.loc.gov/cgi-bin/query/r?ammem/calbkbib:@field(AUTHOR+@band(Scharmann,+Hermann+B.,b.+1838.+))

Schoolcraft

Schoolcraft, Henry Rowe. *Narrative Journal of Travels through the Northwestern Regions of the United States, Extending from Detroit through the Great Chain of American Lakes to the Sources of the Mississippi River, Performed as a Member of the Expedition under Governor Cass in the Year 1820.* Albany, NY: Hosford, 1821. 423p.
http://memory.loc.gov/cgi-bin/query/r?ammem/lhbum:@field(DOCID+@lit(01453T000)):@@@REF

————. *Narrative of an Expedition through the Upper Mississippi to Itasca Lake, the Actual Source of This River Embracing an Exploratory Trip through the St. Croix and Burntwood (or Broule) Rivers in 1832.* New York, NY: Harper, 1834. 308p.
http://memory.loc.gov/cgi-bin/query/r?ammem/lhbum:@field(DOCID+@lit(08794T000)):@@@REF

————. *Personal Memoirs of a Residence of Thirty Years with the Indian Tribes on the American Frontiers with Brief Notices of Passing Events, Facts, and Opinions, A.D. 1812 to A.D. 1842.* Philadelphia, PA: Lippincott, 1851. 703p.
http://memory.loc.gov/cgi-bin/query/r?ammem/lhbum:@field(DOCID+@lit(15006T000)):@@@REF

Scudder

Bunker, Mary Powell. *Long Island Genealogies, Families of Albertson, Andrews, Bedell, Birdsall, Bowne, Carman, Carr, Clowes, Cock, Cornelius, Covert, Dean, Doughty, Duryea, Feke, Frost, Haff, Hallock, Haydock, Hicks, Hopkins, Jackson, Jones, Keese, Ketcham, Kirby, Liones, Marvin, Merritt, Moore, Mott, Oakley, Onderdonck, Pearsall, Post, Powell, Prior, Robbins, Rodman, Rowland, Rushmore, Sands, Scudder, Seaman, Searing, Smith, Strickland,*

Titus, Townsend, Underhill, Valentine, Vanderdonk, Weeks, Whitman, Whitson, Willets, Williams, Willis, Wright, and other Families. Being Kindred Descendants of Thomas Powell of Bethpage, L.I., 1688. Albany, NY: Munsell's, 1895. 350p.
http://moa.cit.cornell.edu/dienst/moabrowse.fly/MOA-JOURNALS2:BUNK-0101/5/1:TIFF2GIF:100

Seaman

Bunker, Mary Powell. *Long Island Genealogies, Families of Albertson, Andrews, Bedell, Birdsall, Bowne, Carman, Carr, Clowes, Cock, Cornelius, Covert, Dean, Doughty, Duryea, Feke, Frost, Haff, Hallock, Haydock, Hicks, Hopkins, Jackson, Jones, Keese, Ketcham, Kirby, Liones, Marvin, Merritt, Moore, Mott, Oakley, Onderdonck, Pearsall, Post, Powell, Prior, Robbins, Rodman, Rowland, Rushmore, Sands, Scudder, Seaman, Searing, Smith, Strickland, Titus, Townsend, Underhill, Valentine, Vanderdonk, Weeks, Whitman, Whitson, Willets, Williams, Willis, Wright, and other Families. Being Kindred Descendants of Thomas Powell of Bethpage, L.I., 1688.* Albany, NY: Munsell's, 1895. 350p.
http://moa.cit.cornell.edu/dienst/moabrowse.fly/MOA-JOURNALS2:BUNK-0101/5/1:TIFF2GIF:100

Searing

Bunker, Mary Powell. *Long Island Genealogies, Families of Albertson, Andrews, Bedell, Birdsall, Bowne, Carman, Carr, Clowes, Cock, Cornelius, Covert, Dean, Doughty, Duryea, Feke, Frost, Haff, Hallock, Haydock, Hicks, Hopkins, Jackson, Jones, Keese, Ketcham, Kirby, Liones, Marvin, Merritt, Moore, Mott, Oakley, Onderdonck, Pearsall, Post, Powell, Prior, Robbins, Rodman, Rowland, Rushmore, Sands, Scudder, Seaman, Searing, Smith, Strickland, Titus, Townsend, Underhill, Valentine, Vanderdonk, Weeks, Whitman, Whitson, Willets, Williams, Willis, Wright, and other Families. Being Kindred Descendants of Thomas Powell of Bethpage, L.I., 1688.* Albany, NY: Munsell's, 1895. 350p.
http://moa.cit.cornell.edu/dienst/moabrowse.fly/MOA-JOURNALS2:BUNK-0101/5/1:TIFF2GIF:100

Sebury

Plato, Ann. *Essays, Including Biographies and Miscellaneous Pieces in Prose and Poetry.* Hartford, CT: Author, 1841. 122p.
http://digilib.nypl.org/dynaweb/digs/wwm97251/

Sevareid

Sevareid, Arnold Eric. *Canoeing with the Cree.* New York, NY: Macmillan, 1935. 201p.
http://memory.loc.gov/cgi-bin/query/r?ammem/lhbumbib:@field(SUBJ+@band(Canoes+and+canoeing.+))

Shaw

Johnson, William Bishop. *Sermons and Addresses. (Including, Eulogy on William J. Simmons, D.D., LL.D.; Religious Status of the Negro; National Perils; the Character and Work of the Apostle Paul; Robert G. Shaw; the Religious and the Secular Press Compared; the Value of Baptist Principles to the American Government; the Church as a Factor in the Race Problem; the Divinity of the Church).* Lynchburg, VA: Virginia Seminary Steam Print, 1899. 51p.
http://memory.loc.gov/cgi-bin/query/r?ammem/murray:@field(FLD001+90898305+):@@@REF

Shaw, Anna Howard. *The Story of a Pioneer.* New York, NY: Harper, 1915. 337p.
http://memory.loc.gov/cgi-bin/query/r?ammem/lhbumbib:@field(SUBJ+@band(Woman--Suffrage--United+States.+))

Shaw, David Augustus. *Eldorado, or California as Seen by a Pioneer, 1850-1900.* Los Angeles, CA: Baumgardt, 1900. 313p.
http://memory.loc.gov/cgi-bin/query/r?ammem/calbkbib:@field(AUTHOR+@band(Shaw,+David+Augustus,1826-1915.+))

Shaw, Pringle. *Ramblings in California, Containing a Description of the Country, Life at the Mines, State of Society etc., interspersed with Characteristic Anecdotes, and Sketches from Life, Being the Five Years Experience of a Gold Digger.* Toronto, Ontario: Bain, 1857. 239p.
http://memory.loc.gov/cgi-bin/query/r?ammem/calbkbib:@field(AUTHOR+@band(Shaw,+Pringle.+))

Shaw, William. *Golden Dreams and Waking Realities, Being the Adventures of a Gold Seeker in California and the Pacific Islands.* London: Smith, Elder & Co., 1851. 316p.
http://memory.loc.gov/cgi-bin/query/r?ammem/calbkbib:@field(AUTHOR+@band(Shaw,+William.+))

Shepherd

Shepherd, Henry Elliot. *Narrative of Prison Life at Baltimore and Johnson's Island, Ohio.* Baltimore, MD: Commercial Printing, 1917. 22p.
http://metalab.unc.edu/docsouth/shepherd/menu.html

Sherman

Plato, Ann. *Essays, Including Biographies and Miscellaneous Pieces in Prose and Poetry.* Hartford, CT: Author, 1841. 122p.
http://digilib.nypl.org/dynaweb/digs/wwm97251/

Sherrill

Sherrill, Miles O. *A Soldier's Story, Prison Life and Other Incidents in the War of 1861-65.* Author, 1904. 20p.
http://metalab.unc.edu/docsouth/sherrill/menu.html

Shufelt

Shufelt, S. *A Letter from a Gold Miner, Placerville, California, October 1850.* San Marino, CA: Friends of the Huntington Library, 1944. 28p.
http://memory.loc.gov/cgi-bin/query/r?ammem/calbkbib:@field(AUTHOR+@band(Shufelt,+S.+))

Sibley

Sibley, Henry Hastings. *The Unfinished Autobiography of Henry Hastings Sibley, together with a Selection of Hitherto Unpublished Letters from the Thirties, Edited by Theodore C. Blegen.* Minneapolis, MN: Voyageur Press, 1932. 75p.
http://memory.loc.gov/cgi-bin/query/r?ammem/lhbumbib:@field(SUBJ+@band(Fur+trade--Northwest,+Old.+))

Simmons

Johnson, William Bishop. *Sermons and Addresses. (Including, Eulogy on William J. Simmons, D.D., LL.D.; Religious Status of the Negro; National Perils; the Character and Work of the Apostle Paul; Robert G. Shaw; the Religious and the Secular Press Compared; the Value of Baptist Principles to the American Government; the Church as a Factor in the Race Problem; the Divinity of the Church).* Lynchburg, VA: Virginia Seminary Steam Print, 1899. 51p.
http://memory.loc.gov/cgi-bin/query/r?ammem/murray:@field(FLD001+90898305+):@@@REF

Smedes

Smedes, Susan Dabney. *Memorials of a Southern Planter*. Baltimore, MD: Cushings & Bailey, 1888. 348p.
http://moa.umdl.umich.edu/cgi-bin/moa/sgml/moa-idx?notisid=AFK4047

Smith

Bunker, Mary Powell. *Long Island Genealogies, Families of Albertson, Andrews, Bedell, Birdsall, Bowne, Carman, Carr, Clowes, Cock, Cornelius, Covert, Dean, Doughty, Duryea, Feke, Frost, Haff, Hallock, Haydock, Hicks, Hopkins, Jackson, Jones, Keese, Ketcham, Kirby, Liones, Marvin, Merritt, Moore, Mott, Oakley, Onderdonck, Pearsall, Post, Powell, Prior, Robbins, Rodman, Rowland, Rushmore, Sands, Scudder, Seaman, Searing, Smith, Strickland, Titus, Townsend, Underhill, Valentine, Vanderdonk, Weeks, Whitman, Whitson, Willets, Williams, Willis, Wright, and other Families. Being Kindred Descendants of Thomas Powell of Bethpage, L.I., 1688.* Albany, NY: Munsell's, 1895. 350p.
http://moa.cit.cornell.edu/dienst/moabrowse.fly/MOA-JOURNALS2:BUNK-0101/5/1:TIFF2GIF:100

Colt, Miriam Davis. *Went to Kansas, Being a Thrilling Account of an Ill Fated Expedition to That Fairy Land and Its Sad Result, together with a Sketch of the Life of the Author and How the World Goes with Her*. Watertown, NY: Ingalls & Co., 1862. 294p.
http://www.ukans.edu/carrie/kancoll/books/colt/

Haviland, Laura Smith. *A Woman's Life-work, Labors and Experiences of Laura S. Haviland*. Cincinnati, OH: Walden & Stowe, 1882. 531p.
http://memory.loc.gov/cgi-bin/query/r?ammem/lhbumbib:@field(SUBJ+@band(Freedmen.+))

Smith, Amanda. *An Autobiography, the Story of the Lord's Dealings with Mrs. Amanda Smith, the Colored Evangelist, Containing an Account of Her Life Work of Faith, and Her Travels in America, England, Ireland, Scotland, India and Africa, as an Independent Missionary*. Chicago, IL: Meyer and Brother, 1893. 506p.
http://digilib.nypl.org/dynaweb/digs/wwm97264/

Smith, Harry. *The Autobiography of Harry Smith*. 1901. 2 vols.
http://homepages.ihug.co.nz/~awoodley/harry/harryintro.html

Smith, Sarah Hathaway Bixby. *Adobe Days, Being the Truthful Narrative of the Events in the Life of a California Girl on a Sheep Ranch and in El Pueblo de Nuestra Senora de Los Angeles while It Was Yet a Small and Humble Town, together with an Account of How Three Young Men from Maine in Eighteen Hundred and Fifty-three Drove Sheep and Cattle across the Plains, Mountains and Deserts from Illinois to the Pacific Coast, and the Strange Prophecy of Admiral Thatcher about San Pedro Harbor*. Cedar Rapids, IA: Torch Press, 1925. 208p.
http://memory.loc.gov/cgi-bin/query/r?ammem/calbkbib:@field(AUTHOR+@band(Smith,+Sarah+Hathaway+Bixby,1871-1935.+))

Smithwick

Smithwick, Noah. *The Evolution of a State or Recollections of Old Texas Days*. Austin, TX: Gammel Book Co., 1900. 354p.
http://www.erols.com/hardeman/lonestar/olbooks/smithwic/otd.htm

Southworth

Webber, Samuel Gilbert. *A Genealogy of the Southworths (Southards) Descendants of Constant Southworth, with a Sketch of the Family in England*. Boston, MA: Fort Hill Press, 1905. 487p.
http://genweb.net/~blackwell/ma/southworth/

Spaulding

Crosby, Elisha Oscar. *Memoirs of Elisha Oscar Crosby, Reminiscences of California and Guatemala from 1849 to 1864.* San Marino, CA: Huntington Library, 1945. 119p.
http://memory.loc.gov/cgi-bin/query/r?ammem/calbkbib:@field(AUTHOR+@band(Crosby,+Elisha+Oscar, 1818-1895.+))

Spofford

Shippen, R. R. *In Memoriam, Sarah Partridge Spofford, Born November 10, 1823, Departed May 11, 1892.* Washington, DC: Author, 1892. 10p.
http://memory.loc.gov/cgi-bin/query/r?ammem/aap:@field(SUBJ+@band(Eulogies--Washington++D.C.+ --1892.+))

Stanford

Stanford, Peter Thomas. *Imaginary Obstructions to True Spiritual Progress, Preached during the Service at the Day Street Congregational Church, August 14, 1898.* West Somerville, MA: Davis Square Printing, Co., 1898. 12p.
http://memory.loc.gov/cgi-bin/query/r?ammem/aap:@field(SUBJ+@band(Day+Street+Congregational+ Church.+))

Stearns

Stearns, Charles Woodward. *The Black Man of the South and the Rebels, or the Characteristics of the Former and the Recent Outrages of the Latter.* New York, NY: American News, 1872. 578p.
http://moa.umdl.umich.edu/cgi-bin/moa/sgml/moa-idx?notisid=ABL5152

Steele

Bidwell, John. *Echoes of the Past about California.* Published with *In Camp and Cabin,* by Rev. John Steele. Chicago, IL: Donnelley, 1928. 377p.
http://memory.loc.gov/ammem/mdbquery.html

Fairchild, Lucius. *California Letters of Lucius Fairchild.* Madison, WI: State Historical Society of Wisconsin, 1931. 212p.
http://memory.loc.gov/cgi-bin/query/r?ammem/calbkbib:@field(AUTHOR+@band(Fairchild,+Lucius, 1831-1896.+))

Steele, James. *Old Californian Days.* Chicago, IL: Belford Clarke, Co., 1889. 227p.
http://memory.loc.gov/cgi-bin/query/r?ammem/calbkbib:@field(AUTHOR+@band(Steele,+James.+))

Stephens

Stephens, Lorenzo Dow. *Life Sketches of a Jayhawker of '49.* San Jose, CA: Nolta Brothers, 1916. 68p.
http://memory.loc.gov/cgi-bin/query/r?ammem/calbkbib:@field(AUTHOR+@band(Stephens,+Lorenzo+ Dow,1827-+))

Stephenson

Stephenson, Isaac. *Recollections of a Long Life, 1829-1915.* Chicago, IL: Donnelley & Sons, 1915. 264p.
http://memory.loc.gov/cgi-bin/query/r?ammem/lhbum:@field(DOCID+@lit(26800T000)):@@@REF

Stevenson

Stevenson, Robert Louis. *The Silverado Squatters*. New York, NY: Lovell Co., 1888. 96p.
http://memory.loc.gov/cgi-bin/query/r?ammem/calbkbib:@field(AUTHOR+@band(Stevenson,+Robert+Louis,1850-1894.+))

Stewart

Stewart, Austin. *Twenty-two Years a Slave and Forty Years a Freeman, Embracing a Correspondence of Several Years, while President of Wilberforce Colony, London, Canada West*. Rochester, NY: Alling, 1857. 360p.
http://metalab.unc.edu/docsouth/steward/menu.html

Stiles

Stiles, Robert. *Four Years under Marse Robert (General Robert E. Lee)*. New York, NY: Neale, 1904. 368p.
http://metalab.unc.edu/docsouth/stiles/menu.html

Stimson

Stimson, Hiram K. *From the Stage Coach to the Pulpit, being an Autobiographical Sketch, with Incidents and Anecdotes of Elder H. K. Stimson, the Veteran Pioneer of Western New York, Now of Kansas*. Saint Louis, MO: Campbell, 1874. 430p.
http://moa.umdl.umich.edu/cgi-bin/moa/sgml/moa-idx?notisid=AJK2081

Stoddard

Stoddard, Charles Warren. *In the Footprints of the Padres*. San Francisco, CA: Robertson, 1902. 335p.
http://memory.loc.gov/cgi-bin/query/r?ammem/calbkbib:@field(AUTHOR+@band(Stoddard,+Charles+Warren,1843-1909.+))

Stone

Perry, Belle McArthur. *Lucinda Hinsdale Stone, Her Life Story and Reminiscences*. Detroit, MI: Blinn Publishing, 1902. 369p.
http://memory.loc.gov/cgi-bin/query/r?ammem/lhbumbib:@field(SUBJ+@band(Stone,+Lucinda+Hinsdale,--1814-1900.+))

Stone, Henry Lane. *Morgan's Men, a Narrative of Personal Experience*. Louisville, KY: Westerfield Bonte Co., 1919. 36p.
http://metalab.unc.edu/docsouth/stone/menu.html

Stoner

Simms, Jeptha Root. *Trappers of New York or a Biography of Nicholas Stoner and Nathaniel Foster, together with Anecdotes of other Celebrated Hunters and Some Account of Sir William Johnson*. Albany, NY: Munsell's, 1850. 280p.
http://moa.cit.cornell.edu/dienst/moabrowse.fly/MOA-JOURNALS2:SIMM-0023/5/1:TIFF2GIF:100

Streeter

Streeter, Milford B. *A Genealogical History of the Descendants of Stephen and Ursula Streeter of Gloucester, Mass., 1642, afterwards of Charlestown, Mass. 1644-1652, with an Account of the Streeters of Goodherst, Kent, England*. Salem, MA: Eben Putnam Publisher, 1896.
http://genweb.net/~blackwell/ma/Streeter1896/

Strickland

Bunker, Mary Powell. *Long Island Genealogies, Families of Albertson, Andrews, Bedell, Birdsall, Bowne, Carman, Carr, Clowes, Cock, Cornelius, Covert, Dean, Doughty, Duryea, Feke, Frost, Haff, Hallock, Haydock, Hicks, Hopkins, Jackson, Jones, Keese, Ketcham, Kirby, Liones, Marvin, Merritt, Moore, Mott, Oakley, Onderdonck, Pearsall, Post, Powell, Prior, Robbins, Rodman, Rowland, Rushmore, Sands, Scudder, Seaman, Searing, Smith, Strickland, Titus, Townsend, Underhill, Valentine, Vanderdonk, Weeks, Whitman, Whitson, Willets, Williams, Willis, Wright, and other Families. Being Kindred Descendants of Thomas Powell of Bethpage, L.I., 1688.* Albany, NY: Munsell's, 1895. 350p.
http://moa.cit.cornell.edu/dienst/moabrowse.fly/MOA-JOURNALS2:BUNK-0101/5/1:TIFF2GIF:100

Stuyvesant

Tuckerman, Bayard. *Peter Stuyvesant, Director General for the West India Company in New Netherland.* New York, NY: Dodd, Mead & Co., 1893. 193p.
http://moa.cit.cornell.edu/dienst/moabrowse.fly/MOA-JOURNALS2:TUCK-0011/5/1:TIFF2GIF:100

Summers

Whipple Haslam, Lee Summers. *Early Days in California, Scenes and Events of the '50s as I Remember Them.* Jamestown, CA: Author, 1925. 34p.
http://memory.loc.gov/cgi-bin/query/r?ammem/calbkbib:@field(AUTHOR+@band(Whipple-Haslam,+Lee,Mrs.+))

Sutter

Sutter, John Augustus. *The Diary of Johann August Sutter.* San Francisco, CA: Grabhorn Press, 1932. 56p.
http://memory.loc.gov/cgi-bin/query/r?ammem/calbkbib:@field(AUTHOR+@band(Sutter,+John+Augustus,1803-1880.+))

Swan

Swan, John Alfred. *A Trip to the Gold Mines of California in 1848.* San Francisco, CA: Book Club of California, 1960. 51p.
http://memory.loc.gov/cgi-bin/query/r?ammem/calbkbib:@field(AUTHOR+@band(Swan,+John+Alfred,1817-1896.+))

Swisshelm

Swisshelm, Jane Grey Cannon. *Half a Century.* Chicago, IL: Author, 1880. 263p.
http://memory.loc.gov/cgi-bin/query/r?ammem/lhbumbib:@field(SUBJ+@band(Slavery+in+the+United+States--Anti-slavery+movements.+))

-T

Tarr

Vinton, John Adams. *The Giles Memorial. Genealogical Memoirs of the Families Bearing the Names of Giles, Gould, Holmes, Jennison, Leonard, Lindall, Curwen, Marshall, Robinson, Sampson and Webb, also Genealogical Sketches of the Pool, Very, Tarr and other Families,*

with a History of Pemaquid, Ancient and Modern, Some Account of Early Settlements in Maine and Some Details of Indian Warfare. Boston, MA: Dutton, 1864. 600p.
http://genweb.net/~blackwell/ma/Gyles1864/

Taylor

McCray, S. J. *Life of Mary F. McCray, Born and Raised a Slave in the State of Kentucky, by Her Husband and Son.* Lima, OH: Author, 1898. 115p.
http://metalab.unc.edu/docsouth/mccray/menu.html

Taylor, Bayard. *Eldorado, or Adventures in the Path of Empire, comprising a Voyage to California, via Panama, Life in San Francisco and Monterey, Pictures of the Gold Region and Experiences of Mexican Travel.* New York, NY: Putnam, 1850. 2 vols.
http://memory.loc.gov/cgi-bin/query/r?ammem/calbk:@field(DOCID+@lit(C122T00)):@@@REF

Taylor, Benjamin Franklin. *Between the Gates.* Chicago, IL: Griggs, 1878. 292p.
http://memory.loc.gov/cgi-bin/query/r?ammem/calbkbib:@field(AUTHOR+@band(Taylor,+Benjamin+F[ranklin],1819-1887.+))

Taylor, Richard. *Destruction and Reconstruction, Personal Experiences of the Late War.* New York, NY: Appleton, 1879. 274p.
http://metalab.unc.edu/docsouth/taylor/menu.html

Taylor, Susie King. *Reminiscences of My Life in Camp with the 33d United States Colored Troops Late 1st S.C. Volunteers.* Boston, MA: Author, 82p.
http://digilib.nypl.org/dynaweb/digs/wwm97267/

Taylor, William. *California Life Illustrated.* New York, NY: Carlton & Porter, 1858. 348p.
http://memory.loc.gov/cgi-bin/query/r?ammem/calbk:@field(DOCID+@lit(C063T00)):@@@REF

————. *Seven Year's Street Preaching in San Francisco, California, Embracing Incidents, Triumphant Death Scenes, etc.* New York, NY: Author, 1857. 394p.
http://memory.loc.gov/cgi-bin/query/r?ammem/calbk:@field(DOCID+@lit(C109T00)):@@@REF

————. 1859 Edition. 418p.
http://moa.umdl.umich.edu/cgi-bin/moa/sgml/moa-idx?notisid=AJG9120

Ten Broeck

Manley, John. *Cattaraugus County, Embracing Its Agricultural Society, Newspapers, Civil List, from the Organization of the County to 1857, Biographies of the Old Pioneers, with Portraits, Benjamin Chamberlain, Peter Ten Broeck, Frederick S. Martin, Chauncey J. Fox, Alson Leavenworth, Stanley N. Clarke, and of Congressmen Francis S. Edwards and Reuben E. Fenton, Colonial and State Governors of New York, Names of Towns and Post Offices with the Statistics of Each Town.* Little Valley, NY: Author, 1857. 140p.
http://moa.cit.cornell.edu/dienst/moabrowse.fly/MOA-JOURNALS2:MANL-0089/3/1:TIFF2GIF:100

Thayer

Thayer, Bezaleel. *Memorial of the Thayer Name from the Massachusetts Colony of Weymouth and Braintree, Embracing Genealogical and Biographical Sketches of Richard and Thomas Thayer and Their Descendants from 1636 to 1874.* Oswego, NY: Oliphant, 1874. 708p.
http://genweb.net/~blackwell/ma/Thayer1874/

Thomas

Hoag, Joseph. *The Transformation of Joseph Hoag.* Philadelphia, PA: Tract Association of Friends. N.p., n.d.
http://people.delphi.com/pdsippel/hoag.htm

Thomas, Edward J. *Memoirs of a Southerner, 1840-1923*. Savannah, GA: Author, 1923. 64p.
http://metalab.unc.edu/docsouth/thomas/menu.html

Thompson

Thompson, George. *Prison Life and Reflections or a Narrative of the Arrest, Trial, Conviction, Imprisonment, Treatment, Observations, Reflections and Deliverance of Work, Burr and Thompson Who Suffered an Unjust and Cruel Imprisonment in Missouri Penitentiary for Attempting to Aid Some Slaves to Liberty*. Hartford, CT: Alanson Work, 1850. 376p.
http://moa.umdl.umich.edu/cgi-bin/moa/sgml/moa-idx?notisid=ACK4077

Thoresby

Thoresby, William. *A Narrative of God's Love to William Thoresby*. 2nd ed. Redruth, England: J. Bennett, 1801. 150p.
http://www.mun.ca/rels/meth/thoresby.html

Titus

Bunker, Mary Powell. *Long Island Genealogies, Families of Albertson, Andrews, Bedell, Birdsall, Bowne, Carman, Carr, Clowes, Cock, Cornelius, Covert, Dean, Doughty, Duryea, Feke, Frost, Haff, Hallock, Haydock, Hicks, Hopkins, Jackson, Jones, Keese, Ketcham, Kirby, Liones, Marvin, Merritt, Moore, Mott, Oakley, Onderdonck, Pearsall, Post, Powell, Prior, Robbins, Rodman, Rowland, Rushmore, Sands, Scudder, Seaman, Searing, Smith, Strickland, Titus, Townsend, Underhill, Valentine, Vanderdonk, Weeks, Whitman, Whitson, Willets, Williams, Willis, Wright, and other Families. Being Kindred Descendants of Thomas Powell of Bethpage, L.I., 1688*. Albany, NY: Munsell's, 1895. 350p.
http://moa.cit.cornell.edu/dienst/moabrowse.fly/MOA-JOURNALS2:BUNK-0101/5/1:TIFF2GIF:100

Todd

Todd, John. *The Sunset Land or the Great Pacific Slope*. Boston, MA: Lee & Shepard, 1870. 322p.
http://memory.loc.gov/cgi-bin/query/r?ammem/calbk:@field(DOCID+@lit(C184T00)):@@@REF

Tower

Tower, Charlemagne. *Tower Genealogy, an Account of the Descendants of John Tower of Hingham, Mass., Compiled under the Direction of Charlemagne Tower, Late of Philadelphia, Deceased*. Cambridge, MA: John Wilson, 1891. 689p.
http://genweb.net/~blackwell/ma/Tower1891/

Townsend

Bunker, Mary Powell. *Long Island Genealogies, Families of Albertson, Andrews, Bedell, Birdsall, Bowne, Carman, Carr, Clowes, Cock, Cornelius, Covert, Dean, Doughty, Duryea, Feke, Frost, Haff, Hallock, Haydock, Hicks, Hopkins, Jackson, Jones, Keese, Ketcham, Kirby, Liones, Marvin, Merritt, Moore, Mott, Oakley, Onderdonck, Pearsall, Post, Powell, Prior, Robbins, Rodman, Rowland, Rushmore, Sands, Scudder, Seaman, Searing, Smith, Strickland, Titus, Townsend, Underhill, Valentine, Vanderdonk, Weeks, Whitman, Whitson, Willets, Williams, Willis, Wright, and other Families. Being Kindred Descendants of Thomas Powell of Bethpage, L.I., 1688*. Albany, NY: Munsell's, 1895. 350p.
http://moa.cit.cornell.edu/dienst/moabrowse.fly/MOA-JOURNALS2:BUNK-0101/5/1:TIFF2GIF:100

Traill

Traill, Catherine Parr. *The Backwoods of Canada, Being Letters from the Wife of an Emigrant Officer, Illustrative of the Domestic Economy of British America.* London: Knight, 1836. 361p.
http://www.canadiana.org/cgi-bin/ECO/mtq?id=04ee01375f&doc=41930

Train

Train, George Francis. *An American Merchant in Europe, Asia and Australia, a Series of Letters from Java, Singapore, China, Bengal, Egypt, the Holy Land, the Crimea, and Its Battle Grounds, England, Melbourne, Sydney etc.* New York, NY: Putnam, 1857. 522p.
http://moa.umdl.umich.edu/cgi-bin/moa/sgml/moa-idx?notisid=AFK6711

Truman

Truman, Benjamin Cummings. *Semi-tropical California, Its Climate, Healthfulness, Productiveness and Scenery.* San Francisco, CA: Bancroft, 1874. 204p.
http://memory.loc.gov/cgi-bin/query/r?ammem/calbkbib:@field(AUTHOR+@band(Truman,+Ben[jamin]+C[ummings],1835-1916.+))

Truth

Gilbert, Olive. *Narrative of Sojourner Truth, a Bonds-woman of Olden Time, Emancipated by the New York Legislature in the Early Part of the Present Century, with a History of Her Labors and Correspondence, Drawn from Her Book of Life.* Battle Creek, MI: Author, 1878. 320p.
http://memory.loc.gov/cgi-bin/query/r?ammem/lhbumbib:@field(SUBJ+@band(Truth,+Sojourner,--d.+1883.+))

Tubman

Bradford, Sarah H. *Harriet, the Moses of Her People.* New York, NY: Lockwood, 1886. 149p.
http://metalab.unc.edu/docsouth/harriet/menu.html

Turrill

Turrill, Charles Beebe. *California Notes.* San Francisco, CA: Bosqui, 1876. 232p.
http://memory.loc.gov/cgi-bin/query/r?ammem/calbkbib:@field(AUTHOR+@band(Turrill,+Charles+B.+))

Tyson

Tyson, James Lawrence. *Diary of a Physician in California, Being the Results of Actual Experience Including Notes of the Journey by Land and Water and Observations on the Climate, Soil, Resources of the Country.* New York, NY: Appleton, 1850. 92p.
http://memory.loc.gov/cgi-bin/query/r?ammem/calbkbib:@field(AUTHOR+@band(Tyson,+James+Lawrence.+))

-U

Underhill

Bunker, Mary Powell. *Long Island Genealogies, Families of Albertson, Andrews, Bedell, Birdsall, Bowne, Carman, Carr, Clowes, Cock, Cornelius, Covert, Dean, Doughty, Duryea, Feke,*

Frost, Haff, Hallock, Haydock, Hicks, Hopkins, Jackson, Jones, Keese, Ketcham, Kirby, Liones, Marvin, Merritt, Moore, Mott, Oakley, Onderdonck, Pearsall, Post, Powell, Prior, Robbins, Rodman, Rowland, Rushmore, Sands, Scudder, Seaman, Searing, Smith, Strickland, Titus, Townsend, Underhill, Valentine, Vanderdonk, Weeks, Whitman, Whitson, Willets, Williams, Willis, Wright, and other Families. Being Kindred Descendants of Thomas Powell of Bethpage, L.I., 1688. Albany, NY: Munsell's, 1895. 350p.
http://moa.cit.cornell.edu/dienst/moabrowse.fly/MOA-JOURNALS2:BUNK-0101/5/1:TIFF2GIF:100

Upham
Upham, Samuel Curtis. *Notes of a Voyage to California via Cape Horn, together with Scenes in El Dorado, in the Years of 1849-50, with an Appendix Containing Reminiscences together with the Articles of Association and Roll of Members of the Associated Pioneers of the Territorial Days of California.* Philadelphia, PA: Author, 1878. 594p.
http://memory.loc.gov/cgi-bin/query/r?ammem/calbkbib:@field(AUTHOR+@band(Upham,+Samuel+Curtis,1819-1885.+))

Vail
Vail, Mary C. *Both Sides Told, or Southern California as It Is.* Pasadena, CA: West Coast Pub. Co., 1888. 23p.
http://memory.loc.gov/cgi-bin/query/r?ammem/calbkbib:@field(AUTHOR+@band(Vail,+Mary+C.+))

Valentine
Bunker, Mary Powell. *Long Island Genealogies, Families of Albertson, Andrews, Bedell, Birdsall, Bowne, Carman, Carr, Clowes, Cock, Cornelius, Covert, Dean, Doughty, Duryea, Feke, Frost, Haff, Hallock, Haydock, Hicks, Hopkins, Jackson, Jones, Keese, Ketcham, Kirby, Liones, Marvin, Merritt, Moore, Mott, Oakley, Onderdonck, Pearsall, Post, Powell, Prior, Robbins, Rodman, Rowland, Rushmore, Sands, Scudder, Seaman, Searing, Smith, Strickland, Titus, Townsend, Underhill, Valentine, Vanderdonk, Weeks, Whitman, Whitson, Willets, Williams, Willis, Wright, and other Families. Being Kindred Descendants of Thomas Powell of Bethpage, L.I., 1688.* Albany, NY: Munsell's, 1895. 350p.
http://moa.cit.cornell.edu/dienst/moabrowse.fly/MOA-JOURNALS2:BUNK-0101/5/1:TIFF2GIF:100

Van Cleve
Van Cleve, Charlotte Ouisconsin Clark. *Three Score Years and Ten, Life-long Memories of Fort Snelling, Minnesota and Other Parts of the West.* Minneapolis, MN: Harrison & Smith, 1888. 176p.
http://memory.loc.gov/cgi-bin/query/r?ammem/lhbumbib:@field(SUBJ+@band(Fort+Snelling,+Minn.+))

Vanderdonk
Bunker, Mary Powell. *Long Island Genealogies, Families of Albertson, Andrews, Bedell, Birdsall, Bowne, Carman, Carr, Clowes, Cock, Cornelius, Covert, Dean, Doughty, Duryea, Feke, Frost, Haff, Hallock, Haydock, Hicks, Hopkins, Jackson, Jones, Keese, Ketcham, Kirby, Liones, Marvin, Merritt, Moore, Mott, Oakley, Onderdonck, Pearsall, Post, Powell, Prior, Robbins, Rodman, Rowland, Rushmore, Sands, Scudder, Seaman, Searing, Smith, Strickland,*

Titus, Townsend, Underhill, Valentine, Vanderdonk, Weeks, Whitman, Whitson, Willets, Williams, Willis, Wright, and other Families. Being Kindred Descendants of Thomas Powell of Bethpage, L.I., 1688. Albany, NY: Munsell's, 1895. 350p.
http://moa.cit.cornell.edu/dienst/moabrowse.fly/MOA-JOURNALS2:BUNK-0101/5/1:TIFF2GIF:100

Vandergon

Vandergon, Gertrude Braat. *Our Pioneer Days in Minnesota.* Author, 1949. 138p.
http://memory.loc.gov/cgi-bin/query/r?ammem/lhbum:@field(DOCID+@lit(03667T000)):@@@REF

Van Hoosen

Van Hoosen, Bertha. *Petticoat Surgeon.* Chicago, IL: Pellegrini & Cudahy, 1947. 324p.
http://memory.loc.gov/cgi-bin/query/r?ammem/lhbumbib:@field(SUBJ+@band(Gynecologists--Illinois--Biography.+))

Velazquez

Worthington, C. J. *The Woman in Battle, a Narrative of the Exploits, Adventures, and Travels of Madame Loreta Janeta Velazquez, otherwise Known as Lieutenant Harry T. Buford, Confederate States Army in which is Given Full Descriptions of the Numerous Battles in Which She Participated as a Confederate Officer.* Richmond, VA: Dustin, Gilman, 1876. 606p.
http://metalab.unc.edu/docsouth/velazquez/menu.html

Veney

Veney, Bethany. *The Narrative of Bethany Veney, a Slave Woman.* Worcester, MA: Author, 1889. 47p.
http://metalab.unc.edu/docsouth/veney/menu.html
http://digilib.nypl.org/dynaweb/digs/wwm97269/

Very

Vinton, John Adams. *The Giles Memorial. Genealogical Memoirs of the Families Bearing the Names of Giles, Gould, Holmes, Jennison, Leonard, Lindall, Curwen, Marshall, Robinson, Sampson and Webb, also Genealogical Sketches of the Pool, Very, Tarr and other Families, with a History of Pemaquid, Ancient and Modern, Some Account of Early Settlements in Maine and Some Details of Indian Warfare.* Boston, MA: Dutton, 1864. 600p.
http://genweb.net/~blackwell/ma/Gyles1864/

Vizetelly

Vizetelly, Henry. *California. Four Months among the Goldfinders, Being the Diary of an Expedition from San Francisco to the Gold Districts.* Paris, France: Galignani, 1849. 136p.
http://memory.loc.gov/cgi-bin/query/r?ammem/calbkbib:@field(AUTHOR+@band(Vizetelly,+Henry,1820-1894.+))

Waldo

Medberry, Rebecca B. Stetson. *Memoir of Mrs. Sarah Emily York, formerly Miss Sarah Emily Waldo, Missionary in Greece.* Boston, MA: Phillips, Sampson and Co., 1863, 434p.
http://moa.umdl.umich.edu/cgi-bin/moa/sgml/moa-idx?notisid=AJG8055

Ward

Ward, Dallas T. *The Last Flag of Truce*. Franklinton, NC: Author, 1915. 16p.
http://metalab.unc.edu/docsouth/ward/menu.html

Ward, David. *The Autobiography of David Ward*. New York, NY: Author, 1912. 194p.
http://memory.loc.gov/cgi-bin/query/r?ammem/lhbumbib:@field(SUBJ+@band(Michigan--Social+life+and+customs.+))

Waring

Jervey, Susan Ravenel and Charlotte St. J. Ravenel. *Two Diaries from Middle St. John's, Berkeley, South Carolina, February-May, 1865. Journals Kept by Miss Susan R. Jervey and Miss Charlotte St. J. Ravenel at Northampton and Pooshee Plantations, and Reminiscences of Mrs. (Waring) Henagan with Two Contemporary Reports from Federal Officials*. Berkeley, CA: St. John's Hunting Club, 1921. 56p.
http://metalab.unc.edu/docsouth/jervey/menu.html

Warner

Warner, Charles Dudley. *Our Italy*. New York, NY: Harper, 1891. 266p.
http://memory.loc.gov/cgi-bin/query/r?ammem/calbkbib:@field(AUTHOR+@band(Warner,+Charles+Dudley,1829-1900.+))

Washington

Washington, Booker Talieferro. *My Larger Eduction, Being Chapters from My Experience*. Garden City, NY: Doubleday, Page & Co., 1911. 313p.
http://metalab.unc.edu/docsouth/washeducation/menu.html

————. *Up from Slavery, an Autobiography*. New York, NY: Doubleday, 1901. 330p.
http://metalab.unc.edu/docsouth/washington/menu.html

Watson

Marston, Benjamin. *Diaries of Benjamin Marston, 1776-1787*. 20 vols. Original manuscript.
http://ultratext.hil.unb.ca/Texts/Marston/Marston.html

Webb

Vinton, John Adams. *The Giles Memorial. Genealogical Memoirs of the Families Bearing the Names of Giles, Gould, Holmes, Jennison, Leonard, Lindall, Curwen, Marshall, Robinson, Sampson and Webb, also Genealogical Sketches of the Pool, Very, Tarr and other Families, with a History of Pemaquid, Ancient and Modern, Some Account of Early Settlements in Maine and Some Details of Indian Warfare*. Boston, MA: Dutton, 1864. 600p.
http://genweb.net/~blackwell/ma/Gyles1864/

Webb, William Edward. *Buffalo Land, an Authentic Account of the Discoveries, Adventures and Mishaps of a Scientific and Sporting Party in the Wild West, with Graphic Descriptions of the Country, the Red Man, Savage and Civilized, Hunting the Buffalo, Antelope etc. Replete with Information, Wit, and Humor. The Appendix Comprising a Complete Guide for Sportsmen and Emigrants*. Cincinnati, OH: Hannaford, 1872. 504p.
http://moa.umdl.umich.edu/cgi-bin/moa/sgml/moa-idx?notisid=AKR1255

Webster

Hall, Linville John and George Gideon Webster. *Around the Horn in '49, Journal of the Hartford Union Mining and Trading Company. Containing the Name, Residence and Occupa-*

tion of Each Member, with Incidents of the Voyage. Wethersfield, CT: L. J. Hall, 1898. 252p.
http://memory.loc.gov/cgi-bin/query/r?ammem/calbkbib:@field(AUTHOR+@band(Hartford+Union+Mining+and+Trading+Company.+))

Webster, Kimball. *The Gold Seekers of '49, a Personal Narrative of the Overland Trail and Adventures in California and Oregon from 1849 to 1854, by Kimball Webster a New England Forty-niner, with an Introduction and Biographical Sketch by George Waldo Browne.* Manchester, NH: Standard Book Co., 1917. 240p.
http://memory.loc.gov/cgi-bin/query/r?ammem/calbkbib:@field(AUTHOR+@band(Webster,+Kimball,+1828-1916.+))

Weeks

Bunker, Mary Powell. *Long Island Genealogies, Families of Albertson, Andrews, Bedell, Birdsall, Bowne, Carman, Carr, Clowes, Cock, Cornelius, Covert, Dean, Doughty, Duryea, Feke, Frost, Haff, Hallock, Haydock, Hicks, Hopkins, Jackson, Jones, Keese, Ketcham, Kirby, Liones, Marvin, Merritt, Moore, Mott, Oakley, Onderdonck, Pearsall, Post, Powell, Prior, Robbins, Rodman, Rowland, Rushmore, Sands, Scudder, Seaman, Searing, Smith, Strickland, Titus, Townsend, Underhill, Valentine, Vanderdonk, Weeks, Whitman, Whitson, Willets, Williams, Willis, Wright, and other Families. Being Kindred Descendants of Thomas Powell of Bethpage, L.I., 1688.* Albany, NY: Munsell's, 1895. 350p.
http://moa.cit.cornell.edu/dienst/moabrowse.fly/MOA-JOURNALS2:BUNK-0101/5/1:TIFF2GIF:100

Weeks, George F. *California Copy.* Washington, DC: Washington College Press, 1928. 346p.
http://memory.loc.gov/cgi-bin/query/r?ammem/calbkbib:@field(AUTHOR+@band(Weeks,+George+F.,+1852?-+))

Whipple

Whipple Haslam, Lee Summers. *Early Days in California, Scenes and Events of the '50s as I Remember Them.* Jamestown, CA: Author, 1925. 34p.
http://memory.loc.gov/cgi-bin/query/r?ammem/calbkbib:@field(AUTHOR+@band(Whipple-Haslam,+Lee,Mrs.+))

Whitaker

Whitaker, Fess. *History of Corporal Fess Whitaker, Life in the Kentucky Mountains, Mexico and Texas.* Louisville, KY: Standard Printing, 1918. 152p.
http://metalab.unc.edu/docsouth/whitaker/menu.html

White

Lothrop, Thomas J. *The Nicholas White Family 1643-1900.* Taunton, MA: Author, 1902. 493p.
http://genweb.net/~blackwell/ma/WhiteNicholas/

A Memorial Souvenir of Rev. J. Wofford White, Pastor of Wesley, M.E. Church, Charleston, S.C. Who Fell Asleep, January 7th, 1890, Aged 33 Years. Charleston, SC: Walker, Evans & Cogswell, 1890. 8p.
http://memory.loc.gov/cgi-bin/query/r?ammem/aap:@field(SUBJ+@band(Wesley+Methodist+Episcopal+Church++Charleston,+S.C.++))

White, Michael Claringbud. *California All the Way Back to 1828.* Los Angeles, CA: Dawson, 1956. 93p.
http://memory.loc.gov/cgi-bin/query/r?ammem/calbkbib:@field(AUTHOR+@band(White,+Michael+Claringbud,1801-1885.+))

White, William Francis. *A Picture of Pioneer Times in California*. San Francisco, CA: Hinton, 1881. 677p.
http://memory.loc.gov/cgi-bin/query/r?ammem/calbkbib:@field(AUTHOR+@band(White,+William+Francis,1829-1891?+))

Whiting

Whiting, William. *Memoir of Rev. Samuel Whiting, D.D. and of His Wife Elizabeth St. John, with References to Some of Their English Ancestors and American Descendants*. Boston, MA: Rand, Avery and Co., 1873. 334p.
http://genweb.net/~books/ma/whiting1873/

Whitman

Bunker, Mary Powell. *Long Island Genealogies, Families of Albertson, Andrews, Bedell, Birdsall, Bowne, Carman, Carr, Clowes, Cock, Cornelius, Covert, Dean, Doughty, Duryea, Feke, Frost, Haff, Hallock, Haydock, Hicks, Hopkins, Jackson, Jones, Keese, Ketcham, Kirby, Liones, Marvin, Merritt, Moore, Mott, Oakley, Onderdonck, Pearsall, Post, Powell, Prior, Robbins, Rodman, Rowland, Rushmore, Sands, Scudder, Seaman, Searing, Smith, Strickland, Titus, Townsend, Underhill, Valentine, Vanderdonk, Weeks, Whitman, Whitson, Willets, Williams, Willis, Wright, and other Families. Being Kindred Descendants of Thomas Powell of Bethpage, L.I., 1688*. Albany, NY: Munsell's, 1895. 350p.
http://moa.cit.cornell.edu/dienst/moabrowse.fly/MOA-JOURNALS2:BUNK-0101/5/1:TIFF2GIF:100

Whitson

Bunker, Mary Powell. *Long Island Genealogies, Families of Albertson, Andrews, Bedell, Birdsall, Bowne, Carman, Carr, Clowes, Cock, Cornelius, Covert, Dean, Doughty, Duryea, Feke, Frost, Haff, Hallock, Haydock, Hicks, Hopkins, Jackson, Jones, Keese, Ketcham, Kirby, Liones, Marvin, Merritt, Moore, Mott, Oakley, Onderdonck, Pearsall, Post, Powell, Prior, Robbins, Rodman, Rowland, Rushmore, Sands, Scudder, Seaman, Searing, Smith, Strickland, Titus, Townsend, Underhill, Valentine, Vanderdonk, Weeks, Whitman, Whitson, Willets, Williams, Willis, Wright, and other Families. Being Kindred Descendants of Thomas Powell of Bethpage, L.I., 1688*. Albany, NY: Munsell's, 1895. 350p.
http://moa.cit.cornell.edu/dienst/moabrowse.fly/MOA-JOURNALS2:BUNK-0101/5/1:TIFF2GIF:100

Wierzbicki

Wierzbicki, Felix Paul. *California as It Is and as It May Be, or a Guide to the Gold Region*. San Francisco, CA: Grabhorn Press, 1933. 100p.
http://memory.loc.gov/cgi-bin/query/r?ammem/calbkbib:@field(AUTHOR+@band(Wierzbicki,+Felix+Paul,1815-1860.+))

Wiggins

Kelly, Fanny Wiggins. *Narrative of My Captivity among the Sioux Indians, with a Brief Account of General Sully's Indian Expedition in 1864, Bearing upon Events Occuring in My Captivity*. Hartford, CT: Mutual Publishing Co., 1871. 310p.
http://moa.umdl.umich.edu/cgi-bin/moa/sgml/moa-idx?notisid=ABB5283

Wilkinson

Wilkinson, Israel. *Memoirs of the Wilkinson Family*. Jacksonville, IL: Davis & Penniman, 1869. 585p.
http://www.fortunecity.com/victorian/stanford/228/wilk1869.html

Willette

Bunker, Mary Powell. *Long Island Genealogies, Families of Albertson, Andrews, Bedell, Birdsall, Bowne, Carman, Carr, Clowes, Cock, Cornelius, Covert, Dean, Doughty, Duryea, Feke, Frost, Haff, Hallock, Haydock, Hicks, Hopkins, Jackson, Jones, Keese, Ketcham, Kirby, Liones, Marvin, Merritt, Moore, Mott, Oakley, Onderdonck, Pearsall, Post, Powell, Prior, Robbins, Rodman, Rowland, Rushmore, Sands, Scudder, Seaman, Searing, Smith, Strickland, Titus, Townsend, Underhill, Valentine, Vanderdonk, Weeks, Whitman, Whitson, Willets, Williams, Willis, Wright, and other Families. Being Kindred Descendants of Thomas Powell of Bethpage, L.I., 1688.* Albany, NY: Munsell's, 1895. 350p.
http://moa.cit.cornell.edu/dienst/moabrowse.fly/MOA-JOURNALS2:BUNK-0101/5/1:TIFF2GIF:100

Willey

Willey, Samuel Hopkins. *Thirty Years in California, a Contribution to the History of the State from 1849 to 1879.* San Francisco, CA: Bancroft, 1879. 76p.
http://memory.loc.gov/cgi-bin/query/r?ammem/calbkbib:@field(AUTHOR+@band(Willey,+Samuel+Hopkins.+))

Williams

Austin, John Osborne. *Ancestry of Thirty-three Rhode Islanders, Born in the Eighteenth Century, Also Twenty-seven Charts of Roger Williams' Descendants to the Fifth Generation and an Account of Lewis Latham, Falconer to King Charles I, with a Chart of His American Descendants to the Fourth Generation and a List of 180 Existing Portraits of Rhode Island Governors, Chief Justices, Senators, etc. and of Certain Military Officers, Divines, Physicians, Authors, Lawyers, Merchants etc.* Albany, NY: Munsell's, 1889. 127p.
http://genweb.net/~blackwell/ri/33ri1889/

Bacon, Edward. *Among the Cotton Thieves.* Detroit, MI: Free Press Steam Book, 1867. 300p.
http://moa.umdl.umich.edu/cgi-bin/moa/sgml/moa-idx?notisid=ACK4755

Bunker, Mary Powell. *Long Island Genealogies, Families of Albertson, Andrews, Bedell, Birdsall, Bowne, Carman, Carr, Clowes, Cock, Cornelius, Covert, Dean, Doughty, Duryea, Feke, Frost, Haff, Hallock, Haydock, Hicks, Hopkins, Jackson, Jones, Keese, Ketcham, Kirby, Liones, Marvin, Merritt, Moore, Mott, Oakley, Onderdonck, Pearsall, Post, Powell, Prior, Robbins, Rodman, Rowland, Rushmore, Sands, Scudder, Seaman, Searing, Smith, Strickland, Titus, Townsend, Underhill, Valentine, Vanderdonk, Weeks, Whitman, Whitson, Willets, Williams, Willis, Wright, and other Families. Being Kindred Descendants of Thomas Powell of Bethpage, L.I., 1688.* Albany, NY: Munsell's, 1895. 350p.
http://moa.cit.cornell.edu/dienst/moabrowse.fly/MOA-JOURNALS2:BUNK-0101/5/1:TIFF2GIF:100

Williams, Albert. *A Pioneer Pastorate and Times Embodying Contemporary Local Transactions and Events by the Rev. Albert Williams, Founder and First Pastor of the First Presbyterian Church, San Francisco.* San Francisco, CA: Wallace & Hassett Printers, 1879. 240p.
http://memory.loc.gov/cgi-bin/query/r?ammem/calbkbib:@field(AUTHOR+@band(Williams,+Albert,1809-1893.+))

Williams, James. *A Narrative of Events Since the First of August, 1834, by James Williams an Apprenticed Labourer in Jamaica.* London: J. Rider, 1837. 26p.
http://metalab.unc.edu/docsouth/williamsjames/menu.html

———. *Narrative of James Williams, an American Slave, Who Was for Several Years a Driver on a Cotton Plantation in Alabama.* New York, NY: American Anti-Slavery Society, 1838. 108p.
http://metalab.unc.edu/docsouth/williams/menu.html

Williamson

Narrative of Facts in the Case of Passmore Williamson. Philadelphia, PA: Pennsylvania Anti-Slavery Society, 1855. 24p.
http://moa.umdl.umich.edu/cgi-bin/moa/sgml/moa-idx?notisid=ABJ1564

Willis

Bunker, Mary Powell. *Long Island Genealogies, Families of Albertson, Andrews, Bedell, Birdsall, Bowne, Carman, Carr, Clowes, Cock, Cornelius, Covert, Dean, Doughty, Duryea, Feke, Frost, Haff, Hallock, Haydock, Hicks, Hopkins, Jackson, Jones, Keese, Ketcham, Kirby, Liones, Marvin, Merritt, Moore, Mott, Oakley, Onderdonck, Pearsall, Post, Powell, Prior, Robbins, Rodman, Rowland, Rushmore, Sands, Scudder, Seaman, Searing, Smith, Strickland, Titus, Townsend, Underhill, Valentine, Vanderdonk, Weeks, Whitman, Whitson, Willets, Williams, Willis, Wright, and other Families. Being Kindred Descendants of Thomas Powell of Bethpage, L.I., 1688.* Albany, NY: Munsell's, 1895. 350p.
http://moa.cit.cornell.edu/dienst/moabrowse.fly/MOA-JOURNALS2:BUNK-0101/5/1:TIFF2GIF:100

Wills

Wills, Mary H. *A Winter in California.* Norristown, PA: Author, 1889. 150p.
http://memory.loc.gov/cgi-bin/query/r?ammem/calbkbib:@field(AUTHOR+@band(Wills,+Mary+H.+))

Wilson

Farrington, Edward Irving and Alfred Rehder. *Ernest H. Wilson, Plant Hunter.* Boston, MA: Stratford Co., 1931. 222p.
http://chla.mannlib.cornell.edu/cgi-bin/chla/viewer.cgi?docid=title2c.chla.mannlib.cornell/0889farr&format=1:75-GIF&section=Title+Page

Wilson, Benjamin Davis. *The Indians of Southern California in 1852.* San Marino, CA: Huntington Library, 1952. 154p.
http://memory.loc.gov/cgi-bin/query/r?ammem/calbkbib:@field(AUTHOR+@band(Wilson,+Benjamin+Davis,1811-1878.+))

Wilson, Luzena Stanley. *Luzena Stanley Wilson, '49er, Memories Recalled Years Later for Her Daughter Correnah Wilson Wright.* Mills College, CA: Eucalyptus Press, 1937. 61p.
http://memory.loc.gov/cgi-bin/query/r?ammem/calbkbib:@field(AUTHOR+@band(Wilson,+Luzena+Stanley,b.+1821?+))

Wise

Hambleton, James Pinkney. *A Biographical Sketch of Henry A. Wise, with a History of the Political Campaign in Virginia in 1855.* Richmond, VA: J. W. Randolph, 1856. 509p.
http://moa.umdl.umich.edu/cgi-bin/moa/sgml/moa-idx?notisid=AFJ9125

Wise, John Sergeant. *The End of an Era.* Boston, MA: Houghton, Mifflin & Co., 1899. 474p.
http://metalab.unc.edu/docsouth/wise/menu.html

Witham

Witham, James W. *Fifty Years on the Firing Line.* Chicago, IL: Author, 1924. 213p.
http://memory.loc.gov/cgi-bin/query/r?ammem/lhbumbib:@field(SUBJ+@band(Agricultural+societies--United+States.+))

Wood

MacLeod, Xavier Donald. *Biography of Hon. Fernando Wood, Mayor of the City of New York.* New York, NY: Parsons, 1856.
http://moa.cit.cornell.edu/dienst/moabrowse.fly/MOA-JOURNALS2:MACL-0018/5/1:TIFF2GIF:100

Wood, Harvey. *Personal Recollections*. Pasadena, CA: John B. Goodman, III, 1955. 27p.
http://memory.loc.gov/cgi-bin/query/r?ammem/calbkbib:@field(AUTHOR+@band(Wood,+Harvey,1828-1895.+))

Wood, James H. *The War, Stonewall Jackson, His Campaigns and Battles, the Regiment as I Saw Them*. Cumberland, MD: Eddy Press, 1910. 181p.
http://metalab.unc.edu/docsouth/wood/menu.html

Woodhouse

Taylor, Susie King. *Reminiscences of My Life in Camp with the 33d United States Colored Troops Late 1st S.C. Volunteers*. Boston, MA: Author, 82p.
http://digilib.nypl.org/dynaweb/digs/wwm97267/

Woods

Woods, Daniel B. *Sixteen Months at the Gold Camps*. New York, NY: Harper, 1851. 199p.
http://memory.loc.gov/cgi-bin/query/r?ammem/calbkbib:@field(AUTHOR+@band(Woods,+Daniel+B.+))

Woods, James. *Recollections of Pioneer Work in California*. San Francisco, CA: Winterburn, 1878. 260p.
http://memory.loc.gov/cgi-bin/query/r?ammem/calbkbib:@field(AUTHOR+@band(Woods,+James,1814+or+5-1886.+))

Wooley

Wooley, Charles. *A Two Years Journal in New York, and Part of Its Territories in America*. New York, NY: William Gowans, 1860. 98p.
http://moa.cit.cornell.edu/dienst/moabrowse.fly/MOA-JOURNALS2:WOOL-0009/5/1:TIFF2GIF:100

Woolley

Woolley, Lell Hawley. *California, 1849-1913, or the Rambling Sketches and Experiences of Sixty-four Years' Residence in That State*. Oakland, CA: De Witt & Snelling, 1913. 48p.
http://memory.loc.gov/cgi-bin/query/r?ammem/calbkbib:@field(AUTHOR+@band(Woolley,+Lell+Hawley,1825-+))

Woolman

Woolman, John. *A Journal of the Life, Gospel Labours and Christian Experiences of That Faithful Minister of Jesus Christ, John Woolman, Late of Mount Holly in the Province of New Jersey*. Philadelphia, PA: Crukshank, 1774. 436p.
http://darkwing.uoregon.edu/~rbear/woolman.html

Work

Thompson, George. *Prison Life and Reflections or a Narrative of the Arrest, Trial, Conviction, Imprisonment, Treatment, Observations, Reflections and Deliverance of Work, Burr and Thompson Who Suffered an Unjust and Cruel Imprisonment in Missouri Penitentiary for Attempting to Aid Some Slaves to Liberty*. Hartford, CT: Alanson Work, 1850. 376p.
http://moa.umdl.umich.edu/cgi-bin/moa/sgml/moa-idx?notisid=ACK4077

Workhoven

Vandergon, Gertrude Braat. *Our Pioneer Days in Minnesota*. Author, 1949. 138p.
http://memory.loc.gov/cgi-bin/query/r?ammem/lhbum:@field(DOCID+@lit(03667T000)):@@@REF

Worsham

Worsham, John H. *One of Jackson's Foot Cavalry, His Experience and What He Saw During the War 1861-1865, including a History of "F Company" Richmond, Va., 21st Regiment Virginia Infantry, Second Brigade, Jackson's Division, Second Corps, A.N.Va.* New York, NY: Neale, 1912. 353p.
http://metalab.unc.edu/docsouth/worsham/menu.html

Wright

Bunker, Mary Powell. *Long Island Genealogies, Families of Albertson, Andrews, Bedell, Birdsall, Bowne, Carman, Carr, Clowes, Cock, Cornelius, Covert, Dean, Doughty, Duryea, Feke, Frost, Haff, Hallock, Haydock, Hicks, Hopkins, Jackson, Jones, Keese, Ketcham, Kirby, Liones, Marvin, Merritt, Moore, Mott, Oakley, Onderdonck, Pearsall, Post, Powell, Prior, Robbins, Rodman, Rowland, Rushmore, Sands, Scudder, Seaman, Searing, Smith, Strickland, Titus, Townsend, Underhill, Valentine, Vanderdonk, Weeks, Whitman, Whitson, Willets, Williams, Willis, Wright, and other Families. Being Kindred Descendants of Thomas Powell of Bethpage, L.I., 1688.* Albany, NY: Munsell's, 1895. 350p.
http://moa.cit.cornell.edu/dienst/moabrowse.fly/MOA-JOURNALS2:BUNK-0101/5/1:TIFF2GIF:100

Wilson, Luzena Stanley. *Luzena Stanley Wilson, '49er, Memories Recalled Years Later for Her Daughter Correnah Wilson Wright.* Mills College, CA: Eucalyptus Press, 1937. 61p.
http://memory.loc.gov/cgi-bin/query/r?ammem/calbkbib:@field(AUTHOR+@band(Wilson,+Luzena+Stanley,b.+1821?+))

Wright, Louise Wigfall. *A Southern Girl in '61, the Wartime Memories of a Confederate Senator's Daughter.* New York, NY: Doubleday, 1905. 258p.
http://metalab.unc.edu/docsouth/wright/menu.html

Wright, Marcus J. *Diary of Brigadier General Marcus J. Wright, C.S.A., April 23, 1861-February 26, 1863.* Author, Date Unknown. 8p.
http://metalab.unc.edu/docsouth/wrightmarcus/menu.html

Wyeth

Wyeth, John Allan. *With Sabre and Scalpel, the Autobiography of a Soldier and Surgeon.* New York, NY: Harper, 1914. 535p.
http://metalab.unc.edu/docsouth/wyeth/menu.html

 -Y ━━━━━━━━━━━━━━━━━━━━

York

Medberry, Rebecca B. Stetson. *Memoir of Mrs. Sarah Emily York, formerly Miss Sarah Emily Waldo, Missionary in Greece.* Boston, MA: Phillips, Sampson and Co., 1863, 434p.
http://moa.umdl.umich.edu/cgi-bin/moa/sgml/moa-idx?notisid=AJG8055

Young

Young, Kenneth M. *As Some Things Appear on the Plains and among the Rockies in Midsummer.* Spartanburg, SC: Fowler, 1890. 15p.
http://memory.loc.gov/cgi-bin/query/r?ammem/aap:@field(SUBJ+@band(Afro-Americans--Travel--United+States.+))

Young, Lot D. *Reminiscences of a Soldier of the Orphan Brigade, by Lieut. L. D. Young, Paris, Kentucky.* Louisville, KY: Courier Journal Print Job, 1918. 99p.
http://metalab.unc.edu/docsouth/young/menu.html

LOCAL HISTORIES BY STATE

Alabama

Baldwin, Joseph Glover. *Flush Times of Alabama and Mississippi, a Series of Sketches*. New York, NY: Appleton, 1854. 366p.
http://metalab.unc.edu/docsouth/baldwin/menu.html
http://moa.umdl.umich.edu/cgi-bin/moa/sgml/moa-idx?notisid=ADS9517

Clay Clopton, Virginia. *A Belle of the Fifties, Memoirs of Mrs. Clay of Alabama*. New York, NY: Doubleday, 1905. 386p.
http://metalab.unc.edu/docsouth/clay/menu.html

Edwards, William James. *Twenty-five Years in the Black Belt*. Boston, MA: Cornhill Co., 1918. 143p.
http://metalab.unc.edu/docsouth/edwards/menu.html

Gordon, John Brown. *Reminiscences of the Civil War*. New York, NY: Scribners, 1904. 474p.
http://metalab.unc.edu/docsouth/gordon/menu.html

Research Outline. Alabama. Salt Lake City, UT: Family History Library, 1997.
http://www.familysearch.com/sg/Alabama.html

Wright, A. J. *Alabama Libraries prior to World War I, a Chronology*. Birmingham, AL: Author, 1997. Unpgd.
http://www.anes.uab.edu/alachron.htm

Greene County
Williams, James. *Narrative of James Williams, an American Slave, Who Was for Several Years a Driver on a Cotton Plantation in Alabama*. New York, NY: American Anti-Slavery Society, 1838. 108p.
http://metalab.unc.edu/docsouth/williams/menu.html

Marshall County
Wyeth, John Allan. *With Sabre and Scalpel, the Autobiography of a Soldier and Surgeon*. New York, NY: Harper, 1914. 535p.
http://metalab.unc.edu/docsouth/wyeth/menu.html

Mobile
Mobile [City Directory]. Mobile, AL: Farrow & Dennett, 1859.
http://www.citydirectories.psmedia.com/city/free_statesort.html

Russell County

Houghton, William Robert. *Two Boys in the Civil War and after*. Montgomery, AL: Paragon Press, 1912. 242p.
http://metalab.unc.edu/docsouth/houghton/menu.html

Alaska

Garland, Hamlin. *The Trail of the Goldseekers, a Record of Travel in Prose and Verse*. New York, NY: Macmillan, 1889. 274p.
http://moa.umdl.umich.edu/cgi-bin/moa/sgml/moa-idx?notisid=AGD5638

Parham, R. Bruce. *How to Find Your Gold Rush Relative, Sources on the Klondike and Alaska Gold Rushes (1896-1914)*. Anchorage, AK: National Archives, Pacific Alaska Region, 1997. Unpgd.
http://www.educ.state.ak.us/lam/library/hist/parham.html

Parkinson, Edward S. *Wonderland or Twelve Weeks In and Out of the United States. Brief Account of a Trip across the Continent, Short Run in Mexico, Ride to the Yosemite Valley, Steamer Voyage to Alaska, the Land of Glaciers, Visit to the Great Shoshone Falls and a Stage Ride through the Yellowstone National Park*. Trenton, NJ: MacCrellish & Quigley, 1894. 259p.
http://memory.loc.gov/cgi-bin/query/r?ammem/calbkbib:@field(AUTHOR+@band(Parkinson,+Edward+S.+))

Research Outline. Alaska. Salt Lake City, UT: Family History Library, 1997.
http://www.familysearch.com/sg/Alaska.html

Arizona

Cozzens, Samuel Woodworth. *The Marvelous Country, or, Three Years in Arizona and New Mexico. Containing an Authentic History of This Wonderful Country and Its Ancient Civilization . . . together with a Full and Complete History of the Apache Tribe of Indians*. Boston, MA: Lee & Shepard, 1876. 606p.
http://moa.umdl.umich.edu/cgi-bin/moa/sgml/moa-idx?notisid=AJA3616

Hodge, Hiram C. *Arizona As It Is; or, the Coming Country. Comp. from Notes of Travel during the Years 1874, 1875, and 1876.* New York, NY: Hurd & Houghton, 1877. 282p.
http://moa.umdl.umich.edu/cgi-bin/moa/sgml/moa-idx?notisid=ABA4801

Mowry, Sylvester. *Arizona and Sonora, the Geography, History, and Resources of the Silver Region of North America.* New York, NY: Author, 1864. 252p.
http://moa.umdl.umich.edu/cgi-bin/moa/sgml/moa-idx?notisid=AFM1971

Preliminary Report Concerning Explorations and Surveys, Principally in Nevada and Arizona. Prosecuted in Accordance with Paragraph 2, Special Orders No. 109, War Dept., March 18, 1871, and Letter of Instructions of March 23, 1871, from Brigadier General A. A. Humphreys, Chief of Engineers. Conducted under the Immediate Direction of 1st Lieut. George M. Wheeler . . . 1871. Washington, DC: Government Printing Office, 1872. 96p.
http://moa.umdl.umich.edu/cgi-bin/moa/sgml/moa-idx?notisid=AJA3663

Research Outline. Arizona. Salt Lake City, UT: Family History Library, 1997.
http://www.familysearch.com/sg/Arizona.html

Yuma

Briggs, Lloyd Vernon. *California and the West, 1881 and later.* Boston, MA: Wright & Potter, 1931. 214p.
http://memory.loc.gov/cgi-bin/query/r?ammem/calbkbib:@field(AUTHOR+@band(Briggs,+Lloyd+Vernon,1863-1941.+))

Stratton, Royal B. *Captivity of the Oatman Girls, Being an Interesting Narrative of Life among the Apache and Mohave Indians, Containing an Interesting Account of the Massacre of the Oatman Family by the Apache Indians in 1851, the Narrow Escape of Lorenze D. Oatman, the Capture of Olive A. and Mary A. Oatman, as Given by Lorenzo D. and Olive A. Oatman.* New York, NY: Carlton & Porter, 1858. 312p.
http://moa.umdl.umich.edu/cgi-bin/moa/sgml/moa-idx?notisid=ABB5623

Arkansas

Henry, James P. *Resources of the State of Arkansas with Descriptions of Counties, Railroads, Mines and the City of Little Rock.* Little Rock, AR: Price & McClure, 1872. 134p.
http://moa.umdl.umich.edu/cgi-bin/moa/sgml/moa-idx?notisid=ABL6083

Parkman, Francis. *The Oregon Trail, Sketches of Prairie and Rocky Mountain Life.* Philadelphia, PA: Winston, 1931. 388p.
http://xroads.virginia.edu/~HYPER/OREGON/oregon.html

Research Outline. Arkansas. Salt Lake City, UT: Family History Library, 1997.
http://www.familysearch.com/sg/Arkansas.html

Little Rock

Proceedings of the Eighth Annual Convocation of the Most Excellent Royal Arch Chapter of Free Masons for the State and Jurisdiction of Arkansas and of a Meeting Preliminary to the Same, Held in the City of Little Rock, Ark., Dec. 16th and 17th Anno Inventionis 2428, A.D. 1898. Pine Bluff, AR: Courier Printing Co., 1899. 14p.
http://memory.loc.gov/cgi-bin/query/r?ammem/aap:@field(SUBJ+@band(Afro-American+freemasons.+))

Pine Bluff

Catalogue and Circular of the Branch Normal College of the Arkansas Industrial University, Located at Pine Bluff, Arkansas. Pine Bluff, AR: College, 1894, 1895.
1892-93. 29p.
http://memory.loc.gov/cgi-bin/query/r?ammem/murray:@field(FLD001+91898260+):@@@REF

1893-94. 32p.
http://memory.loc.gov/cgi-bin/query/r?ammem/murray:@field(FLD001+91898259+):@@@REF

California

Bates, D. B. *Incidents on Land and Water, or Four Years on the Pacific Coast. Being a Narrative of the Burning of the Ships Nonantum, Humayoon and Fanchon, together with Many Startling and Interesting Adventures on Sea and Land.* Boston, MA: Author, 1861. 344p.
http://moa.umdl.umich.edu/cgi-bin/moa/sgml/moa-idx?notisid=AJL3457

Chinese Immigration. The Social, Moral, and Political Effect of Chinese Immigration. Testimony Taken before a Committee of the Senate of the State of California, Appointed April 3d, 1876. Sacramento, CA: State Printing Office, 1876. 182p.
http://moa.umdl.umich.edu/cgi-bin/moa/sgml/moa-idx?notisid=AEX5872

Colton, Walter. *Three Years in California.* New York, NY: A. S. Barnes, 1850. 480p.
http://moa.umdl.umich.edu/cgi-bin/moa/sgml/moa-idx?notisid=ABE2329

Cone, Mary. *Two Years in California.* Chicago, IL: Griggs, 1876. 238p.
http://memory.loc.gov/cgi-bin/query/r?ammem/calbkbib:@field(AUTHOR+@band(Cone,+Mary.+))

Cronise, Titus Fey. *The Natural Wealth of California, Comprising Duly History, Geography, Topography and Scenery, Climate, Agriculture and Commercial Products, Geology, Zoology and Botany, Minerology, Mines, and Mining Processes, Manufactures, Steamship Lines, Railroads, and Commerce, Immigration, a Detailed Description of Each County.* San Francisco, CA: Hancroft, 1868. 744p.
http://moa.umdl.umich.edu/cgi-bin/moa/sgml/moa-idx?notisid=AJL3430

Fremont, John Charles. *The Life of Col. John Charles Fremont and His Narrative of Explorations and Adventures in Kansas, Nebraska, Oregon and California.* New York, NY: Auburn, Miller, Orton & Mulligan, 1856. 514p.
http://moa.umdl.umich.edu/cgi-bin/moa/sgml/moa-idx?notisid=AAZ9580

Helper, Hinton Rowan. *The Land of Gold, Reality Versus Fiction.* Baltimore, MD: Taylor, 1855. 300p.
http://memory.loc.gov/cgi-bin/query/r?ammem/calbkbib:@field(AUTHOR+@band(Helper,+Hinton+Rowan,1829-1909.+))

Hittell, John Shertzer. *The Resources of California, Comprising, Agriculture, Mining, Geography, Climate, Commerce, etc. and the Past and Future Developments of the State.* San Francisco, CA: Roman, 1863. 480p.
http://moa.umdl.umich.edu/cgi-bin/moa/sgml/moa-idx?notisid=ABA5343

The Industrial Interests of California, Being a Series of Letters Relating to Our Home Manufactures, Industrial Labor, Agricultural Progress and Material Interests. San Francisco, CA: Towne & Bacon, 1862. 96p.
http://moa.umdl.umich.edu/cgi-bin/moa/sgml/moa-idx?notisid=AJL3450

McClellan, Rolander Guy. *The Golden State, a History of the Region West of the Rocky Mountains, Embracing California, Oregon, Nevada, Utah, Arizona, Idaho, Washington Territory, British Columbia, and Alaska, from the Earliest Period to the Present Time, with a History of Mormonism and the Mormons.* Philadelphia, PA: Flint, 1872. 844p.
http://moa.umdl.umich.edu/cgi-bin/moa/sgml/moa-idx?notisid=ABA5033

Nordhoff, Charles. *California for Health, Pleasure and Residence. A Book for Travelers and Settlers.* New York, NY: Harper, 1873. 255p.
http://memory.loc.gov/cgi-bin/query/r?ammem/calbkbib:@field(AUTHOR+@band(Nordhoff,+Charles,1830-1901.+))

————. *Northern California, Oregon, and the Sandwich Islands.* New York, NY: Harper, 1875. 256p.
http://moa.umdl.umich.edu/cgi-bin/moa/sgml/moa-idx?notisid=AJL3484

Palmer, John Williamson. *The New and the Old, or California and India in Romantic Aspects.* New York, NY: Rudd & Carleton, 1859. 433p.
http://memory.loc.gov/cgi-bin/query/r?ammem/calbkbib:@field(AUTHOR+@band(Palmer,+J[ohn]+W[illiamson],1825-1906.+))

Parkman, Francis. *The Oregon Trail, Sketches of Prairie and Rocky Mountain Life.* Philadelphia, PA: Winston, 1931. 388p.
http://xroads.virginia.edu/~HYPER/OREGON/oregon.html

Phillips, David L. *Letters from California, Its Mountains, Valleys, Plains, Lakes, Rivers, Climate and Productions. Also Its Railroads, Cities, Towns and People, as Seen in 1876.* Springfield, IL: Illinois State Journal, 1877. 171p.
http://memory.loc.gov/cgi-bin/query/r?ammem/calbkbib:@field(AUTHOR+@band(Pond,+William+Chauncey,1830-1925.+))

Pond, William Chauncey. *Gospel Pioneering, Reminiscences of Early Congregationalism in California, 1833-1920.* Oberlin, OH: New Printing Co., 1921. 191p.
http://memory.loc.gov/cgi-bin/query/r?ammem/calbkbib:@field(AUTHOR+@band(Pond,+William+Chauncey,1830-1925.+))

Research Outline. California. Salt Lake City, UT: Family History Library, 1997.
http://www.familysearch.com/sg/California.html

Taylor, William. *California Life Illustrated.* New York, NY: Carlton & Potter, 1858. 350p.
http://memory.loc.gov/cgi-bin/query/r?ammem/calbk:@field(DOCID+@lit(C063T00)):@@@REF

Upham, Samuel Curtis. *Notes of a Voyage to California via Cape Horn, together with Scenes in El Dorado, in the Years of 1849-50, with an Appendix Containing Reminiscences together*

with the Articles of Association and Roll of Members of the Associated Pioneers of the Territorial Days of California. Philadelphia, PA: Author, 1878. 594p.
http://memory.loc.gov/cgi-bin/query/r?ammem/calbkbib:@field(AUTHOR+@band(Upham,+Samuel+Curtis,1819-1885.+))

Alameda
Weeks, George F. *California Copy.* Washington, DC: Washington College Press, 1928. 346p.
http://memory.loc.gov/cgi-bin/query/r?ammem/calbkbib:@field(AUTHOR+@band(Weeks,+George+F.,1852?-+))

Azusa
Ayers, James J. *Gold and Sunshine, Reminiscences of Early California.* Boston, MA: Badger, 1922. 359p.
http://memory.loc.gov/cgi-bin/query/r?ammem/calbkbib:@field(AUTHOR+@band(Ayers,+James+J.+))

Bakersfield
Weeks, George F. *California Copy.* Washington, DC: Washington College Press, 1928. 346p.
http://memory.loc.gov/cgi-bin/query/r?ammem/calbkbib:@field(AUTHOR+@band(Weeks,+George+F.,1852?-+))

Calaveras County
Wood, Harvey. *Personal Recollections.* Pasadena, CA: John B. Goodman, III, 1955. 27p.
http://memory.loc.gov/cgi-bin/query/r?ammem/calbkbib:@field(AUTHOR+@band(Wood,+Harvey,1828-1895.+))

Chico
Bidwell, John. *Echoes of the Past about California.* Published with *In Camp and Cabin,* by Rev. John Steele. Chicago, IL: Donnelley, 1928. 377p.
http://memory.loc.gov/cgi-bin/query/r?ammem/calbkbib:@field(AUTHOR+@band(Bidwell,+John,1819-1900.+))

Moak, Sim. *The Last of the Mill Creeks and Early Life in Northern California.* Chico, CA: Author, 1923. 47p.
http://memory.loc.gov/cgi-bin/query/r?ammem/calbkbib:@field(AUTHOR+@band(Moak,+Sim,1845-+))

Royce, Charles C. *Addresses, Reminiscences, etc. of General John Bidwell.* Chico, CA: Charles C. Royce, 1906. 221p.
http://memory.loc.gov/cgi-bin/query/r?ammem/calbkbib:@field(AUTHOR+@band(Bidwell,+John,1819-1900.+))

Cold Spring
Tyson, James Lawrence. *Diary of a Physician in California, Being the Results of Actual Experience Including Notes of the Journey by Land and Water and Observations on the Climate, Soil, Resources of the Country.* New York, NY: Appleton, 1850. 92p.
http://memory.loc.gov/cgi-bin/query/r?ammem/calbkbib:@field(AUTHOR+@band(Tyson,+James+Lawrence.+))

Coloma
Harlan, Jacob Wright. *California '46 to '88.* San Francisco, CA: Bancroft, 1888. 242p.
http://memory.loc.gov/cgi-bin/query/r?ammem/calbkbib:@field(AUTHOR+@band(Harlan,+Jacob+Wright,1828-+))

Crescent City

Bancroft, Hubert Howe. *Literary Industries, a Memoir*. San Francisco, CA: History Company, 1891. 808p.
http://memory.loc.gov/cgi-bin/query/r?ammem/calbkbib:@field(AUTHOR+@band(Bancroft,+Hubert+Howe,1832-1918.+))

Culomma

Johnson, Theodore Taylor. *Sights in the Gold Region and Scenes by the Way*. New York, NY: Baker & Scribner, 1849. 278p.
http://memory.loc.gov/cgi-bin/query/r?ammem/calbkbib:@field(AUTHOR+@band(Johnson,+Theodore+Taylor,b.+1818.+))

Eldorado County

Bryan, George W. *The Lure of the Past, the Present and Future*. Los Angeles, CA: Newton, 1911. 139p.
http://memory.loc.gov/cgi-bin/query/r?ammem/calbkbib:@field(AUTHOR+@band(Bryan,+George+W.+))

Hangtown

Borthwick, John David. *Three Years in California*. Edinburgh: Blackwood, 1857. 384p.
http://memory.loc.gov/cgi-bin/query/r?ammem/calbkbib:@field(AUTHOR+@band(Borthwick,+J.+D.+))

Gaer, Joseph. *Index, Three Years in California*. Author, 1935. 16p.
http://memory.loc.gov/cgi-bin/query/r?ammem/calbkbib:@field(AUTHOR+@band(Gaer,+Joseph,1897-ed.+))

Healdsburg

Norton, Lewis Adelbert. *Life and Adventures of Col. L. A. Norton*. Oakland, CA: Pacific Press, 1887. 492p.
http://memory.loc.gov/cgi-bin/query/r?ammem/calbkbib:@field(AUTHOR+@band(Norton,+Lewis+Adelbert,b.+1819.+))

Jackson

Peters, Charles. *The Autobiography of Charles Peters in 1915 the Oldest Pioneer Living in California, Who Mined in the Days of '49. Also Historical Happenings, Interesting Incidents and Illustrations of the Old Mining Towns in the Good Luck Era, the Placer Mining Days of the '50s*. Sacramento, CA: LaGrave, 1915. 231p.
http://memory.loc.gov/cgi-bin/query/r?ammem/calbkbib:@field(AUTHOR+@band(Peters,+Charles,b.+1825.+))

Los Angeles

Adams, Emma Hildreth. *To and Fro in Southern California*. Cincinnati, OH: W.M.B.C. Press, 1887. 288p.
http://memory.loc.gov/cgi-bin/query/r?ammem/calbkbib:@field(AUTHOR+@band(Adams,+Emma+H.+Emma+Hildreth++))

Bell, Horace. *Reminiscences of a Ranger or Early Times in Southern California*. Los Angeles, CA: Yarnell, Caystile & Mathes, 1881. 457p.
http://memory.loc.gov/cgi-bin/query/r?ammem/calbkbib:@field(AUTHOR+@band(Bell,+Horace,1830-1918.+))

Briggs, Lloyd Vernon. *California and the West, 1881 and later*. Boston, MA: Wright & Potter, 1931. 214p.
http://memory.loc.gov/cgi-bin/query/r?ammem/calbkbib:@field(AUTHOR+@band(Briggs,+Lloyd+Vernon,1863-1941.+))

Bryan, George W. *The Lure of the Past, the Present and Future*. Los Angeles, CA: Newton, 1911. 139p.
http://memory.loc.gov/cgi-bin/query/r?ammem/calbkbib:@field(AUTHOR+@band(Bryan,+George+W.+))

Graves, Jackson Alpheus. *My Seventy Years in California, 1857-1927*. Los Angeles, CA: Times Mirror Press, 1927. 478p.
http://memory.loc.gov/cgi-bin/query/r?ammem/calbkbib:@field(AUTHOR+@band(Graves,+Jackson+Alpheus,1852-1933.+))

Hayes, Benjamin Ignatius. *Pioneer Notes from the Diaries of Judge Benjamin Hayes, 1849-1875*. Los Angeles, CA: Author, 1929. 307p.
http://memory.loc.gov/cgi-bin/query/r?ammem/calbkbib:@field(AUTHOR+@band(Hayes,+Benjamin+Ignatius,1815-1877.+))

Lecouvreur, Frank. *From East Prussia to the Golden Gate. Letters and Diary of the California Pioneer*. New York, NY: Angelina Book, 1906. 355p.
http://memory.loc.gov/cgi-bin/query/r?ammem/calbkbib:@field(AUTHOR+@band(Lecouvreur,+Frank,1829-1901.+))

Newmark, Harris. *Sixty Years in Southern California, 1853-1913, containing the Reminiscences of Harris Newmark*. New York, NY: Knickerbocker Press, 1916. 732p.
http://memory.loc.gov/cgi-bin/query/r?ammem/calbkbib:@field(AUTHOR+@band(Newmark,+Harris,1834-1916.+))

Reid, Hugo. *The Indians of Los Angeles County, Hugh Reid's Letters of 1852*. Los Angeles, CA: Southwest Museum, 1968. 142p.
http://memory.loc.gov/cgi-bin/query/r?ammem/calbkbib:@field(AUTHOR+@band(Reid,+Hugo,1811?-1853.+))

Warner, Charles Dudley. *Our Italy*. New York, NY: Harper, 1891. 266p.
http://memory.loc.gov/cgi-bin/query/r?ammem/calbkbib:@field(AUTHOR+@band(Warner,+Charles+Dudley,1829-1900.+))

Marysville

Field, Stephen Johnson. *Personal Reminiscences of Early Days in California, with Other Sketches*. San Francisco, CA: Author, 1880. 248p.
http://memory.loc.gov/cgi-bin/query/r?ammem/calbkbib:@field(AUTHOR+@band(Field,+Stephen+Johnson,1816-1899.+))

Graves, Jackson Alpheus. *My Seventy Years in California, 1857-1927*. Los Angeles, CA: Times Mirror Press, 1927. 478p.
http://memory.loc.gov/cgi-bin/query/r?ammem/calbkbib:@field(AUTHOR+@band(Graves,+Jackson+Alpheus,1852-1933.+))

Huntly, Henry Veel. *California, Its Gold and Its Inhabitants*. London: Newby, 1856. 2 vols.
http://memory.loc.gov/cgi-bin/query/r?ammem/calbkbib:@field(AUTHOR+@band(Huntley,+Henry+Veel,Sir,1795-1864.+))

Mereced

Dowsett, Charles Finch. *A Start in Life. A Journey across America, Fruit Farming in California*. London: Dowsett & Co., 1891. 112p.
http://memory.loc.gov/cgi-bin/query/r?ammem/calbkbib:@field(AUTHOR+@band(Dowsett,+Charles+Finch,1835+or+6-1915.+))

Monterey

Colton, Walter. *Three Years in California*. New York, NY: A. S. Barnes, 1850. 480p.
http://moa.umdl.umich.edu/cgi-bin/moa/sgml/moa-idx?notisid=ABE2329

Swan, John Alfred. *A Trip to the Gold Mines of California in 1848*. San Francisco, CA: Book Club of California, 1960. 51p.
http://memory.loc.gov/cgi-bin/query/r?ammem/calbkbib:@field(AUTHOR+@band(Swan,+John+Alfred, 1817-1896.+))

New Helvetia

Lienhard, Heinrich. *A Pioneer at Sutter's Fort, 1846-1850, the Adventures of Heinrich Lienhard, Translated, Edited and Annotated by Marguerite Eyer Wilbur from the Original German Script*. Los Angeles, CA: Calafia Society, 1941. 291p.
http://memory.loc.gov/cgi-bin/query/r?ammem/calbkbib:@field(AUTHOR+@band(Lienhard,+Heinrich, 1822-1903.+))

Oakland

Browne, John Ross. *Crusoe's Island*. New York, NY: Harper, 1864. 436p.
http://memory.loc.gov/cgi-bin/query/r?ammem/calbkbib:@field(AUTHOR+@band(Browne,+John+Ross, 1821-1875.+))

Leach, Frank Aleamon. *Recollections of a Newspaperman, a Record of Life and Events in California*. San Francisco, CA: Levinson, 1917. 416p.
http://memory.loc.gov/cgi-bin/query/r?ammem/calbkbib:@field(AUTHOR+@band(Leach,+Frank+ Aleamon,1846-+))

Orange County

Smithwick, Noah. *The Evolution of a State or Recollections of Old Texas Days*. Austin, TX: Gammel Book Co., 1900. 354p.
http://www.erols.com/hardeman/lonestar/olbooks/smithwic/otd.htm

Pasadena

Holder, Charles Frederick. *Life in the Open, Sport with Rod, Gun Horse, and Hound in Southern California*. New York, NY: Putnam's, 1906. 401p.
http://memory.loc.gov/cgi-bin/query/r?ammem/calbkbib:@field(AUTHOR+@band(Holder,+Charles+ Frederick,1851-1915.+))

Piedmont

Crumpton, Hezekiah John and Washington Bryan Crumpton. *The Adventure of Two Alabama Boys (California Gold Rush)*. Montgomery, AL: Paragon Press, 1912. 238p.
http://metalab.unc.edu/docsouth/crumpton/menu.html

Placerville

Shufelt, S. *A Letter from a Gold Miner, Placerville, California, October 1850*. San Marino, CA: Friends of the Huntington Library, 1944. 28p.
http://memory.loc.gov/cgi-bin/query/r?ammem/calbkbib:@field(AUTHOR+@band(Shufelt,+S.+))

Sacramento

Cross, Lillian A. *Appreciation of Loved Ones Who Made Life Rich for Many. My Father, John Francis Cross, My Mother, Sarah Jane Cross*. Oakland, CA: Tribune Press, 1933. 101p.
http://memory.loc.gov/cgi-bin/query/r?ammem/calbkbib:@field(AUTHOR+@band(Cross,+Lilian+A.+))

Delano, Alonzo. *Alonzo Delano's California Correspondence, being Letters Hitherto Uncollected from the Ottawa (Illinois) Free Trader and the New Orleans True Delta, 1849-1952.* Sacramento, CA: Sacramento Book Collector's Club, 1952. 155p.
http://memory.loc.gov/cgi-bin/query/r?ammem/calbk:@field(DOCID+@lit(C073T00)):@@@REF

————. *Life on the Plains and among the Diggings, Being Scenes and Adventures of an Overland Journey to California, with Particular Incidents of the Route, Mistakes and Sufferings of the Emigrants, the Indian Tribes, the Present and Future of the Great West.* New York, NY: Miller, Orton & Co., 1857. 384p.
http://memory.loc.gov/cgi-bin/query/r?ammem/calbk:@field(DOCID+@lit(C171T00)):@@@REF

Field, Stephen Johnson. *Personal Reminiscences of Early Days in California, with Other Sketches.* San Francisco, CA: Author, 1880. 248p.
http://memory.loc.gov/cgi-bin/query/r?ammem/calbkbib:@field(AUTHOR+@band(Field,+Stephen+Johnson,1816-1899.+))

Houghton, Eliza Poor Donner. *The Expedition of the Donner Party and Its Tragic Fate.* Chicago, IL: McClurg, 1911. 374p.
http://memory.loc.gov/cgi-bin/query/r?ammem/calbkbib:@field(AUTHOR+@band(Houghton,+Eliza+Poor+Donner,1843-1922.+))

Huntly, Henry Veel. *California, Its Gold and Its Inhabitants.* London: Newby, 1856. 2 vols.
http://memory.loc.gov/cgi-bin/query/r?ammem/calbkbib:@field(AUTHOR+@band(Huntley,+Henry+Veel,Sir,1795-1864.+))

Lienhard, Heinrich. *A Pioneer at Sutter's Fort, 1846-1850, the Adventures of Heinrich Lienhard, Translated, Edited and Annotated by Marguerite Eyer Wilbur from the Original German Script.* Los Angeles, CA: Calafia Society, 1941. 291p.
http://memory.loc.gov/cgi-bin/query/r?ammem/calbkbib:@field(AUTHOR+@band(Lienhard,+Heinrich,1822-1903.+))

Sacramento 1859-60 [City Directory]. Sacramento, CA: Cutter, 1859.
http://www.citydirectories.psmedia.com/city/free_statesort.html

Sutter, John Augustus. *The Diary of Johann August Sutter.* San Francisco, CA: Grabhorn Press, 1932. 56p.
http://memory.loc.gov/cgi-bin/query/r?ammem/calbkbib:@field(AUTHOR+@band(Sutter,+John+Augustus,1803-1880.+))

Upham, Samuel Curtis. *Notes of a Voyage to California via Cape Horn, together with Scenes in El Dorado, in the Years of 1849-50, with an Appendix Containing Reminiscences together with the Articles of Association and Roll of Members of the Associated Pioneers of the Territorial Days of California.* Philadelphia, PA: Author, 1878. 594p.
http://memory.loc.gov/cgi-bin/query/r?ammem/calbkbib:@field(AUTHOR+@band(Upham,+Samuel+Curtis,1819-1885.+))

Wilson, Luzena Stanley. *Luzena Stanley Wilson, '49er, Memories Recalled Years Later for Her Daughter Correnah Wilson Wright.* Mills College, CA: Eucalyptus Press, 1937. 61p.
http://memory.loc.gov/cgi-bin/query/r?ammem/calbkbib:@field(AUTHOR+@band(Wilson,+Luzena+Stanley,b.+1821?+))

San Diego

Hayes, Benjamin Ignatius. *Pioneer Notes from the Diaries of Judge Benjamin Hayes, 1849-1875.* Los Angeles, CA: Author, 1929. 307p.
http://memory.loc.gov/cgi-bin/query/r?ammem/calbkbib:@field(AUTHOR+@band(Hayes,+Benjamin+Ignatius,1815-1877.+))

Wilson, Benjamin Davis. *The Indians of Southern California in 1852*. San Marino, CA: Huntington Library, 1952. 154p.
http://memory.loc.gov/cgi-bin/query/r?ammem/calbkbib:@field(AUTHOR+@band(Wilson,+Benjamin+ Davis,1811-1878.+))

San Francisco

Bancroft, Hubert Howe. *Literary Industries, a Memoir*. San Francisco, CA: History Company, 1891. 808p.
http://memory.loc.gov/cgi-bin/query/r?ammem/calbkbib:@field(AUTHOR+@band(Bancroft,+Hubert+ Howe,1832-1918.+))

Barry, Theodore Augustus and Benjamin Ada Patten. *Men and Memories of San Francisco, in the Spring of '50*. San Francisco, CA: Bancroft, 1873. 296p.
http://memory.loc.gov/cgi-bin/query/r?ammem/calbkbib:@field(AUTHOR+@band(Barry,+Theodore+ Augustus,1825-1881.+))

Bemis, Stephen Allen. *Recollections of a Long and Somewhat Uneventful Life*. St. Louis, MO: Author, 1932. 92p.
http://memory.loc.gov/cgi-bin/query/r?ammem/calbkbib:@field(AUTHOR+@band(Bemis,+Stephen+ Allen,1828-1919.+))

Brewer, William Henry. *Up and Down California in 1860-1864, the Journal of William H. Brewer*. New Haven, CT: Yale, 1930. 601p.
http://memory.loc.gov/cgi-bin/query/r?ammem/calbkbib:@field(AUTHOR+@band(Brewer,+William+ Henry,1828-1910.+))

Brown, John Henry. *Reminiscences and Incidents of the Early Days of San Francisco*. San Francisco, CA: Mission Journal Publishing, 1886. 106p.
http://memory.loc.gov/cgi-bin/query/r?ammem/calbkbib:@field(AUTHOR+@band(Brown,+John+Henry, 1810-1905.+))

Chambliss, William H. *Chambliss' Diary or Society as It Really Is*. New York, NY: Chambliss & Co., 1895. 408p.
http://memory.loc.gov/cgi-bin/query/r?ammem/calbkbib:@field(AUTHOR+@band(Chambliss,+William+ H.,+1865++))

Crosby, Elisha Oscar. *Memoirs of Elisha Oscar Crosby, Reminiscences of California and Guatemala from 1849 to 1864*. San Marino, CA: Huntington Library, 1945. 119p.
http://memory.loc.gov/cgi-bin/query/r?ammem/calbkbib:@field(AUTHOR+@band(Crosby,+Elisha+Oscar, 1818-1895.+))

Davis, William Heath. *Seventy-five Years in California, a History of Events and Life in California, Personal, Political and Military, under the Mexican Regime, during the Quasi-military Government of the Territory by the United States and after the Admission of the State to the Union*. San Francisco, CA: Howell, 1929. 422p.
http://memory.loc.gov/cgi-bin/query/r?ammem/calbkbib:@field(AUTHOR+@band(Davis,+William+ Heath,1822-1909.+))

Ellis, Henry Hiram. *From the Kennebec to California, Reminiscences of a California Pioneer*. Los Angeles, CA: Lewis, 1959. 88p.
http://memory.loc.gov/cgi-bin/query/r?ammem/calbkbib:@field(AUTHOR+@band(Ellis,+Henry+Hiram, 1829-1909.+))

Evans, Albert S. *A la California, Sketch of Life in the Golden State*. San Francisco, CA: Bancroft, 1873. 379p.
http://memory.loc.gov/cgi-bin/query/r?ammem/calbkbib:@field(AUTHOR+@band(Evans,+Albert+S.+))

Kip, William Ingraham. *The Early Days of My Episcopate*. New York, NY: Whittaker, 1892. 263p.
http://memory.loc.gov/cgi-bin/query/r?ammem/calbkbib:@field(AUTHOR+@band(Kip,+William+Ingraham,bp.,1811-1893.+))

Knower, Daniel. *The Adventures of a Forty-niner. An Historic Description of California, with Events and Ideas of San Francisco and Its People in Those Early Days*. Albany, NY: Weed Parsons, 1894. 200p.
http://memory.loc.gov/cgi-bin/query/r?ammem/calbkbib:@field(AUTHOR+@band(Knower,+Daniel.+))

Leach, Frank Aleamon. *Recollections of a Newspaperman, a Record of Life and Events in California*. San Francisco, CA: Levinson, 1917. 416p.
http://memory.loc.gov/cgi-bin/query/r?ammem/calbkbib:@field(AUTHOR+@band(Leach,+Frank+Aleamon,1846-+))

Likins, James W., Mrs. *Six Years' Experience as a Book Agent in California, Including My Trip from New York to San Francisco via Nicaragua*. San Francisco, CA: Women's Union Book and Job Printing Office, 1874. 168p.
http://memory.loc.gov/cgi-bin/query/r?ammem/calbkbib:@field(AUTHOR+@band(Likins,+J.+W.,Mrs.+))

McGowan, Edward. *Narrative of Edward McGowan, Including a Full Account of the Author's Adventures and Perils while Persecuted by the San Francisco Vigilance Committee of 1856, together with a Report of His Trial, which Resulted in His Acquittal*. San Francisco, CA: Russell, 1917. 240p.
http://memory.loc.gov/cgi-bin/query/r?ammem/calbkbib:@field(AUTHOR+@band(McGowan,+Edward,1813-1893.+))

Murdock, Charles Albert. *A Backward Glance at Eighty, Recollections and Comments by Charles A. Murdock, Massachusetts 1841, Humboldt Bay 1855, San Francisco, 1864*. San Francisco, CA: Elder, 1921. 275p.
http://memory.loc.gov/cgi-bin/query/r?ammem/calbkbib:@field(AUTHOR+@band(Murdock,+Charles+Albert,1841-+))

Natale, Valerie. "Angel Island, Guardian of the Western Gate." Prologue. Vol. 30, No. 2 (Summer 1998).
http://www.nara.gov/publications/prologue/angel1.html

Older, Fremont. *My Own Story*. San Francisco, CA: Call Publishing, 1919. 197p.
http://memory.loc.gov/cgi-bin/query/r?ammem/calbkbib:@field(AUTHOR+@band(Older,+Fremont,1856-1935+))

San Francisco 1859[City Directory]. San Francisco, CA: Herrick & Hoogs, 1859.
http://www.citydirectories.psmedia.com/city/free_statesort.html

San Francisco [City Directory]. San Francisco, CA: Valentine & Co., various. 1859-60; 1860-61; 1861; 1862.
http://www.citydirectories.psmedia.com/city/free_statesort.html

San Francisco [City Directory]. San Francisco, CA: Towne & Bacon, various. 1863; 1864.
http://www.citydirectories.psmedia.com/city/free_statesort.html

San Francisco [City Directory]. San Francisco, CA: Directory Company. 1880 edition.
http://www.citydirectories.psmedia.com/city/free_statesort.html

San Francisco [City Directory]. San Francisco, CA: Crocker. 1905; 1908.
http://www.citydirectories.psmedia.com/city/free_statesort.html

Taylor, William. *California Life Illustrated*. New York, NY: Carlton & Porter, 1858. 348p.
http://memory.loc.gov/cgi-bin/query/r?ammem/calbk:@field(DOCID+@lit(C063T00)):@@@REF

————. *Seven Year's Street Preaching in San Francisco, California, Embracing Incidents, Triumphant Death Scenes, etc.* New York, NY: Author, 1857. 394p.
http://memory.loc.gov/cgi-bin/query/r?ammem/calbk:@field(DOCID+@lit(C109T00)):@@@REF

————. 1859 Edition. 418p.
http://moa.umdl.umich.edu/cgi-bin/moa/sgml/moa-idx?notisid=AJG9120

Wierzbicki, Felix Paul. *California as It Is and as It May Be, or a Guide to the Gold Region*. San Francisco, CA: Grabhorn Press, 1933. 100p.
http://memory.loc.gov/cgi-bin/query/r?ammem/calbkbib:@field(AUTHOR+@band(Wierzbicki,+Felix+Paul,1815-1860.+))

Willey, Samuel Hopkins. *Thirty Years in California, a Contribution to the History of the State from 1849 to 1879*. San Francisco, CA: Bancroft, 1879. 76p.
http://memory.loc.gov/cgi-bin/query/r?ammem/calbkbib:@field(AUTHOR+@band(Willey,+Samuel+Hopkins.+))

Williams, Albert. *A Pioneer Pastorate and Times Embodying Contemporary Local Transactions and Events by the Rev. Albert Williams, Founder and First Pastor of the First Presbyterian Church, San Francisco*. San Francisco, CA: Wallace & Hassett Printers, 1879. 240p.
http://memory.loc.gov/cgi-bin/query/r?ammem/calbkbib:@field(AUTHOR+@band(Williams,+Albert,1809-1893.+))

San Joaquin Valley

Austin, Mary Hunter. *The Land of Little Rain*. Boston, MA: Houghton, Mifflin, 1903. 280p.
http://memory.loc.gov/cgi-bin/query/r?ammem/calbkbib:@field(AUTHOR+@band(Austin,+Mary+Hunter,1868-1934.+))

San Jose

Burnett, Peter Hardeman. *Recollections and Opinions of an Old Pioneer*. New York, NY: Appleton, 1880. 448p.
http://memory.loc.gov/cgi-bin/query/r?ammem/calbkbib:@field(AUTHOR+@band(Burnett,+Peter+H[ardeman],1807-1895.+))

Carroll, Mary Bowden. *Ten Years in Paradise. Leaves from a Society Reporter's Notebook*. San Jose, CA: Popp & Hogan, 1903. 212p.
http://memory.loc.gov/cgi-bin/query/r?ammem/calbkbib:@field(AUTHOR+@band(Carroll,+Mary+Bowden.+))

Churchill, Caroline M. Nichols. *Little Sheaves Gathered while Gleaning after Reapers. Being Letters of Travel Commencing in 1870 and Ending in 1873*. San Francisco, CA: Author, 1874. 110p.
http://memory.loc.gov/cgi-bin/query/r?ammem/calbk:@field(DOCID+@lit(C091T00)):@@@REF

Harlan, Jacob Wright. *California '46 to '88*. San Francisco, CA: Bancroft, 1888. 242p.
http://memory.loc.gov/cgi-bin/query/r?ammem/calbkbib:@field(AUTHOR+@band(Harlan,+Jacob+Wright,1828-+))

Woolley, Lell Hawley. *California, 1849-1913, or the Rambling Sketches and Experiences of Sixty-four Years' Residence in That State*. Oakland, CA: De Witt & Snelling, 1913. 48p.
http://memory.loc.gov/cgi-bin/query/r?ammem/calbkbib:@field(AUTHOR+@band(Woolley,+Lell+Hawley,1825-+))

San Juan Bautista

Mylar, Isaac L. *Early Days at the Mission San Juan Bautista*. Watsonville, CA: Evening Pajarorian, 1929. 195p.

http://memory.loc.gov/cgi-bin/query/r?ammem/calbkbib:@field(AUTHOR+@band(Mylar,+Isaac+L.+))

Smith, Sarah Hathaway Bixby. *Adobe Days, Being the Truthful Narrative of the Events in the Life of a California Girl on a Sheep Ranch and in El Pueblo de Nuestra Senora de Los Angeles while It Was Yet a Small and Humble Town, together with an Account of How Three Young Men from Maine in Eighteen Hundred and Fifty-three Drove Sheep and Cattle across the Plains, Mountains and Deserts from Illinois to the Pacific Coast, and the Strange Prophecy of Admiral Thatcher about San Pedro Harbor*. Cedar Rapids, IA: Torch Press, 1925. 208p.

http://memory.loc.gov/cgi-bin/query/r?ammem/calbkbib:@field(AUTHOR+@band(Smith,+Sarah+Hathaway+Bixby,1871-1935.+))

San Juan Capistrano

Janssens, Victor Eugene August. *The Life and Adventures in California of Don Agustin Janssens, 1834-1856*. San Marino, CA: Huntington, 1953. 165p.

http://memory.loc.gov/cgi-bin/query/r?ammem/calbkbib:@field(AUTHOR+@band(Janssens,+Victor+Eugene+August,1817-1894.+))

San Mateo

Graves, Jackson Alpheus. *My Seventy Years in California, 1857-1927*. Los Angeles, CA: Times Mirror Press, 1927. 478p.

http://memory.loc.gov/cgi-bin/query/r?ammem/calbkbib:@field(AUTHOR+@band(Graves,+Jackson+Alpheus,1852-1933.+))

San Pedro

Smith, Sarah Hathaway Bixby. *Adobe Days, Being the Truthful Narrative of the Events in the Life of a California Girl on a Sheep Ranch and in El Pueblo de Nuestra Senora de Los Angeles while It Was Yet a Small and Humble Town, together with an Account of How Three Young Men from Maine in Eighteen Hundred and Fifty-three Drove Sheep and Cattle across the Plains, Mountains and Deserts from Illinois to the Pacific Coast, and the Strange Prophecy of Admiral Thatcher about San Pedro Harbor*. Cedar Rapids, IA: Torch Press, 1925. 208p.

http://memory.loc.gov/cgi-bin/query/r?ammem/calbkbib:@field(AUTHOR+@band(Smith,+Sarah+Hathaway+Bixby,1871-1935.+))

Santa Anna

Smithwick, Noah. *The Evolution of a State or Recollections of Old Texas Days*. Austin, TX: Gammel Book Co., 1900. 354p.

http://www.erols.com/hardeman/lonestar/olbooks/smithwic/otd.htm

Santa Barbara

Roberts, Edwards. *Santa Barbara and around There*. Boston, MA: Roberts Brothers, 1886. 191p.

http://memory.loc.gov/cgi-bin/query/r?ammem/calbkbib:@field(AUTHOR+@band(Roberts,+Edwards.+))

Santa Clara County

Hines, Joseph Wilkinson. *Touching Incidents in the Life and Labors of a Pioneer on the Pacific Coast since 1853.* San Jose, CA: Eaton & Co., 1911. 198p.
http://memory.loc.gov/cgi-bin/query/r?ammem/calbkbib:@field(AUTHOR+@band(Hines,+Joseph+Wilkinson+))

Santa Cruz

Farnham, Eliza Woodson Burhans. *California, Indoors and Out, or How We Farm, Mine and Live Generally in the Golden State.* New York, NY: Dix, Edwards, 1856. 508p.
http://memory.loc.gov/cgi-bin/query/r?ammem/calbkbib:@field(AUTHOR+@band(Farnham,+Eliza+Woodson+Burhans,1815-1864.+))

White, William Francis. *A Picture of Pioneer Times in California.* San Francisco, CA: Hinton, 1881. 677p.
http://memory.loc.gov/cgi-bin/query/r?ammem/calbkbib:@field(AUTHOR+@band(White,+William+Francis,1829-1891?+))

Santa Monica

Rindge, Frederick Hastings. *Happy Days in Southern California.* Cambridge, MA: Author, 1898. 199p.
http://memory.loc.gov/cgi-bin/query/r?ammem/calbkbib:@field(AUTHOR+@band(Rindge,+Frederick+Hastings,1857-1905.+))

Scott Valley

Fairchild, Lucius. *California Letters of Lucius Fairchild.* Madison, WI: State Historical Society of Wisconsin, 1931. 212p.
http://memory.loc.gov/cgi-bin/query/r?ammem/calbkbib:@field(AUTHOR+@band(Fairchild,+Lucius,1831-1896.+))

Silverado

Stevenson, Robert Louis. *The Silverado Squatters.* New York, NY: Lovell Co., 1888. 96p.
http://memory.loc.gov/cgi-bin/query/r?ammem/calbkbib:@field(AUTHOR+@band(Stevenson,+Robert+Louis,1850-1894.+))

Sonoma

Christman, Enos. *One Man's Gold, the Letters & Journal of a Forty-niner, Enos Christman.* New York, NY: Whittlesey House, 1930. 278p.
http://memory.loc.gov/cgi-bin/query/r?ammem/calbkbib:@field(AUTHOR+@band(Christman,+Enos,1828-1912.+))

Gregson, Eliza Marshall. *The Gregson Memoirs, Containing Mrs. Eliza Gregson's Memory and the Statement of James Gregson.* San Francisco, CA: Kennedy, 1940. 31p.
http://memory.loc.gov/cgi-bin/query/r?ammem/calbkbib:@field(AUTHOR+@band(Gregson,+Eliza+Marshall,1824-+))

Houghton, Eliza Poor Donner. *The Expedition of the Donner Party and Its Tragic Fate.* Chicago, IL: McClurg, 1911. 374p.
http://memory.loc.gov/cgi-bin/query/r?ammem/calbkbib:@field(AUTHOR+@band(Houghton,+Eliza+Poor+Donner,1843-1922.+))

Sonora

Booth, Edmund. *Edmund Booth (1810-1905), Forty-niner, the Life Story of a Deaf Pioneer, including Portions of His Autobiographical Notes and Gold Rush Diary, and Selections from Family Letters and Reminiscences.* Stockton, CA: San Joaquin Pioneer and Historical Society, 1953. 72p.
http://memory.loc.gov/cgi-bin/query/r?ammem/calbkbib:@field(AUTHOR+@band(Booth,+Edmund,1810-1905.+))

Gunn, Lewis Carstairs. *Records of a California Family, Journals and Letters of Lewis C. Gunn and Elizabeth Le Breton Gunn.* San Diego, CA: Johnck and Seeger, 1928. 279p.
http://memory.loc.gov/cgi-bin/query/r?ammem/calbkbib:@field(AUTHOR+@band(Gunn,+Lewis+Carstairs,1813-1892.+))

Stanislaus

Ryan, William Redmond. *Personal Adventures in Upper and Lower California in 1848-9, with the Author's Experience at the Mines.* London: Shoberl, 1850. 2 vols.
http://memory.loc.gov/cgi-bin/query/r?ammem/calbkbib:@field(AUTHOR+@band(Ryan,+William+Redmond,1791-1855.+))

Stockton

Woods, James. *Recollections of Pioneer Work in California.* San Francisco, CA: Winterburn, 1878. 260p.
http://memory.loc.gov/cgi-bin/query/r?ammem/calbkbib:@field(AUTHOR+@band(Woods,+James,1814+or+5-1886.+))

Tulare

Carson, James H. *Early Recollections of the Mines and a Description of the Great Tulare Valley.* Tarrytown, NY: Abbatt, 1931. 82p.
http://memory.loc.gov/cgi-bin/query/r?ammem/calbkbib:@field(AUTHOR+@band(Carson,+James+H.,d.+1853.+))

Tuolumne County

Wood, Harvey. *Personal Recollections.* Pasadena, CA: John B. Goodman, III, 1955. 27p.
http://memory.loc.gov/cgi-bin/query/r?ammem/calbkbib:@field(AUTHOR+@band(Wood,+Harvey,1828-1895.+))

Vacaville

Wilson, Luzena Stanley. *Luzena Stanley Wilson, '49er, Memories Recalled Years Later for Her Daughter Correnah Wilson Wright.* Mills College, CA: Eucalyptus Press, 1937. 61p.
http://memory.loc.gov/cgi-bin/query/r?ammem/calbkbib:@field(AUTHOR+@band(Wilson,+Luzena+Stanley,b.+1821?+))

Weaverville

Abbey, James. *California. A Trip across the Plains in the Spring of 1850, Being a Daily Record of Incidents of the Trip and Containing Valuable Information to Emigrants.* New Albany, IN: Kent & Norman, 1850. 63p.
http://memory.loc.gov/cgi-bin/query/r?ammem/calbkbib:@field(AUTHOR+@band(Abbey,+James.+))

Buck, Franklin Agustus. A Yankee Trader in the Gold Rush, the Letters of Franklin A. Buck. Boston, MA: Houghton, Mifflin, 1930. 294p.
http://memory.loc.gov/cgi-bin/query/r?ammem/calbkbib:@field(AUTHOR+@band(Buck,+Franklin+Agustus,1826-1909.+))

Buffum, Edward Gould. *Six Months in the Gold Mines from a Journal of Three Years' Residence in Upper and Lower California, 1847-8-9.* Philadelphia, PA: Lea & Blanchard, 1850. 172p.
http://memory.loc.gov/cgi-bin/query/r?ammem/calbkbib:@field(AUTHOR+@band(Buffum,+Edward+Gould,1820-1867.+))

Yosemite

Bunnell, Lafayette Houghton. *Discovery of the Yosemite and the Indian War of 1851, which Led to That Event.* New York, NY: Revell, 1892. 359p.
http://memory.loc.gov/cgi-bin/query/r?ammem/calbkbib:@field(AUTHOR+@band(Bunnell,+Lafayette+Houghton,1824-1903.+))

Yuba County

Ellis, William Turner. *Memories, My Seventy-two Years in the Romantic County of Yuba, California.* Eugene, OR: University of Oregon, 1939. 308p.
http://memory.loc.gov/cgi-bin/query/r?ammem/calbkbib:@field(AUTHOR+@band(Ellis,+William+Turner,1866-+))

Colorado

Bird, Isabella L. *Life in the Rocky Mountains.* New York, NY: Putnam's, 1881. 296p.
http://www.indiana.edu/~letrs/vwwp/bird/rocky.html

Research Outline. Colorado. Salt Lake City, UT: Family History Library, 1997.
http://www.familysearch.com/sg/Colorado.html

Denver

Denver [City Directory]. Denver, CO., 1859.
http://www.citydirectories.psmedia.com/city/free_statesort.html

Jackson, Helen Maria Fiske Hunt. *Glimpses of California and the Mission.* Boston, MA: Little, Brown & Co., 1902. 292p.
http://memory.loc.gov/cgi-bin/query/r?ammem/calbkbib:@field(AUTHOR+@band(Jackson,+Helen+[Maria+Fiske]+Hunt,1831-1885.+))

Connecticut

Clubb, Henry S. *Results of Prohibition in Connecticut, Being Special Returns from Every County as to the Effects of the Maine Liquor Law, Containing Contributions from the Governor and Upward of Fifty Clergymen, Judges, Editors and Private Citizens.* New York, NY: Fowlers and Wells, 1855. 82p.
http://moa.umdl.umich.edu/cgi-bin/moa/sgml/moa-idx?notisid=AHL9039

Douglass, William. *A Discourse Concerning the Currencies of the British Plantations in America, Especially with Regard to Their Paper Money, More Particularly in Relation to the Province of Massachusetts Bay in New England.* Unknown. 1740. 3p.
http://www.people.virginia.edu/~rwm3n/webdoc2.html

Field, Stephen Johnson. *Personal Reminiscences of Early Days in California, with Other Sketches.* San Francisco, CA: Author, 1880. 248p.
http://memory.loc.gov/cgi-bin/query/r?ammem/calbkbib:@field(AUTHOR+@band(Field,+Stephen+Johnson,1816-1899.+))

Research Outline. Connecticut. Salt Lake City, UT: Family History Library, 1997.
http://www.familysearch.com/sg/Connecticut.html

Talcott, Sebastian Visscher. *Genealogical Notes of New York and New England Families.* Albany, NY: Weed, Parsons & Co., 1883. 747p.
http://moa.cit.cornell.edu/dienst/moabrowse.fly/MOA-JOURNALS2:TALC-0006/3/1:TIFF2GIF:100

Branford
Abbot, Abiel and Ephraim Abbot. *Genealogical Register of the Descendants of George Abbot of Andover, George Abbot of Rowley, Thomas Abbot of Andover, Arthur Abbot of Ipswich, Robert Abbot of Branford, CT and George Abbot, of Norwalk, CT.* Boston, MA: James Munroe, 1847. 197p.
http://genweb.net/~books/ma/abbot1847/

Canaan
Perry, Belle McArthur. *Lucinda Hinsdale Stone, Her Life Story and Reminiscences.* Detroit, MI: Blinn Publishing, 1902. 369p.
http://memory.loc.gov/cgi-bin/query/r?ammem/lhbumbib:@field(SUBJ+@band(Stone,+Lucinda+Hinsdale,--1814-1900.+))

Cornwall
Memoir of Thomas Hamitah Patoo, a Native of the Marqueas Islands, Who Died June 19, 1823, while a Member of the Foreign Mission School in Cornwall, Connecticut. New York, NY: New York Religious Tract Society, 1823. 48p.
http://memory.loc.gov/cgi-bin/query/r?ammem/aap:@field(SUBJ+@band(Biographies--New+York++N.Y.+--1825.+))

Greenwich (Fairfield County)

Mead, Solomon. *Notes of Two Trips to California and Return, Taken in 1883 and 1886-7*. Greenwich, CT: Author, 1890. 144p.
http://memory.loc.gov/cgi-bin/query/r?ammem/calbkbib:@field(AUTHOR+@band(Mead,+Solomon,1808-1897.+))

Groton

Mitchel, Cora. *Reminiscences of the Civil War*. Providence, RI: Snow & Farnham, 1916. 43p.
http://metalab.unc.edu/docsouth/mitchel/menu.html

Hartford

Hall, Linville John and George Gideon Webster. *Around the Horn in '49, Journal of the Hartford Union Mining and Trading Company. Containing the Name, Residence and Occupation of Each Member, with Incidents of the Voyage*. Wethersfield, CT: L. J. Hall, 1898. 252p.
http://memory.loc.gov/cgi-bin/query/r?ammem/calbkbib:@field(AUTHOR+@band(Hartford+Union+Mining+and+Trading+Company.+))

Hammon, Jupiter. *An Address to the Negroes in the State of New York, by Jupiter Hammon, Servant of John Lloyd, Jun., Esq. of the Manor of Queen's Village, Long Island*. New York, NY: Carroll and Patterson, 1787. 20p.
http://www.lib.virginia.edu/etext/readex/20400.html

Hartford 1859-60 [City Directory]. Hartford, CT: Elihu Greer, 1859.
http://www.citydirectories.psmedia.com/city/free_statesort.html

Hartford, 1859 [City Directory]. Hartford, CT: Bartlett, 1859.
http://www.citydirectories.psmedia.com/city/free_statesort.html

Warner, Charles Dudley. *Our Italy*. New York, NY: Harper, 1891. 266p.
http://memory.loc.gov/cgi-bin/query/r?ammem/calbkbib:@field(AUTHOR+@band(Warner,+Charles+Dudley,1829-1900.+))

New Haven

Bagg, Lyman Hotchkiss. *Four Years at Yale*. New Haven, CT: Chatfield, 1871. 728p.
http://moa.umdl.umich.edu/cgi-bin/moa/sgml/moa-idx?notisid=AGE3953

Brewer, William Henry. *Up and Down California in 1860-1864, the Journal of William H. Brewer*. New Haven, CT: Yale, 1930. 601p.
http://memory.loc.gov/cgi-bin/query/r?ammem/calbkbib:@field(AUTHOR+@band(Brewer,+William+Henry,1828-1910.+))

New Haven, 1859-60 [City Directory]. New Haven, CT: Benham, various.
http://www.citydirectories.psmedia.com/city/free_statesort.html

New London

New London, 1859-60 [City Directory]. New London, CT: Starr & Co., various.
http://www.citydirectories.psmedia.com/city/free_statesort.html

Norwalk

Abbot, Abiel and Ephraim Abbot. *Genealogical Register of the Descendants of George Abbot of Andover, George Abbot of Rowley, Thomas Abbot of Andover, Arthur Abbot of Ipswich, Robert Abbot of Branford, CT and George Abbot, of Norwalk, CT.* Boston, MA: James Munroe, 1847. 197p.
http://genweb.net/~books/ma/abbot1847/

Stamford

Marcus, Ronald. *Stamford, Connecticut, a Bibliography.* Stamford, CT: Stamford Historical Society, 1995. 284p.
http://www.cslnet.ctstateu.edu/stamford/Biblio.htm

Delaware

Delaware Genealogy: A Guide to Research in the Historical Society of Delaware Research Library. Wilmington, DE: Historical Society of Delaware. Unpgd.
http://www.hsd.org/gengd.htm

Delaware State Directory, 1859-60 [City Directory]. Wilmington, DE: Boyd, various.
http://www.citydirectories.psmedia.com/city/free_statesort.html

Research Outline. Delaware. Salt Lake City, UT: Family History Library, 1997.
http://www.familysearch.com/sg/Delaware.html

Newark

Newark, Delaware, Selected Primary Sources. Newark, DE: University of Delaware, Special Collections Department. Unpgd.
http://www.lib.udel.edu/ud/spec/guides/newark.htm

District of Columbia

Episcopal Church, Commission of Home Missions to Colored People. New York, NY: Church, 1875, 1876.

9th Annual Report, 1873-74. 20p.
http://memory.loc.gov/cgi-bin/query/r?ammem/murray:@field(FLD001+91898515+):@@@REF

11th Annual Report, 1875-76. 24p.
http://memory.loc.gov/cgi-bin/query/r?ammem/murray:@field(FLD001+91898514+):@@@REF

Heger, Kenneth W. "Strategies for Reconstructing Careers of Foreign Service Officers, 1869-1887." *Prologue*. Vol. 31, No. 1 (Spring 1999).
http://www.nara.gov/publications/prologue/fso.html

Hunter, Alfred. *The Washington and Georgetown Directory, Strangers' Guide-book for Washington, and Congressional and Clerk's Register*. Washington, DC: Kirkwood & McGill, 1853. 126p.
http://moa.umdl.umich.edu/cgi-bin/moa/sgml/moa-idx?notisid=AFJ8697

Matchette, Robert B. *Guide to Federal Records in the National Archives of the United States*. Washington, DC: National Archives, 1995.
http://www.nara.gov/guide/

National Association for the Relief of Destitute Colored Women and Children. Annual Report. Washington, DC: The Association, 1883, 1887, 1895, 1900.
20th Annual Report, 1883. 16p.
http://memory.loc.gov/cgi-bin/query/r?ammem/murray:@field(FLD001+91898518+):@@@REF

24th Annual Report, 1887. 16p.
http://memory.loc.gov/cgi-bin/query/r?ammem/murray:@field(FLD001+91898517+):@@@REF

32nd Annual Report, 1895. 20p.
http://memory.loc.gov/cgi-bin/query/r?ammem/murray:@field(FLD001+91898480+):@@@REF

37th Annual Report, 1900. 24p.
http://memory.loc.gov/cgi-bin/query/r?ammem/murray:@field(FLD001+91898495+):@@@REF

Phillips, Henry L. *In Memoriam of the Late Rev. Alex Crummell, D.D. of Washington, D.C., an Address Delivered before the American Negro Historical Society of Philadelphia*. Philadelphia, PA: Coleman Printery, 1899. 21p.
http://memory.loc.gov/cgi-bin/query/r?ammem/murray:@field(FLD001+91898532+):@@@REF

Report of the Board of the Freedmen's Hospital to the Secretary of the Interior. Washington, DC: Government Printing Office, 1899. 21p.
http://memory.loc.gov/cgi-bin/query/r?ammem/aap:@field(SUBJ+@band(Freedmen's+Hospital++Washington,+D.C.++))

Research Outline. District of Columbia. Salt Lake City, UT: Family History Library, 1997.
http://www.familysearch.com/sg/District_of_Columbia.html

Trustees of Colored Schools of Washington and Georgetown, D.C., Made in Compliance with a Resolution of the Senate of the United States, Passed December 8, 1870. Washington, DC: McGill & Witherow, 1871. 56p.
http://memory.loc.gov/ammem/mdbquery.html

Waller, Owen Meredith. *The Episcopal Church and the Colored People, a Statement of Facts*. Washington, DC: Emmett C. Jones & Co., 1898. 14p.
http://memory.loc.gov/cgi-bin/query/r?ammem/aap:@field(SUBJ+@band(Afro-American+Episcopalians.+))

Wyeth, Samuel Douglas. *Roose's Companion and Guide to Washington and Vicinity*. Washington, DC: Gibson Brothers Printers, 1876. 142p.
http://moa.umdl.umich.edu/cgi-bin/moa/sgml/moa-idx?notisid=AAV9985

Florida

Eppes, Susan Bradford. *Through Some Eventful Years*. Macon, GA: Burke, 1926. 382p.
http://moa.umdl.umich.edu/cgi-bin/moa/sgml/moa-idx?notisid=AFJ8883

Florida Libraries. Serial. Vol. 40, No. 1, (January-February 1997- .).
http://www.flalib.org/library/fla/florlibs/florlibs.htm

Hallock, Charles. *Camp Life in Florida, a Handbook for Sportsmen and Settlers*. New York, NY: Forest and Stream Publishing Co., 1876. 364p.
http://moa.umdl.umich.edu/cgi-bin/moa/sgml/moa-idx?notisid=AFJ9563

Lanier, Sidney. *Florida, Its Scenery, Climate and History, with an Account of Charleston, Savannah, Augusta and Aiken, a Chapter for Consumptives, Various Papers on Fruit Culture and a Complete Handbook and Guide*. Philadelphia, PA: Lippincott, 1876. 346p.
http://moa.umdl.umich.edu/cgi-bin/moa/sgml/moa-idx?notisid=AFJ9565

Ledyard, Bill. *A Winter in Florida; or, Observations on the Soil, Climate, and Products of Our Semi-tropical State; with Sketches of the Principal Towns and Cities in Eastern Florida. To which is Added a Brief Historical Summary; together with Hints to the Tourist, Invalid, and Sportsman*. New York, NY: Wood & Holbrook, 1869. 238p.
http://moa.umdl.umich.edu/cgi-bin/moa/sgml/moa-idx?notisid=AAW2336

Research Outline. Florida. Salt Lake City, UT: Family History Library, 1997.
http://www.familysearch.com/sg/Florida.html

Apalachicola
Mitchel, Cora. *Reminiscences of the Civil War*. Providence, RI: Snow & Farnham, 1916. 43p.
http://metalab.unc.edu/docsouth/mitchel/menu.html

Miami
Gordon, John Brown. *Reminiscences of the Civil War*. New York, NY: Scribners, 1904. 474p.
http://metalab.unc.edu/docsouth/gordon/menu.html

Georgia

Andrews, Sidney. *The South since the War, as Shown by Fourteen Weeks of Travel and Observation in Georgia and the Carolinas.* Boston, MA: Ticknor & Fields, 1866. 408p.
http://moa.umdl.umich.edu/cgi-bin/moa/sgml/moa-idx?notisid=AAW0193

Chappell, Absalom Harris. *Miscellanies of Georgia, Historical, Biographical, Descriptive, etc.* Atlanta, GA: J. F. Meegan, 1874. 240p.
http://moa.umdl.umich.edu/cgi-bin/moa/sgml/moa-idx?notisid=AFK4125

Leigh, Frances Butler. *Ten Years on a Georgia Plantation since the War.* London: Richard Bentley & Son, 1883. 347p.
http://metalab.unc.edu/docsouth/leigh/menu.html

Love, Emanuel K. *Annual Address to the Missionary Baptist Convention of Georgia (Containing History of the Church).* Nashville, TN: National Baptist Publishing Board, 1899. 44p.
http://memory.loc.gov/cgi-bin/query/r?ammem/aap:@field(SUBJ+@band(Afro-American+Baptists--Georgia.+))

Radical Rule, Military Outrage in Georgia. Arrest of Columbus Prisoners, with Facts Connected with Their Imprisonment and Release. Louisville, KY: Morton, 1868. 200p.
http://moa.umdl.umich.edu/cgi-bin/moa/sgml/moa-idx?notisid=AFJ9489

Research Outline. Georgia. Salt Lake City, UT: Family History Library, 1997.
http://www.familysearch.com/sg/Georgia.html

Stearns, Charles Woodward. *The Black Man of the South and the Rebels, or the Characteristics of the Former and the Recent Outrages of the Latter.* New York, NY: American News, 1872. 578p.
http://moa.umdl.umich.edu/cgi-bin/moa/sgml/moa-idx?notisid=ABL5152

Taylor, Susie King. *Reminiscences of My Life in Camp with the 33d United States Colored Troops Late 1st S.C. Volunteers.* Boston, MA: Author, 82p.
http://digilib.nypl.org/dynaweb/digs/wwm97267/

Wells Barnett, Ida B. *Lynch Law in Georgia.* Chicago, IL: Author, 1899. 18p.
http://memory.loc.gov/cgi-bin/query/r?ammem/aap:@field(SUBJ+@band(Hose,+Samuel.+))

Albany
Andrews, Eliza Frances. *The Wartime Journal of a Georgia Girl, 1864-1865.* New York, NY: Appleton, 1908. 387p.
http://metalab.unc.edu/docsouth/andrews/menu.html

Athens
Howard, Wiley C. *Sketch of Cobb Legion Cavalry and Some Incidents and Scenes Remembered.* Author, 1901. 20p.
http://metalab.unc.edu/docsouth/howard/menu.html

Atlanta

Atlanta, 1859-60 [City Directory]. Atlanta, GA: Williams, various.
http://www.citydirectories.psmedia.com/city/free_statesort.html

Augusta

Augusta, 1859 [City Directory]. Augusta, GA: Watkins, various.
http://www.citydirectories.psmedia.com/city/free_statesort.html

Lanier, Sidney. *Florida, Its Scenery, Climate and History, with an Account of Charleston, Savannah, Augusta and Aiken, a Chapter for Consumptives, Various Papers on Fruit Culture and a Complete Handbook and Guide.* Philadelphia, PA: Lippincott, 1876. 346p.
http://moa.umdl.umich.edu/cgi-bin/moa/sgml/moa-idx?notisid=AFJ9565

Columbus

Columbus, 1859-60 [City Directory]. Columbus, GA: Directory Co., 1859.
http://www.citydirectories.psmedia.com/city/free_statesort.html

Radical Rule, Military Outrage in Georgia. Arrest of Columbus Prisoners, with Facts Connected with Their Imprisonment and Release. Louisville, KY: Morton, 1868. 200p.
http://moa.umdl.umich.edu/cgi-bin/moa/sgml/moa-idx?notisid=AFJ9489

Covington

Burge, Dolly Sumner Lunt. *A Woman's Wartime Journal, an Account of the Passage over Georgia's Plantation of Sherman's Army on the March to the Sea, as Recorded in the Diary of Dolly Sumner Lunt (Mrs. Thomas Burge).* New York, NY: Century Co., 1918. 54p.
http://metalab.unc.edu/docsouth/burge/menu.html

Columbus (Muscogee County)

The Marvelous Musical Prodigy, Blind Tom, the Negro Boy Pianist, Whose Performances at the Great St. James and Egyptian Halls, London and Salle Hertz, Paris, Have Created Such a Profound Sensation. Anecdotes, Songs, Sketches of the Life, Testimonials of Musicians and Savans, and Opinions of the American and English Press of Blind Tom (Thomas Greene Bethune). New York, NY: French & Wheat, 1868. 30p.
http://memory.loc.gov/cgi-bin/query/r?ammem/aap:@field(SUBJ+@band(Bethune,+Thomas+Greene,--1849-1908.+))

McIntosh County

Kell, John McIntosh. *Recollections of a Naval Life, Including the Cruises of the Confederate States Steamers, Sumter and Alabama.* Washington, DC: Neale, 1900. 307p.
http://metalab.unc.edu/docsouth/kell/menu.html

Macon

Burton, Annie L. *Memories of Childhood's Slavery Days.* Boston, MA: Ross Publishing, 1909. 97p.
http://metalab.unc.edu/docsouth/burton/menu.html
http://digilib.nypl.org/dynaweb/digs/wwm97252/

Morgan County

Felton, Rebecca Latimer. *County Life in Georgia in the Days of My Youth.* Atlanta, GA: Index Printing Co., 1919. 303p.
http://metalab.unc.edu/docsouth/felton/menu.html

Murray County

Branham, Levi. *My Life and Travels*. Dalton, GA: Showalter, 1929. 64p.
http://metalab.unc.edu/docsouth/branham/menu.html

Muskogee County

The Marvelous Musical Prodigy, Blind Tom, the Negro Boy Pianist, Whose Performances at the Great St. James and Egyptian Halls, London and Salle Hertz, Paris, Have Created Such a Profound Sensation. Anecdotes, Songs, Sketches of the Life, Testimonials of Musicians and Savans, and Opinions of the American and English Press of Blind Tom (Thomas Greene Bethune). New York, NY: French & Wheat, 1868. 30p.
http://memory.loc.gov/cgi-bin/query/r?ammem/aap:@field(SUBJ+@band(Bethune,+Thomas+Greene,--1849-1908.+))

Savannah

Doesticks, Q. K. Philander. *What Became of the Slaves on a Georgia Plantation? Great Auction Sale of Slaves, at Savannah, Georgia, March 2d & 3d, 1859. A Sequel to Mrs. Kemble's Journal*. Author, 1863. 20p.
http://memory.loc.gov/cgi-bin/query/r?ammem/murray:@field(FLD001+11003986+):@@@REF

Episcopal Church, Commission of Home Missions to Colored People. New York, NY: Church, 1875, 1876.
9th Annual Report, 1873-74. 20p.
http://memory.loc.gov/cgi-bin/query/r?ammem/murray:@field(FLD001+91898515+):@@@REF

11th Annual Report, 1875-76. 24p.
http://memory.loc.gov/cgi-bin/query/r?ammem/murray:@field(FLD001+91898514+):@@@REF

Jones, Charles Colcock. *The Siege of Savannah in December, 1864, and the Confederate Operations in Georgia, and the Third Military District of South Carolina during General Sherman's March from Atlanta to the Sea*. Albany, NY: Munsell, 1874. 184p.
http://metalab.unc.edu/docsouth/jonescharles/menu.html

Lanier, Sidney. *Florida, Its Scenery, Climate and History, with an Account of Charleston, Savannah, Augusta and Aiken, a Chapter for Consumptives, Various Papers on Fruit Culture and a Complete Handbook and Guide*. Philadelphia, PA: Lippincott, 1876. 346p.
http://moa.umdl.umich.edu/cgi-bin/moa/sgml/moa-idx?notisid=AFJ9565

Love, Emanuel K. *Introductory Sermon of Rev. Emanuel K. Love, on Entering the Pastorate of the First African Baptist Church, Savannah, Georgia*. Augusta, GA: Sentinel Print, 1885. 11p.
http://memory.loc.gov/cgi-bin/query/r?ammem/aap:@field(SUBJ+@band(Installation+sermons--Georgia--Savannah--1885.+))

————. *Learning of Christ, the Anniversary Sermon of the First Bryan Baptist Church, West Broad Street, Savannah, Georgia*. Augusta, GA: Georgia Baptist Printing Co., 1882. 19p.
http://memory.loc.gov/cgi-bin/query/r?ammem/aap:@field(SUBJ+@band(Anniversary+sermons--Georgia--Savannah--1883.+))

Savannah, 1859 [City Directory]. Savannah, GA: Cooper & Co., 1859.
http://www.citydirectories.psmedia.com/city/free_statesort.html

Thomas, Edward J. *Memoirs of a Southerner, 1840-1923*. Savannah, GA: Author, 1923. 64p.
http://metalab.unc.edu/docsouth/thomas/menu.html

Hawaii

Anderson, Rufus. *The Hawaiian Islands Their Progress and Condition under Missionary Labors.* Boston, MA: Gould and Lincoln, 1865. 460p.
http://moa.umdl.umich.edu/cgi-bin/moa/sgml/moa-idx?notisid=ALQ8090

————. *History of the Sandwich Islands Mission.* Boston, MA: Congregational Publishing Society, 1870. 436p.
http://moa.umdl.umich.edu/cgi-bin/moa/sgml/moa-idx?notisid=AGA4514

Bartlett, Samuel Colcord. *Historical Sketch of the Hawaiian Mission, and the Missions to Micronesia and the Marquesas Islands.* Boston, MA: American Board of Commissioners for Foreign Missions, 1871. 36p.
http://moa.umdl.umich.edu/cgi-bin/moa/sgml/moa-idx?notisid=AJG8986

Baxley, Henry Willis. *What I Saw on the West Coast of South and North America and at the Hawaiian Islands.* New York, NY: Appleton, 1865. 646p.
http://moa.umdl.umich.edu/cgi/sgml/moa-idx?notisid=ABF7940

Bird, Isabella L. *The Hawaiian Archipelago, Six Months among the Palm Groves, Coral Reefs and Volcanoes of the Sandwich Islands.* London: Murray, 1875. 473p.
http://www.indiana.edu/~letrs/vwwp/bird/hawaii.html

Cheever, Henry T. *The Island World of the Pacific, Being Travel through the Sandwich or Hawaiian Islands and Other Parts of Polynesia.* New York, NY: Harper, 1856. 418p.
http://moa.umdl.umich.edu/cgi-bin/moa/sgml/moa-idx?notisid=ABA2734

Damon, Samuel Chenery. Puritan Missions in the Pacific, a Discourse Delivered at Honolulu, on the Anniversary of the Hawaiian Evangelical Association, Sabbath Evening, June 17, 1866. New Haven, CT: Hunnewell, 1868. 52p.
http://moa.umdl.umich.edu/cgi-bin/moa/sgml/moa-idx?notisid=AJG8991

Ellis, William. *The American Mission in the Sandwich Islands, a Vindication and an Appeal in Relation to the Proceedings of the Reformed Catholic Mission at Honolulu.* Honolulu, HI: Whitney, 1866. 78p.
http://moa.umdl.umich.edu/cgi-bin/moa/sgml/moa-idx?notisid=AGA4516

Nordhoff, Charles. *Northern California, Oregon, and the Sandwich Islands.* New York, NY: Harper, 1875. 256p.
http://moa.umdl.umich.edu/cgi-bin/moa/sgml/moa-idx?notisid=AJL3484

Parker, E. M. Wills. *The Sandwich Islands as They Are, Not as They Should Be.* San Francisco, CA: Burgess, Gilbert & Still, 1852. 18p.
http://moa.umdl.umich.edu/cgi-bin/moa/sgml/moa-idx?notisid=AFJ6736

Research Outline. Hawaii. Salt Lake City, UT: Family History Library, 1997.
http://www.familysearch.com/sg/Hawaii.html

Honolulu

Briggs, Lloyd Vernon. *California and the West, 1881 and Later*. Boston, MA: Wright & Potter, 1931. 214p.
http://memory.loc.gov/cgi-bin/query/r?ammem/calbkbib:@field(AUTHOR+@band(Briggs,+Lloyd+Vernon,1863-1941.+))

The Oahu College at the Sandwich Islands. Boston, MA: Marvin, 1857. 18p.
http://moa.umdl.umich.edu/cgi-bin/moa/sgml/moa-idx?notisid=AJL9076

Idaho

Research Outline. Idaho. Salt Lake City, UT: Family History Library, 1997.
http://www.familysearch.com/sg/Idaho.html

Illinois

Gerhard, Frederick. *Illinois as It Is, Its History, Geography, Statistics, Constitution, Laws, Government*. Chicago, IL: Keen & Lee, 1857. 466p.
http://moa.umdl.umich.edu/cgi-bin/moa/sgml/moa-idx?notisid=AFK4275

Research Outline. Illinois. Salt Lake City, UT: Family History Library, 1997.
http://www.familysearch.com/sg/Illinois.html

Stewart, Charles Leslie. *Land Tenure in the United States, with Special Reference to Illinois*. Urbana, IL: University of Illinois, 1916. 142p.
http://chla.mannlib.cornell.edu/cgi-bin/chla/viewer.cgi?docid=title2c.chla.mannlib.cornell/0391stew&format=1:75-GIF&section=Title+Page

Chicago (Cook County)

Bemis, Stephen Allen. *Recollections of a Long and Somewhat Uneventful Life*. St. Louis, MO: Author, 1932. 92p.
http://memory.loc.gov/cgi-bin/query/r?ammem/calbkbib:@field(AUTHOR+@band(Bemis,+Stephen+Allen,1828-1919.+))

Chicago [City Directory]. Chicago, IL: Cooke & Co., various.
1859-60; 1861-62.
http://www.citydirectories.psmedia.com/city/free_statesort.html

Chicago, 1859-60 [City Directory]. Chicago, IL: Hellier & Co., 1859.
http://www.citydirectories.psmedia.com/city/free_statesort.html

Chicago, 1859-60 [City Directory]. Chicago, IL: Smith & Du Moulin, 1859.
http://www.citydirectories.psmedia.com/city/free_statesort.html

Chicago, 1859 [City Directory]. Chicago, IL: Griggs & Co., 1859.
http://www.citydirectories.psmedia.com/city/free_statesort.html

Chicago [City Directory]. Chicago, IL: Halpin & Bailey, various.
1861-62; 1862-63; 1864; 1865; 1867-68.
http://www.citydirectories.psmedia.com/city/free_statesort.html

Chicago [City Directory]. Chicago, IL: Edwards, various.
1866-67; 1871; 1873.
http://www.citydirectories.psmedia.com/city/free_statesort.html

Chicago Magazine, the West as It Is. Chicago, IL: Gager, 1857. 458p.
http://moa.umdl.umich.edu/cgi-bin/moa/sgml/moa-idx?notisid=AFK4278

Churchill, Caroline M. Nichols. *Little Sheaves Gathered while Gleaning after Reapers. Being Letters of Travel Commencing in 1870 and Ending in 1873*. San Francisco, CA: Author, 1874. 110p.
http://memory.loc.gov/cgi-bin/query/r?ammem/calbk:@field(DOCID+@lit(C091T00)):@@@REF

Curtiss, Daniel S. *Western Portraiture, and Emigrants' Guide, a Description of Wisconsin, Illinois, and Iowa with Remarks on Minnesota and Other Territories*. New York, NY: Colton, 1852. 370p.
http://moa.umdl.umich.edu/cgi-bin/moa/sgml/moa-idx?notisid=AJA3436

Goodsell, James H. *History of the Great Chicago Fire, October 8, 9, and 10, 1871*. New York, NY: Author, 1871. 32p.
http://moa.umdl.umich.edu/cgi-bin/moa/sgml/moa-idx?notisid=AJA3021

Report of the Chicago Relief and Aid Society of Disbursement of Contributions for the Sufferers by the Chicago Fire. Chicago, IL: Chicago Relief and Aid Society, 1874. 458p.
http://moa.umdl.umich.edu/cgi-bin/moa/sgml/moa-idx?notisid=AAZ9846

Sheahan, James W. *The Great Conflagration. Chicago, Its Past, Present and Future. Embracing a Detailed Narrative of the Great Conflagration in the North, South, and West Divisions: Also, a Condensed History of Chicago, Its Population, Growth and Great Public Works. And a Statement of all the Great Fires of the World*. Chicago, IL: Union Publishing, 1872. 534p.
http://moa.umdl.umich.edu/cgi-bin/moa/sgml/moa-idx?notisid=AJA3022

Taylor, Benjamin Franklin. *Between the Gates*. Chicago, IL: Griggs, 1878. 292p.
http://memory.loc.gov/cgi-bin/query/r?ammem/calbkbib:@field(AUTHOR+@band(Taylor,+Benjamin+F[ranklin],1819-1887.+))

Wright, John S. *Chicago, Past, Present, Future. Relations to the Great Interior, and to the Continent*. Chicago, IL: Horton & Leonard Printers, 1870. 496p.
http://moa.umdl.umich.edu/cgi-bin/moa/sgml/moa-idx?notisid=ACK8117

Delavan

Sanders, Sue A. Pike. *A Journey to, on and from the Golden Shore*. Delavan, IL: Times Printing Office, 1887. 118p.

http://memory.loc.gov/cgi-bin/query/r?ammem/calbkbib:@field(AUTHOR+@band(Sanders,+Sue+A.+Pike,1842-1931.+))

Kane County

Kane County Directory, 1859-60 [City Directory]. Chicago, IL: Bailey, 1859.

http://www.citydirectories.psmedia.com/city/free_statesort.html

Merango

Shaw, David Augustus. *Eldorado, or California as Seen by a Pioneer, 1850-1900*. Los Angeles, CA: Baumgardt, 1900. 313p.

http://memory.loc.gov/cgi-bin/query/r?ammem/calbkbib:@field(AUTHOR+@band(Shaw,+David+Augustus,1826-1915.+))

Ottawa

Delano, Alonzo. *Alonzo Delano's California Correspondence, Being Letters Hitherto Uncollected from the Ottawa (Illinois) Free Trader and the New Orleans True Delta, 1849-1952*. Sacramento, CA: Sacramento Book Collector's Club, 1952. 155p.

http://memory.loc.gov/cgi-bin/query/r?ammem/calbk:@field(DOCID+@lit(C073T00)):@@@REF

————. *Life on the Plains and among the Diggings, Being Scenes and Adventures of an Overland Journey to California, with Particular Incidents of the Route, Mistakes and Sufferings of the Emigrants, the Indian Tribes, the Present and Future of the Great West*. New York, NY: Miller, Orton & Co., 1857. 384p.

http://memory.loc.gov/cgi-bin/query/r?ammem/calbk:@field(DOCID+@lit(C171T00)):@@@REF

Peoria

Peoria [City Directory]. Peoria, IL: Root, 1859.

http://www.citydirectories.psmedia.com/city/free_statesort.html

Putnam

Dally, Nathan. *Tracks and Trails, or Incidents in the Life of a Minnesota Territorial Pioneer*. Walker, MN: Cass County Pioneer, 1931. 138p.

http://memory.loc.gov/ammem/mdbquery.html

Quincy

Quincy, 1859-60 [City Directory]. Quincy, IL: Williams, 1859.

http://www.citydirectories.psmedia.com/city/free_statesort.html

Randolph County

Randolph County Directory [City Directory]. Randolph County, IL: Montague, 1859.

http://www.citydirectories.psmedia.com/city/free_statesort.html

Rockford

Rockford, 1859-60 [City Directory]. Rockford, IL: Williams', 1859.

http://www.citydirectories.psmedia.com/city/free_statesort.html

Springfield

Houghton, Eliza Poor Donner. *The Expedition of the Donner Party and Its Tragic Fate*. Chicago, IL: McClurg, 1911. 374p.
http://memory.loc.gov/cgi-bin/query/r?ammem/calbkbib:@field(AUTHOR+@band(Houghton,+Eliza+Poor+Donner,1843-1922.+))

Phillips, David L. *Letters from California, Its Mountains, Valleys, Plains, Lakes, Rivers, Climate and Productions. Also Its Railroads, Cities, Towns and People, as Seen in 1876*. Springfield, IL: Illinois State Journal, 1877. 171p.
http://memory.loc.gov/cgi-bin/query/r?ammem/calbkbib:@field(AUTHOR+@band(Phillips,+David+L., 1823-1880.+))

Springfield [City Directory]. Springfield, IL: Buck & Kriegh, 1859.
http://www.citydirectories.psmedia.com/city/free_statesort.html

Will County

Will County Directory, 1859 [City Directory]. Will County, IL: Bailey, 1859.
http://www.citydirectories.psmedia.com/city/free_statesort.html

Indiana

Bell, Horace. *Reminiscences of a Ranger or Early Times in Southern California*. Los Angeles, CA: Yarnell, Caystile & Mathes, 1881. 457p.
http://memory.loc.gov/cgi-bin/query/r?ammem/calbkbib:@field(AUTHOR+@band(Bell,+Horace,1830-1918.+))

Fisher, Richard Swainson. *Indiana in Relation to Its Geography, Statistics, Institutions, County, Topography, etc. with a Reference Index to Colton's Maps of Indiana*. New York, NY: Colton, 1852. 144p.
http://moa.umdl.umich.edu/cgi-bin/moa/sgml/moa-idx?notisid=AFK4266

Holliday, Fernandez C. *Indiana Methodism Being an Account of the Introduction, Progress, and Present Position of Methodism in the State; and also a History of the Literary Institutions under the Care of the Church, with Sketches of the Principal Methodist Educators in the State down to 1872*. Cincinnati, OH: Hitchcock and Walden, 1873. 378p.
http://moa.umdl.umich.edu/cgi-bin/moa/sgml/moa-idx?notisid=AGV9056

Research Outline. Indiana. Salt Lake City, UT: Family History Library, 1997.
http://www.familysearch.com/sg/Indiana.html

Indianapolis

Holloway, William Robeson. *Indianapolis. A Historical and Statistical Sketch of the Railroad City, a Chronicle of Its Social, Municipal, Commercial and Manufacturing Progress, with Full Statistical Tables*. Indianapolis, IN: Indianapolis Journal Print, 1870. 452p.
http://moa.umdl.umich.edu/cgi-bin/moa/sgml/moa-idx?notisid=AJA2982

Indianapolis, 1859-60 [City Directory]. Indianapolis, IN: McEvoy, 1859.
http://www.citydirectories.psmedia.com/city/free_statesort.html

Jefferson County

Jefferson County Directory [City Directory]. Jefferson County, IN: Webb, 1859.
http://www.citydirectories.psmedia.com/city/free_statesort.html

Kosciusko County

Harlan, Jacob Wright. *California '46 to '88*. San Francisco, CA: Bancroft, 1888. 242p.
http://memory.loc.gov/cgi-bin/query/r?ammem/calbkbib:@field(AUTHOR+@band(Harlan,+Jacob+Wright,1828-+))

Lawrenceburgh

Lawrenceburgh, 1859-60 [City Directory]. Lawrenceburgh, IL: McEvoy, 1859.
http://www.citydirectories.psmedia.com/city/free_statesort.html

Logansport

Logansport, 1859-60 [City Directory]. Logansport, IN: Talbott, 1859.
http://www.citydirectories.psmedia.com/city/free_statesort.html

Madison

Madison, 1859-60 [City Directory]. Madison, IN: Williams, 1859.
http://www.citydirectories.psmedia.com/city/free_statesort.html

New Albany

Abbey, James. *California. A Trip across the Plains in the Spring of 1850, Being a Daily Record of Incidents of the Trip and Containing Valuable Information to Emigrants*. New Albany, IN: Kent & Norman, 1850. 63p.
http://memory.loc.gov/cgi-bin/query/r?ammem/calbkbib:@field(AUTHOR+@band(Abbey,+James.+))

New Albany, 1859 [City Directory]. New Albany, IN: Hawes, 1859.
http://www.citydirectories.psmedia.com/city/free_statesort.html

Putnam County

Stone, Henry Lane. *Morgan's Men, a Narrative of Personal Experience*. Louisville, KY: Westerfield Bonte Co., 1919. 36p.
http://metalab.unc.edu/docsouth/stone/menu.html

St. Joseph Valley

Turner, Timothy G. *Gazetteer of the St. Joseph Valley, Michigan and Indiana*. Chicago, IL: Hazlitt & Reed, 1867. 168p.
http://moa.umdl.umich.edu/cgi-bin/moa/sgml/moa-idx?notisid=AFK0736

South Bend

Leeper, David Rohrer. *The Argonauts of 'Forty-nine, some Recollections of the Plains and the Diggings*. South Bend, IN: Stoll, 1894. 146p.
http://memory.loc.gov/cgi-bin/query/r?ammem/calbkbib:@field(AUTHOR+@band(Leeper,+David+Rohrer,1832-1900.+))

Wayne County

Harlan, Jacob Wright. *California '46 to '88*. San Francisco, CA: Bancroft, 1888. 242p.
http://memory.loc.gov/cgi-bin/query/r?ammem/calbkbib:@field(AUTHOR+@band(Harlan,+Jacob+
Wright,1828-+))

Iowa

Curtiss, Daniel S. *Western Portraiture, and Emigrants' Guide, a Description of Wisconsin, Illinois, and Iowa with Remarks on Minnesota and Other Territories*. New York, NY: Colton,
1852. 370p.
http://moa.umdl.umich.edu/cgi-bin/moa/sgml/moa-idx?notisid=AJA3436

Parker, Nathan Howe. *Iowa as It Is in 1855*. Chicago, IL: Keen & Lee, 1855. 282p.
http://moa.umdl.umich.edu/cgi-bin/moa/sgml/moa-idx?notisid=AFK4426

————. *Iowa as It Is in 1856*. Chicago, IL: Keen & Lee, 1856. 356p.
http://moa.umdl.umich.edu/cgi-bin/moa/sgml/moa-idx?notisid=AFK4427

Research Outline. Iowa. Salt Lake City, UT: Family History Library, 1997.
http://www.familysearch.com/sg/Iowa.html

Burlington

Burlington [City Directory]. Burlington, IA: Corse & Son, 1859.
http://www.citydirectories.psmedia.com/city/free_statesort.html

Cedar County

Witham, James W. *Fifty Years on the Firing Line*. Chicago, IL: Author, 1924. 213p.
http://memory.loc.gov/cgi-bin/query/r?ammem/lhbumbib:@field(SUBJ+@band(Agricultural+societies--
United+States.+))

Centerdale (Cedar County)

Witham, James W. *Fifty Years on the Firing Line*. Chicago, IL: Author, 1924. 213p.
http://memory.loc.gov/cgi-bin/query/r?ammem/lhbumbib:@field(SUBJ+@band(Agricultural+societies--
United+States.+))

Davenport

Wilkie, Franc B. *Davenport Past and Present, Including the Early History and Personal and
Anecdotal Reminiscences of Davenport, together with Biographies, Likenesses of Its Prominent Men, Compendious Articles upon Physical, Industrial, Social and Political Characteristics of the City, Statistics of Every Department of Note or Interest*. Davenport, IA:
Luse, Lane & Co., 1858. 376p.
http://moa.umdl.umich.edu/cgi-bin/moa/sgml/moa-idx?notisid=AFK4431

Henry County
Henry County, 1859-60 [City Directory]. Henry County, IN: Bowron, 1859.
http://www.citydirectories.psmedia.com/city/free_statesort.html

Iowa City
Booth, Edmund. *Edmund Booth (1810-1905), Forty-niner, the Life Story of a Deaf Pioneer, Including Portions of His Autobiographical Notes and Gold Rush Diary, and Selections from Family Letters and Reminiscences.* Stockton, CA: San Joaquin Pioneer and Historical Society, 1953. 72p.
http://memory.loc.gov/cgi-bin/query/r?ammem/calbkbib:@field(AUTHOR+@band(Booth,+Edmund,1810-1905.+))

Keokuk
Keokuk, 1859-1860 [City Directory]. Keokuk, IA: Williams, 1859.
http://www.citydirectories.psmedia.com/city/free_statesort.html

Muscatine
Muscatine, 1859-60 [City Directory]. Muscatine, IA: Williams, 1859.
http://www.citydirectories.psmedia.com/city/free_statesort.html

Kansas

Boynton, Charles Brandon. *Journey through Kansas; with Sketches of Nebraska.* Cincinnati, OH: Moore, Wilstach, Keys & Co., 1855. 230p.
http://moa.umdl.umich.edu/cgi-bin/moa/sgml/moa-idx?notisid=ABE4921

Brewerton, George Douglas. *The War in Kansas. A Rough Trip to the Border, among New Homes and a Strange People.* New York, NY: Derby & Jackson, 1856. 424p.
http://moa.umdl.umich.edu/cgi-bin/moa/sgml/moa-idx?notisid=AFK4439

Colt, Miriam Davis. *Went to Kansas, Being a Thrilling Account of an Ill Fated Expedition to That Fairy Land and Its Sad Result, together with a Sketch of the Life of the Author and How the World Goes with Her.* Watertown, NY: Ingalls & Co., 1862. 294p.
http://www.ukans.edu/carrie/kancoll/books/colt/

Cordley, Richard. *Pioneer Days in Kansas.* New York, NY: Pilgrim Press, 1903. 274p.
http://www.ukans.edu/carrie/kancoll/books/cordley_pioneer/cordley.00.html

Crevecoeur, Ferdinand Francis. *Old Settler's Tales, Historical and Biographical Sketches of the Early Settlement and Settlers of Northeastern Pottawatomie and Southwestern Nemaha Counties, Kansas, from Earliest Settlement to the Year 1877.* KS: Onaga Republican, 1902. 162p.
http://www.ukans.edu/carrie/kancoll/books/crevecr/ost.htm

Cutler, William G. *History of the State of Kansas*. Chicago, IL: Andreas, 1883. 1,616p.
http://www.ukans.edu/carrie/kancoll/books/cutler/index.html

Ebbutt, Percy G. *Emigrant Life in Kansas*. London: Swan Sonnenschein and Co., 1886. 237p.
http://www.ukans.edu/carrie/kancoll/books/ebbutt/ebtitle.htm

Fremont, John Charles. *The Life of Col. John Charles Fremont and His Narrative of Explorations and Adventures in Kansas, Nebraska, Oregon and California*. New York, NY: Auburn, Miller, Orton & Mulligan, 1856. 514p.
http://moa.umdl.umich.edu/cgi-bin/moa/sgml/moa-idx?notisid=AAZ9580

Gihon, John H. *Geary and Kansas. Governor Geary's Administration in Kansas, with a Complete History of the Territory until July 1857, Embracing a Full Account of Its Discovery, Geography, Soil, Rivers, Climate, Products, Its Organization as a Territory*. Philadelphia, PA: Rhodes, 1857. 348p.
http://moa.umdl.umich.edu/cgi-bin/moa/sgml/moa-idx?notisid=ABA0699

Gladstone, Thomas H. *The Englishman in Kansas, or Squatter Life and Border Warfare*. New York, NY: Miller & Co., 1857. 384p.
http://moa.umdl.umich.edu/cgi-bin/moa/sgml/moa-idx?notisid=AFK1368

Goodell, William. *The Kansas Struggle of 1856, in Congress and in the Presidential Campaign*. New York, NY: American Abolition Society, 1857. 80p.
http://moa.umdl.umich.edu/cgi-bin/moa/sgml/moa-idx?notisid=ABJ4853

Gregg, Josiah. *Commerce of the Prairies*. New York, NY: Langley, 1844. 2 vols.
http://www.ukans.edu/carrie/kancoll/books/gregg/

Hale, Edward Everett. *Kansas and Nebraska, the History, Geography and Physical Characteristics and Political Position of Those Territories, an Account of the Emigrant Aid Companies and Directions to Emigrants*. Boston, MA: Philips, Sampson and Co., 1854. 262p.
http://moa.umdl.umich.edu/cgi-bin/moa/sgml/moa-idx?notisid=AFK4441

Hutchinson, Clinton Carter. *Resources of Kansas. Fifteen Years Experience*. Topeka, KS: Author, 1871. 288p.
http://moa.umdl.umich.edu/cgi-bin/moa/sgml/moa-idx?notisid=ABA1237

In Perils by Mine Own Countrymen, Three Years on the Kansas Border, by a Clergyman of the Episcopal Church. New York, NY: Auburn, Miller, Orton & Mulligan, 1856. 242p.
http://moa.umdl.umich.edu/cgi-bin/moa/sgml/moa-idx?notisid=ABA0775

Parkman, Francis. *The Oregon Trail, Sketches of Prairie and Rocky Mountain Life*. Philadelphia, PA: Winston, 1931. 388p.
http://xroads.virginia.edu/~HYPER/OREGON/oregon.html

Phillips, William Addison. *The Conquest of Kansas, by Missouri and Her Allies. A History of the Troubles in Kansas, from the Passage of the Organic Act until the Close of July, 1856*. Boston, MA: Philips, Sampson and Co., 1856. 422p.
http://moa.umdl.umich.edu/cgi-bin/moa/sgml/moa-idx?notisid=AFK4442

Research Outline. Kansas. Salt Lake City, UT: Family History Library, 1997.
http://familysearch.org/sg/Kansas.html

Reynolds, John N. *The Twin Hells, A Thrilling Narrative of Life in the Kansas and Missouri Penitentiaries*. Chicago, IL: Donohue, 1890. 331p.
http://www.ukans.edu/carrie/kancoll/books/twnhells/

Robinson, Sarah Tappan Doolittle. *Kansas, Its Interior and Exterior Life, Including a Full View of Its Settlement, Political History, Social Life, Climate, Soil, Productions, Scenery etc.* Boston, MA: Crosby, Nichols and Co., 1856. 386p.
http://moa.umdl.umich.edu/cgi-bin/moa/sgml/moa-idx?notisid=AJA3508
http://www.ukans.edu/carrie/kancoll/books/robinson/r_intro.htm

Ropes, Hannah Anderson. *Six Months in Kansas.* Boston, MA: Jewett, 1856.
http://www.ukans.edu/carrie/kancoll/books/ropes/index.html

Spring, Leverett Wilson. *Kansas, the Prelude to the War for the Union.* Boston, MA: Houghton Mifflin, 1907. 340p.
http://www.ukans.edu/carrie/kancoll/books/spring/

Stimson, Hiram K. *From the Stage Coach to the Pulpit, Being an Autobiographical Sketch, with Incidents and Anecdotes of Elder H. K. Stimson, the Veteran Pioneer of Western New York, Now of Kansas.* Saint Louis, MO: Campbell, 1874. 430p.
http://moa.umdl.umich.edu/cgi-bin/moa/sgml/moa-idx?notisid=AJK2081

Thayer, William Makepeace. *Marvels of the New West. A Vivid Portrayal of the Stupendous Marvels in the Vast Wonderland West of the Missouri River.* Norwich, CT: Henry Bill Publishing Co., 1890. 715p.
http://www.ukans.edu/carrie/kancoll/books/thayer/index.html

Webb, William Edward. *Buffalo Land, an Authentic Account of the Discoveries, Adventures and Mishaps of a Scientific and Sporting Party in the Wild West, with Graphic Descriptions of the Country, the Red Man, Savage and Civilized, Hunting the Buffalo, Antelope etc. Replete with Information, Wit, and Humor. The Appendix Comprising a Complete Guide for Sportsmen and Emigrants.* Cincinnati, OH: Hannaford, 1872. 504p.
http://moa.umdl.umich.edu/cgi-bin/moa/sgml/moa-idx?notisid=AKR1255

Atichson

Atchison, 1859-60 [City Directory]. Atchison, KS: Sutherland & McEvoy, 1859.
http://www.citydirectories.psmedia.com/city/free_statesort.html

Johnson County

Blair, Ed. *History of Johnson County, Kansas.* Lawrence, KS: Standard Publishing Co., 1915. 469p.
http://www.ukans.edu/carrie/kancoll/books/spring/

Lawrence

Cordley, Richard. *The Lawrence Massacre by a Band of Missouri Ruffians under Quantrell, August 21, 1863, 150 Men Killed, Eighty Women Made Widows and 250 Children Made Orphans.* Lawrence, KS: Broughton Publisher, 1865. 36p.
http://www.ukans.edu/carrie/kancoll/books/cordley_massacre/quantrel.raid.html

Doy, John. *The Narrative of John Doy, of Lawrence, Kansas.* New York, NY: Holman, 1860. 136p.
http://moa.umdl.umich.edu/cgi-bin/moa/sgml/moa-idx?notisid=ABJ5091

Kentucky

Browne, John Ross. *Crusoe's Island*. New York, NY: Harper, 1864. 436p.
http://memory.loc.gov/cgi-bin/query/r?ammem/calbkbib:@field(AUTHOR+@band(Browne,+John+Ross, 1821-1875.+))

Kentucky State Directory, 1859-60 [City Directory]. Lexington, KY: Williams, 1859.
http://www.citydirectories.psmedia.com/city/free_statesort.html

Research Outline. Kentucky. Salt Lake City, UT: Family History Library, 1997.
http://familysearch.org/sg/Kentucky.html

Bath County
Stone, Henry Lane. *Morgan's Men, a Narrative of Personal Experience*. Louisville, KY: Westerfield Bonte Co., 1919. 36p.
http://metalab.unc.edu/docsouth/stone/menu.html

Berea
Fee, John Gregg. *Autobiography of John G. Fee, Berea, Kentucky*. Chicago, IL: National Christian Association, 1891. 211p.
http://metalab.unc.edu/docsouth/fee/menu.html

Carthage
Bryan, George W. *The Lure of the Past, the Present and Future*. Los Angeles, CA: Newton, 1911. 139p.
http://memory.loc.gov/cgi-bin/query/r?ammem/calbkbib:@field(AUTHOR+@band(Bryan,+George+W.+))

Henderson County
McCray, S. J. *Life of Mary F. McCray, Born and Raised a Slave in the State of Kentucky, By Her Husband and Son*. Lima, OH: Author, 1898. 115p.
http://metalab.unc.edu/docsouth/mccray/menu.html

Knott County
Burton, Thomas William. *What Experience Has Taught Me, an Autobiography of Thomas William Burton, Doctor of Medicine, Springfield, Ohio*. Cincinnati, OH: Jennings and Graham, 1910, 126p.
http://metalab.unc.edu/docsouth/burtont/menu.html

Letcher County
Burton, Thomas William. *What Experience Has Taught Me, an Autobiography of Thomas William Burton, Doctor of Medicine, Springfield, Ohio*. Cincinnati, OH: Jennings and Graham, 1910, 126p.
http://metalab.unc.edu/docsouth/burtont/menu.html

Lexington

Brown, Josephine. *Biography of an American Bondsman, Written by His Daughter.* Boston, MA: Wallcut, 1856. 104p.
http://digilib.nypl.org/dynaweb/digs/wwm975/

Brown, William Wells. *Narrative of William W. Brown, an American Slave.* 3rd ed. London: Charles Gilpin, 1849. 168p.
http://metalab.unc.edu/docsouth/brownw/menu.html

Graves, Jackson Alpheus. *My Seventy Years in California, 1857-1927.* Los Angeles, CA: Times Mirror Press, 1927. 478p.
http://memory.loc.gov/cgi-bin/query/r?ammem/calbkbib:@field(AUTHOR+@band(Graves,+Jackson+Alpheus,1852-1933.+))

Lexington, 1859-60 [City Directory]. Lexington, KY: Williams, 1859.
http://www.citydirectories.psmedia.com/city/free_statesort.html

Louisville

Louisville, 1859-60 [City Directory]. Louisville, KY: Tanner, 1859.
http://www.citydirectories.psmedia.com/city/free_statesort.html

Madison County

Burton, Thomas William. *What Experience Has Taught Me, an Autobiography of Thomas William Burton, Doctor of Medicine, Springfield, Ohio.* Cincinnati, OH: Jennings and Graham, 1910, 126p.
http://metalab.unc.edu/docsouth/burtont/menu.html

Paris

Young, Lot D. *Reminiscences of a Soldier of the Orphan Brigade, by Lieut. L. D. Young, Paris, Kentucky.* Louisville, KY: Courier Journal Print Job, 1918. 99p.
http://metalab.unc.edu/docsouth/young/menu.html

Louisiana

Dennett, Daniel. *Louisiana as It Is, Its Topography and Material Resources; Its Cotton, Sugar Cane, Rice and Tobacco Fields; Its Corn and Grain Lands . . . Reliable Information for . . . Any Who May Desire to Settle or Purchase Lands in the Gulf States.* New Orleans, LA: Eureka Press, 1876. 288p.
http://moa.umdl.umich.edu/cgi-bin/moa/sgml/moa-idx?notisid=AAW3265

Marcy, Randolph Barnes. *Exploration of the Red River of Louisiana in the Year 1852.* Washington, DC: Tucker, 1854. 390p.
http://moa.umdl.umich.edu/cgi-bin/moa/sgml/moa-idx?notisid=ABB2532

Northup, Solomon. *Narrative of Solomon Northup, a Citizen of New York, Kidnapped in Washington City in 1841, Rescued in 1853, from a Cotton Plantation near the Red River, in Louisiana*. Auburn, NY: Derby and Miller, 1853. 336p.
http://metalab.unc.edu/docsouth/northup/menu.html

Research Outline. Louisiana. Salt Lake City, UT: Family History Library, 1997.
http://familysearch.org/sg/Louisiana.html

Taylor, Richard. *Destruction and Reconstruction, Personal Experiences of the Late War*. New York, NY: Appleton, 1879. 274p.
http://metalab.unc.edu/docsouth/taylor/menu.html

Baton Rouge
Dawson, Sarah Morgan. *A Confederate Girl's Diary*. Boston, MA: Houghton, Mifflin, 1913. 441p.
http://metalab.unc.edu/docsouth/dawson/menu.html

Bayou Lafourche
Fearn, Frances Hewitt. *Diary of a Refugee*. New York, NY: Moffat, Yard and Co. 1910. 149p.
http://metalab.unc.edu/docsouth/fearn/menu.html

East Feliciana Parish
Merrick, Caroline Elizabeth Thomas. *Old Times in Dixie Land, a Southern Matron's Memories*. New York, NY: Grafton, 1901. 241p.
http://metalab.unc.edu/docsouth/merrick/menu.html

New Orleans
Delano, Alonzo. *Alonzo Delano's California Correspondence, Being Letters Hitherto Uncollected from the Ottawa (Illinois) Free Trader and the New Orleans True Delta, 1849-1952*. Sacramento, CA: Sacramento Book Collector's Club, 1952. 155p.
http://memory.loc.gov/cgi-bin/query/r?ammem/calbk:@field(DOCID+@lit(C073T00)):@@@REF

————. *Life on the Plains and among the Diggings, Being Scenes and Adventures of an Overland Journey to California, with Particular Incidents of the Route, Mistakes and Sufferings of the Emigrants, the Indian Tribes, the Present and Future of the Great West*. New York, NY: Miller, Orton & Co., 1857. 384p.
http://memory.loc.gov/cgi-bin/query/r?ammem/calbk:@field(DOCID+@lit(C171T00)):@@@REF

Episcopal Church, Commission of Home Missions to Colored People. New York, NY: Church, 1875, 1876.
9th Annual Report, 1873-74. 20p.
http://memory.loc.gov/cgi-bin/query/r?ammem/murray:@field(FLD001+91898515+):@@@REF

11th Annual Report, 1875-76. 24p.
http://memory.loc.gov/cgi-bin/query/r?ammem/murray:@field(FLD001+91898514+):@@@REF

Mallard, Robert Q. *Plantation Life before Emancipation*. Richmond, VA: Whittet & Shepperson, 1892. 237p.
http://metalab.unc.edu/docsouth/mallard/menu.html

Morgan, James Morris. *Recollections of a Rebel Reefer*. Boston, MA: Houghton Mifflin, 1917. 492p.
http://metalab.unc.edu/docsouth/morganjames/menu.html

New Orleans [City Directory]. New Orleans, LA: Gardner, various.
1859; 1860; 1861; 1866.
http://www.citydirectories.psmedia.com/city/free_statesort.html

New Orleans, 1860-61 [City Directory]. New Orleans, LA: Hellier, 1860.
http://www.citydirectories.psmedia.com/city/free_statesort.html

Ripley, Eliza Moore Chinn McHatton. *From Flag to Flag, a Woman's Adventures and Experiences in the South during the War, in Mexico and in Cuba*. New York, NY: Appleton, 1889. 296p.
http://metalab.unc.edu/docsouth/ripleyflag/menu.html

———. *Social Life in Old New Orleans, Being Recollections of My Girlhood*. New York, NY: Appleton, 1912. 332p.
http://metalab.unc.edu/docsouth/ripley/menu.html

Port Hudson
Bacon, Edward. *Among the Cotton Thieves*. Detroit, MI: Free Press Steam Book, 1867. 300p.
http://moa.umdl.umich.edu/cgi-bin/moa/sgml/moa-idx?notisid=ACK4755

Maine

Clubb, Henry S. *Results of Prohibition in Connecticut, Being Special Returns from Every County as to the Effects of the Maine Liquor Law, containing Contributions from the Governor and Upward of Fifty Clergymen, Judges, Editors and Private Citizens*. New York, NY: Fowlers and Wells, 1855. 82p.
http://moa.umdl.umich.edu/cgi-bin/moa/sgml/moa-idx?notisid=AHL9039

Research Outline. Maine. Salt Lake City, UT: Family History Library, 1997.
http://familysearch.org/sg/Maine.html

Talcott, Sebastian Visscher. *Genealogical Notes of New York and New England Families*. Albany, NY: Weed, Parsons & Co., 1883. 747p.
http://moa.cit.cornell.edu/dienst/moabrowse.fly/MOA-JOURNALS2:TALC-0006/3/1:TIFF2GIF:100

Vinton, John Adams. *The Giles Memorial. Genealogical Memoirs of the Families Bearing the Names of Giles, Gould, Holmes, Jennison, Leonard, Lindall, Curwen, Marshall, Robinson, Sampson and Webb, also Genealogical Sketches of the Pool, Very, Tarr and other Families, with a History of Pemaquid, Ancient and Modern, Some Account of Early Settlements in Maine and Some Details of Indian Warfare*. Boston, MA: Dutton, 1864. 600p.
http://genweb.net/~blackwell/ma/Gyles1864/

Bangor
Bangor [City Directory]. Bangor, ME: Smith, 1859.
http://www.citydirectories.psmedia.com/city/free_statesort.html

Pond, William Chauncey. *Gospel Pioneering, Reminiscences of Early Congregationalism in California, 1833-1920*. Oberlin, OH: New Printing Co., 1921. 191p.
http://memory.loc.gov/cgi-bin/query/r?ammem/calbkbib:@field(AUTHOR+@band(Pond,+William+ Chauncey,1830-1925.+))

Stephenson, Isaac. *Recollections of a Long Life, 1829-1915*. Chicago, IL: Donnelley & Sons, 1915. 264p.
http://memory.loc.gov/ammem/mdbquery.html

Belfast

Cross, Lillian A. *Appreciation of Loved Ones Who Made Life Rich for Many. My Father, John Francis Cross, My Mother, Sarah Jane Cross*. Oakland, CA: Tribune Press, 1933. 101p.
http://memory.loc.gov/cgi-bin/query/r?ammem/calbkbib:@field(AUTHOR+@band(Cross,+Lilian+A.+))

Bloomfield

Folsom, William Henry Carman. *Fifty Years in the Northwest*. St. Paul, MN: Pioneer Press Co., 1888. 763p.
http://memory.loc.gov/cgi-bin/query/r?ammem/lhbum:@field(DOCID+@lit(01070T000)):@@@REF

Bucksport

Buck, Franklin Agustus. *A Yankee Trader in the Gold Rush, the Letters of Franklin A. Buck*. Boston, MA: Houghton, Mifflin, 1930. 294p.
http://memory.loc.gov/cgi-bin/query/r?ammem/calbkbib:@field(AUTHOR+@band(Buck,+Franklin+ Agustus,1826-1909.+))

Eastport

Grimke, Francis J. *Anne M. Purvis*. Washington, DC: Colored Orphans Home, 1899. 18p.
http://memory.loc.gov/cgi-bin/query/r?ammem/aap:@field(SUBJ+@band(Funeral+addresses--Washington ++D.C.+--1899.+))

Norridgewock

Smith, Sarah Hathaway Bixby. *Adobe Days, Being the Truthful Narrative of the Events in the Life of a California Girl on a Sheep Ranch and in El Pueblo de Nuestra Senora de Los Angeles while It Was Yet a Small and Humble Town, together with an Account of How Three Young Men from Maine in Eighteen Hundred and Fifty-three Drove Sheep and Cattle across the Plains, Mountains and Deserts from Illinois to the Pacific Coast, and the Strange Prophecy of Admiral Thatcher about San Pedro Harbor*. Cedar Rapids, IA: Torch Press, 1925. 208p.
http://memory.loc.gov/cgi-bin/query/r?ammem/calbkbib:@field(AUTHOR+@band(Smith,+Sarah+ Hathaway+Bixby,1871-1935.+))

Waterville

Ellis, Henry Hiram. *From the Kennebec to California, Reminiscences of a California Pioneer*. Los Angeles, CA: Lewis, 1959. 88p.
http://memory.loc.gov/cgi-bin/query/r?ammem/calbkbib:@field(AUTHOR+@band(Ellis,+Henry+Hiram, 1829-1909.+))

Maryland

Bluett, Thomas. *Some Memoirs of the Life of Job, the Son of Solomon the Highest Priest of Boonda in Africa, Who Was a Slave about Two Years in Maryland, and afterwards Being Brought to England Was Set Free and Sent to His Native Land in the Year 1734.* London: Ford, 1734. 63p.
http://metalab.unc.edu/docsouth/bluett/menu.html

Felton, Rebecca Latimer. *County Life in Georgia in the Days of My Youth.* Atlanta, GA: Index Printing Co., 1919. 303p.
http://metalab.unc.edu/docsouth/felton/menu.html

Lame, J. S. *Maryland Slavery and Maryland Chivalry, Containing the Letters of Junius, Originally Published in Zion's Herald, together with a Brief History of the Circumstances that Prompted the Publication of Those Letters. Also a Short Account of the Persecution Suffered by the Author at the Hands of Southern Slaveholders.* Philadelphia, PA: Collins, 1858. 60p.
http://moa.umdl.umich.edu/cgi-bin/moa/sgml/moa-idx?notisid=ABJ5141

Memoir of Old Elizabeth a Coloured Woman. Philadelphia, PA: Collins Printer, 1863. 19p.
http://digilib.nypl.org/dynaweb/digs/wwm97259/

Research Outline. Maryland. Salt Lake City, UT: Family History Library, 1997.
http://familysearch.org/sg/Maryland.html

Baltimore

Baltimore, 1859-60 [City Directory]. Baltimore, MD: Directory Co., 1859.
http://www.citydirectories.psmedia.com/city/free_statesort.html

Catalogue of Pupils of Saint Frances' Academy for Colored Girls, under the Direction of the Sisters of Providence, for the Academic Year 1867-8, Incorporated 1867. Baltimore, MD: John Murphy & Co., 1868. 24p.
http://memory.loc.gov/cgi-bin/query/r?ammem/murray:@field(FLD001+91898522+):@@@REF

Hayes, Benjamin Ignatius. *Pioneer Notes from the Diaries of Judge Benjamin Hayes, 1849-1875.* Los Angeles, CA: Author, 1929. 307p.
http://memory.loc.gov/cgi-bin/query/r?ammem/calbkbib:@field(AUTHOR+@band(Hayes,+Benjamin+Ignatius,1815-1877.+))

Hughes, Thomas. *A Boy's Experience in the Civil War, 1860-1865.* Baltimore, MD: Daily Record Co., 1904. 55p.
http://metalab.unc.edu/docsouth/hughest/menu.html

Shepherd, Henry Elliot. *Narrative of Prison Life at Baltimore and Johnson's Island, Ohio.* Baltimore, MD: Commercial Printing, 1917. 22p.
http://metalab.unc.edu/docsouth/shepherd/menu.html

Tyson, James Lawrence. *Diary of a Physician in California, Being the Results of Actual Experience Including Notes of the Journey by Land and Water and Observations on the Climate, Soil, Resources of the Country*. New York, NY: Appleton, 1850. 92p.
http://memory.loc.gov/cgi-bin/query/r?ammem/calbkbib:@field(AUTHOR+@band(Tyson,+James+Lawrence.+))

Calvert County

Ball, Charles. *Fifty Years in Chains, or the Life of an American Slave*. New York, NY: Dayton, 1859. 430p.
http://metalab.unc.edu/docsouth/ball/menu.html

Cambridge

Bradford, Sarah H. *Harriet, the Moses of Her People*. New York, NY: Lockwood, 1886. 149p.
http://metalab.unc.edu/docsouth/harriet/menu.html

Emmitsburg

Bunkley, Josephine M. *The Testimony of an Escaped Novice from the Sisterhood of St. Joseph, Emmittsburg, Maryland, the Mother House of the Sisters of Charity in the United States*. New York, NY: Harper, 1855. 348p.
http://moa.umdl.umich.edu/cgi-bin/moa/sgml/moa-idx?notisid=AGU6805

Frederick

Frederick, 1859-60 [City Directory]. Frederick, MD: Williams, 1859.
http://www.citydirectories.psmedia.com/city/free_statesort.html

Schaeffer, Luther Melanchthon. *Sketches of Travels in South America, Mexico and California*. New York, NY: Egbert, 1860. 247p.
http://memory.loc.gov/cgi-bin/query/r?ammem/calbkbib:@field(AUTHOR+@band(Schaeffer,+Luther+Melanchthon.+))

Kent County

Mason, Isaac. *Life of Isaac Mason as a Slave*. Worcester, MA: Author, 1893. 74p.
http://metalab.unc.edu/docsouth/mason/menu.html

Long Green

Smith, Amanda. *An Autobiography, the Story of the Lord's Dealings with Mrs. Amanda Smith, the Colored Evangelist, Containing an Account of Her Life Work of Faith, and Her Travels in America, England, Ireland, Scotland, India and Africa, as an Independent Missionary*. Chicago, IL: Meyer and Brother, 1893. 506p.
http://digilib.nypl.org/dynaweb/digs/wwm97264/

Mount Auburn

Ellis, William Turner. *Memories, My Seventy-two Years in the Romantic County of Yuba, California*. Eugene, OR: University of Oregon, 1939. 308p.
http://memory.loc.gov/cgi-bin/query/r?ammem/calbkbib:@field(AUTHOR+@band(Ellis,+William+Turner,1866-+))

Talbot County

Douglass, Frederick. *Life and Times of Frederick Douglass, His Early Life as a Slave, His Escape from Bondage and His Complete History to the Present Time.* Hartford, CT: Park, 1881. 516p.
http://metalab.unc.edu/docsouth/douglasslife/menu.html

Washington County

Green, Fletcher M. *Ferry Hill Plantation Journal, January 4, 1838-January 15, 1839 (by John Blackford, 1771-1839).* Chapel Hill, NC: University of North Carolina Press, 1961. 139p.
http://metalab.unc.edu/docsouth/blackford/menu.html

Massachusetts

Adams, Brooks. *The Emancipation of Massachusetts.* Boston, MA: Houghton Mifflin, 1887. 388p.
http://moa.cit.cornell.edu/dienst/moabrowse.fly/MOA-JOURNALS2:ADAM-0033/3/1:TIFF2GIF:100?,,

Bacon, Leonard. *The Genesis of the New England Churches.* New York, NY: Harper, 1874. 485p.
http://moa.cit.cornell.edu/dienst/moabrowse.fly/MOA-JOURNALS2:BACO-0030/5/1:TIFF2GIF:100

Bay State Monthly (1884-1886). Boston, MA: J. N. McClintock & Co. 3 vols.
http://moa.cit.cornell.edu/MOA/MOA-JOURNALS2/BAY.html

Bradford, William. *Of Plymouth Plantation, 1620-1647.* New York, NY: Knopf, 1952. 448p.
http://members.aol.com/calebj/bradford_journal.html

Douglass, William. *A Discourse Concerning the Currencies of the British Plantations in America, Especially with Regard to Their Paper Money, More Particularly in Relation to the Province of Massachusetts Bay in New England.* 1740. Unknown. 3p.
http://www.people.virginia.edu/~rwm3n/webdoc2.html

Drake, Samuel Adams. *Nooks and Corners of the New England Coast.* New York, NY: Harper & Brothers, 1875. 464p.
http://moa.umdl.umich.edu/cgi-bin/moa/sgml/moa-idx?notisid=AJA1974

Ellis, George Edward. *The Puritan Age and Rule in the Colony of the Massachusetts Bay, 1629-1685.* Boston, MA: Houghton, Mifflin, 1888. 576p.
http://moa.cit.cornell.edu/dienst/moabrowse.fly/MOA-JOURNALS2:ELLI-0036/5/1:TIFF2GIF:100

Hallowell, Norwood Penrose. *The Negro as a Soldier in the War of the Rebellion.* Boston, MA: Little, Brown & Co., 1897. 29p.
http://memory.loc.gov/cgi-bin/query/r?ammem/murray:@field(FLD001+22002319+):@@@REF

History of the Massachusetts Horticultural Society, 1829-1878. Boston, MA: Society, 1880. 564p.
http://chla.mannlib.cornell.edu/cgi-bin/chla/viewer.cgi?docid=title2c.chla.mannlib.cornell/0656mass&
format=1:75-GIF&section=Title+Page

Hosmer, James Kendall. *The Life of Thomas Hutchinson, Royal Governor of the Province of Massachusetts Bay.* Boston, MA: Houghton Mifflin, 1896. 454p.
http://moa.cit.cornell.edu/dienst/moabrowse.fly/MOA-JOURNALS2:HOSM-0221/5/1:TIFF2GIF:100

Howe, Daniel Wait. *The Puritan Republic of the Massachusetts Bay in New England.* Indianapolis, IN: Bowen, Merrill Co., 1899. 424p.
http://moa.cit.cornell.edu/dienst/moabrowse.fly/MOA-JOURNALS2:HOWE-0039/5/1:TIFF2GIF:100

Jones, Augustine. *The Life and Work of Thomas Dudley, the Second Governor of Massachusetts.* Boston, MA: Houghton, Mifflin, 1899. 486p.
http://moa.cit.cornell.edu/dienst/moabrowse.fly/MOA-JOURNALS2:JONE-0212/5/1:TIFF2GIF:100

Knapp, Samuel L. *Biographical Sketches of Eminent Lawyers, Statesmen, and Men of Letters.* Boston, MA: Richardson and Lord, 1821. 360p.
http://moa.cit.cornell.edu/dienst/moabrowse.fly/MOA-JOURNALS2:KNAP-0031/3/1:TIFF2GIF:100

Massachusetts Anti-Slavery Society Board of Managers. Boston, MA: Andrews, Prentiss & Studley, 1845.
13th *Annual Report.* 1845. 81p.
http://memory.loc.gov/cgi-bin/query/r?ammem/aap:@FIELD(AUTHOR+@band(+Massachusetts+Anti+
Slavery+Society.++Board+of+Managers.))

Massachusetts State Directory [City Directory]. Boston, MA: Adams, Sampson & Co., 1859.
http://www.citydirectories.psmedia.com/city/free_statesort.html

Research Outline. Massachusetts. Salt Lake City, UT: Family History Library, 1997.
http://familysearch.org/sg/Massachusetts.html

Talcott, S. V. *Genealogical Notes of New York and New England Families.* Albany, NY: Weed, Parsons & Co., 1883. 747p.
http://moa.cit.cornell.edu/dienst/moabrowse.fly/MOA-JOURNALS2:TALC-0006/3/1:TIFF2GIF:100

Amherst

Clappe, Louise Amelia Knapp Smith. *The Shirley Letters from California Mines in 1851-52.* San Francisco, CA: Russell, 1922. 350p.
http://memory.loc.gov/cgi-bin/query/r?ammem/calbkbib:@field(AUTHOR+@band(Clappe,+Louise+
Amelia+Knapp+Smith,1819-1906.+))

Jackson, Helen Maria Fiske Hunt. *Glimpses of California and the Mission.* Boston, MA: Little, Brown & Co., 1902. 292p.
http://memory.loc.gov/cgi-bin/query/r?ammem/calbkbib:@field(AUTHOR+@band(Jackson,+Helen+
[Maria+Fiske]+Hunt,1831-1885.+))

Andover

Abbot, Abiel and Ephraim Abbot. *Genealogical Register of the Descendants of George Abbot of Andover, George Abbot of Rowley, Thomas Abbot of Andover, Arthur Abbot of Ipswich, Robert Abbot of Branford, CT and George Abbot, of Norwalk, CT.* Boston, MA: James Munroe, 1847. 197p.
http://genweb.net/~books/ma/abbot1847/

Raymond, Samuel. *The Record of Andover in the Revolution*. Andover, MA: R. W. Draper, 1875. 240p.
http://moa.umdl.umich.edu/cgi-bin/moa/sgml/moa-idx?notisid=AFJ7552

Attleboro

Daggett, John. *A Sketch of the History of Attleborough, from Its Settlement to the Division*. Boston, MA: Samuel Usher, 1894. 788p.
http://genweb.net/~blackwell/ma/attleboro1894/

Vital Records of Attleborough, Massachusetts to the End of the Year 1849. Salem, MA: Essex Institute, 1934. 479p.
http://genweb.net/~blackwell/ma/attleboroVR/

Boston

Boston [City Directory]. Boston, MA: Adams, Sampson & Co., various. 1859-1866.
http://www.citydirectories.psmedia.com/city/free_statesort.html

Boston [City Directory]. Boston, MA: Damrell, various.
1859; 1860-61.
http://www.citydirectories.psmedia.com/city/free_statesort.html

Boston Slave Riot, and Trial of Anthony Burns, Containing the Report of the Faneuil Hall Meeting, the Murder of Batchelder, Theodore Parker's Lesson for the Day, Speeches of Counsel on Both Sides, Corrected by Themselves, a Verbatim Report of Judge Loring's Decision and Detailed Account of the Embarkation. Boston, MA: Fetridge and Co., 1854. 98p.
http://moa.umdl.umich.edu/cgi-bin/moa/sgml/moa-idx?notisid=ABT7939

Briggs, Lloyd Vernon. *California and the West, 1881 and later*. Boston, MA: Wright & Potter, 1931. 214p.
http://memory.loc.gov/cgi-bin/query/r?ammem/calbkbib:@field(AUTHOR+@band(Briggs,+Lloyd+Vernon,1863-1941.+))

Drake, Samuel Adams. *Old Landmarks and Historic Personages of Boston*. Boston: Osgood, 1873. 502p.
http://moa.umdl.umich.edu/cgi-bin/moa/sgml/moa-idx?notisid=AFJ7482

Roper, Moses. *A Narrative of the Adventures and Escape of Moses Roper, from American Slavery*. Philadelphia, PA: Merrihew & Gunn, 1838. 89p.
http://metalab.unc.edu/docsouth/roper/menu.html

Rowlandson, Mary. *Narrative of the Captivity and Restoration of Mrs. Mary Rowlandson*. 1862. 316p.
ftp://uiarchive.cso.uiuc.edu/pub/etext/gutenberg/etext97/crmmr10.txt
http://tom.cs.cmu.edu/cgi-bin/book/lookup?num=851

The Stranger's New Guide through Boston and Vicinity. Being a Complete Handbook, Directing Visitors Where to Go, When to Go, and How to Go. Boston, MA: Williams, 1869. 100p.
http://moa.umdl.umich.edu/cgi-bin/moa/sgml/moa-idx?notisid=AFJ7520

Braintree

Bates, Samuel A. *Records of the Town of Braintree, 1640 to 1793*. Randolph, MA: Huxford, 1886. 939p.
http://genweb.net/~braintree/

Pattee, William S. *A History of Old Braintree and Quincy, with a Sketch of Randolph and Holbrook*. Quincy, MA: Green & Prescott, 1878. 600p.
http://genweb.net/~blackwell/ma/braintree1876/brntr001.htm

Bridgewater

Kingman, Bradford. *History of North Bridgewater, Plymouth County, Massachusetts, from Its First Settlement to the Present Time with Family Registers*. Boston, MA: Author, 1866, 696p.
http://genweb.net/~blackwell/ma/bridgewaternorth/brdgwtrintro.html

Bristol

Hurd, Duane Hamilton. *History of Bristol County, Massachusetts, with Biographical Sketches of Many of Its Pioneers and Prominent Men*. Philadelphia, PA: Philadelphia, J. W. Lewis & Co., 1883. 922p.
http://genweb.net/~blackwell/ma/bristol/b000toc.html

Brockton

Kingman, Bradford. *History of North Bridgewater, Plymouth County, Massachusetts, from Its First Settlement to the Present Time with Family Registers*. Boston, MA: Author, 1866, 696p.
http://genweb.net/~blackwell/ma/bridgewaternorth/brdgwtrintro.html

Cambridge

Cambridge [City Directory]. Boston, MA: Baldwin, 1859.
http://www.citydirectories.psmedia.com/city/free_statesort.html

Clark, Susie Champney. *The Round Trip from the Hub to the Golden Gate*. Boston, MA: Lee & Shepard, 1890. 193p.
http://memory.loc.gov/cgi-bin/query/r?ammem/calbkbib:@field(AUTHOR+@band(Clark,+Susie+Champney,1856-+))

Harvard Alumni Association. *The Necrology of Harvard College. 1869-1872*. Cambridge, MA: J. Wilson & Son, 1872. 134p.
http://moa.umdl.umich.edu/cgi-bin/moa/sgml/moa-idx?notisid=AGE3372

Palmer, Joseph. Necrology of Alumni of Harvard College, 1851-52 to 1862-63. Boston, MA: J. Wilson and Son, 1864. 544p.
http://moa.umdl.umich.edu/cgi-bin/moa/sgml/moa-idx?notisid=AGE3371

Pond, William Chauncey. *Gospel Pioneering, Reminiscences of Early Congregationalism in California, 1833-1920*. Oberlin, OH: New Printing Co., 1921. 191p.
http://memory.loc.gov/cgi-bin/query/r?ammem/calbkbib:@field(AUTHOR+@band(Pond,+William+Chauncey,1830-1925.+))

Rindge, Frederick Hastings. *Happy Days in Southern California*. Cambridge, MA: Author, 1898. 199p.
http://memory.loc.gov/cgi-bin/query/r?ammem/calbkbib:@field(AUTHOR+@band(Rindge,+Frederick+Hastings,1857-1905.+))

Chicopee

Booth, Edmund. *Edmund Booth (1810-1905), Forty-niner, the Life Story of a Deaf Pioneer, Including Portions of His Autobiographical Notes and Gold Rush Diary, and Selections*

from Family Letters and Reminiscences. Stockton, CA: San Joaquin Pioneer and Historical
  Society, 1953. 72p.
http://memory.loc.gov/cgi-bin/query/r?ammem/calbkbib:@field(AUTHOR+@band(Booth,+Edmund,1810-1905.+))

Cohasset
Baldwin, Thomas W. *Vital Records of Cohasset, Massachusetts to the Year 1850.* Boston, MA:
  New England Historic Genealogical Society, 1916. 237p.
http://genweb.net/~blackwell/ma/cohassetVR/

Davenport, George Lyman and Elizabeth Osgood Davenport. *The Genealogies of the Families
  of Cohasset, Massachusetts.* Cohasset, MA: Committee of Town History, 1909. 631p.
http://genweb.net/~blackwell/ma/cohasset/c1909.html

Dorchester
Frothingham, Richard. *Oration Delivered before the City Government and Citizens of Boston.*
  Boston, MA: Rockwell & Churchill, printers, 1874. 56p.
http://moa.umdl.umich.edu/cgi-bin/moa/sgml/moa-idx?notisid=ABP2857

Harland, Marion. *Marion Harland's Autobiography, the Story of a Long Life.* New York, NY:
  Harper, 1910. 498p.
http://metalab.unc.edu/docsouth/harland/menu.html

Dover
Smith, Frank. *The Genealogical History of Dover, Massachusetts, Tracing all Families Previous to 1850 and Many Families That Have Lived in the Town Since with an Account of the Habits and Customs of the People.* Dover, MA: Historical and Natural History Society,
  1917. 268p.
http://genweb.net/~blackwell/ma/dover/

Essex
Felt, Joseph Barlow. *History of Ipswich, Essex and Hamilton.* Cambridge, MA: C. Folsom,
  1834. 304p.
http://www.geocities.com/~jslaughter/HistoryOfIpswich.html

Fall River
Fall River [City Directory]. Boston, MA: Adams, Sampson & Co., 1859.
http://www.citydirectories.psmedia.com/city/free_statesort.html

Fitchburg
Fitchburg [City Directory]. Fitchburg, MA: Brown's, 1859.
http://www.citydirectories.psmedia.com/city/free_statesort.html

Framingham
Barry, William. *A History of Framingham, Massachusetts, Including the Plantation from 1640 to the Present Time, with an Appendix Containing a Notice of Sudbury and Its First Proprietors, also a Register of the Inhabitants of Framingham before 1800 with Genealogical Sketches.* Boston, MA: James Monroe, 1847. 456p.
http://genweb.net/~blackwell/ma/framingham/

Temple, J. H. *A Genealogical Register of Framingham Families Including All Who Took Up Residence in Town before AD 1860.* Framingham, MA: Town of Framingham, 1867.
http://genweb.net/~blackwell/ma/framinghamgen/

Franklin
Blake, Mortimer. *A History of the Town of Franklin, Mass., from Its Settlement to the Completion of Its First Century, 2d March, 1878 with Genealogical Notices of Its Earliest Families, Sketches of Its Professional Men, and a Report of the Centennial Celebration.* Franklin, MA: Town of Franklin, 1879. 289p.
http://genweb.net/~blackwell/ma/franklin1878/

Freetown
Herbert, Mary Phillips. *Freetown, Mass. Marriage Records, (Bristol County), 1686-1844.* Glendale, CA: Margaret Phillips Creer, 1934. 63p.
http://genweb.net/~blackwell/ma/freetown1934/

Hamilton
Felt, Joseph Barlow. *History of Ipswich, Essex and Hamilton.* Cambridge, MA: C. Folsom, 1834. 304p.
http://www.geocities.com/~jslaughter/HistoryOfIpswich.html

Haverhill
Haverhill [City Directory]. Haverhill, MA: Harriman, 1859.
http://www.citydirectories.psmedia.com/city/free_statesort.html

Hingham
History of Hingham. Hingham, MA: Town of Hingham, 1893. 3 vols.
http://genweb.net/~blackwell/ma/hingham/Hingham1893.html

Tower, Charlemagne. *Tower Genealogy, an Account of the Descendants of John Tower of Hingham, Mass., Compiled under the Direction of Charlemagne Tower, Late of Philadelphia, Deceased.* Cambridge, MA: John Wilson, 1891. 689p.
http://genweb.net/~blackwell/ma/Tower1891/

Holbrook
Pattee, William S. *A History of Old Braintree and Quincy, with a Sketch of Randolph and Holbrook.* Quincy, MA: Green & Prescott, 1878. 600p.
http://genweb.net/~blackwell/ma/braintree1876/brntr001.htm

Ipswich
Abbot, Abiel and Ephraim Abbot. *Genealogical Register of the Descendants of George Abbot of Andover, George Abbot of Rowley, Thomas Abbot of Andover, Arthur Abbot of Ipswich, Robert Abbot of Branford, CT and George Abbot, of Norwalk, CT.* Boston, MA: James Munroe, 1847. 197p.
http://genweb.net/~books/ma/abbot1847/

Felt, Joseph Barlow. *History of Ipswich, Essex and Hamilton.* Cambridge, MA: C. Folsom, 1834. 304p.
http://www.geocities.com/~jslaughter/HistoryOfIpswich.html

Lancaster

Rowlandson, Mary. *Narrative of the Captivity and Restoration of Mrs. Mary Rowlandson.* 1862.
ftp://uiarchive.cso.uiuc.edu/pub/etext/gutenberg/etext97/crmmr10.txt
http://tom.cs.cmu.edu/cgi-bin/book/lookup?num=851

Lawrence

Lawrence [City Directory]. Boston, MA: Adams, Sampson & Co., 1859.
http://www.citydirectories.psmedia.com/city/free_statesort.html

Leominster

Murdock, Charles Albert. *A Backward Glance at Eighty, Recollections and Comments by Charles A. Murdock, Massachusetts 1841, Humboldt Bay 1855, San Francisco, 1864.* San Francisco, CA: Elder, 1921. 275p.
http://memory.loc.gov/cgi-bin/query/r?ammem/calbkbib:@field(AUTHOR+@band(Murdock,+Charles+Albert,1841-+))

Lowell

Lowell [City Directory]. Lowell, MA: Directory Co., 1859.
http://www.citydirectories.psmedia.com/city/free_statesort.html

Marshfield

Morrison, George Austin, Jr. *King Genealogy, Clement King of Marshfield, Mass., 1668 and His Descendants.* Albany, NY: Munsell, 1898. 65p.
http://genweb.net/~blackwell/ma/King1898/

Richards, Lysander Salmon. *History of Marshfield.* Plymouth, MA: Memorial Press, 1901. 2 vols.
http://www.rootsweb.com/~macmarsh/marshhis.html

Middleborough

Emery, Samuel Hopkins. *The History of the Church of North Middleborough, Massachusetts in Six Discourses.* Middleborough, MA: Harlow & Thatcher, Steam Book and Job Printers, 1876. 106p.
http://genweb.net/~blackwell/ma/middleborochurch/

New Bedford

New Bedford [City Directory]. New Bedford, MA: Taber, 1859. Unpgd.
http://www.citydirectories.psmedia.com/city/free_statesort.html

Newburyport

Prince, Nancy. *A Narrative of the Life and Travels of Mrs. Nancy Prince.* 2nd ed. Boston, MA: Author, 1853. 89p.
http://digilib.nypl.org/dynaweb/digs/wwm97263/

Norton

Vital Records of Norton, Massachusetts to the Year 1850. Boston, MA: New England Historic Genealogical Society, 1906. 405p.
http://genweb.net/~blackwell/ma/nortonVR/

Pittsfield

Pittsfield, 1859-60 [City Directory]. Pittsfield, MA: Renne & Chickering, 1859.
http://www.citydirectories.psmedia.com/city/free_statesort.html

Todd, John. *The Sunset Land or the Great Pacific Slope*. Boston, MA: Lee & Shepard, 1870.
322p.
http://memory.loc.gov/cgi-bin/query/r?ammem/calbk:@field(DOCID+@lit(C184T00)):@@@REF

Plymouth

Banvard, Joseph. *Plymouth and the Pilgrims or Incidents of Adventure in the History of the
First Settlers*. Boston, MA: Lothrop, 1886. 304p.
http://moa.cit.cornell.edu/dienst/moabrowse.fly/MOA-JOURNALS2:BANV-0028/5/1:TIFF2GIF:100

Bradford, William. *Of Plymouth Plantation, 1620-1647*. New York, NY: Knopf, 1952. 448p.
http://members.aol.com/calebj/bradford_journal/html

Goodwin, John Abbot. *The Pilgrim Republic, an Historical Review of the Colony of New Plymouth, with Sketches of the Rise of Other New England Settlements, the History of Congregationalism and the Creeds of the Period*. Boston, MA: Ticknor, 1888. 662p.
http://moa.cit.cornell.edu/dienst/moabrowse.fly/MOA-JOURNALS2:GOOD-0032/7/1:TIFF2GIF:100

Higginson, Thomas Wentworth. *Life of Francis Higginson, First Minister in the Massachusetts
Bay Colony and Author of New England's Plantation (1630)*. New York, NY: Dodd, Mead
and Co., 1891. 158p.
http://moa.cit.cornell.edu/dienst/moabrowse.fly/MOA-JOURNALS2:HIGG-0038/3/1:TIFF2GIF:100

Kingman, Bradford. *History of North Bridgewater, Plymouth County, Massachusetts, from Its
First Settlement to the Present Time with Family Registers*. Boston, MA: Author, 1866,
696p.
http://genweb.net/~blackwell/ma/bridgewaternorth/brdgwtrintro.html

Quincy

Pattee, William S. *A History of Old Braintree and Quincy, with a Sketch of Randolph and
Holbrook*. Quincy, MA: Green & Prescott, 1878. 600p.
http://genweb.net/~blackwell/ma/braintree1876/brntr001.htm

Randolph

Pattee, William S. *A History of Old Braintree and Quincy, with a Sketch of Randolph and
Holbrook*. Quincy, MA: Green & Prescott, 1878. 600p.
http://genweb.net/~blackwell/ma/braintree1876/brntr001.htm

Rochester

Vital Records of Rochester, Massachusetts, to the Year 1850. Boston, MA: New England Historic Genealogical Society, 1914. 2 vols.
http://genweb.net/~blackwell/ma/rochesterVR/

Rowley

Abbot, Abiel and Ephraim Abbot. *Genealogical Register of the Descendants of George Abbot
of Andover, George Abbot of Rowley, Thomas Abbot of Andover, Arthur Abbot of Ipswich,
Robert Abbot of Branford, CT and George Abbot, of Norwalk, CT*. Boston, MA: James
Munroe, 1847. 197p.
http://genweb.net/~books/ma/abbot1847/

Salem

Salem [City Directory]. Boston, MA: Adams, Sampson & Co., 1859.
http://www.citydirectories.psmedia.com/city/free_statesort.html

Scituate

Deane, Samuel. *History of Scituate, Massachusetts from Its First Settlement to 1831.* Boston, MA: James Loring, 1831, 408p.
http://genweb.net/~blackwell/ma/scituate1831dean/

Pratt, Harvey Hunter. *Early Planters of Scituate, a History of the Town of Scituate, Massachusetts from Its Establishment to the End of the Revolutionary War.* Scituate, MA: Scituate Historical Society, 1929. 396p.
http://genweb.net/~blackwell/ma/Scituate1929Pratt/sct000.htm

Vital Records of Scituate, Massachusetts to the Year 1850. Boston, MA: New England Historic Genealogical Society, 1909. 2 vols.
http://genweb.net/~blackwell/ma/ScituateVR/

Springfield

Springfield 1859-60 [City Directory]. Springfield, MA: Samuel Bowles, 1859.
http://www.citydirectories.psmedia.com/city/free_statesort.html

Sudbury

Barry, William. *A History of Framingham, Massachusetts, Including the Plantation from 1640 to the Present Time, with an Appendix Containing a Notice of Sudbury and Its First Proprietors, also a Register of the Inhabitants of Framingham before 1800 with Genealogical Sketches.* Boston, MA: James Monroe, 1847. 456p.
http://genweb.net/~blackwell/ma/framingham/

Rowlandson, Mary. *Narrative of the Captivity and Restoration of Mrs. Mary Rowlandson.* Unknown, 1862. 316p.
ftp://uiarchive.cso.uiuc.edu/pub/etext/gutenberg/etext97/crmmr10.txt
http://tom.cs.cmu.edu/cgi-bin/book/lookup?num=851

Vital Records of Sudbury, Massachusetts to the Year 1850. Boston, MA: New England Historical Genealogical Society, 1903. 332p.
http://genweb.net/~blackwell/ma/sudburyVR/

Taunton

Allen, Florence T. *Index, History of Taunton, Massachusetts by Samuel Hopkins Emery, D.D.* Worcester, MA: Author, 1951. Unpgd.
http://genweb.net/~blackwell/ma/tauntonindex/

Chase, Ethel Savage and Elizabeth Fuller Staples. *Cemetery Records, Taunton, Massachusetts, Compiled by Ethel Savage Chase and Elizabeth Fuller Staples, 1935-1938.* Taunton, MA: Daughters of the American Revolution, Lydia Cobb Chapter, 1938. Unpgd.
http://genweb.net/~blackwell/ma/tauntoncemetaries1938/

Emery, Samuel Hopkins. *History of Taunton, Massachusetts from Its Settlement to the Present Time.* Syracuse, NY: Mason, 1893. 768p.
http://genweb.net/~blackwell/ma/taunton1893/

Presbrey, Wendell B., Mrs. *Inscriptions from Eleven Cemeteries in Taunton.* Taunton, MA: Daughters of the American Revolution, Lydia Cobb Chapter, 1973. Unpgd.
http://genweb.net/~blackwell/ma/tauntoncemetaries1973/

Taunton [City Directory]. Boston, MA: Adams, Sampson & Co., 1859.
http://www.citydirectories.psmedia.com/city/free_statesort.html

Vital Records of Taunton, Massachusetts to the Year 1850. Boston, MA: New England Historic
    Genealogical Society, 1909. 3 vols.
http://genweb.net/~blackwell/ma/tauntonVR/

Weymouth

History of Weymouth, Massachusetts. Weymouth, MA: Weymouth Historical Society, 1923.
    4 vols.
http://genweb.net/~blackwell/ma/weymouth/

Thayer, Bezaleel. *Memorial of the Thayer Name from the Massachusetts Colony of Weymouth
    and Braintree, Embracing Genealogical and Biographical Sketches of Richard and Thomas
    Thayer and Their Descendants from 1636 to 1874*. Oswego, NY: Oliphant, 1874. 708p.
http://genweb.net/~blackwell/ma/Thayer1874/

Worcester

*Celebration by the Inhabitants of Worcester, Mass., of the Centennial Anniversary of the Dec-
    laration of Independence, July 4, 1876, to Which Are Added Historical and Chronological
    Notes*. Worcester, MA: City Council, 1876. 150p.
http://moa.umdl.umich.edu/cgi-bin/moa/sgml/moa-idx?notisid=AAR9561

Worcester [City Directory]. Worcester, MA: Howland, 1859.
http://www.citydirectories.psmedia.com/city/free_statesort.html

Wrenthem

Baldwin, Thomas W. *Vital Records of Wrenthem, Massachusetts, to the Year 1850*. Boston,
    MA: Stanhope Press, 1910. 2 vols.
http://genweb.net/~blackwell/ma/wrenthamVR/

Michigan

Blackbird, Andrew J. *History of the Ottawa and Chippewa Indians of Michigan, a Grammar of
    Their Language and Personal and Family History of the Author*. Ypsilanti, MI: Ypsilantian
    Job Printing House, 1887. 128p.
http://memory.loc.gov/cgi-bin/query/r?ammem/lhbum:@field(DOCID+@lit(16465T000)):@@@REF

Blois, John T. *Gazetteer of the State of Michigan, in Three Parts, with a Succinct History of the
    State, from the Earliest Period to the Present Time, with an Appendix, Containing the Usual
    Statistical Tables and a Directory for Emigrants*. Detroit, MI: Rood, 1839. 418p.
http://memory.loc.gov/cgi-bin/query/r?ammem/lhbum:@field(DOCID+@lit(18627T000)):@@@REF

Bramhall, Frank James. *Facts and Figures about Michigan, a Handbook of the State, Statistical, Political, Financial, Economical, Commercial.* Chicago, IL: Poole Brothers, 1885. 88p.
http://memory.loc.gov/cgi-bin/query/r?ammem/lhbumbib:@field(SUBJ+@band(Michigan--Registers.+))

Brown, Charles R. *The Government of Michigan.* Kalamazoo, MI: Moore & Quale, 1874. 200p.
http://moa.umdl.umich.edu/cgi-bin/moa/sgml/moa-idx?notisid=AEW7795

A Gallery of Pen Sketches in Black and White of Our Michigan Friends, as We See 'Em, by Newspaper Cartoonists' Association of Michigan. Detroit, MI: Graham Printing, 1905. 640p.
http://memory.loc.gov/cgi-bin/query/r?ammem/lhbumbib:@field(SUBJ+@band(Michigan--Biography--Portraits.+))

King, John Lyle. *Trouting on the Brule River, or Lawyers' Summer-wayfaring in the Northern Wilderness.* Chicago, IL: Chicago Legal News Co., 1879. 272p.
http://memory.loc.gov/cgi-bin/query/r?ammem/lhbumbib:@field(SUBJ+@band(Trout+fishing--Michigan.+))

Lanman, Charles. *The Red Book of Michigan; a Civil, Military and Biographical History.* Detroit, MI: E. B. Smith & Co., 1871. 560p.
http://moa.umdl.umich.edu/cgi-bin/moa/sgml/moa-idx?notisid=ACL1814

Look, Henry M. *Masonic Trials and Michigan Digest, a Treatise upon the Law and Practice of Masonic Trials with Forms and Precedents.* Pontiac, MI: Rann & Turner, 1869. 232p.
http://moa.umdl.umich.edu/cgi-bin/moa/sgml/moa-idx?notisid=AEM6372

Medical History of Michigan. Minneapolis, MN: Bruce Publishing, 1930. 2 vols.
http://memory.loc.gov/cgi-bin/query/r?ammem/lhbum:@field(DOCID+@lit(1995aT000)):@@@REF
http://memory.loc.gov/cgi-bin/query/r?ammem/lhbum:@field(DOCID+@lit(1995bT000)):@@@REF

Men of Progress, Embracing Biographical Sketches of Representative Michigan Men, with an Outline History of the State. Detroit, MI: Evening News Assn., 1900. 440p.
http://memory.loc.gov/cgi-bin/query/r?ammem/lhbum:@field(DOCID+@lit(29692T000)):@@@REF

Michigan Biographies, Including Members of Congress, Elective State Officers, Justices of the Supreme Court, Members of the Michigan Legislature, Board of Regents of the University of Michigan, State Board of Agriculture and State Board of Education. Lansing, MI: Michigan Historical Commission, 1924. 2 vols.
http://memory.loc.gov/cgi-bin/query/r?ammem/lhbum:@field(DOCID+@lit(7004aT000)):@@@REF
http://memory.loc.gov/cgi-bin/query/r?ammem/lhbum:@field(DOCID+@lit(7004bT000)):@@@REF

Michigan State Historical Society. *Historical Collections.* Lansing, MI: The Society, various.
Vol. 8 **http://memory.loc.gov/cgi-bin/query/r?ammem/lhbum:@field(DOCID+@lit(5298aT000)):@@@REF**
Vol. 9 **http://memory.loc.gov/cgi-bin/query/r?ammem/lhbum:@field(DOCID+@lit(5298bT000)):@@@REF**
Vol. 10 **http://memory.loc.gov/cgi-bin/query/r?ammem/lhbum:@field(DOCID+@lit(5298cT000)):@@@REF**
Vol. 11 **http://memory.loc.gov/cgi-bin/query/r?ammem/lhbum:@field(DOCID+@lit(5298dT000)):@@@REF**
Vol. 12 **http://memory.loc.gov/cgi-bin/query/r?ammem/lhbum:@field(DOCID+@lit(5298eT000)):@@@REF**
Vol. 15 **http://memory.loc.gov/cgi-bin/query/r?ammem/lhbum:@field(DOCID+@lit(5298fT000)):@@@REF**
Vol. 16 **http://memory.loc.gov/cgi-bin/query/r?ammem/lhbum:@field(DOCID+@lit(5298gT000)):@@@REF**
Vol. 19 **http://memory.loc.gov/cgi-bin/query/r?ammem/lhbum:@field(DOCID+@lit(5298hT000)):@@@REF**
Vol. 20 **http://memory.loc.gov/cgi-bin/query/r?ammem/lhbum:@field(DOCID+@lit(5298iT000)):@@@REF**

Michigan State Gazetteer and Business Directory for 1863-4. Detroit, MI: C. F. Clark, 1863. 694p.
http://memory.loc.gov/cgi-bin/query/r?ammem/lhbumbib:@field(SUBJ+@band(Michigan--Description+and+travel--Gazetteers.+))

The Michigan University Magazine Devoted to College Literature and Education. Ann Arbor, MI: Dr. Chase's Steam Printing House, 1867. 492p.
http://moa.umdl.umich.edu/cgi-bin/moa/sgml/moa-idx?notisid=AJL9091b

Research Outline. Michigan. Salt Lake City, UT: Family History Library, 1997.
http://familysearch.org/sg/Michigan.html

Saint John, John R. *A True Description of the Lake Superior Country, with Bayfield's Chart, also a Minute Account of the Copper Mines and Working Companies, containing a Concise Mode of Assaying, Treating, Smelting and Refining Copper Ores.* New York, NY: Graham, 1846. 118p.
http://memory.loc.gov/ammem/mdbquery.html

Schoolcraft, Henry Rowe. *Narrative Journal of Travels through the Northwestern Regions of the United States, Extending from Detroit through the Great Chain of American Lakes to the Sources of the Mississippi River, Performed as a Member of the Expedition under Governor Cass in the Year 1820.* Albany, NY: Hosford, 1821. 423p.
http://memory.loc.gov/cgi-bin/query/r?ammem/lhbum:@field(DOCID+@lit(01453T000)):@@@REF

———. *Narrative of an Expedition through the Upper Mississippi to Itasca Lake, the Actual Source of This River Embracing an Exploratory Trip through the St. Croix and Burntwood (or Broule) Rivers in 1832.* New York, NY: Harper, 1834. 308p.
http://memory.loc.gov/cgi-bin/query/r?ammem/lhbum:@field(DOCID+@lit(08794T000)):@@@REF

———. *Personal Memoirs of a Residence of Thirty Years with the Indian Tribes on the American Frontiers with Brief Notices of Passing Events, Facts, and Opinions, A.D. 1812 to A.D. 1842.* Philadelphia, PA: Lippincott, 1851. 703p.
http://memory.loc.gov/cgi-bin/query/r?ammem/lhbum:@field(DOCID+@lit(15006T000)):@@@REF

Tuttle, Charles R. *General History of the State of Michigan, with Biographical Sketches, Portrait Engravings, and Numerous Illustrations.* Detroit, MI: Tyler, 1873. 744p.
http://moa.umdl.umich.edu/cgi-bin/moa/sgml/moa-idx?notisid=AFK0671

Ann Arbor

Catalogue of the Academic Senate of the University of Michigan and of Those Who Have Received Its Regular and Honorary Degrees. Ann Arbor, MI: University of Michigan, 1871. 90p.
http://moa.umdl.umich.edu/cgi-bin/moa/sgml/moa-idx?notisid=AJL7763

Duffield, Samuel Willoughby. *A Farewell Sermon Delivered in the First Presbyterian Church, Ann Arbor, Michigan.* Ann Arbor, MI: Courier Steam Printing, 1874. 20p.
http://moa.umdl.umich.edu/cgi-bin/moa/sgml/moa-idx?notisid=AAM7378

Benzie County

Howard, John Harris. *A History of Herring Lake, with an Introductory Legend, the Bride of Mystery by the Bard of Benzie.* Boston, MA: Christopher Publishing House, 1929. 84p.
http://memory.loc.gov/cgi-bin/query/r?ammem/lhbumbib:@field(SUBJ+@band(Benzie+Co.,+Mich.--Biography.+))

Dearborn

Nowlin, William. *The Bark Covered House, or Back in the Woods Again, Being a Graphic and Thrilling Description of Real Pioneer Life in the Wilderness of Michigan.* Detroit, MI: Author, 1876. 253p.
http://memory.loc.gov/cgi-bin/query/r?ammem/lhbumbib:@field(SUBJ+@band(Dearborn,+Mich.--History.+))

Detroit

Darby, William. *A Tour from the City of New York to Detroit in the Michigan Territory Made between the 22d of September 1818. The Tour is Accompanied with a Map upon Which the Route Will be Designated, a Particular Map of the Falls and River of Niagara, and the Environs of the City of Detroit.* New York, NY: Kirk & Mercein, 1819. 300p.
http://memory.loc.gov/cgi-bin/query/r?ammem/lhbumbib:@field(SUBJ+@band(New+York++State+--Description+and+travel.+))

Detroit [City Directory]. Detroit, MI: Johnston, various.
1859; 1861.
http://www.citydirectories.psmedia.com/city/free_statesort.html

Detroit 1860-61 [City Directory]. Detroit, MI: Umberyhine, various.
http://www.citydirectories.psmedia.com/city/free_statesort.html

Detroit [City Directory]. Detroit, MI: Clark, various.
1862-67.
http://www.citydirectories.psmedia.com/city/free_statesort.html

Detroit [City Directory]. Detroit, MI: Johnston, various.
1859; 1861.
http://www.citydirectories.psmedia.com/city/free_statesort.html

Detroit [City Directory]. Detroit, MI: Weeks, 1880.
http://www.citydirectories.psmedia.com/city/free_statesort.html

Detroit [City Directory]. R. L. Polk, various.
1890; 1910.
http://www.citydirectories.psmedia.com/city/free_statesort.html

Hubbard, Bela. *Memorials of a Half Century.* New York, NY: Putnam's, 1887. 581p.
http://memory.loc.gov/cgi-bin/query/r?ammem/lhbumbib:@field(SUBJ+@band(Michigan--History--1837-+))

The Revised Charter and Ordinances of the City of Detroit. Detroit, MI: Storey, 1855. 320p.
http://moa.umdl.umich.edu/cgi-bin/moa/sgml/moa-idx?notisid=AHM9803

Roberts, Robert E. *Sketches of the City of Detroit, State of Michigan, Past and Present.* Detroit, MI: Johnsone, 1855. 68p.
http://moa.umdl.umich.edu/cgi-bin/moa/sgml/moa-idx?notisid=AFK0798

Sibley, Henry Hastings. *The Unfinished Autobiography of Henry Hastings Sibley, together with a Selection of Hitherto Unpublished Letters from the Thirties, Edited by Theodore C. Blegen.* Minneapolis, MN: Voyageur Press, 1932. 75p.
http://memory.loc.gov/cgi-bin/query/r?ammem/lhbumbib:@field(SUBJ+@band(Fur+trade--Northwest,+Old.+))

Ward, David. *The Autobiography of David Ward.* New York, NY: Author, 1912. 194p.
http://memory.loc.gov/cgi-bin/query/r?ammem/lhbumbib:@field(SUBJ+@band(Michigan--Social+life+and+customs.+))

Grand Rapids

Grand Rapids, 1859-61 [City Directory]. Grand Rapids, MI: Williams' 1859.
http://www.citydirectories.psmedia.com/city/free_statesort.html

Immen, Looraine Pratt. *Letters of Travel in California in the Winter and Spring of 1896.* Grand Rapids, MI: Author, 1896. 53p.
http://memory.loc.gov/cgi-bin/query/r?ammem/calbkbib:@field(AUTHOR+@band(Immen,+Loraine+[Pratt],1840-+))

Kalamazoo

In Memoriam William S. Huggins, Three Sermons to Young Men, Preached by Rev. William S. Huggins of Kalamazoo, Michigan, and a Funeral Discourse by Rev. Samuel Haskell, with an Account of the Funeral and Memorial Meeting. Philadelphia, PA: Presbyterian Publication Committee, 1862. 150p.
http://moa.umdl.umich.edu/cgi-bin/moa/sgml/moa-idx?notisid=AJK3161

Perry, Belle McArthur. *Lucinda Hinsdale Stone, Her Life Story and Reminiscences.* Detroit, MI: Blinn Publishing, 1902. 369p.
http://memory.loc.gov/cgi-bin/query/r?ammem/lhbumbib:@field(SUBJ+@band(Stone,+Lucinda+Hinsdale,--1814-1900.+))

Lansing

Mevis, Daniel Stafford. *Pioneer Recollections, Semi-historic Side Lights on the Early Days of Lansing.* Lansing, MI: Robert Smith Printing, 1911. 129p.
http://memory.loc.gov/cgi-bin/query/r?ammem/lhbum:@field(DOCID+@lit(10313T000)):@@@REF

Lenawee County

Haviland, Laura Smith. *A Woman's Life-work, Labors and Experiences of Laura S. Haviland.* Cincinnati, OH: Walden & Stowe, 1882. 531p.
http://memory.loc.gov/cgi-bin/query/r?ammem/lhbumbib:@field(SUBJ+@band(Freedmen.+))

Mackinac Island

Childs, B. F. *Marquette, Mackinac Island and the Soo.* New York, NY: Albertype, 1889. 12p.
http://memory.loc.gov/cgi-bin/query/r?ammem/lhbumbib:@field(SUBJ+@band(Marquette+co.,+Mich.--Description+and+travel--Views.+))

The Standard Guide, Mackinac Island and Northern Lake Resorts. New York, NY: Foster & Reynolds, 1899. 88p.
http://memory.loc.gov/cgi-bin/query/r?ammem/lhbumbib:@field(SUBJ+@band(Great+Lakes--Description+and+travel--Guide-books.+))

Strickland, William Peter. *Old Mackinaw, or the Fortress of the Lakes and Its Surroundings.* Philadelphia, PA: Chalten & Son, 1860. 404p.
http://moa.umdl.umich.edu/cgi-bin/moa/sgml/moa-idx?notisid=AJJ9793

Marquette County

Childs, B. F. *Marquette, Mackinac Island and the Soo.* New York, NY: Albertype, 1889. 12p.
http://memory.loc.gov/cgi-bin/query/r?ammem/lhbumbib:@field(SUBJ+@band(Marquette+co.,+Mich.--Description+and+travel--Views.+))

Oakland County

Ward, David. *The Autobiography of David Ward.* New York, NY: Author, 1912. 194p.
http://memory.loc.gov/cgi-bin/query/r?ammem/lhbumbib:@field(SUBJ+@band(Michigan--Social+life+and+customs.+))

Raisin (Lenawee County)

Haviland, Laura Smith. *A Woman's Life-work, Labors and Experiences of Laura S. Haviland.* Cincinnati, OH: Walden & Stowe, 1882. 531p.
http://memory.loc.gov/cgi-bin/query/r?ammem/lhbumbib:@field(SUBJ+@band(Freedmen.+))

Saginaw

The Charter of the City of East Saginaw as Enacted and Amended by the Legislature of the State of Michigan, together with Other Acts of the Legislature, for the Use of the Officers of the City. East Saginaw, MI: Enterprise Printing, 1869. 150p.
http://moa.umdl.umich.edu/cgi-bin/moa/sgml/moa-idx?notisid=AHM9972

Saint Joseph Valley

Turner, Timothy G. *Gazetteer of the St. Joseph Valley, Michigan and Indiana.* Chicago, IL: Hazlitt & Reed, 1867. 168p.
http://moa.umdl.umich.edu/cgi-bin/moa/sgml/moa-idx?notisid=AFK0736

Vermontville

Barber, Edward W. *The Vermontville Colony, Its Genesis and History, with Personal Sketches of the Colonists.* Lansing, MI: Smith, 1897. 93p.
http://memory.loc.gov/cgi-bin/query/r?ammem/lhbumbib:@field(SUBJ+@band(Vermontville,+Mich.+))

Ypsilanti

Foster, G. L. *The Past of Ypsilanti a Discourse Delivered on Leaving the Old Presbyterian Church Edifice, Lord's Day, September 20th, 1857, Also an Appendix Containing a History of Schools, Secret Societies etc.* Detroit, MI: Author, 1857. 48p.
http://moa.umdl.umich.edu/cgi-bin/moa/sgml/moa-idx?notisid=AJA3288

Minnesota

Andrews, Christopher Columbus. *Minnesota and Dacotah, in Letters Descriptive of a Tour through the Northwest, in the Autumn of 1856. With Information Relative to Public Lands, and a Table of Statistics.* 2nd ed. Washington, DC: Farnham, 1857. 215p.
http://memory.loc.gov/cgi-bin/query/r?ammem/lhbumbib:@field(SUBJ+@band(Andrews,+Christopher+Columbus,-1829-1922.+))
http://moa.umdl.umich.edu/cgi-bin/moa/sgml/moa-idx?notisid=ABA0383

Bill, Ledyard. *Minnesota, Its Character and Climate. Likewise Sketches of Other Resorts Favorable to Invalids, together with Copious Notes on Health, also Hints to Tourists and Emigrants.* New York, NY: Wood & Holbrook, 1871. 214p.
http://memory.loc.gov/cgi-bin/query/r?ammem/lhbum:@field(DOCID+@lit(01079T000)):@@@REF

Bishop, Harriet E. *Floral Home, or, First Years of Minnesota Early Sketches, Later Settlements, and Further Developments.* New York, NY: Sheldon, Blakeman and Co., 1857. 360p.
http://moa.umdl.umich.edu/cgi-bin/moa/sgml/moa-idx?notisid=AFK4418

Bond, J. Wesley. *Minnesota and Its Resources; to which Are Appended Camp-fire Sketches, or, Notes of a Trip from St. Paul to Pembina and Selkirk Settlement on the Red River of the North.* New York, NY: Redfield, 1853. 388p.
http://moa.umdl.umich.edu/cgi-bin/moa/sgml/moa-idx?notisid=ABA0387

Coffin, Charles Carleton. *The Seat of Empire.* Boston, MA: Fields, Osgood & Co., 1870. 262p.
http://moa.umdl.umich.edu/cgi-bin/moa/sgml/moa-idx?notisid=AFK4419

Farrar, J. Maurice. *Five Years in Minnesota. Sketches of Life in a Western State.* London: Low, Marston, Searle & Rivington, 1880. 269p.
http://memory.loc.gov/cgi-bin/query/r?ammem/lhbum:@field(DOCID+@lit(05676T000)):@@@REF

Folsom, William Henry Carman. *Fifty Years in the Northwest.* St. Paul, MN: Pioneer Press Co., 1888. 763p.
http://memory.loc.gov/cgi-bin/query/r?ammem/lhbum:@field(DOCID+@lit(01070T000)):@@@REF

Hanson, Glenn. *The Frontier Holiday, Being a Collection of Writings by Minnesota Pioneers Who Recorded Their Diverse Ways of Observing Christmas, Thanksgiving and New Year's.* St. Paul, MN: North Central Pub. Co., 1948. 47p.
http://memory.loc.gov/cgi-bin/query/r?ammem/lhbum:@field(DOCID+@lit(48053T000)):@@@REF

Hewitt, Girart. *Minnesota, Its Advantages to Settlers. 1868. Being a Brief Synopsis of Its History and Progress, Climate, Soil, Agricultural and Manufacturing Facilities, Commercial Capacities, and Social Status; Its Lakes, Rivers and Railroads; Homestead and Exemption Laws, Embracing a Concise Treatise on Its Climatology, in a Hygienic and Sanitary Point of View.* St. Paul, MN: St. Paul Press, 1869. 52p.
http://memory.loc.gov/cgi-bin/query/r?ammem/lhbum:@field(DOCID+@lit(15369T000)):@@@REF
http://moa.umdl.umich.edu/cgi-bin/moa/sgml/moa-idx?notisid=ABA0393

Keating, William Hypolitus. *Narrative of an Expedition to the Source of St. Peter's River, Lake Winnepeck, Lake of the Woods, Performed in the Year 1823, by Order of the Hon. J. C. Calhoun, Secretary of War, under the Command of Stephen H. Long, Major, USTE.* Philadelphia, PA: Carey & Lea, 1824. 2 vols.
http://memory.loc.gov/cgi-bin/query/r?ammem/lhbum:@field(DOCID+@lit(1607aT000)):@@@REF

McClung, John W. *Minnesota as It Is in 1870. Its General Resources and Attractions with Special Descriptions of all Its Counties and Towns.* St. Paul, MN: Author, 1870. 300p.
http://memory.loc.gov/cgi-bin/query/r?ammem/lhbum:@field(DOCID+@lit(01092T000)):@@@REF

Mayer, Francis Blackwell. *With Pen and Pencil on the Frontier in 1851, the Diary and Sketches of Frank Blackwell Mayer.* Saint Paul, MN: Minnesota Historical Society, 1932. 214p.
http://memory.loc.gov/cgi-bin/query/r?ammem/lhbum:@field(DOCID+@lit(17122T000)):@@@REF

Minnesota, the Empire State of the New Northwest, the Commercial, Manufacturing and Geographical Centre of the American Continent. St. Paul, MN: Smyth, 1878. 88p.
http://memory.loc.gov/cgi-bin/query/r?ammem/lhbum:@field(DOCID+@lit(09183T000)):@@@REF

Minnesota Historical Society. *Collections of the Minnesota Historical Society.* St. Paul, MN: Society, varies.
Vol. 1 **http://memory.loc.gov/cgi-bin/query/r?ammem/lhbum:@field(DOCID+@lit(0866aT000)):@@@REF**
Vol. 5 **http://memory.loc.gov/cgi-bin/query/r?ammem/lhbum:@field(DOCID+@lit(0866bT000)):@@@REF**
Vol. 7 **http://memory.loc.gov/cgi-bin/query/r?ammem/lhbum:@field(DOCID+@lit(0866cT000)):@@@REF**
Vol. 9 **http://memory.loc.gov/cgi-bin/query/r?ammem/lhbum:@field(DOCID+@lit(0866dT000)):@@@REF**

Vol. 10 http://memory.loc.gov/cgi-bin/query/r?ammem/lhbum:@field(DOCID+@lit(0866eT000)):@@@REF
        http://memory.loc.gov/cgi-bin/query/r?ammem/lhbum:@field(DOCID+@lit(0866fT000)):@@@REF
Vol. 12 http://memory.loc.gov/cgi-bin/query/r?ammem/lhbum:@field(DOCID+@lit(0866gT000)):@@@REF
Vol. 15 http://memory.loc.gov/cgi-bin/query/r?ammem/lhbum:@field(DOCID+@lit(0866hT000)):@@@REF

Neill, Edward D. *A Hand Book for the Presbyterian Church in Minnesota, Designed to Promote Order in and Love for the Sanctuary.* Philadelphia, PA: Ashmead, 1856. 72p.
http://moa.umdl.umich.edu/cgi-bin/moa/sgml/moa-idx?notisid=AJK3012

Old Rail Fence Corners, the ABC's of Minnesota History. Austin, MN: McCulloch Printing Co., 1914. 333p. [No author]
http://memory.loc.gov/cgi-bin/query/r?ammem/lhbum:@field(DOCID+@lit(19293T000)):@@@REF

Parker, Nathan Howe. *The Minnesota Handbook 1856-7, with a New and Accurate Map.* Boston, MA: Jewett, 1857. 160p.
http://moa.umdl.umich.edu/cgi-bin/moa/sgml/moa-idx?notisid=AJA3458

Research Outline. Minnesota. Salt Lake City, UT: Family History Library, 1997.
http://familysearch.org/sg/Minnesota.html

Seymour, E. S. *Sketches of Minnesota, the New England of the West, with Incidents of Travels in That Territory during the Summer of 1849.* New York, NY: Harper, 1850. 281p.
http://memory.loc.gov/cgi-bin/query/r?ammem/lhbum:@field(DOCID+@lit(01108T000)):@@@REF

Shutter, Marion Daniel. *Progressive Men of Minnesota. Biographical Sketches and Portraits of the Leaders in Business, Politics and the Professions, together with an Historical and Descriptive Sketch of the State.* Minneapolis, MN: Minneapolis Journal, 1897. 514p.
http://memory.loc.gov/cgi-bin/query/r?ammem/lhbum:@field(DOCID+@lit(19129T000)):@@@REF

Blue Earth County
George, Alice Mendenhall. *The Story of My Childhood, Written for My Children.* Whittier, CA: Smith, 1923. 87p.
http://memory.loc.gov/cgi-bin/query/r?ammem/lhbum:@field(DOCID+@lit(04681T000)):@@@REF

Buffalo Lake
Carriagan, Wilhelmina Bruce. *Captured by the Indians, Reminiscences of Pioneer Life in Minnesota.* Buffalo Lake, MN: News Print, 1912. 68p.
http://memory.loc.gov/cgi-bin/query/r?ammem/lhbumbib:@field(SUBJ+@band(Carrigan,+Wilhelmina+Buce.+))

Chatfield
Manahan, James. *Trials of a Lawyer, Autobiography.* Minneapolis, MN: Farnaham Printing, 1933. 248p.
http://memory.loc.gov/cgi-bin/query/r?ammem/lhbumbib:@field(SUBJ+@band(Lawyers--Minnesota--Correspondence,+reminiscences,+etc.+))

Clearwater Lake (Stearns County)
Dally, Nathan. *Track and Trails, or Incidents in the Life of a Minnesota Territorial Pioneer.* Walker, MN: Cass County Pioneer, 1931. 138p.
http://memory.loc.gov/ammem/mdbquery.html

Fort Snelling
Eastman, Mary Henderson. *Dahcotah or Life and Legends of the Sioux around Fort Snelling.* New York, NY: Wiley, 1849. 293p.
http://www.canadiana.org/cgi-bin/ECO/mtq?id=04ee01375f&doc=35037

Van Cleve, Charlotte Ouisconsin Clark. *Three Score Years and Ten, Life-long Memories of Fort Snelling, Minnesota and Other Parts of the West*. Minneapolis, MN: Harrison & Smith, 1888. 176p.
http://memory.loc.gov/cgi-bin/query/r?ammem/lhbumbib:@field(SUBJ+@band(Fort+Snelling,+Minn.+))

Iron River
Reimann, Lewis Charles. *Between the Iron and the Pine, a Biography of a Pioneer Family and a Pioneer Town*. Ann Arbor, MI: Edwards Brothers, 1951. 225p.
http://memory.loc.gov/cgi-bin/query/r?ammem/lhbumbib:@field(SUBJ+@band(Frontier+and+pioneer+life--Michigan,+Upper+Peninsula.+))

Le Sueur County
George, Alice Mendenhall. *The Story of My Childhood, Written for My Children*. Whittier, CA: Smith, 1923. 87p.
http://memory.loc.gov/cgi-bin/query/r?ammem/lhbum:@field(DOCID+@lit(04681T000)):@@@REF

Minneapolis
Douthit, Davis. *Nobody Owns Us, the Story of Joe Gilbert, Midwestern Rebel*. Chicago, IL: Cooperative League of the USA, 1948. 240p.
http://memory.loc.gov/cgi-bin/query/r?ammem/lhbumbib:@field(SUBJ+@band(Gilbert,+Joseph,--1865-+))

Sevareid, Arnold Eric. *Canoeing with the Cree*. New York, NY: Macmillan, 1935. 201p.
http://memory.loc.gov/cgi-bin/query/r?ammem/lhbumbib:@field(SUBJ+@band(Canoes+and+canoeing.+))

Nininger
Le Sueur, Meridel. *Crusaders*. New York, NY: Blue Heron Press, 1955. 94p.
http://memory.loc.gov/cgi-bin/query/r?ammem/lhbumbib:@field(SUBJ+@band(Le+Sueur,+Arthur,--1867-1950.+))

Northfield
Grose, Ingebrikt F. *Fifty Memorable Years at St. Olaf, Marking the History of the College on the Hill from Its Founding in 1874 to Its Golden Jubilee Celebration in 1925*. Northfield, MN: Northfield News, 1925. 46p.
http://memory.loc.gov/cgi-bin/query/r?ammem/lhbumbib:@field(SUBJ+@band(St.+Olaf+college,+Northfield,+Minn.+))

Ramsey County
Moore, Frank. *Reminiscences of Pioneer Days in St. Paul*. St. Paul, MN: Author, 1908. 134p.
http://memory.loc.gov/cgi-bin/query/r?ammem/lhbum:@field(DOCID+@lit(00866T000)):@@@REF

Williams, J. Fletcher *A History of the City of Saint Paul, and of the County of Ramsey, Minnesota*. Collections of the Minnesota Historical Society, Vol. 4. St. Paul, MN: Minnesota Historical Society, 1876. 490p.
http://moa.umdl.umich.edu/cgi-bin/moa/sgml/moa-idx?notisid=AFK4424

Rapidan (Blue Earth County)
George, Alice Mendenhall. *The Story of My Childhood, Written for My Children*. Whittier, CA: Smith, 1923. 87p.
http://memory.loc.gov/cgi-bin/query/r?ammem/lhbum:@field(DOCID+@lit(04681T000)):@@@REF

Saint Anthony

St. Anthony [City Directory]. St. Anthony, MN: Chamberlin, 1859.
http://www.citydirectories.psmedia.com/city/free_statesort.html

Saint Paul (Ramsey County)

Hall, Harlan Page. *H.P. Hall's Observations, Being More or Less a History of Political Contests in Minnesota from 1849 to 1904*. St. Paul, MN: Author, 1904. 384p.
http://memory.loc.gov/cgi-bin/query/r?ammem/lhbumbib:@field(SUBJ+@band(Minnesota--Politics+and+government--1858-1950.+))

Moore, Frank. *Reminiscences of Pioneer Days in St. Paul*. St. Paul, MN: Author, 1908. 134p.
http://memory.loc.gov/cgi-bin/query/r?ammem/lhbum:@field(DOCID+@lit(00866T000)):@@@REF

Williams, J. Fletcher. *A History of the City of Saint Paul, and of the County of Ramsey, Minnesota*. Collections of the Minnesota Historical Society, Vol. 4. St. Paul, MN: Minnesota Historical Society, 1876. 490p.
http://moa.umdl.umich.edu/cgi-bin/moa/sgml/moa-idx?notisid=AFK4424

Silver Creek (Wayne County)

Vandergon, Gertrude Braat. *Our Pioneer Days in Minnesota*. Author, 1949. 138p.
http://memory.loc.gov/cgi-bin/query/r?ammem/lhbum:@field(DOCID+@lit(03667T000)):@@@REF

Stearns County

Dally, Nathan. *Track and Trails, or Incidents in the Life of a Minnesota Territorial Pioneer*. Walker, MN: Cass County Pioneer, 1931. 138p.
http://memory.loc.gov/ammem/mdbquery.html

Wayne County

Vandergon, Gertrude Braat. *Our Pioneer Days in Minnesota*. Author, 1949. 138p.
http://memory.loc.gov/cgi-bin/query/r?ammem/lhbum:@field(DOCID+@lit(03667T000)):@@@REF

Mississippi

Baldwin, Joseph Glover. *Flush Times of Alabama and Mississippi, a Series of Sketches*. New York, NY: Appleton, 1854. 366p.
http://moa.umdl.umich.edu/cgi-bin/moa/sgml/moa-idx?notisid=ADS9517

Chambliss, William H. *Chambliss' Diary or Society as It Really Is*. New York, NY: Chambliss & Co., 1895. 408p.
http://memory.loc.gov/cgi-bin/query/r?ammem/calbkbib:@field(AUTHOR+@band(Chambliss,+William+H.,+1865++))

Hughes, Louis. *Thirty Years a Slave, from Bondage to Freedom, the Institution of Slavery as Seen on the Plantation and in the Home of the Planter.* Milwaukee, WI: South Side Printing Co., 1897. 210p.
http://metalab.unc.edu/docsouth/hughes/menu.html

Research Outline. Mississippi. Salt Lake City, UT: Family History Library, 1997.
http://familysearch.org/sg/Mississippi.html

Adams County
Montgomery, Frank Alexander. *Reminiscences of a Mississippian in Peace and War.* Cincinnati, OH: Robert Clarke Press, 1901. 305p.
http://metalab.unc.edu/docsouth/montgomery/menu.html

Dry Grove
Episcopal Church, Commission of Home Missions to Colored People. New York, NY: Church, 1875, 1876.
9th Annual Report, 1873-74. 20p.
http://memory.loc.gov/cgi-bin/query/r?ammem/murray:@field(FLD001+91898515+):@@@REF

11th Annual Report, 1875-76. 24p.
http://memory.loc.gov/cgi-bin/query/r?ammem/murray:@field(FLD001+91898514+):@@@REF

Tupelo
Aughey, John Hill. *Tupelo.* Chicago, IL: Rhodes & McLure Publishing, 1905. Unpgd.
http://metalab.unc.edu/docsouth/aughey/menu.html

Vernon
Kearney, Belle. *A Slaveholder's Daughter.* New York, NY: Abbey Press, 1900. 269p.
http://metalab.unc.edu/docsouth/kearney/menu.html

Missouri

Brown, Josephine. *Biography of an American Bondsman, Written by His Daughter.* Boston, MA: Wallcut, 1856. 104p.
http://digilib.nypl.org/dynaweb/digs/wwm975/

Brown, William Wells. *Narrative of William W. Brown, an American Slave.* 3rd ed. London: Charles Gilpin, 1849. 168p.
http://metalab.unc.edu/docsouth/brownw/menu.html

Leftwich, William M. *Martyrdom in Missouri, a History of Religious Proscription, the Seizure of Churches and the Persecution of Ministers of the Gospel in the State of Missouri during the Late Civil War and under the Test Oath of the New Constitution.* St. Louis, MO: Author, 1870. 438p.
http://moa.umdl.umich.edu/cgi-bin/moa/sgml/moa-idx?notisid=AGU9422b

Research Outline. Missouri. Salt Lake City, UT: Family History Library, 1997.
http://familysearch.org/sg/missouri.html

Reynolds, John N. *The Twin Hells, a Thrilling Narrative of Life in the Kansas and Missouri Penitentiaries.* Chicago, IL: Donohue, 1890. 331p.
http://www.ukans.edu/carrie/kancoll/books/twnhells/

Thompson, George. *Prison Life and Reflections or a Narrative of the Arrest, Trial, Conviction, Imprisonment, Treatment, Observations, Reflections and Deliverance of Work, Burr and Thompson Who Suffered an Unjust and Cruel Imprisonment in Missouri Penitentiary for Attempting to Aid Some Slaves to Liberty.* Hartford, CT: Alanson Work, 1850. 376p.
http://moa.umdl.umich.edu/cgi-bin/moa/sgml/moa-idx?notisid=ACK4077

Chariton County

Bruce, Henry Clay. *The New Man, Twenty-nine Years a Slave, Twenty-nine Years a Free Man, Recollections of H. C. Bruce.* York, PA: Anstadt & Sons, 1895. 176p.
http://metalab.unc.edu/docsouth/bruce/menu.html

Howard County

Burnett, Peter Hardeman. *Recollections and Opinions of an Old Pioneer.* New York, NY: Appleton, 1880. 448p.
http://memory.loc.gov/cgi-bin/query/r?ammem/calbkbib:@field(AUTHOR+@band(Burnett,+Peter+H[ardeman],1807-1895.+))

Kansas City

Hamilton, James Gillespie. *Notebooks of James Gillespie Hamilton, a Merchant of Old Westport, Missouri (1844-1858).* Fresno, CA: Katharine Jones Moore, 1953. 301p.
http://memory.loc.gov/cgi-bin/query/r?ammem/calbkbib:@field(AUTHOR+@band(Hamilton,+James+Gillespie,1816-1869.+))

Kansas City, Missouri, 1859-60 [City Directory]. Sutherland & McEvoy,
http://www.citydirectories.psmedia.com/city/free_statesort.html

St. Joseph Valley

Turner, Timothy G. *Gazetteer of the St. Joseph Valley, Michigan and Indiana.* Chicago, IL: Hazlitt & Reed, 1867. 168p.
http://moa.umdl.umich.edu/cgi-bin/moa/sgml/moa-idx?notisid=AFK0736

St. Louis

Ayers, James J. *Gold and Sunshine, Reminiscences of Early California.* Boston, MA: Badger, 1922. 359p.
http://memory.loc.gov/cgi-bin/query/r?ammem/calbkbib:@field(AUTHOR+@band(Ayers,+James+J.+))

Bemis, Stephen Allen. *Recollections of a Long and Somewhat Uneventful Life.* St. Louis, MO: Author, 1932. 92p.
http://memory.loc.gov/cgi-bin/query/r?ammem/calbkbib:@field(AUTHOR+@band(Bemis,+Stephen+Allen,1828-1919.+))

Delany, Lucy A. *From the Darkness Cometh the Light, or Struggles for Freedom.* St. Louis, MO: J. T. Smith, unknown. 64p.
http://digilib.nypl.org/dynaweb/digs/wwm97254/

Inventory of the Homans Family Papers, 1850-1938. New York, NY: New York Public Library, Manuscripts and Archives Division, 1997. Unpgd.
http://digilib.nypl.org/dynaweb/ead/human/homans/@Generic__BookView

Reavis, L. U. *Saint Louis, the Future Great City of the World.* St. Louis, MO: St. Louis County Court, 1871. 218p.
http://moa.umdl.umich.edu/cgi-bin/moa/sgml/moa-idx?notisid=AFK4236

St. Louis [City Directory]. St. Louis, MO: Kennedy, various.
1859, 1860, 1863-65.
http://www.citydirectories.psmedia.com/city/free_statesort.html

Westport

Hamilton, James Gillespie. *Notebooks of James Gillespie Hamilton, a Merchant of Old Westport, Missouri (1844-1858).* Fresno, CA: Katharine Jones Moore, 1953. 301p.
http://memory.loc.gov/cgi-bin/query/r?ammem/calbkbib:@field(AUTHOR+@band(Hamilton,+James+Gillespie,1816-1869.+))

Montana

Ludlow, William. *Report of a Reconnaissance from Carroll, Montana Territory, on the Upper Missouri to the Yellowstone National Park and Return Made in the Summer of 1875.* Washington, DC: Government Printing Office, 1876. 160p.
http://moa.umdl.umich.edu/cgi-bin/moa/sgml/moa-idx?notisid=ADQ3957

Parkman, Francis. *The Oregon Trail, Sketches of Prairie and Rocky Mountain Life.* Philadelphia, PA: Winston, 1931. 388p.
http://xroads.virginia.edu/~HYPER/OREGON/oregon.html

Research Outline. Montana. Salt Lake City, UT: Family History Library, 1997.
http://familysearch.org/sg/Montana.html

Nebraska

Boynton, Charles Brandon. *Journey through Kansas; with Sketches of Nebraska.* Cincinnati, OH: Moore, Wilstach, Keys & Co., 1855. 230p.
http://moa.umdl.umich.edu/cgi-bin/moa/sgml/moa-idx?notisid=ABE4921

Fremont, John Charles. *The Life of Col. John Charles Fremont and His Narrative of Explorations and Adventures in Kansas, Nebraska, Oregon and California.* New York, NY: Auburn, Miller, Orton & Mulligan, 1856. 514p.
http://moa.umdl.umich.edu/cgi-bin/moa/sgml/moa-idx?notisid=AAZ9580

Hale, Edward Everett. *Kansas and Nebraska, the History, Geography and Physical Characteristics and Political Position of Those Territories, an Account of the Emigrant Aid Companies and Directions to Emigrants.* Boston, MA: Philips, Sampson and Co., 1854. 262p.
http://moa.umdl.umich.edu/cgi-bin/moa/sgml/moa-idx?notisid=AFK4441

Parkman, Francis. *The Oregon Trail, Sketches of Prairie and Rocky Mountain Life.* Philadelphia, PA: Winston, 1931. 388p.
http://xroads.virginia.edu/~HYPER/OREGON/oregon.html

Research Outline. Nebraska. Salt Lake City, UT: Family History Library, 1997.
http://familysearch.org/sg/Nebraska.html

Knox County

Draper, Solomon. *An Historical Sketch of Knox County, Nebraska.* Niobrara, NE: Pioneer Pub. House, 1876. 16p.
http://moa.umdl.umich.edu/cgi-bin/moa/sgml/moa-idx?notisid=ABA0690

Nevada

Parkman, Francis. *The Oregon Trail, Sketches of Prairie and Rocky Mountain Life.* Philadelphia, PA: Winston, 1931. 388p.
http://xroads.virginia.edu/~HYPER/OREGON/oregon.html

Preliminary Report Concerning Explorations and Surveys, Principally in Nevada and Arizona. Prosecuted in Accordance with Paragraph 2, Special Orders No. 109, War Dept., March 18, 1871, and Letter of Instructions of March 23, 1871, from Brigadier General A. A. Humphreys, Chief of Engineers. Conducted under the Immediate Direction of 1st Lieut. George M. Wheeler . . . 1871. Washington, DC: Government Printing Office, 1872. 96p.
http://moa.umdl.umich.edu/cgi-bin/moa/sgml/moa-idx?notisid=AJA3663

Research Outline. Nevada. Salt Lake City, UT: Family History Library, 1997.
http://familysearch.org/sg/Nevada.html

Pioche

Buck, Franklin Agustus. *A Yankee Trader in the Gold Rush, the Letters of Franklin A. Buck.* Boston, MA: Houghton, Mifflin, 1930. 294p.
http://memory.loc.gov/cgi-bin/query/r?ammem/calbkbib:@field(AUTHOR+@band(Buck,+Franklin+Agustus,1826-1909.+))

New England

Bacon, Leonard. *The Genesis of the New England Churches*. New York, NY: Harper, 1874. 485p.
http://moa.cit.cornell.edu/dienst/moabrowse.fly/MOA-JOURNALS2:BACO-0030/5/1:TIFF2GIF:100

Drake, Samuel Adams. *Nooks and Corners of the New England Coast*. New York, NY: Harper & Brothers, 1875. 464p.
http://moa.umdl.umich.edu/cgi-bin/moa/sgml/moa-idx?notisid=AJA1974

Lilly, Lambert. *History of New England, Illustrated by Tales, Sketches and Anecdotes, with Numerous Engravings*. Boston, MA: Ticknor, 1847. 184p.
http://www.antiquebooks.net/cgi-bin/bookfront?book=1

New England Emigrant Aid Company. *History of the New England Emigrant Aid Company. With a Report on its Future Operations*. Boston, MA: J. Wilson and Son, 1862. 33p.
http://moa.umdl.umich.edu/cgi-bin/moa/sgml/moa-idx?notisid=ABA0781Jam

Savage, James. *A Genealogical Dictionary of the First Settlers of New England, Showing Three Generations of Those Who Came before May 1692*. Boston, MA: Little Brown & Co., 1860-62. 4 vols.
http://genweb.net/~books/savage/savage.htm

Talcott, Sebastian Visscher. *Genealogical Notes of New York and New England Families*. Albany, NY: Weed, Parsons & Co., 1883. 747p.
http://moa.cit.cornell.edu/dienst/moabrowse.fly/MOA-JOURNALS2:TALC-0006/3/1:TIFF2GIF:100

New Hampshire

Burt, Henry M. *Burt's Illustrated Guide of the Connecticut Valley, Containing Descriptions of Mount Holyoke, Mount Mansfield, White Mountains, Lake Memphremagog, Lake Willoughby, Montreal, Quebec*. Northampton: New England Publishing Co., 1867. 294p.
http://moa.umdl.umich.edu/cgi-bin/moa/sgml/moa-idx?notisid=AAB2140

Douglass, William. *A Discourse Concerning the Currencies of the British Plantations in America, Especially with Regard to Their Paper Money, more Particularly in Relation to the Province of Massachusetts Bay in New England*. 1740. Unknown. 3p.
http://www.people.virginia.edu/~rwm3n/webdoc2.html

Evans, Albert S. *A la California, Sketch of Life in the Golden State*. San Francisco, CA: Bancroft, 1873. 379p.
http://memory.loc.gov/cgi-bin/query/r?ammem/calbkbib:@field(AUTHOR+@band(Evans,+Albert+S.+))

Holton, Edward Dwight. *Travels with Jottings. From Midland to the Pacific*. Milwaukee, WI: Trayser Brothers, 1880. 94p.
http://memory.loc.gov/cgi-bin/query/r?ammem/calbkbib:@field(AUTHOR+@band(Holton,+Edward+D.+))

Meader, J. W. *The Merrimack River; Its Source and Its Tributaries. Embracing a History of Manufactures, and of the Towns along Its Course; Their Geography, Topography, and Products, with a Description of the Magnificent Natural Scenery about its Upper Waters*. Boston, MA: B. B. Russell, 1869. 308p.
http://moa.umdl.umich.edu/cgi-bin/moa/sgml/moa-idx?notisid=AFJ7467

Research Outline. New Hampshire. Salt Lake City, UT: Family History Library, 1997.
http://familysearch.org/sg/New_Hampshire.html

Talcott, Sebastian Visscher. *Genealogical Notes of New York and New England Families*. Albany, NY: Weed, Parsons & Co., 1883. 747p.
http://moa.cit.cornell.edu/dienst/moabrowse.fly/MOA-JOURNALS2:TALC-0006/3/1:TIFF2GIF:100

Chesterfield

Colt, Miriam Davis. *Went to Kansas, Being a Thrilling Account of an Ill Fated Expedition to That Fairy Land and Its Sad Result, together with a Sketch of the Life of the Author and How the World Goes with Her*. Watertown, NY: Ingalls & Co., 1862. 294p.
http://www.ukans.edu/carrie/kancoll/books/colt/

Dover

Dover [City Directory]. Dover, NH: Hayes, 1859.
http://www.citydirectories.psmedia.com/city/free_statesort.html

Exeter

Cross, Lillian A. *Appreciation of Loved Ones Who Made Life Rich for Many. My Father, John Francis Cross, My Mother, Sarah Jane Cross*. Oakland, CA: Tribune Press, 1933. 101p.
http://memory.loc.gov/cgi-bin/query/r?ammem/calbkbib:@field(AUTHOR+@band(Cross,+Lilian+A.+))

Nashua

Davis, Stephen Chapin. *California Gold Rush Merchant, the Journal of Stephen Chapin Davis*. San Marino, CA: Huntington Library, 1956. 124p.
http://memory.loc.gov/cgi-bin/query/r?ammem/calbkbib:@field(AUTHOR+@band(Davis,+Stephen+Chapin,1833-1856.+))

Pelham

Webster, Kimball. *The Gold Seekers of '49, a Personal Narrative of the Overland Trail and Adventures in California and Oregon from 1849 to 1854, by Kimball Webster a New England Forty-niner, with an Introduction and Biographical Sketch by George Waldo Browne*. Manchester, NH: Standard Book Co., 1917. 240p.
http://memory.loc.gov/cgi-bin/query/r?ammem/calbkbib:@field(AUTHOR+@band(Webster,+Kimball,1828-1916.+))

New Jersey

Douglass, William. *A Discourse Concerning the Currencies of the British Plantations in America, Especially with Regard to Their Paper Money, more Particularly in Relation to the Province of Massachusetts Bay in New England.* 1740. Unknown. 3p.
http://www.people.virginia.edu/~rwm3n/webdoc2.html

Research Outline. New Jersey. Salt Lake City, UT: Family History Library, 1997.
http://familysearch.org/sg/New_Jersey.html

Burlington County
Woolman, John. *A Journal of the Life, Gospel Labours and Christian Experiences of That Faithful Minister of Jesus Christ, John Woolman, Late of Mount Holly in the Province of New Jersey.* Philadelphia, PA: Crukshank, 1774. 436p.
http://darkwing.uoregon.edu/~rbear/woolman.html

Cape May
Lee, Jarena. *Religious Life and Experience and Journal of Mrs. Jarena Lee, Giving an Account of Her Call to Preach the Gospel.* Philadelphia, PA: Author, 1849. 97p.
http://digilib.nypl.org/dynaweb/digs/wwm9716/

Clifton
Williams, Albert. *A Pioneer Pastorate and Times Embodying Contemporary Local Transactions and Events by the Rev. Albert Williams, Founder and First Pastor of the First Presbyterian Church, San Francisco.* San Francisco, CA: Wallace & Hassett Printers, 1879. 240p.
http://memory.loc.gov/cgi-bin/query/r?ammem/calbkbib:@field(AUTHOR+@band(Williams,+Albert, 1809-1893.+))

Essex County
Essex, Hudson & Union Counties, Directory, [City Directory]. William H. Boyd, 1859.
http://www.citydirectories.psmedia.com/city/free_statesort.html

Hoboken
Jersey City and Hoboken, 1859-60 [City Directory]. James Gopsill, 1859.
http://www.citydirectories.psmedia.com/city/free_statesort.html

Hudson County
Essex, Hudson & Union Counties, Directory, [City Directory]. William H. Boyd, 1859.
http://www.citydirectories.psmedia.com/city/free_statesort.html

Jersey City
Jersey City and Hoboken, 1859-60 [City Directory]. James Gopsill, 1859.
http://www.citydirectories.psmedia.com/city/free_statesort.html

Lebanon

Johnson, Theodore Taylor. *Sights in the Gold Region and Scenes by the Way*. New York, NY: Baker & Scribner, 1849. 278p.
http://memory.loc.gov/cgi-bin/query/r?ammem/calbkbib:@field(AUTHOR+@band(Johnson,+Theodore+Taylor,b.+1818.+))

Morris County

Stephens, Lorenzo Dow. *Life Sketches of a Jayhawker of '49*. San Jose, CA: Nolta Brothers, 1916. 68p.
http://memory.loc.gov/cgi-bin/query/r?ammem/calbkbib:@field(AUTHOR+@band(Stephens,+Lorenzo+Dow,1827-+))

Newark

Levy, Edgar Mortimer. *History of the Newark Baptist City Mission from Its Origin in 1851 to Its Seventeenth Anniversary in 1868*. New York, NY: Hurd and Houghton, 1869. 144p.
http://moa.umdl.umich.edu/cgi-bin/moa/sgml/moa-idx?notisid=AJG8034

Newark, 1859-60 [City Directory]. Pierson, 1859.
http://www.citydirectories.psmedia.com/city/free_statesort.html

Patterson

Patterson [City Directory]. William H. Boyd, 1859.
http://www.citydirectories.psmedia.com/city/free_statesort.html

Trenton

Parkinson, Edward S. *Wonderland or Twelve Weeks in and Out of the United States. Brief Account of a Trip across the Continent, Short Run in Mexico, Ride to the Yosemite Valley, Steamer Voyage to Alaska, the Land of Glaciers, Visit to the Great Shoshone Falls and a Stage Ride through the Yellowstone National Park*. Trenton, NJ: MacCrellish & Quigley, 1894. 259p.
http://memory.loc.gov/cgi-bin/query/r?ammem/calbkbib:@field(AUTHOR+@band(Parkinson,+Edward+S.+))

Trenton [City Directory]. William H. Boyd, 1859.
http://www.citydirectories.psmedia.com/city/free_statesort.html

Union County

Essex, Hudson & Union Counties, Directory, [City Directory]. William H. Boyd, 1859.
http://www.citydirectories.psmedia.com/city/free_statesort.html

New Mexico

Cozzens, Samuel Woodworth. *The Marvelous Country, or, Three Years in Arizona and New Mexico. Containing an Authentic History of This Wonderful Country and Its Ancient*

Civilization . . . together with a Full and Complete History of the Apache Tribe of Indians. Boston, MA: Lee & Shepard, 1876. 606p.
http://moa.umdl.umich.edu/cgi-bin/moa/sgml/moa-idx?notisid=AJA3616

Research Outline. New Mexico. Salt Lake City, UT: Family History Library, 1997.
http://familysearch.org/sg/New_Mexico.html

Wilson, Benjamin Davis. *The Indians of Southern California in 1852.* San Marino, CA: Huntington Library, 1952. 154p.
http://memory.loc.gov/cgi-bin/query/r?ammem/calbkbib:@field(AUTHOR+@band(Wilson,+Benjamin+Davis,1811-1878.+))

Santa Fe

Austin, Mary Hunter. *The Land of Little Rain.* Boston, MA: Houghton, Mifflin, 1903. 280p.
http://memory.loc.gov/cgi-bin/query/r?ammem/calbkbib:@field(AUTHOR+@band(Austin,+Mary+Hunter,1868-1934.+))

Taos

Abbott, John S. C. *Christopher Carson, Familiarly Known as Kit Carson.* New York, NY: Dodd, Mead, 1874. 362p.
http://moa.umdl.umich.edu/cgi-bin/moa/sgml/moa-idx?notisid=ABE2513

New York

Barber, John W. *Historical Collections of the State of New York, Being a General Collection of the Most Interesting Facts, Biographical Sketches, Varied Descriptions etc., Relating to the Past and Present with Geographical Descriptions of the Counties, Cities and Principal Villages throughout the State.* New York, NY: Austin, 1851. 418p.
http://moa.cit.cornell.edu/dienst/moabrowse.fly/MOA-JOURNALS2:BARB-0007/5/1:TIFF2GIF:100

Boyd, Andrew. *Boyd's Business Directory of the One Hundred Cities and Villages in New York State, together with Post Offices, Postmasters' Names, Money Order Post Offices and Telegraph and Express Stations throughout the States, History of the States and Territories, and Brief Sketches of the Places Contained in the Directory, Incorporated and Manufacturing Companies, Railroads, Newspapers, etc. United States, New York State, County, City Officers. 1869-1870.* Albany, NY: Van Benthuysen, 1869. 864p.
http://moa.cit.cornell.edu/dienst/moabrowse.fly/MOA-JOURNALS2:BOYD-0001/3/1:TIFF2GIF:100

————. *New York State Business Directory and Gazetteer.* Albany, NY: Boyds, 1,410p.
http://moa.cit.cornell.edu/dienst/moabrowse.fly/MOA-JOURNALS2:BOYD-0002/3/1:TIFF2GIF:100

Colt, S. S. *The Tourist's Guide through the Empire State, Embracing all Cities, Towns and Watering Places, by Hudson River and New York Central Route.* Albany, NY: Colt, 1871. 332p.
http://moa.umdl.umich.edu/cgi-bin/moa/sgml/moa-idx?notisid=AJA2210

Douglass, William. *A Discourse Concerning the Currencies of the British Plantations in America, Especially with Regard to Their Paper Money, more Particularly in Relation to the Province of Massachusetts Bay in New England.* 1740. Unknown. 3p.
http://www.people.virginia.edu/~rwm3n/webdoc2.html

Franks, David. *The New York Directory, 1786.* New York, NY: Patterson, 1786, 1874.
http://moa.cit.cornell.edu/dienst/moabrowse.fly/MOA-JOURNALS2:NEWY-0053/3/1:TIFF2GIF:100

Jenkins, John S. *Lives of the Governors of the State of New York.* Auburn, NY: Derby and Miller, 1851. 832p.
http://moa.cit.cornell.edu/dienst/moabrowse.fly/MOA-JOURNALS2:JENK-0004/5/1:TIFF2GIF:100

Macleod, William. *Harper's New York and Erie Railroad Guide Book . . . with One Hundred and Thirty-six Engravings, by Lossing and Barritt.* 8th ed., New York, NY: Harper, 1855. 190p.
http://moa.umdl.umich.edu/cgi-bin/moa/sgml/moa-idx?notisid=AJA2207

Murray, W. H. H. *Lake Champlain and Its Shores.* Boston, MA: De Wolfe, Fiske, Co., 1890. 262p.
http://moa.cit.cornell.edu/dienst/moabrowse.fly/MOA-JOURNALS2:MURR-0090/7/1:TIFF2GIF:100

Names of Persons for Whom Marriage Licenses were Issued by the Secretary of the Province of New York Previous to 1784. Albany, NY: Weed, Parsons, and Co., 1860. 480p.
http://moa.cit.cornell.edu/dienst/moabrowse.fly/MOA-JOURNALS2:TUCK-0005/3/1:TIFF2GIF:100

New York State Archives and Records Administration. *Records Relating to African Americans in the New York State Archives.* Albany, NY: Author, 1997. Unpgd.
http://www.sara.nysed.gov/holding/fact/leaf8.htm

Randall, Samuel Sidwell. *History of the State of New York, for the use of Common Schools, Academies, Normal and High Schools.* New York, NY: Ford, 1871. 370p.
http://moa.cit.cornell.edu/dienst/moabrowse.fly/MOA-JOURNALS2:RAND-0073/3/1:TIFF2GIF:100

Research Outline. New York. Salt Lake City, UT: Family History Library, 1997.
http://familysearch.org/sg/New_York.html

Satterlee, Herbert Livingston. *The Political History of the Province of New York.* New York, NY: Pearson, 1885. 108p.
http://moa.cit.cornell.edu/dienst/moabrowse.fly/MOA-JOURNALS2:SATT-0044/5/1:TIFF2GIF:100

Simms, Jeptha Root. *Trappers of New York or a Biography of Nicholas Stoner and Nathaniel Foster, together with Anecdotes of other Celebrated Hunters and Some Account of Sir William Johnson.* Albany, NY: Munsell's, 1850. 280p.
http://moa.cit.cornell.edu/dienst/moabrowse.fly/MOA-JOURNALS2:SIMM-0023/5/1:TIFF2GIF:100

Talcott, S. V. *Genealogical Notes of New York and New England Families.* Albany, NY: Weed, Parsons & Co., 1883. 747p.
http://moa.cit.cornell.edu/dienst/moabrowse.fly/MOA-JOURNALS2:TALC-0006/3/1:TIFF2GIF:100

Wooley, Charles. *A Two Years Journal in New York, and Part of Its Territories in America.* New York, NY: William Gowans, 1860. 98p.
http://moa.cit.cornell.edu/dienst/moabrowse.fly/MOA-JOURNALS2:WOOL-0009/5/1:TIFF2GIF:100

Adirondacks

Byron Curtiss, Arthur Lester Byron. *The Life and Adventures of Nat Foster, Trapper and Hunter of the Adirondacks.* Utica, NY: Griffiths, 1897. 286p.
http://moa.cit.cornell.edu/dienst/moabrowse.fly/MOA-JOURNALS2:CURT-0015/5/1:TIFF2GIF:100

DeCosta, Benjamin Franklin. *Lake George, Its Scenes and Characteristics with Glimpses of the Olden Times, to which Is Added Some Account of Ticonderoga, Lake Luzerne, Schroon Lake and the Adirondacks, with an Appendix Containing Notes on Lake Champlain.* 3rd ed. New York, NY: Randolph, 1868. 181p.
http://moa.cit.cornell.edu/dienst/moabrowse.fly/MOA-JOURNALS2:DECO-0095/5/1:TIFF2GIF:100

Hammond, Samuel H. *Hunting Adventures in the Northern Wilds, or a Tramp in the Chateaugay, over Hills, Lakes and Forest Streams.* Philadelphia, PA: Keystone Publishing Co., 1890. 340p.
http://moa.cit.cornell.edu/dienst/moabrowse.fly/MOA-JOURNALS2:HAMM-0076/5/1:TIFF2GIF:100

————, and L. W. Mansfield. *Country Margins and Rambles of a Journalist.* New York, NY: Derby, 1855. 356p.
http://moa.cit.cornell.edu/dienst/moabrowse.fly/MOA-JOURNALS2:HAMM-0022/5/1:TIFF2GIF:100

Headley, Joel Tyler. *The Adirondack, or, Life in the Woods.* New York, NY: Baker & Scribner, 1853. 316p.
http://moa.umdl.umich.edu/cgi-bin/moa/sgml/moa-idx?notisid=AAS0215

Albany

Albany [City Directory]. Adams, Sampson & Co., 1859.
http://www.citydirectories.psmedia.com/city/free_statesort.html

Bryan, George J. *Biographies of Attorney General George P. Barker, John C. Lord, D.D., Mrs. John C. Lord and William G. Bryan, Esq. Also Lecture on Journalism.* Buffalo, NY: Courier Co., 1886. 232p.
http://moa.cit.cornell.edu/dienst/moabrowse.fly/MOA-JOURNALS2:BRYN-0003/5/1:TIFF2GIF:100

Kip, Leonard. *California Sketches, with Recollections of the Gold Mines.* Los Angeles, CA: Kovach, 1946. 58p.
http://memory.loc.gov/cgi-bin/query/r?ammem/calbkbib:@field(AUTHOR+@band(Kip,+Leonard,1826-1906.+))

Knower, Daniel. *The Adventures of a Forty-niner. An Historic Description of California, with Events and Ideas of San Francisco and Its People in Those Early Days.* Albany, NY: Weed Parsons, 1894. 200p.
http://memory.loc.gov/cgi-bin/query/r?ammem/calbkbib:@field(AUTHOR+@band(Knower,+Daniel.+))

Moak, Sim. *The Last of the Mill Creeks and Early Life in Northern California.* Chico, CA: Author, 1923. 47p.
http://memory.loc.gov/cgi-bin/query/r?ammem/calbkbib:@field(AUTHOR+@band(Moak,+Sim,1845-+))

Rogers, E. P. *A Historical Discourse on the Reformed Protestant Dutch Church of Albany.* New York, NY: Church, 1858. 120p.
http://moa.cit.cornell.edu/dienst/moabrowse.fly/MOA-JOURNALS2:ROGE-0062/5/1:TIFF2GIF:100

Allegany County

Turner, O. *History of the Pioneer Settlement of Phelps and Gorham's Purchase and Morris' Reserve, Embracing the Counties of Monroe, Ontario, Livingston, Yates, Steuben, Most of Wayne and Allegany and Parts of Orleans, Genesee and Wyoming, to which is Added a Supplement or Extension of the Pioneer History of Monroe County.* Rochester, NY: William Alling 1851. 624p.
http://moa.cit.cornell.edu/dienst/moabrowse.fly/MOA-JOURNALS2:TURN-0092/3/1:TIFF2GIF:100

Auburn

Auburn, 1859-60 [City Directory]. William H. Boyd, 1859.
http://www.citydirectories.psmedia.com/city/free_statesort.html

Aurora

Delano, Alonzo. *Alonzo Delano's California Correspondence, being Letters Hitherto Uncollected from the Ottawa (Illinois) Free Trader and the New Orleans True Delta, 1849-1952*. Sacramento, CA: Sacramento Book Collector's Club, 1952. 155p.
http://memory.loc.gov/cgi-bin/query/r?ammem/calbk:@field(DOCID+@lit(C073T00)):@@@REF

———. *Life on the Plains and among the Diggings, Being Scenes and Adventures of an Overland Journey to California, with Particular Incidents of the Route, Mistakes and Sufferings of the Emigrants, the Indian Tribes, the Present and Future of the Great West*. New York, NY: Miller, Orton & Co., 1857. 384p.
http://memory.loc.gov/cgi-bin/query/r?ammem/calbk:@field(DOCID+@lit(C171T00)):@@@REF

Bedford (Westchester County)

Wood, Harvey. *Personal Recollections*. Pasadena, CA: John B. Goodman, III, 1955. 27p.
http://memory.loc.gov/cgi-bin/query/r?ammem/calbkbib:@field(AUTHOR+@band(Wood,+Harvey,1828-1895.+))

Binghamton

Binghamton, 1859-60 [City Directory]. William H. Boyd, 1859.
http://www.citydirectories.psmedia.com/city/free_statesort.html

Brookhaven

Records of the Town of Brookhaven, Suffolk County, N.Y., This Volume Contains the Entire Records from 1796 to March 1856, inclusive, Copied from the Original Records in Their Order, under the Direction of the Supervisor and Justices of the Peace and Established by the Authority of the Town. Port Jefferson, NY: Times Steam Job Print, 1888. 552p.
http://moa.cit.cornell.edu/dienst/moabrowse.fly/MOA-JOURNALS2:BROO-0063/3/1:TIFF2GIF:100

Records of the Town of Brookhaven, Suffolk County, N.Y. This Volume Contains the Entire Records from 1856 to December 1885, inclusive, Copied from the Original Records in Their Order, under the Direction of the Supervisor and Justices of the Peace, and Published by the Authority of the Town. New York, NY: Burr Printing House, 1893. 1,118p.
http://moa.cit.cornell.edu/dienst/moabrowse.fly/MOA-JOURNALS2:BROO-0064/3/1:TIFF2GIF:100

Brooklyn (Kings County)

Brooklyn [City Directory]. Brooklyn, NY: Lain, various.
1860; 1880-81; 1890-91.
http://www.citydirectories.psmedia.com/city/free_statesort.html

Ostrander, Stephen M. *A History of the City of Brooklyn and Kings County*. Brooklyn, NY: Annie A. Ostrander, 1894. 2 vols.
http://moa.cit.cornell.edu/dienst/moabrowse.fly/MOA-JOURNALS2:OSTR-0065/5/1:TIFF2GIF:100

Buffalo

Bancroft, Hubert Howe. *Literary Industries, a Memoir*. San Francisco, CA: History Company, 1891. 808p.
http://memory.loc.gov/cgi-bin/query/r?ammem/calbkbib:@field(AUTHOR+@band(Bancroft,+Hubert+Howe,1832-1918.+))

Buffalo [City Directory]. Buffalo, NY: Jewett, 1859.
http://www.citydirectories.psmedia.com/city/free_statesort.html

Clarke, Walter. *Half Century Discourse, the First Church in Buffalo.* Buffalo, NY: Theodore Butler, 1862. 92p.
http://moa.cit.cornell.edu/dienst/moabrowse.fly/MOA-JOURNALS2:CLAR-0067/3/1:TIFF2GIF:100

Welch, Samuel Manning. *Home History, Recollections of Buffalo during the Decade from 1830 to 1840 or Fifty Years Since.* Buffalo, NY: Peter Paul & Bro., 1891. 424p.
http://moa.cit.cornell.edu/dienst/moabrowse.fly/MOA-JOURNALS2:WELC-0069/5/1:TIFF2GIF:100

Wilkeson, John. *The Manufacture of Iron in Buffalo.* Buffalo, NY: Wheeler, Matthews & Warren, 1864. 8p.
http://moa.umdl.umich.edu/cgi-bin/moa/sgml/moa-idx?notisid=AFT1331

Canajoharie
James, Thomas. *Wonderful Eventful Life of Rev. Thomas James.* Rochester, NY: Post Express Printing Co., 1887. 24p.
http://memory.loc.gov/cgi-bin/query/r?ammem/aap:@field(SUBJ+@band(Autobiographies--New+York++State+--1887.+))

Cape Vincent
Pratt, Elizur H. *A Historical Sketch of the Town of Cape Vincent, Read at the Centennial Celebration of the Township, July 4, 1876.* Cape Vincent, NY: Warren W. Ames, 1876. 50p.
http://moa.cit.cornell.edu/dienst/moabrowse.fly/MOA-JOURNALS2:PRAT-0070/3/1:TIFF2GIF:100

Catskill
Pinckney, James D. *Reminiscences of Catskill, Local Sketches.* Catskill, NY: Hall, 1868. 80p.
http://moa.cit.cornell.edu/dienst/moabrowse.fly/MOA-JOURNALS2:PINC-0071/5/1:TIFF2GIF:100

Cattaraugus County
Manley, John. *Cattaraugus County, Embracing Its Agricultural Society, Newspapers, Civil List, from the Organization of the County to 1857, Biographies of the Old Pioneers, with Portraits, Benjamin Chamberlain, Peter Ten Broeck, Frederick S. Martin, Chauncey J. Fox, Alson Leavenworth, Stanley N. Clarke, and of Congressmen Francis S. Edwards and Reuben E. Fenton, Colonial and State Governors of New York, Names of Towns and Post Offices with the Statistics of Each Town.* Little Valley, NY: Author, 1857. 140p.
http://moa.cit.cornell.edu/dienst/moabrowse.fly/MOA-JOURNALS2:MANL-0089/3/1:TIFF2GIF:100

Cayuga County
Leach, Frank Aleamon. *Recollections of a Newspaperman, a Record of Life and Events in California.* San Francisco, CA: Levinson, 1917. 416p.
http://memory.loc.gov/cgi-bin/query/r?ammem/calbkbib:@field(AUTHOR+@band(Leach,+Frank+Aleamon,1846-+))

Chateaugay (Franklin County)
Norton, Lewis Adelbert. *Life and Adventures of Col. L. A. Norton.* Oakland, CA: Pacific Press, 1887. 492p.
http://memory.loc.gov/cgi-bin/query/r?ammem/calbkbib:@field(AUTHOR+@band(Norton,+Lewis+Adelbert,b.+1819.+))

Chautauqua County

Bidwell, John. *Echoes of the Past about California.* Published with *In Camp and Cabin,* by Rev. John Steele. Chicago, IL: Donnelley, 1928. 377p.
http://memory.loc.gov/cgi-bin/query/r?ammem/calbkbib:@field(AUTHOR+@band(Bidwell,+John,1819-1900.+))

Hazeltine, Gilbert W. *The Early History of the Town of Ellicott, Chautauqua County, N.Y., Compiled Largely from the Personal Recollections of the Author.* Jamestown, NY: Journal Printing, 1887. 556p.
http://moa.cit.cornell.edu/dienst/moabrowse.fly/MOA-JOURNALS2:HAZE-0113/3/1:TIFF2GIF:100

Royce, Charles C. *Addresses, Reminiscences, etc. of General John Bidwell.* Chico, CA: Charles C. Royce, 1906. 221p.
http://memory.loc.gov/cgi-bin/query/r?ammem/calbkbib:@field(AUTHOR+@band(Bidwell,+John,1819-1900.+))

Chenango County

Bundy, Charles Smith. *Early Days in the Chippewa Valley.* Menominie, WI: Flint Douglas Printing, 1916. 16p.
http://memory.loc.gov/cgi-bin/query/r?ammem/lhbum:@field(DOCID+@lit(16807T000)):@@@REF

Cherry Valley

Sawyer John. *History of Cherry Valley, from 1740 to 1898.* Cherry Valley, NY: Gazette Print, 1898. 156p.
http://moa.cit.cornell.edu/dienst/moabrowse.fly/MOA-JOURNALS2:SAWY-0072/3/1:TIFF2GIF:100

Clarendon

Copeland, David Sturges. *History of Clarendon from 1810 to 1888.* Buffalo, NY: Courier, 1889. 382p.
http://moa.cit.cornell.edu/dienst/moabrowse.fly/MOA-JOURNALS2:COPE-0109/3/1:TIFF2GIF:100

Cohoes

Masten, Arthur H. *The History of Cohoes, New York, from Its Earliest Settlement to the Present Time.* Albany, NY: Munsell's, 1877. 328p.
http://moa.cit.cornell.edu/dienst/moabrowse.fly/MOA-JOURNALS2:MAST-0105/5/1:TIFF2GIF:100

Collins

Briggs, Erasmus. *History of the Original Town of Concord, Being the Present Towns of Concord, Collins, North Collins and Sardinia.* Rochester, NY: Union and Advertisers Company's Print, 1883. 992p.
http://moa.cit.cornell.edu/dienst/moabrowse.fly/MOA-JOURNALS2:BRIG-0106/3/1:TIFF2GIF:100

Columbia County

Raymond, William. *Biographical Sketches of the Distinguished Men of Columbia County, Including an Account of the Most Important Offices They Have Filled in the State and General Governments, and in the Army and Navy.* Albany, NY: Weed, Parsons, and Co., 1851. 120p.
http://moa.cit.cornell.edu/dienst/moabrowse.fly/MOA-JOURNALS2:RAYM-0019/5/1:TIFF2GIF:100

Concord

Briggs, Erasmus. *History of the Original Town of Concord, Being the Present Towns of Concord, Collins, North Collins and Sardinia.* Rochester, NY: Union and Advertisers Company's Print, 1883. 992p.
http://moa.cit.cornell.edu/dienst/moabrowse.fly/MOA-JOURNALS2:BRIG-0106/3/1:TIFF2GIF:100

Conesus (Livingston County)

Boyd, William. *History of the Town of Conesus, Livingston Co., NY, from Its First Settlement in 1793 to 1887, with a Brief Genealogical Record of the Conesus Families.* Conesus, NY: Boyd's, 1887. 198p.
http://moa.cit.cornell.edu/dienst/moabrowse.fly/MOA-JOURNALS2:BOYD-0107/5/1:TIFF2GIF:100

Cooperstown

Shaw, S. M. *A Centennial Offering, Being a Brief History of Cooperstown, with a Biographical Sketch of James Fenimore Cooper by Hon. Isaac H. Arnold.* Cooperstown, NY: Freeman's Journal Office, 1886. 240p.
http://moa.cit.cornell.edu/dienst/moabrowse.fly/MOA-JOURNALS2:SHAW-0108/3/1:TIFF2GIF:100

Cornwall

Beech, Louis. *Cornwall, a History.* Newburgh, NY: Ruttenber, 1873. 200p.
http://moa.cit.cornell.edu/dienst/moabrowse.fly/MOA-JOURNALS2:BEAC-0110/3/1:TIFF2GIF:Fit Window?,,

Cortland County

Child, Hamilton. *Gazetteer and Business Directory of Cortland County, New York, for 1869.* Syracuse, NY: Journal Office, 1869. 204p.
http://moa.cit.cornell.edu/dienst/moabrowse.fly/MOA-JOURNALS2:CHIL-0078/9/1:TIFF2GIF:100?,,

Goodwin, H. C. *Pioneer History of Cortland County and the Border Wars of New York from the Earliest Period to the Present Time.* New York, NY: Burdick, 1850. 456p.
http://moa.cit.cornell.edu/dienst/moabrowse.fly/MOA-JOURNALS2:GOOD-0079/5/1:TIFF2GIF:100

Crown Point (Essex County)

Colt, Miriam Davis. *Went to Kansas, Being a Thrilling Account of an Ill Fated Expedition to That Fairy Land and Its Sad Result, together with a Sketch of the Life of the Author and How the World Goes with Her.* Watertown, NY: Ingalls & Co., 1862. 294p.
http://www.ukans.edu/carrie/kancoll/books/colt/

Watson, Winslow Cossoul. *The Military and Civil History of the County of Essex, New York and a General Survey of Its Physical Geography, Its Mines and Minerals and Industrial Pursuits. Embracing an Account of the Northern Wilderness and also the Military Annals of the Fortresses of Crown Point and Ticonderoga.* New York, NY: Munsell, 1869. 504p.
http://moa.cit.cornell.edu/dienst/moabrowse.fly/MOA-JOURNALS2:WATS-0094/5/1:TIFF2GIF:100

Deerpark (Orange County)

Gumaer, Peter E. *A History of Deerpark in Orange County, N.Y.* Port Jervis, NY: Union Print, 1890. 206p.
http://moa.cit.cornell.edu/dienst/moabrowse.fly/MOA-JOURNALS2:GUMA-0111/5/1:TIFF2GIF:100

Delaware County

The Sidney Centennial Jubilee at Sidney Plains, Delaware County, NY, June 13, 1872. Ann Arbor, MI: Chase's Steam Printing House, 1875. 100p.
http://moa.umdl.umich.edu/cgi-bin/moa/sgml/moa-idx?notisid=AJA2325

Dutchess County

Bailey, Henry D. B. *Local Tales and Historical Sketches.* Fishkill Landing, NY: Spaight, 1874. 432p.
http://moa.cit.cornell.edu/dienst/moabrowse.fly/MOA-JOURNALS2:BAIL-0081/3/1:TIFF2GIF:100

Smith, Philip Henry. *General History of Dutchess County from 1609 to 1876, inclusive.* Pawling, NY: Author, 1877. 508p.
http://moa.cit.cornell.edu/dienst/moabrowse.fly/MOA-JOURNALS2:SMIT-0080/5/1:TIFF2GIF:100

East Hampton

Hedges, Henry Parsons. *A History of the Town of East Hampton, N.Y., Including an Address Delivered at the Celebration of the Bi-Centennial Anniversary of Its Settlement in 1849, Introductions to the Four Printed Volumes of Its Records with other Historic Material, an Appendix and Genealogical Notes.* Sag Harbor, NY: Hunt, 1897. 344p.
http://moa.cit.cornell.edu/dienst/moabrowse.fly/MOA-JOURNALS2:HEDG-0112/5/1:TIFF2GIF:100

Ellicott (Chautauqua County)

Hazeltine, Gilbert W. *The Early History of the Town of Ellicott, Chautauqua County, N.Y., Compiled Largely from the Personal Recollections of the Author.* Jamestown, NY: Journal Printing, 1887. 556p.
http://moa.cit.cornell.edu/dienst/moabrowse.fly/MOA-JOURNALS2:HAZE-0113/3/1:TIFF2GIF:100

Erie County

Johnson, Crisfield. *Centennial History of Erie County, New York, Being Its Annals from the Earliest Recorded Events to the Hundredth Year of American Independence.* Buffalo, NY: Matthews & Warren, 1876. 512p.
http://moa.cit.cornell.edu/dienst/moabrowse.fly/MOA-JOURNALS2:JOHN-0082/3/1:TIFF2GIF:100

Essex County

Colt, Miriam Davis. *Went to Kansas, Being a Thrilling Account of an Ill Fated Expedition to That Fairy Land and Its Sad Result, together with a Sketch of the Life of the Author and How the World Goes with Her.* Watertown, NY: Ingalls & Co., 1862. 294p.
http://www.ukans.edu/carrie/kancoll/books/colt/

Northup, Solomon. *Narrative of Solomon Northup, a Citizen of New York, Kidnapped in Washington City in 1841, Rescued in 1853, from a Cotton Plantation near the Red River, in Louisiana.* Auburn, NY: Derby and Miller, 1853. 336p.
http://metalab.unc.edu/docsouth/northup/menu.html

Ward, David. *The Autobiography of David Ward.* New York, NY: Author, 1912. 194p.
http://memory.loc.gov/cgi-bin/query/r?ammem/lhbumbib:@field(SUBJ+@band(Michigan--Social+life+and+customs.+))

Watson, Winslow Cossoul. *The Military and Civil History of the County of Essex, New York and a General Survey of Its Physical Geography, Its Mines and Minerals and Industrial Pursuits. Embracing an Account of the Northern Wilderness and also the Military Annals of the Fortresses of Crown Point and Ticonderoga.* New York, NY: Munsell's, 1869. 504p.
http://moa.cit.cornell.edu/dienst/moabrowse.fly/MOA-JOURNALS2:WATS-0094/5/1:TIFF2GIF:100

Genesee County

Turner, O. *History of the Pioneer Settlement of Phelps and Gorham's Purchase and Morris' Reserve, Embracing the Counties of Monroe, Ontario, Livingston, Yates, Steuben, Most of Wayne and Allegany and Parts of Orleans, Genesee and Wyoming, to which is Added a Supplement or Extension of the Pioneer History of Monroe County.* Rochester, NY: William Alling 1851. 624p.
http://moa.cit.cornell.edu/dienst/moabrowse.fly/MOA-JOURNALS2:TURN-0092/3/1:TIFF2GIF:100

Greenwich

Thurston, Elisha P. *History of the Town of Greenwich, from the Earliest Settlement.* Salem, NY: H. D. Morris, Book and Job Printer, 1876. 78p.
http://moa.cit.cornell.edu/dienst/moabrowse.fly/MOA-JOURNALS2:THUR-0115/5/1:TIFF2GIF:100

Groton (Tompkins County)

Crosby, Elisha Oscar. *Memoirs of Elisha Oscar Crosby, Reminiscences of California and Guatemala from 1849 to 1864.* San Marino, CA: Huntington Library, 1945. 119p.
http://memory.loc.gov/cgi-bin/query/r?ammem/calbkbib:@field(AUTHOR+@band(Crosby,+Elisha+Oscar,1818-1895.+))

Hamilton (Madison County)

Schoolcraft, Henry Rowe. *Narrative Journal of Travels through the Northwestern Regions of the United States, Extending from Detroit through the Great Chain of American Lakes to the Sources of the Mississippi River, Performed as a Member of the Expedition under Governor Cass in the Year 1820.* Albany, NY: Hosford, 1821. 423p.
http://memory.loc.gov/cgi-bin/query/r?ammem/lhbum:@field(DOCID+@lit(01453T000)):@@@REF

————. *Narrative of an Expedition through the Upper Mississippi to Itasca Lake, the Actual Source of This River Embracing an Exploratory Trip through the St. Croix and Burntwood (or Broule) Rivers in 1832.* New York, :NY: Harper, 1834. 308p.
http://memory.loc.gov/cgi-bin/query/r?ammem/lhbum:@field(DOCID+@lit(08794T000)):@@@REF

————. *Personal Memoirs of a Residence of Thirty Years with the Indian Tribes on the American Frontiers with Brief Notices of Passing Events, Facts, and Opinions, A.D. 1812 to A.D. 1842.* Philadelphia, PA: Lippincott, 1851. 703p.
http://memory.loc.gov/cgi-bin/query/r?ammem/lhbum:@field(DOCID+@lit(15006T000)):@@@REF

Hurley (Ulster County)

Gilbert, Olive. *Narrative of Sojourner Truth, a Bonds-woman of Olden Time, Emancipated by the New York Legislature in the Early Part of the Present Century, with a History of Her Labors and Correspondence, Drawn from Her Book of Life.* Battle Creek, MI: Author, 1878. 320p.
http://memory.loc.gov/cgi-bin/query/r?ammem/lhbumbib:@field(SUBJ+@band(Truth,+Sojourner,--d.+1883.+))

Jefferson County

Rogers, Frank D. *Folk Stories of the Northern Border.* Jefferson County, NY: Author, 1897. 274p.
http://moa.cit.cornell.edu/dienst/moabrowse.fly/MOA-JOURNALS2:ROGE-0086/5/1:TIFF2GIF:100

Keene (Essex County)

Ward, David. *The Autobiography of David Ward.* New York, NY: Author, 1912. 194p.
http://memory.loc.gov/cgi-bin/query/r?ammem/lhbumbib:@field(SUBJ+@band(Michigan--Social+life+and+customs.+))

Keesville

Inventory of the William Henry Jackson Papers. New York, NY: New York Public Library, Manuscripts and Archives Division, 1998. Unpgd.
http://digilib.nypl.org/dynaweb/ead/human/jacksonw/@Generic__BookView

Kings County

Bergen, Teunis G. *Register in Alphabetical Order of the Early Settlers of Kings County, Long Island, New York, from Its First Settlement by Europeans to 1700, with Contributions to Their Biographies and Genealogies, Compiled from Various Sources.* New York, NY: Green's Son, 1881. 454p.
http://moa.cit.cornell.edu/dienst/moabrowse.fly/MOA-JOURNALS2:BERG-0085/3/1:TIFF2GIF:100

Ostrander, Stephen M. *A History of the City of Brooklyn and Kings County.* Brooklyn, NY: Annie A. Ostrander, 1894. 2 vols.
http://moa.cit.cornell.edu/dienst/moabrowse.fly/MOA-JOURNALS2:OSTR-0065/5/1:TIFF2GIF:100

Livingston County

Boyd, William. *History of the Town of Conesus, Livingston Co., NY, from Its First Settlement in 1793 to 1887, with a Brief Genealogical Record of the Conesus Families.* Conesus, NY: Boyd's, 1887. 198p.
http://moa.cit.cornell.edu/dienst/moabrowse.fly/MOA-JOURNALS2:BOYD-0107/5/1:TIFF2GIF:100

Doty, Lockwood Lyon. *A History of Livingston County, New York, from Its Earliest Traditions to Its Part in the War for Our Union, with an Account of the Seneca Nation of Indians and Biographical Sketches of Earliest Settlers and Prominent Public Men.* Geneseo, NY: Edward E. Doty, 1876. 686p.
http://moa.cit.cornell.edu/dienst/moabrowse.fly/MOA-JOURNALS2:DOTY-0102/5/1:TIFF2GIF:100
http://genweb.net/~braintree/livingston/

A History of the Treaty of Big Tree, and an Account of Celebration of the One Hundredth Anniversary of the Making of the Treaty, Held at Geneseo, N.Y., September the Fifteenth, Eighteen Hundred Ninety Seven. Dansville, NY: Bunnell, 1897. 104p.
http://moa.cit.cornell.edu/dienst/moabrowse.fly/MOA-JOURNALS2:LIVI-0045/7/1:TIFF2GIF:100

Stetson, G. Emmet. *New Gazetteer and Business Directory for Livingston County, N.Y. for 1868.* Geneva, NY: Adams, 1868. 246p.
http://moa.cit.cornell.edu/dienst/moabrowse.fly/MOA-JOURNALS2:STET-0047/3/1:TIFF2GIF:100

Turner, O. *History of the Pioneer Settlement of Phelps and Gorham's Purchase and Morris' Reserve, Embracing the Counties of Monroe, Ontario, Livingston, Yates, Steuben, Most of Wayne and Allegany and Parts of Orleans, Genesee and Wyoming, to which is Added a Supplement or Extension of the Pioneer History of Monroe County.* Rochester, NY: William Alling 1851. 624p.
http://moa.cit.cornell.edu/dienst/moabrowse.fly/MOA-JOURNALS2:TURN-0092/3/1:TIFF2GIF:100

Madison County

Child, Hamilton. *Gazetteer and Business Directory of Madison County, New York, for 1868-9.* Syracuse, NY: Journal Office, 1868. 234p.
http://moa.cit.cornell.edu/dienst/moabrowse.fly/MOA-JOURNALS2:CHIL-0021/7/1:TIFF2GIF:100?,,

Mendon (Monroe County)

Stimson, Hiram K. *From the Stage Coach to the Pulpit, being an Autobiographical Sketch, with Incidents and Anecdotes of Elder H. K. Stimson, the Veteran Pioneer of Western New York, Now of Kansas.* Saint Louis, MO: Campbell, 1874. 430p.
http://moa.umdl.umich.edu/cgi-bin/moa/sgml/moa-idx?notisid=AJK2081

Middletown (Orange County)

Laskaris, Peter A. *Middletown, a Photographic History*. Middletown, NY: Middletown Centennial Committee, 1988. Unpgd.
http://www.thrall.org/middletown/

Minerva (Essex County)

Northup, Solomon. *Narrative of Solomon Northup, a Citizen of New York, Kidnapped in Washington City in 1841, Rescued in 1853, from a Cotton Plantation near the Red River, in Louisiana*. Auburn, NY: Derby and Miller, 1853. 336p.
http://metalab.unc.edu/docsouth/northup/menu.html

Monroe County

Child, Hamilton. *Gazetteer and Business Directory of Monroe County, New York, for 1869-70*. Syracuse, NY: Journal Office, 1869. 420p.
http://moa.cit.cornell.edu/dienst/moabrowse.fly/MOA-JOURNALS2:CHIL-0104/9/1:TIFF2GIF:100?,,

Turner, O. *History of the Pioneer Settlement of Phelps and Gorham's Purchase and Morris' Reserve, Embracing the Counties of Monroe, Ontario, Livingston, Yates, Steuben, Most of Wayne and Allegany and Parts of Orleans, Genesee and Wyoming, to which is Added a Supplement or Extension of the Pioneer History of Monroe County*. Rochester, NY: William Alling 1851. 624p.
http://moa.cit.cornell.edu/dienst/moabrowse.fly/MOA-JOURNALS2:TURN-0092/3/1:TIFF2GIF:100

New York City

Association for the Benefit of Colored Orphans. Annual Report. New York, NY: Trow's Printing and Bookbinding, 1879. 23p.
http://memory.loc.gov/cgi-bin/query/r?ammem/murray:@field(FLD001+91898249+):@@@REF

Barnes, David M. *The Draft Riots in New York, July 1863. The Metropolitan Police, Their Services During the Riot Week, Their Honorable Record*. New York, NY: Baker & Godwin, 1863. 120p.
http://moa.umdl.umich.edu/cgi-bin/moa/sgml/moa-idx?notisid=AFJ8114
http://moa.cit.cornell.edu/dienst/moabrowse.fly/MOA-JOURNALS2:BARN-0060/3/1:TIFF2GIF:100

Booth, Mary L. *History of the City of New York from Its Earliest Settlement to the Present Time*. New York, NY: Clark, 1860. 852p.
http://moa.cit.cornell.edu/dienst/moabrowse.fly/MOA-JOURNALS2:BOOT-0055/5/1:TIFF2GIF:100

Browne, Junius Henri. *The Great Metropolis, a Mirror of New York*. Hartford, CT: American Publishing Co., 1869. 734p.
http://moa.umdl.umich.edu/cgi-bin/moa/sgml/moa-idx?notisid=AFK3938

Buffum, Edward Gould. *Six Months in the Gold Mines from a Journal of Three Years' Residence in Upper and Lower California, 1847-8-9*. Philadelphia, PA: Lea & Blanchard, 1850. 172p.
http://memory.loc.gov/cgi-bin/query/r?ammem/calbkbib:@field(AUTHOR+@band(Buffum,+Edward+Gould,1820-1867.+))

Davis, Ashable. *History of New Amsterdam or New York as It Was in the Days of the Dutch Governors, together with Papers on Events Connected with the American Revolution and on Philadelphia in the Times of William Penn*. New York, NY: Young, 1854. 240p.
http://moa.cit.cornell.edu/dienst/moabrowse.fly/MOA-JOURNALS2:DAVI-0057/5/1:TIFF2GIF:100

Francis, John W. *Old New York or Reminiscences of the Past Sixty Years*. New York, NY: Roe, 1858. 384p.
http://moa.cit.cornell.edu/dienst/moabrowse.fly/MOA-JOURNALS2:FRAN-0061/5/1:TIFF2GIF:100

Gunn, Thomas Butler. *The Physiology of New York Boarding Houses*. New York, NY: Mason Brothers, 1857. 300p.
http://moa.cit.cornell.edu/dienst/moabrowse.fly/MOA-JOURNALS2:GUNN-0157/3/1:TIFF2GIF:100

Headley, Joel Tyler. *The Great Riots of New York, 1712 to 1873, Including a Full and Complete Account of the Four Days' Draft Riot of 1863*. New York, NY: Treat, 1873. 358p.
http://moa.umdl.umich.edu/cgi-bin/moa/sgml/moa-idx?notisid=AFJ8079

Hemstreet, Charles. *Nooks and Corners of Old New York*. New York, NY: Scribners, 1899. 228p.
http://moa.cit.cornell.edu/dienst/moabrowse.fly/MOA-JOURNALS2:HEMS-0056/5/1:TIFF2GIF:100

Knapp, Shepherd. *Gideon Lee Knapp and Augusta Murray Spring, His Wife, Extracts from Letters and Journal, ed. By One of Their Grandsons*. Author, 1909. 66p.
http://memory.loc.gov/cgi-bin/query/r?ammem/calbkbib:@field(AUTHOR+@band(Knapp,+Gideon+Lee,1822?-1875.+))

Letts, John M. *California Illustrated, Including a Description of the Panama and Nicaragua Routes*. New York, NY: Young, 1853. 224p.
http://memory.loc.gov/cgi-bin/query/r?ammem/calbkbib:@field(AUTHOR+@band(Letts,+John+M.+))

MacLeod, Xavier Donald. *Biography of Hon. Fernando Wood, Mayor of the City of New York*. New York, NY: Parsons, 1856. 335p.
http://moa.cit.cornell.edu/dienst/moabrowse.fly/MOA-JOURNALS2:MACL-0018/5/1:TIFF2GIF:100

McManus, Blanche. *How the Dutch Came to Manhattan*. New York, NY: Herrick, 1897. 82p.
http://moa.cit.cornell.edu/dienst/moabrowse.fly/MOA-JOURNALS2:MCMA-0058/5/1:TIFF2GIF:100

A Narrative of Some Recent Occurrences in the Church of the Puritans, New York with Documents Relating thereto. New York, NY: Dorr, 1857. 50p.
http://moa.umdl.umich.edu/cgi-bin/moa/sgml/moa-idx?notisid=AJK2271

New York City [City Directory]. New York, NY: Trow, various.
1859-1866; 1880-81; 1890.
http://www.citydirectories.psmedia.com/city/free_statesort.html

New York City [City Directory]. New York, NY: Carroll, 1859.
http://www.citydirectories.psmedia.com/city/free_statesort.html

New York City [City Directory]. New York, NY: Ensign, Bridgman & Fanning, 1860.
http://www.citydirectories.psmedia.com/city/free_statesort.html

O'Callaghan, E. B. *Laws and Ordinances of New Netherland, 1638-1674*. Albany, NY: Weed, Parsons and Co., 1868. 602p.
http://moa.cit.cornell.edu/dienst/moabrowse.fly/MOA-JOURNALS2:NEWY-0010/3/1:TIFF2GIF:100

Proceedings of a Council of Congregational Churches, Relative to the Privileges of Members of the Church of the Puritans, New York. New York, NY: Jenkins, 1859. 92p.
http://moa.umdl.umich.edu/cgi-bin/moa/sgml/moa-idx?notisid=AJK2272

Proceedings of a Council of Congregational Churches, Relative to the Church of the Puritans, New York, and to the Privileges of Members Thereof, May, 1861. New York, NY: Gray, 1861. 132p.
http://moa.umdl.umich.edu/cgi-bin/moa/sgml/moa-idx?notisid=AJK2273

Report of the Committee of Merchants for the Relief of Colored People, Suffering from the Late Riots in the City of New York. New York, NY: Whitehorne, 1863. 48p.
http://memory.loc.gov/cgi-bin/query/r?ammem/aap:@field(SUBJ+@band(Draft+Riot,+1863.+))

Riker, James. *Harlem, Its Origin and Early Annals, Prefaced by Home Scenes in the Fatherlands, or Notices of Its Founders before Emigration also, Sketches of Numerous Families and the Recovered History of the Land Titles.* New York, NY: Author, 1881. 636p.
http://moa.cit.cornell.edu/dienst/moabrowse.fly/MOA-JOURNALS2:RIKE-0161/3/1:TIFF2GIF:100

Smith, Matthew Hale. *Sunshine and Shadow in New York.* Hartford, CT: Burr, 1868. 718p.
http://moa.cit.cornell.edu/dienst/moabrowse.fly/MOA-JOURNALS2:SMIT-0155/5/1:TIFF2GIF:100

Stone, William Leete. *The Centennial History of New York City, from the Discovery to the Present.* New York, NY: R. D. Cooke, 1876. 252p.
http://moa.cit.cornell.edu/dienst/moabrowse.fly/MOA-JOURNALS2:STON-0054/5/1:TIFF2GIF:100

Thompson, Mary W. *Broken Gloom, Sketches of the History, Character, and Dying Testimony of Beneficiaries of the Colored Home in the City of New York.* New York, NY: John F. Trow, 1851. 78p.
http://metalab.unc.edu/docsouth/thompson/menu.html

Tuckerman, Bayard. *Peter Stuyvesant, Director General for the West India Company in New Netherland.* New York, NY: Dodd, Mead & Co., 1893. 193p.
http://moa.cit.cornell.edu/dienst/moabrowse.fly/MOA-JOURNALS2:TUCK-0011/5/1:TIFF2GIF:100

Niagara County

Bigelow, Timothy. *Journal of a Tour to Niagara Falls in the Year 1805.* Boston, MA: John Wilson and Son, 1876. 144p.
http://moa.cit.cornell.edu/dienst/moabrowse.fly/MOA-JOURNALS2:BIGE-0075/3/1:TIFF2GIF:100

Darby, William. *A Tour from the City of New York to Detroit in the Michigan Territory Made between the 22d of September 1818. The Tour is Accompanied with a Map upon Which the Route Will be Designated, a Particular Map of the Falls and River of Niagara, and the Environs of the City of Detroit.* New York, NY: Kirk & Mercein, 1819. 300p.
http://memory.loc.gov/cgi-bin/query/r?ammem/lhbumbib:@field(SUBJ+@band(New+York++State+--Description+and+travel.+))

Hunter, William S. *Hunter's Panoramic Guide from Niagara Falls to Quebec.* Boston, MA: Jewett, 1857. 68p.
http://moa.umdl.umich.edu/cgi-bin/moa/sgml/moa-idx?notisid=ABT1030

McCollum, William S. *California as I Saw It. Pencillings by the Way of Its Gold and Gold Diggers and Incidents of Travel by Land and Water. With Five Letters from the Isthmus.* Los Gatos, CA: Talisman Press, 1960. 219p.
http://memory.loc.gov/cgi-bin/query/r?ammem/calbkbib:@field(AUTHOR+@band(M'Collum,+William+S.+))

Severance, Frank H. *Old Trails on the Niagara Frontier.* Buffalo, NY: Complete Art Printing, 1899. 322p.
http://moa.cit.cornell.edu/dienst/moabrowse.fly/MOA-JOURNALS2:SEVE-0020/5/1:TIFF2GIF:100

Oneida County

Hines, Joseph Wilkinson. *Touching Incidents in the Life and Labors of a Pioneer on the Pacific Coast since 1853.* San Jose, CA: Eaton & Co., 1911. 198p.
http://memory.loc.gov/cgi-bin/query/r?ammem/calbkbib:@field(AUTHOR+@band(Hines,+Joseph+Wilkinson+))

Ontario County

Turner, O. *History of the Pioneer Settlement of Phelps and Gorham's Purchase and Morris' Reserve, Embracing the Counties of Monroe, Ontario, Livingston, Yates, Steuben, Most of Wayne and Allegany and Parts of Orleans, Genesee and Wyoming, to which is Added a Supplement or Extension of the Pioneer History of Monroe County.* Rochester, NY: William Alling 1851. 624p.
http://moa.cit.cornell.edu/dienst/moabrowse.fly/MOA-JOURNALS2:TURN-0092/3/1:TIFF2GIF:100

Orange County

Gumaer, Peter E. *A History of Deerpark in Orange County, N.Y.* Port Jervis, NY: Union Print, 1890. 206p.
http://moa.cit.cornell.edu/dienst/moabrowse.fly/MOA-JOURNALS2:GUMA-0111/5/1:TIFF2GIF:100

Orleans County

Turner, O. *History of the Pioneer Settlement of Phelps and Gorham's Purchase and Morris' Reserve, Embracing the Counties of Monroe, Ontario, Livingston, Yates, Steuben, Most of Wayne and Allegany and Parts of Orleans, Genesee and Wyoming, to which is Added a Supplement or Extension of the Pioneer History of Monroe County.* Rochester, NY: William Alling 1851. 624p.
http://moa.cit.cornell.edu/dienst/moabrowse.fly/MOA-JOURNALS2:TURN-0092/3/1:TIFF2GIF:100

Otswego County

Beardsley, Levi. *Reminiscences, Personal and Other Incidents, Early Settlement of Otsego County, Notices and Anecdotes of Public Men, Judicial, Legal, and Legislative Matters, Field Sports, Dissertations and Discussions.* New York, NY: Vinten, 1852. 592p.
http://moa.cit.cornell.edu/dienst/moabrowse.fly/MOA-JOURNALS2:BEAR-0027/5/1:TIFF2GIF:100

Carroll, Mary Bowden. *Ten Years in Paradise. Leaves from a Society Reporter's Notebook.* San Jose, CA: Popp & Hogan, 1903. 212p.
http://memory.loc.gov/cgi-bin/query/r?ammem/calbkbib:@field(AUTHOR+@band(Carroll,+Mary+Bowden.+))

Oxford (Chenango County)

Bundy, Charles Smith. *Early Days in the Chippewa Valley.* Menomenee, WI: Flint Douglas Printing, 1916. 16p.
http://memory.loc.gov/cgi-bin/query/r?ammem/lhbum:@field(DOCID+@lit(16807T000)):@@@REF

Poughkeepsie

Farnham, Eliza Woodson Burhans. *California, Indoors and Out, or How We Farm, Mine and Live Generally in the Golden State.* New York, NY: Dix, Edwards, 1856. 508p.
http://memory.loc.gov/cgi-bin/query/r?ammem/calbkbib:@field(AUTHOR+@band(Farnham,+Eliza+Woodson+Burhans,1815-1864.+))

Poughkeepsie, 1859-60 [City Directory]. Poughkeepsie, NY: Lent, 1859.
http://www.citydirectories.psmedia.com/city/free_statesort.html

Putnam County

Nowlin, William. *The Bark Covered House, or Back in the Woods again, Being a Graphic and Thrilling Description of Real Pioneer Life in the Wilderness of Michigan.* Detroit, MI: Author, 1876. 253p.
http://memory.loc.gov/cgi-bin/query/r?ammem/lhbumbib:@field(SUBJ+@band(Dearborn,+Mich.--History.+))

Rochester

James, Thomas. *Wonderful Eventful Life of Rev. Thomas James*. Rochester, NY: Post Express Printing Co., 1887. 24p.
http://memory.loc.gov/cgi-bin/query/r?ammem/aap:@field(SUBJ+@band(Autobiographies--New+York++State+--1887.+))

Rochester [City Directory]. Rochester, NY: Curtis, Butts & Co., 1859.
http://www.citydirectories.psmedia.com/city/free_statesort.html

Stoddard, Charles Warren. *In the Footprints of the Padres*. San Francisco, CA: Robertson, 1902. 335p.
http://memory.loc.gov/cgi-bin/query/r?ammem/calbkbib:@field(AUTHOR+@band(Stoddard,+Charles+Warren,1843-1909.+))

Rome

Rome, 1859-60 [City Directory]. William H. Boyd, 1859.
http://www.citydirectories.psmedia.com/city/free_statesort.html

Sag Harbor

Mulford, Prentice. *Life by Land and Sea*. New York, NY: Needham, 1889. 299p.
http://memory.loc.gov/cgi-bin/query/r?ammem/calbkbib:@field(AUTHOR+@band(Mulford,+Prentice,1834-1891.+))

Saratoga Springs (Monroe County)

Stimson, Hiram K. *From the Stage Coach to the Pulpit, being an Autobiographical Sketch, with Incidents and Anecdotes of Elder H. K. Stimson, the Veteran Pioneer of Western New York, Now of Kansas*. Saint Louis, MO: Campbell, 1874. 430p.
http://moa.umdl.umich.edu/cgi-bin/moa/sgml/moa-idx?notisid=AJK2081

Sardinia

Briggs, Erasmus. *History of the Original Town of Concord, Being the Present Towns of Concord, Collins, North Collins and Sardinia*. Rochester, NY: Union and Advertisers Company's Print, 1883. 992p.
http://moa.cit.cornell.edu/dienst/moabrowse.fly/MOA-JOURNALS2:BRIG-0106/3/1:TIFF2GIF:100

Schenectady

Foote, Julia A. J. *A Brand Plucked from the Fire, an Autobiographical Sketch*. Cleveland, OH: Lauer & Yost, 1879. 124p.
http://digilib.nypl.org/dynaweb/digs/wwm978/

Sidney

The Sidney Centennial Jubilee at Sidney Plains, Delaware County, NY, June 13, 1872. Ann Arbor, MI: Chase's Steam Printing House, 1875. 100p.
http://moa.umdl.umich.edu/cgi-bin/moa/sgml/moa-idx?notisid=AJA2325

Steuben (Oneida County)

Hines, Joseph Wilkinson. *Touching Incidents in the Life and Labors of a Pioneer on the Pacific Coast since 1853*. San Jose, CA: Eaton & Co., 1911. 198p.
http://memory.loc.gov/cgi-bin/query/r?ammem/calbkbib:@field(AUTHOR+@band(Hines,+Joseph+Wilkinson+))

Turner, O. *History of the Pioneer Settlement of Phelps and Gorham's Purchase and Morris' Reserve, Embracing the Counties of Monroe, Ontario, Livingston, Yates, Steuben, Most of Wayne and Allegany and Parts of Orleans, Genesee and Wyoming, to which is Added a Supplement or Extension of the Pioneer History of Monroe County.* Rochester, NY: William Alling 1851. 624p.
http://moa.cit.cornell.edu/dienst/moabrowse.fly/MOA-JOURNALS2:TURN-0092/3/1:TIFF2GIF:100

Suffolk County

Furman, Gabriel. *Antiquities of Long Island to which is Added a Bibliography by Henry Onderdonk, Jr.* New York, NY: Bouton, 1874. 478p.
http://moa.cit.cornell.edu/dienst/moabrowse.fly/MOA-JOURNALS2:FURM-0103/3/1:TIFF2GIF:100

Hammon, Jupiter. *An Address to the Negroes in the State of New York, by Jupiter Hammon, Servant of John Lloyd, Jun., Esq. of the Manor of Queen's Village, Long Island.* New York, NY: Carroll and Patterson, 1787. 20p.
http://www.lib.virginia.edu/etext/readex/20400.html

Records of the Town of Brookhaven, Suffolk County, N.Y., This Volume Contains the Entire Records from 1796 to March 1856, Inclusive, Copied from the Original Records in Their Order, under the Direction of the Supervisor and Justices of the Peace and Established by the Authority of the Town. Port Jefferson, NY: Times Steam Job Print, 1888. 552p.
http://moa.cit.cornell.edu/dienst/moabrowse.fly/MOA-JOURNALS2:BROO-0063/3/1:TIFF2GIF:100

Records of the Town of Brookhaven, Suffolk County, N.Y. This Volume Contains the Entire Records from 1856 to December 1885, Inclusive, Copied from the Original Records in Their Order, under the Direction of the Supervisor and Justices of the Peace, and Published by the Authority of the Town. New York, NY: Burr Printing House, 1893. 1,118p.
http://moa.cit.cornell.edu/dienst/moabrowse.fly/MOA-JOURNALS2:BROO-0064/3/1:TIFF2GIF:100

Syracuse

Syracuse, 1859-60 [City Directory]. William H. Boyd, 1859.
http://www.citydirectories.psmedia.com/city/free_statesort.html

Ticonderoga

DeCosta, Benjamin Franklin. *Lake George, Its Scenes and Characteristics with Glimpses of the Olden Times, to which Is Added Some Account of Ticonderoga, Lake Luzerne, Schroon Lake and the Adirondacks, with an Appendix Containing Notes on Lake Champlain.* 3rd ed. New York, NY: Randolph, 1868. 181p.
http://moa.cit.cornell.edu/dienst/moabrowse.fly/MOA-JOURNALS2:DECO-0095/5/1:TIFF2GIF:100

Watson, Winslow Cossoul. *The Military and Civil History of the County of Essex, New York and a General Survey of Its Physical Geography, Its Mines and Minerals and Industrial Pursuits. Embracing an Account of the Northern Wilderness and also the Military Annals of the Fortresses of Crown Point and Ticonderoga.* New York, NY: Munsell's, 1869. 504p.
http://moa.cit.cornell.edu/dienst/moabrowse.fly/MOA-JOURNALS2:WATS-0094/5/1:TIFF2GIF:100

Tompkins County

Crosby, Elisha Oscar. *Memoirs of Elisha Oscar Crosby, Reminiscences of California and Guatemala from 1849 to 1864.* San Marino, CA: Huntington Library, 1945. 119p.
http://memory.loc.gov/cgi-bin/query/r?ammem/calbkbib:@field(AUTHOR+@band(Crosby,+Elisha+Oscar,1818-1895.+))

Troy

Inventory of the William Henry Jackson Papers. New York, NY: New York Public Library, Manuscripts and Archives Division, 1998. Unpgd.
http://digilib.nypl.org/dynaweb/ead/human/jacksonw/@Generic__BookView

Pierce, Hiram Dwight. *A Forty-niner Speaks, a Chronological Record of a New Yorker and His Adventures in Various Mining Localities in California, His Return Trip across Nicaragua, Including Several Descriptions of the Changes in San Francisco and other Mining Centers from March 1849 to January 1851.* Oakland, CA: Keystone Inglett Printing, 1930. 74p.
http://memory.loc.gov/cgi-bin/query/r?ammem/calbkbib:@field(AUTHOR+@band(Pierce,+Hiram+Dwight,b.+1810.+))

Troy [City Directory]. Adams, Sampson & Co, 1859.
http://www.citydirectories.psmedia.com/city/free_statesort.html

Ulster County

Gilbert, Olive. *Narrative of Sojourner Truth, a Bonds-woman of Olden Time, Emancipated by the New York Legislature in the Early Part of the Present Century, with a History of Her Labors and Correspondence, Drawn from Her Book of Life.* Battle Creek, MI: Author, 1878. 320p.
http://memory.loc.gov/cgi-bin/query/r?ammem/lhbumbib:@field(SUBJ+@band(Truth,+Sojourner,--d.+1883.+))

Utica

Utica, 1859-60 [City Directory]. Utica, NY: Arnott, 1859.
http://www.citydirectories.psmedia.com/city/free_statesort.html

Wayne County

Clark, L. H. *Military History of Wayne County, N.Y., the County in the Civil War.* Syracuse, NY: Truair, Smith & Bruce, 1883. 936p.
http://moa.cit.cornell.edu/dienst/moabrowse.fly/MOA-JOURNALS2:CLAR-0048/3/1:TIFF2GIF:100

Turner, O. *History of the Pioneer Settlement of Phelps and Gorham's Purchase and Morris' Reserve, Embracing the Counties of Monroe, Ontario, Livingston, Yates, Steuben, Most of Wayne and Allegany and Parts of Orleans, Genesee and Wyoming, to which is Added a Supplement or Extension of the Pioneer History of Monroe County.* Rochester, NY: William Alling 1851. 624p.
http://moa.cit.cornell.edu/dienst/moabrowse.fly/MOA-JOURNALS2:TURN-0092/3/1:TIFF2GIF:100

Westchester County

Pelletreau, William S. *Early Wills of Westchester County, New York, from 1864 to 1784.* New York, NY: Francis P. Harper, 1898. 488p.
http://moa.cit.cornell.edu/dienst/moabrowse.fly/MOA-JOURNALS2:PELL-0049/7/1:TIFF2GIF:100

Waldron, William Watson. *Huguenots of Westchester and Parish of Fordham.* New York, NY: Kelley & Brother, Publishers, 1864. 126p.
http://moa.cit.cornell.edu/dienst/moabrowse.fly/MOA-JOURNALS2:WALD-0050/5/1:TIFF2GIF:100

Wood, Harvey. *Personal Recollections.* Pasadena, CA: John B. Goodman, III, 1955. 27p.
http://memory.loc.gov/cgi-bin/query/r?ammem/calbkbib:@field(AUTHOR+@band(Wood,+Harvey,1828-1895.+))

Yonkers, 1859-60 [City Directory]. New York, NY: Smith, 1859.
http://www.citydirectories.psmedia.com/city/free_statesort.html

Windham
Shufelt, S. *A Letter from a Gold Miner, Placerville, California, October 1850*. San Marino, CA: Friends of the Huntington Library, 1944. 28p.
http://memory.loc.gov/cgi-bin/query/r?ammem/calbkbib:@field(AUTHOR+@band(Shufelt,+S.+))

Wyoming County
Turner, O. *History of the Pioneer Settlement of Phelps and Gorham's Purchase and Morris' Reserve, Embracing the Counties of Monroe, Ontario, Livingston, Yates, Steuben, Most of Wayne and Allegany and Parts of Orleans, Genesee and Wyoming, to which is Added a Supplement or Extension of the Pioneer History of Monroe County*. Rochester, NY: William Alling 1851. 624p.
http://moa.cit.cornell.edu/dienst/moabrowse.fly/MOA-JOURNALS2:TURN-0092/3/1:TIFF2GIF:100

Yates County
Graham, Robert H. *Yates County's Boys in Blue, 1861-1865, Who They Were and What They Did*. Penn Yan, NY: Author, 1926. 204p.
http://moa.cit.cornell.edu/dienst/moabrowse.fly/MOA-JOURNALS2:GRAH-0051/3/1:TIFF2GIF:100

Turner, O. *History of the Pioneer Settlement of Phelps and Gorham's Purchase and Morris' Reserve, Embracing the Counties of Monroe, Ontario, Livingston, Yates, Steuben, Most of Wayne and Allegany and Parts of Orleans, Genesee and Wyoming, to which is Added a Supplement or Extension of the Pioneer History of Monroe County*. Rochester, NY: William Alling 1851. 624p.
http://moa.cit.cornell.edu/dienst/moabrowse.fly/MOA-JOURNALS2:TURN-0092/3/1:TIFF2GIF:100

Wolcott, Walter. *The Military History of Yates County, N.Y., Containing a Record of the Services Rendered by Citizens of the County in the Army and Navy, from the Foundation of the Government to the Present Time*. Penn Van, NY: Express Book and Job Printing House, 1895. 158p.
http://moa.cit.cornell.edu/dienst/moabrowse.fly/MOA-JOURNALS2:WOLC-0052/3/1:TIFF2GIF:100

North Carolina

Biggs, Asa. *Autobiography of Asa Biggs, Including a Journal of a Trip from North Carolina to New York in 1832*. Raleigh, NC: Edwards and Broughton Printing Co., 1915. 51p.
http://metalab.unc.edu/docsouth/biggs/menu.html

Bryan, Mary Norcott. *A Grandmother's Recollection of Dixie*. New Bern, NC: Dunn, 1912. 43p.
http://metalab.unc.edu/docsouth/bryan/menu.html

Douglass, William. *A Discourse Concerning the Currencies of the British Plantations in America, Especially with Regard to Their Paper Money, more Particularly in Relation to the Province of Massachusetts Bay in New England.* 1740. Unknown. 3p.
http://www.people.virginia.edu/~rwm3n/webdoc2.html

General Military Hospital for the North Carolina Troops in Petersburg, Virginia. Raleigh, NC: Strother & Marcom Book and Job Printers, 1861. 8p.
http://metalab.unc.edu/docsouth/generalhospital/menu.html

Malone, Bartlett Yancey. *The Diary of Bartlett Yancey Malone.* Vol. 16, No. 2 , James Sprunt Historical Publications, North Carolina Historical Society. 58p.
http://metalab.unc.edu/docsouth/malone/menu.html

Pyatt, Timothy D. *Guide to African-American Documentary Resources in North Carolina.* Charlottesville, VA: University of Virginia, 1996. Unpgd.
http://www.upress.virginia.edu/epub/pyatt/index.html

Research Outline. North Carolina. Salt Lake City, UT: Family History Library, 1997.
http://familysearch.org/sg/North_Carolina.html

Wager, Paul Woodford. *County Government and Administration in North Carolina.* Chapel Hill, NC: University of North Carolina Press, 1928. 474p.
http://chla.mannlib.cornell.edu/cgi-bin/chla/viewer.cgi?docid=title2c.chla.mannlib.cornell/0224wage&format=1:75-GIF&section=Title+Page

Asheville

Episcopal Church, Commission of Home Missions to Colored People. New York, NY: Church, 1875, 1876.
9th Annual Report, 1873-74. 20p.
http://memory.loc.gov/cgi-bin/query/r?ammem/murray:@field(FLD001+91898515+):@@@REF

11th Annual Report, 1875-76. 24p.
http://memory.loc.gov/cgi-bin/query/r?ammem/murray:@field(FLD001+91898514+):@@@REF

Camden County

Grandy, Moses. *Narrative of the Life of Moses Grandy, Late a Slave in the United States of America.* London: Gilpin, 1843. 72p.
http://metalab.unc.edu/docsouth/grandy/menu.html

Casswell County

Roper, Moses. *A Narrative of the Adventures and Escape of Moses Roper, from American Slavery.* Philadelphia, PA: Merrihew & Gunn, 1838. 89p.
http://metalab.unc.edu/docsouth/roper/menu.html

Charlotte

Leon, Louis. *Diary of a Tar Heel Confederate Soldier.* Charlotte, NC: Stone Publishing Co., 1913. 87p.
http://metalab.unc.edu/docsouth/leon/menu.html

Chatham County

Horton, George Moses. *Life of George M. Horton, the Colored Bard of North Carolina.* Hillsborough, NC: Heartt, 1845. 20p.
http://metalab.unc.edu/docsouth/hortonlife/menu.html

Fayetteville

Episcopal Church, Commission of Home Missions to Colored People. New York, NY: Church, 1875, 1876.
9th Annual Report, 1873-74. 20p.
http://memory.loc.gov/cgi-bin/query/r?ammem/murray:@field(FLD001+91898515+):@@@REF

11th Annual Report, 1875-76. 24p.
http://memory.loc.gov/cgi-bin/query/r?ammem/murray:@field(FLD001+91898514+):@@@REF

United Daughters of the Confederacy, J. E. B. Stuart Chapter. *War Days in Fayetteville, North Carolina, Reminiscences of 1861-1865.* Fayetteville, NC: Judge Print Co., 1910. 60p.
http://metalab.unc.edu/docsouth/chapter/menu.html

Franklinton

Ward, Dallas T. *The Last Flag of Truce.* Franklinton, NC: Author, 1915. 16p.
http://metalab.unc.edu/docsouth/ward/menu.html

Halifax County

Branch, Mary Jones Polk. *Memoirs of a Southern Woman, "Within the Lines," and a Genealogical Table.* Chicago, IL: Joseph G. Branch Publishing, 1912. 107p.
http://metalab.unc.edu/docsouth/branch/menu.html

Haywood County

Compton, Lucius Bunyan. *Life of Lucius B. Compton, the Mountain Evangelist, or from the Depths of Sin to the Heights of Holiness.* Cincinnati, OH: Author, 1903. 102p.
http://metalab.unc.edu/docsouth/compton/menu.html

Martin County

Smithwick, Noah. *The Evolution of a State or Recollections of Old Texas Days.* Austin, TX: Gammel Book Co., 1900. 354p.
http://www.erols.com/hardeman/lonestar/olbooks/smithwic/otd.htm

Newberne

Episcopal Church, Commission of Home Missions to Colored People. New York, NY: Church, 1875, 1876.
9th Annual Report, 1873-74. 20p.
http://memory.loc.gov/cgi-bin/query/r?ammem/murray:@field(FLD001+91898515+):@@@REF

11th Annual Report, 1875-76. 24p.
http://memory.loc.gov/cgi-bin/query/r?ammem/murray:@field(FLD001+91898514+):@@@REF

Northampton County

Horton, George Moses. *Life of George M. Horton, the Colored Bard of North Carolina.* Hillsborough, NC: Heartt, 1845. 20p.
http://metalab.unc.edu/docsouth/hortonlife/menu.html

Pitt County

Grimes, Bryan. *Extracts of Letters of Major General Bryan Grimes to His Wife, Written While in Active Service in the Army of Northern Virginia, together with Some Personal Recollections of the War, Written by Him after Its Close.* Raleigh, NC: Broughton, 1883. 137p.
http://metalab.unc.edu/docsouth/grimes/menu.html

Raleigh

Episcopal Church, Commission of Home Missions to Colored People. New York, NY: Church, 1875, 1876.
9th Annual Report, 1873-74. 20p.
http://memory.loc.gov/cgi-bin/query/r?ammem/murray:@field(FLD001+91898515+):@@@REF

11th Annual Report, 1875-76. 24p.
http://memory.loc.gov/cgi-bin/query/r?ammem/murray:@field(FLD001+91898514+):@@@REF

Lane, Lunsford. *The Narrative of Lunsford Lane, formerly of Raleigh, NC. Embracing an Account of His Early Life, the Redemption by Purchase of Himself and Family from Slavery, and His Banishment from the Place of His Birth for the Crime of Wearing a Colored Skin.* 2nd ed. Boston, MA: Torrey, 1842. 56p.
http://metalab.unc.edu/docsouth/lanelunsford/menu.html

Salisbury

Helper, Hinton Rowan. *The Land of Gold, Reality Versus Fiction.* Baltimore, MD: Taylor, 1855. 300p.
http://memory.loc.gov/cgi-bin/query/r?ammem/calbkbib:@field(AUTHOR+@band(Helper,+Hinton+Rowan,1829-1909.+))

Wake County

Olive, Johnson. *One of the Wonders of the Age or the Life and Times of Rev. Johnson Olive, Wake County, North Carolina, Written by Himself, at the Solicitation of Friends and for the Benefit of All Who Read It, with Supplement by His Son, H. C. Olive.* Raleigh, NC: Edwards, Broughton, 1886. 314p.
http://metalab.unc.edu/docsouth/olive/menu.html

Warren County

Green, Wharton Jackson. *Recollections and Reflections, an Auto of Half a Century and More.* Raleigh, NC: Edwards & Broughton Printing, 1906. 349p.
http://metalab.unc.edu/docsouth/green/menu.html

Wilmington

Episcopal Church, Commission of Home Missions to Colored People. New York, NY: Church, 1875, 1876.
9th Annual Report, 1873-74. 20p.
http://memory.loc.gov/cgi-bin/query/r?ammem/murray:@field(FLD001+91898515+):@@@REF

11th Annual Report, 1875-76. 24p.
http://memory.loc.gov/cgi-bin/query/r?ammem/murray:@field(FLD001+91898514+):@@@REF

Jones, Thomas H. *The Experience of Thomas H. Jones, Who Was a Slave for Forty-Three Years.* Boston, MA: Bazin & Chandler, 1862. 48p.
http://metalab.unc.edu/docsouth/jones/menu.html

Robinson, William H. *From Log Cabin to Pulpit, or Fifteen Years in Slavery.* 3rd ed. Eau Claire, WI: Tifft, 1913. 200p.
http://metalab.unc.edu/docsouth/robinson/menu.html

The Quarterly Almanac. Wilmington, NC.
1893. 32p.
http://memory.loc.gov/cgi-bin/query/r?ammem/aap:@field(SUBJ+@band(Almanacs,+American--North+Carolina.+))

1894. 32p.
http://memory.loc.gov/cgi-bin/query/r?ammem/murray:@field(FLD001+91898155+):@@@REF

North Dakota

Andrews, Christopher Columbus. *Minnesota and Dacotah, in Letters Descriptive of a Tour through the Northwest, in the Autumn of 1856.* Washington, DC: Farnham, 1857. 215p.
http://memory.loc.gov/cgi-bin/query/r?ammem/lhbumbib:@field(SUBJ+@band(Andrews,+Christopher+Columbus,-1829-1922.+))

Heard, Isaac V. D. *History of the Sioux War and Massacres of 1862 and 1863.* New York, NY: Harper, 1864. 360p.
http://moa.umdl.umich.edu/cgi-bin/moa/sgml/moa-idx?notisid=ACK0828

Parkman, Francis. *The Oregon Trail, Sketches of Prairie and Rocky Mountain Life.* Philadelphia, PA: Winston, 1931. 388p.
http://xroads.virginia.edu/~HYPER/OREGON/oregon.html

Research Outline. North Dakota. Salt Lake City, UT: Family History Library, 1997.
http://familysearch.org/sg/North_Dakota.html

Tostlebe, Alvin Samuel. *The Bank of North America, an Experiment in Agrarian Banking.* New York, NY: Columbia University, 1924. 234p.
http://chla.mannlib.cornell.edu/cgi-bin/chla/viewer.cgi?docid=title2c.chla.mannlib.cornell/0201tost&format=1:75-GIF&section=Title+Page

Minot
Le Sueur, Meridel. *Crusaders.* New York, NY: Blue Heron Press, 1955. 94p.
http://memory.loc.gov/cgi-bin/query/r?ammem/lhbumbib:@field(SUBJ+@band(Le+Sueur,+Arthur,--1867-1950.+))

Ohio

Arnett, Benjamin William. *The Black Laws.* Columbus, OH: Ohio State Journal, 1886. 40p.
http://memory.loc.gov/cgi-bin/query/r?ammem/aap:@field(SUBJ+@band(Afro-Americans--Legal+status,+laws,+etc.--Ohio--History.+))

The Biographical Encyclopedia of Ohio of the Nineteenth Century. Cincinnati, OH: Galaxy
    Publishing Company, 1876. 868p.
    http://moa.umdl.umich.edu/cgi-bin/moa/sgml/moa-idx?notisid=AHU5132

Hawes, George W. *Ohio State Gazetteer and Business Directory for 1860-61*. Indianapolis, IN:
    Author, 1860. 958p.
    http://moa.umdl.umich.edu/cgi-bin/moa/sgml/moa-idx?notisid=AJA2907

Howe, Henry. *Historical Collections of Ohio; Containing a Collection of the Most Interesting
    Facts, Traditions, Biographical Sketches, Anecdotes, etc., Relating to Its General and Lo-
    cal History; with Descriptions of Its Counties, Principal Towns and Villages*. Cincinnati,
    OH: E. Morgan & Co., 1851. 636p.
    http://moa.umdl.umich.edu/cgi-bin/moa/sgml/moa-idx?notisid=AJA2910

*Ohio Boys in Dixie, the Adventures of Twenty-two Scouts Sent by Gen. O.M. Mitchell to De-
    stroy a Railroad, with a Narrative of Their Barbarous Treatment by the Rebels and Judge
    Holt's Report*. New York, NY: Miller & Mathews, 1863. 48p.
    http://moa.umdl.umich.edu/cgi-bin/moa/sgml/moa-idx?notisid=ACR4661

Ohio Rural Life Survey. New York, NY: Presbyterian Church in the USA, Board of Home Mis-
    sions, 1912. 6 vols.
    http://chla.mannlib.cornell.edu/cgi-bin/chla/viewer.cgi?docid=title2c.chla.mannlib.cornell/1046pres&
    format=1:75-GIF&section=Title+Page

Ohio State Directory, 1859-60 [City Directory]. George W. Hawes, 1859.
    http://www.citydirectories.psmedia.com/city/free_statesort.html

Research Outline. Ohio. Salt Lake City, UT: Family History Library, 1997.
    http://familysearch.org/sg/Ohio.html

Akron

Akron, Wooster & Cuyahoga, 1859-60 [City Directory]. C.S. Williams, 1859.
    http://www.citydirectories.psmedia.com/city/free_statesort.html

Likins, James W., Mrs. *Six Years Experience as a Book Agent in California, Including My Trip
    from New York to San Francisco via Nicaragua*. San Francisco, CA: Women's Union Book
    and Job Printing Office, 1874. 168p.
    http://memory.loc.gov/cgi-bin/query/r?ammem/calbkbib:@field(AUTHOR+@band(Likins,+J.+W.,Mrs.+))

Bennington (Morrow County)

Witham, James W. *Fifty Years on the Firing Line*. Chicago, IL: Author, 1924. 213p.
    http://memory.loc.gov/cgi-bin/query/r?ammem/lhbumbib:@field(SUBJ+@band(Agricultural+societies--
    United+States.+))

Cincinnati

Akron, Wooster & Cuyahoga, 1859-60 [City Directory]. C.S. Williams, 1859.
    http://www.citydirectories.psmedia.com/city/free_statesort.html

Cincinnati [City Directory]. C.S. Williams, 1859.
    http://www.citydirectories.psmedia.com/city/free_statesort.html

Cist, Charles. *Sketches and Statistics of Cincinnati in 1851*. Cincinnati, OH: W. H. Moore &
    Co., 1851. 402p.
    http://moa.umdl.umich.edu/cgi-bin/moa/sgml/moa-idx?notisid=AJA2929

Mattison, Hiram. *Louisa Picquet, the Octoroon, a Tale of Southern Slave Life*. New York, NY: Author, 1861. 60p.
http://digilib.nypl.org/dynaweb/digs/wwm97258/

Nordhoff, Charles. *California for Health, Pleasure and Residence. A Book for Travelers and Settlers*. New York, NY: Harper, 1873. 255p.
http://memory.loc.gov/cgi-bin/query/r?ammem/calbkbib:@field(AUTHOR+@band(Nordhoff,+Charles,1830-1901.+))

————. *Northern California, Oregon, and the Sandwich Islands*. New York, NY: Harper, 1875. 256p.
http://moa.umdl.umich.edu/cgi-bin/moa/sgml/moa-idx?notisid=AJL3484

Proceedings of the Semi-centenary Celebration of the African Methodist Episcopal Church of Cincinnati, Held in Allen Temple, February 8th, 9th, and 10th, 1874, with an Account of the Rise and Progress of the Colored Schools, also a List of the Charitable and Benevolent Societies of the City. Cincinnati, OH: Watkin, 1874. 136p.
http://memory.loc.gov/cgi-bin/query/r?ammem/murray:@field(FLD001+91898101+):@@@REF

Circleville

Circleville and Lancaster [City Directory]. C.S. Williams, 1859.
http://www.citydirectories.psmedia.com/city/free_statesort.html

Cleveland

Adams, Emma Hildreth. *To and Fro in Southern California*. Cincinnati, OH: W.M.B.C. Press, 1887. 288p.
http://memory.loc.gov/cgi-bin/query/r?ammem/calbkbib:@field(AUTHOR+@band(Adams,+Emma+H.+Emma+Hildreth++))

Cleveland, 1859-60 [City Directory]. Cleveland, OH: Williston, 1859.
http://www.citydirectories.psmedia.com/city/free_statesort.html

Cleveland, 1861-62 [City Directory]. Cleveland, OH: Ben Franklin, 1861.
http://www.citydirectories.psmedia.com/city/free_statesort.html

Cleveland, 1861 [City Directory]. Cleveland, OH: Herald, 1861.
http://www.citydirectories.psmedia.com/city/free_statesort.html

Cleveland, 1863-64 [City Directory]. Cleveland, OH: Andrew Boyd, 1863.
http://www.citydirectories.psmedia.com/city/free_statesort.html

Cleveland, 1864-65 [City Directory]. Cleveland, OH: Baker, 1864.
http://www.citydirectories.psmedia.com/city/free_statesort.html

Cleveland, 1865-66 [City Directory]. Cleveland, OH: Cowles, 1865.
http://www.citydirectories.psmedia.com/city/free_statesort.html

Cleveland [City Directory]. Cleveland, OH: Cleveland Leader Co., various. 1866-67; 1867-68.
http://www.citydirectories.psmedia.com/city/free_statesort.html

Rice, Harvey. *Letters from the Pacific Slope or First Impressions*. New York, NY: Appleton, 1870. 135p.
http://memory.loc.gov/cgi-bin/query/r?ammem/calbkbib:@field(AUTHOR+@band(Rice,+Harvey,1800-1891.+))

Cuyahoga Falls

Akron, Wooster & Cuyahoga, 1859-60 [City Directory]. C.S. Williams, 1859.
http://www.citydirectories.psmedia.com/city/free_statesort.html

Dayton

Dayton, 1859-60 [City Directory]. Dayton, OH: Hawes, 1859.
http://www.citydirectories.psmedia.com/city/free_statesort.html

Delaware

Delaware, 1859-60 [City Directory]. Delaware, OH: Williams, 1859.
http://www.citydirectories.psmedia.com/city/free_statesort.html

Johnson's Island

Shepherd, Henry Elliot. *Narrative of Prison Life at Baltimore and Johnson's Island, Ohio.*
Baltimore, MD: Commercial Printing, 1917. 22p.
http://metalab.unc.edu/docsouth/shepherd/menu.html

Lancaster

Circleville and Lancaster [City Directory]. C.S. Williams, 1859.
http://www.citydirectories.psmedia.com/city/free_statesort.html

McNeil, Samuel. *McNeil's Travels in 1849, to, through and from the Gold Regions in California.* Columbus, OH: Scott & Sascom, 1850. 40p.
http://memory.loc.gov/cgi-bin/query/r?ammem/calbkbib:@field(AUTHOR+@band(McNeil,+Samuel.+))

Lima

McCray, S. J. *Life of Mary F. McCray, Born and Raised a Slave in the State of Kentucky, By Her Husband and Son.* Lima, OH: Author, 1898. 115p.
http://metalab.unc.edu/docsouth/mccray/menu.html

Marietta

Cone, Mary. *Two Years in California.* Chicago, IL: Griggs, 1876. 238p.
http://memory.loc.gov/cgi-bin/query/r?ammem/calbkbib:@field(AUTHOR+@band(Cone,+Mary.+))

Morrow County

Witham, James W. *Fifty Years on the Firing Line.* Chicago, IL: Author, 1924. 213p.
http://memory.loc.gov/cgi-bin/query/r?ammem/lhbumbib:@field(SUBJ+@band(Agricultural+societies--United+States.+))

Springfield

Springfield and Urbana, 1859-60 [City Directory]. Springfield, OH: C.S. Williams, 1859.
http://www.citydirectories.psmedia.com/city/free_statesort.html

Toledo

Funeral Services in Respect to the Memory of Rev. William Paul Quinn, Late Senior Bishop of the African M.E. Church, Held at Warren Chapel, Toledo, Ohio, March 9th, 1873. Toledo, OH: Warren Chapel, 1873. 52p.
http://memory.loc.gov/cgi-bin/query/r?ammem/aap:@field(SUBJ+@band(Quinn,+William+Paul,--1799-1873.+))

Wooster
Akron, Wooster & Cuyahoga, 1859-60 [City Directory]. C.S. Williams, 1859.
http://www.citydirectories.psmedia.com/city/free_statesort.html

Oklahoma

Directory of Oklahoma Public Libraries and Systems. Oklahoma City, OK: Oklahoma Department of Libraries.
http://www.odl.state.ok.us/go/pl.asp

Research Outline. Oklahoma. Salt Lake City, UT: Family History Library, 1997.
http://familysearch.org/sg/Oklahoma.html

Oregon

Fremont, John Charles. *The Life of Col. John Charles Fremont and His Narrative of Explorations and Adventures in Kansas, Nebraska, Oregon and California.* New York, NY: Auburn, Miller, Orton & Mulligan, 1856. 514p.
http://moa.umdl.umich.edu/cgi-bin/moa/sgml/moa-idx?notisid=AAZ9580

Hines, Gustavus. *A Voyage Round the World, with a History of the Oregon Mission, to which Is Appended a Full Description of Oregon Territory, Its Geography, History and Religion, Designed for the Benefit of Emigrants to That Rising Country.* Buffalo, NY: Derby, 1850. 436p.
http://moa.umdl.umich.edu/cgi-bin/moa/sgml/moa-idx?notisid=ABE0943

Kane, Paul. *Wanderings of an Artist among the Indians of North America from Canada to Vancouver's Island and Oregon through the Hudson's Bay Company's Territory and Back Again.* London: Longman, Brown, Green, Longmans and Roberts, 1859. 515p.
http://www.canadiana.org/cgi-bin/ECO/mtq?id=985701065f&doc=35931

Nordhoff, Charles. *Northern California, Oregon, and the Sandwich Islands.* New York, NY: Harper, 1875. 256p.
http://moa.umdl.umich.edu/cgi-bin/moa/sgml/moa-idx?notisid=AJL3484

Parkman, Francis. *The Oregon Trail, Sketches of Prairie and Rocky Mountain Life.* Philadelphia, PA: Winston, 1931. 388p.
http://xroads.virginia.edu/~HYPER/OREGON/oregon.html

Research Outline. Oregon. Salt Lake City, UT: Family History Library, 1997.
http://familysearch.org/sg/Oregon.html

Oregon City

Burnett, Peter Hardeman. *Recollections and Opinions of an Old Pioneer.* New York, NY: Appleton, 1880. 448p.
http://memory.loc.gov/cgi-bin/query/r?ammem/calbkbib:@field(AUTHOR+@band(Burnett,+Peter+H[ardeman],1807-1895.+))

Pennsylvania

Douglass, William. *A Discourse Concerning the Currencies of the British Plantations in America, Especially with Regard to Their Paper Money, more Particularly in Relation to the Province of Massachusetts Bay in New England.* 1740. Unknown. 3p.
http://www.people.virginia.edu/~rwm3n/webdoc2.html

Research Outline. Pennsylvania. Salt Lake City, UT: Family History Library, 1997.
http://familysearch.org/sg/Pennsylvania.html

Chester

Whitehead, William: *Directory of the Borough of Chester, for the Years 1859-60, Containing a Concise History of the Borough from its First Settlement the Present Time, the Names of all the Inhabitants Alphabetically Arranged, Their Occupations, Places of Business, and Dwelling Houses: A List of the Streets of the Borough, Statistics of Public and Private Schools.* West Chester, PA: E. F. James, 1859. 128p.
http://moa.umdl.umich.edu/cgi-bin/moa/sgml/moa-idx?notisid=AFJ8568
http://www.citydirectories.psmedia.com/city/free_statesort.html

Erie County

Erie, 1859-60 [City Directory]. Hulbert, 1859.
http://www.citydirectories.psmedia.com/city/free_statesort.html

Erie County, 1859-60 [City Directory]. Lints, 1859.
http://www.citydirectories.psmedia.com/city/free_statesort.html

Harrisburg

Maclay, William. *The Journal of William Maclay, United States Senator from Pennsylvania, 1789-1791.* New York, NY: Appleton, 1890. 438p.
http://memory.loc.gov/ammem/amlaw/lwmj.html

Lancaster

Lancaster County, 1859-60 [City Directory]. William H. Boyd, 1859.
http://www.citydirectories.psmedia.com/city/free_statesort.html

Monongahela Valley

Monongahela and Youghiogheny Valleys [City Directory]. Thurston, 1859.
http://www.citydirectories.psmedia.com/city/free_statesort.html

Norristown

Wills, Mary H. *A Winter in California.* Norristown, PA: Author, 1889. 150p.
http://memory.loc.gov/cgi-bin/query/r?ammem/calbkbib:@field(AUTHOR+@band(Wills,+Mary+H.+))

Philadelphia

Davis, Ashable. *History of New Amsterdam or New York as It Was in the Days of the Dutch Governors, together with Papers on Events Connected with the American Revolution and on Philadelphia in the Times of William Penn.* New York, NY: Young, 1854. 240p.
http://moa.cit.cornell.edu/dienst/moabrowse.fly/MOA-JOURNALS2:DAVI-0057/5/1:TIFF2GIF:100

Freedley, Edwin T. *Philadelphia and Its Manufactures, a Handbook of the Great Manufactories and Representative Mercantile Houses of Philadelphia in 1857.* Philadelphia, PA: Young, 1858. 500p.
http://moa.umdl.umich.edu/cgi-bin/moa/sgml/moa-idx?notisid=AKX4165

————. *Philadelphia and Its Manufactures, a Handbook of the Great Manufactories and Representative Mercantile Houses of Philadelphia in 1867.* Philadelphia, PA: Young, 1867. 638p.
http://moa.umdl.umich.edu/cgi-bin/moa/sgml/moa-idx?notisid=AFR2748

Gunn, Lewis Carstairs. *Records of a California Family, Journals and Letters of Lewis C. Gunn and Elizabeth Le Breton Gunn.* San Diego, CA: Johnck and Seeger, 1928. 279p.
http://memory.loc.gov/cgi-bin/query/r?ammem/calbkbib:@field(AUTHOR+@band(Gunn,+Lewis+Carstairs,1813-1892.+))

Hoag, Joseph. *The Transformation of Joseph Hoag.* Philadelphia, PA: Tract Association of Friends. N.d., n.p.
http://people.delphi.com/pdsippel/hoag.htm
http://memory.loc.gov/ammem/mdbquery.html

Home for the Aged and Infirm Colored Persons. Annual Report of the Board of Managers. Philadelphia, PA: Various,
2nd Annual Meeting, 1866. 28p.
http://memory.loc.gov/cgi-bin/query/r?ammem/murray:@field(FLD001+91898494+):@@@REF

5th Annual Meeting, 1869. 20p.
http://memory.loc.gov/cgi-bin/query/r?ammem/murray:@field(FLD001+91898492+):@@@REF

6th Annual Meeting, 1870. 24p.
http://memory.loc.gov/cgi-bin/query/r?ammem/murray:@field(FLD001+91898491+):@@@REF

9th Annual Meeting, 1873. 32p.
http://memory.loc.gov/cgi-bin/query/r?ammem/murray:@field(FLD001+91898493+):@@@REF

35th Annual Report, 1899. 38p.
http://memory.loc.gov/cgi-bin/query/r?ammem/murray:@field(FLD001+91898490+):@@@REF

Kenderdine, Thaddeus S. *California Revisited, 1858-1897*. Doylestown, PA: Doylestown Publishing, 1898. 310p.
http://memory.loc.gov/cgi-bin/query/r?ammem/calbk:@field(DOCID+@lit(C164T00)):@@@REF

————. *A California Tramp and Later Footprints, or Life on the Plains and in the Golden State Thirty Years Ago, with Miscellaneous Sketches in Prose and Verse*. Philadelphia, PA: Globe Printing, 1888. 415p.
http://memory.loc.gov/cgi-bin/query/r?ammem/calbk:@field(DOCID+@lit(C005T00)):@@@REF

Hunt, B. P. *Why Colored People in Philadelphia are Excluded from the Street Cars*. Philadelphia, PA: Merrihew & Son, 1866. 28p.
http://moa.umdl.umich.edu/cgi-bin/moa/sgml/moa-idx?notisid=AJA2395

Lee, Jarena. *Religious Life and Experience and Journal of Mrs. Jarena Lee, Giving an Account of Her Call to Preach the Gospel*. Philadelphia, PA: Author, 1849. 97p.
http://digilib.nypl.org/dynaweb/digs/wwm9716/

McGowan, Edward. *Narrative of Edward McGowan, Including a Full Account of the Author's Adventures and Perils while Persecuted by the San Francisco Vigilance Committee of 1856, together with a Report of His Trial, which Resulted in His Acquittal*. San Francisco, CA: Russell, 1917. 240p.
http://memory.loc.gov/cgi-bin/query/r?ammem/calbkbib:@field(AUTHOR+@band(McGowan,+Edward, 1813-1893.+))

Narrative of Facts in the Case of Passmore Williamson. Philadelphia, PA: Pennsylvania Anti-Slavery Society, 1855. 24p.
http://moa.umdl.umich.edu/cgi-bin/moa/sgml/moa-idx?notisid=ABJ1564

Palmer, John M. *Was Richard Allen Great?* Philadelphia, PA: Weekly Astonisher Print, 1898. 9p.
http://memory.loc.gov/cgi-bin/query/r?ammem/aap:@field(SUBJ+@band(Allen,+Richard,-1760-1831.+))

Philadelphia [City Directory]. William H. Boyd, various.
1859-60; 1860-61; 1910.
http://www.citydirectories.psmedia.com/city/free_statesort.html

Philadelphia [City Directory]. Biddle, various.
1859-64.
http://www.citydirectories.psmedia.com/city/free_statesort.html

Philadelphia [City Directory]. Cohen, 1859
http://www.citydirectories.psmedia.com/city/free_statesort.html

Philadelphia [City Directory]. Philadelphia, PA: Cowell, 1860.
http://www.citydirectories.psmedia.com/city/free_statesort.html

Philadelphia [City Directory]. James Gopsill, 1880.
http://www.citydirectories.psmedia.com/city/free_statesort.html

Philadelphia Relief Committee to Collect Funds for the Sufferers by Yellow Fever. *Report of the Philadelphia Relief Committee, Appointed to Collect Funds for the Sufferers of Yellow Fever at Norfolk and Portsmouth, VA, 1855*. Philadelphia, PA: Inquirer, 1856. 142p.
http://moa.umdl.umich.edu/cgi-bin/moa/sgml/moa-idx?notisid=AAW1577

A Statistical Inquiry into the Condition of the People of Colour of the City and Districts of Philadelphia. Philadelphia, PA: Kite & Walton, 1849. 44p.
http://memory.loc.gov/cgi-bin/query/r?ammem/murray:@field(FLD001+12014690+):@@@REF

Statistics of the Colored People of Philadelphia. Philadelphia, PA: Pennsylvania Society for Promoting the Abolition of Slavery, Board of Education, 1859. 24p.
http://memory.loc.gov/cgi-bin/query/r?ammem/murray:@field(FLD001+12014692+):@@@REF

Tower, Charlemagne. *Tower Genealogy, an Account of the Descendants of John Tower of Hingham, Mass., Compiled under the Direction of Charlemagne Tower, Late of Philadelphia, Deceased*. Cambridge, MA: John Wilson, 1891. 689p.
http://genweb.net/~blackwell/ma/Tower1891/

Upham, Samuel Curtis. *Notes of a Voyage to California via Cape Horn, together with Scenes in El Dorado, in the Years of 1849-50, with an Appendix Containing Reminiscences together with the Articles of Association and Roll of Members of the Associated Pioneers of the Territorial Days of California*. Philadelphia, PA: Author, 1878. 594p.
http://memory.loc.gov/cgi-bin/query/r?ammem/calbkbib:@field(AUTHOR+@band(Upham,+Samuel+Curtis,1819-1885.+))

Wetherill, Charles. *History of the Religious Society of Friends Called by Some the Free Quakers in the City of Philadelphia*. Philadelphia, PA: Society of Friends, 1894. 10p.
http://people.delphi.com/pdsippel/fq-a1.htm

Woods, Daniel B. *Sixteen Months at the Gold Camps*. New York, NY: Harper, 1851. 199p.
http://memory.loc.gov/cgi-bin/query/r?ammem/calbkbib:@field(AUTHOR+@band(Woods,+Daniel+B.+))

Pittsburgh

Pittsburgh, 1859-60 [City Directory]. George H. Thurston, 1859.
http://www.citydirectories.psmedia.com/city/free_statesort.html

Swisshelm, Jane Grey Cannon. *Half a Century*. Chicago, IL: Author, 1880. 263p.
http://memory.loc.gov/cgi-bin/query/r?ammem/lhbumbib:@field(SUBJ+@band(Slavery+in+the+United+States--Anti-slavery+movements.+))

York County

Maclay, William. *The Journal of William Maclay, United States Senator from Pennsylvania, 1789-1791*. New York, NY: Appleton, 1890. 438p.
http://memory.loc.gov/ammem/amlaw/lwmj.html

Washington County

Commemorative Biographical Record, Washington County, Pennsylvania, Biographical Sketches of Prominent and Representative Citizens, and of Many of the Early Settled Families. Chicago, IL: Beers, 1893. 1,468p.
http://www.chartiers.com/beers-project/beers.html

West Chester

Christman, Enos. *One Man's Gold, the Letters & Journal of a Forty-niner, Enos Christman.* New York, NY: Whittlesey House, 1930. 278p.
http://memory.loc.gov/cgi-bin/query/r?ammem/calbkbib:@field(AUTHOR+@band(Christman,+Enos,+1828-1912.+))

Rhode Island

Arnold, James N. *Narragansett Historical Register, a Magazine Devoted to the Antiquities, Genealogy and Historical Matter Illustrating the History of the State of Rhode Island and Providence Plantation.* Vol. 6. Providence, RI: Narragansett Historical Publishing Co., various. 1888.
http://members.xoom.com/daveblql/

Austin, John Osborne. *Ancestry of Thirty-three Rhode Islanders, Born in the Eighteenth Century, Also Twenty-seven Charts of Roger Williams' Descendants to the Fifth Generation and an Account of Lewis Latham, Falconer to King Charles I, with a Chart of His American Descendants to the Fourth Generation and a List of 180 Existing Portraits of Rhode Island Governors, Chief Justices, Senators, etc. and of Certain Military Officers, Divines, Physicians, Authors, Lawyers, Merchants etc.* Albany, NY: Munsell's, 1889. 127p.
http://genweb.net/~blackwell/ri/33ri1889/

Douglass, William. *A Discourse Concerning the Currencies of the British Plantations in America, Especially with Regard to Their Paper Money, more Particularly in Relation to the Province of Massachusetts Bay in New England.* 1740. 3p.
http://www.people.virginia.edu/~rwm3n/webdoc2.html

Research Outline. Rhode Island. Salt Lake City, UT: Family History Library, 1997.
http://familysearch.org/sg/Rhode_Island.html

Talcott, S. V. *Genealogical Notes of New York and New England Families.* Albany, NY: Weed, Parsons & Co., 1883. 747p.
http://moa.cit.cornell.edu/dienst/moabrowse.fly/MOA-JOURNALS2:TALC-0006/3/1:TIFF2GIF:100

Providence

Providence [City Directory]. H. H. Brown, 1859.
http://www.citydirectories.psmedia.com/city/free_statesort.html

Truman, Benjamin Cummings. *Semi-tropical California, Its Climate, Healthfulness, Productiveness and Scenery.* San Francisco, CA: Bancroft, 1874. 204p.
http://memory.loc.gov/cgi-bin/query/r?ammem/calbkbib:@field(AUTHOR+@band(Truman,+Ben[jamin]+C[ummings],1835-1916.+))

Wierzbicki, Felix Paul. *California as It Is and as It May Be, or a Guide to the Gold Region.* San Francisco, CA: Grabhorn Press, 1933. 100p.
http://memory.loc.gov/cgi-bin/query/r?ammem/calbkbib:@field(AUTHOR+@band(Wierzbicki,+Felix+Paul,1815-1860.+))

South Carolina

Chestnut, Mary Boykin Miller. *A Diary from Dixie, as Written by Mary Boykin Chestnut, Wife of James Chestnut, Jr., United States Senator from South Carolina, 1859-1861, and afterward an Aide to Jefferson Davis and a Brigadier General in the Confederate Army.* New York, NY: Appleton, 1905. 424p.
http://metalab.unc.edu/docsouth/chesnut/menu.html

Edwards, William James. *Twenty-five Years in the Black Belt.* Boston, MA: Cornhill Co., 1918. 143p.
http://metalab.unc.edu/docsouth/edwards/menu.html

Ford, Arthur Peronneau. *Life in the Confederate Army, Being Personal Experience of a Private Soldier in the Confederate Army and Some Experiences and Sketches of Southern Life and Marion Johnstone Ford.* New York, NY: Neale, 1905. 136p.
http://metalab.unc.edu/docsouth/ford/menu.html

Jacobs, Harriet A. *Incidents in the Life of a Slave Girl.* Boston, MA: Author, 1861. 306p.
http://digilib.nypl.org/dynaweb/digs/wwm97255/

Jones, Charles Colcock. *The Siege of Savannah in December, 1864, and the Confederate Operations in Georgia, and the Third Military District of South Carolina during General Sherman's March from Atlanta to the Sea.* Albany, NY: Munsell's, 1874. 184p.
http://metalab.unc.edu/docsouth/jonescharles/menu.html

Pike, James Shepherd. *The Prostrate State, South Carolina under Negro Government.* New York, NY: Appleton, 1874. 288p.
http://moa.umdl.umich.edu/cgi-bin/moa/sgml/moa-idx?notisid=AFK4119

Research Outline. South Carolina. Salt Lake City, UT: Family History Library, 1997.
http://familysearch.org/sg/South_Carolina.html

Taylor, Susie King. *Reminiscences of My Life in Camp with the 33d United States Colored Troops Late 1st S.C. Volunteers.* Boston, MA: Author, 82p.
http://digilib.nypl.org/dynaweb/digs/wwm97267/

Aiken

Lanier, Sidney. *Florida, Its Scenery, Climate and History, with an Account of Charleston, Savannah, Augusta and Aiken, a Chapter for Consumptives, Various Papers on Fruit Culture and a Complete Handbook and Guide.* Philadelphia, PA: Lippincott, 1876. 346p.
http://moa.umdl.umich.edu/cgi-bin/moa/sgml/moa-idx?notisid=AFJ9565

Anderson County

Pickens, William. *The Heir of Slaves, an Autobiography.* Boston, MA: Pilgrim Press, 1911. 138p.
http://metalab.unc.edu/docsouth/pickens/menu.html

Berkeley

Jervey, Susan Ravenel and Charlotte St. J. Ravenel. *Two Diaries from Middle St. John's, Berkeley, South Carolina, February-May, 1865. Journals Kept by Miss Susan R. Jervey and Miss Charlotte St. J. Ravenel at Northampton and Pooshee Plantations, and Reminiscences of Mrs. (Waring) Henagan with Two Contemporary Reports from Federal Officials.* Berkeley, SC: St. John's Hunting Club, 1921. 56p.
http://metalab.unc.edu/docsouth/jervey/menu.html

Charleston

Charleston [City Directory]. Charleston, SC: Mears & Turnbull, 1859.
1859-60; 1860-61; 1910.
http://www.citydirectories.psmedia.com/city/free_statesort.html

Collis, Septima Maria Levy. *A Woman's War Record, 1861-1865.* New York, NY: Putnam, 1889. 78p.
http://metalab.unc.edu/docsouth/collis/menu.html

Lanier, Sidney. *Florida, Its Scenery, Climate and History, with an Account of Charleston, Savannah, Augusta and Aiken, a Chapter for Consumptives, Various Papers on Fruit Culture and a Complete Handbook and Guide.* Philadelphia, PA: Lippincott, 1876. 346p.
http://moa.umdl.umich.edu/cgi-bin/moa/sgml/moa-idx?notisid=AFJ9565

A Memorial Souvenir of Rev. J. Wofford White, Pastor of Wesley, M.E. Church, Charleston, S.C. Who Fell Asleep, January 7th, 1890, Aged 33 Years. Charleston, SC: Walker, Evans & Cogswell, 1890. 8p.
http://memory.loc.gov/cgi-bin/query/r?ammem/aap:@field(SUBJ+@band(Wesley+Methodist+Episcopal+Church++Charleston,+S.C.++))

Columbia

Columbia [City Directory]. Columbia, SC: Hershman, 1859.
http://www.citydirectories.psmedia.com/city/free_statesort.html

Episcopal Church, Commission of Home Missions to Colored People. New York, NY: Church, 1875, 1876.
9th Annual Report, 1873-74. 20p.
http://memory.loc.gov/cgi-bin/query/r?ammem/murray:@field(FLD001+91898515+):@@@REF

11th Annual Report, 1875-76. 24p.
http://memory.loc.gov/cgi-bin/query/r?ammem/murray:@field(FLD001+91898514+):@@@REF

Straker, David Augustus. *Bethel, A.M.E. Church Case, in Columbia, S.C., the State of South Carolina, Richland County, J. W. Morris et. al. Plaintiffs, against S. B. Wallace, et. al. Defendants, Action for Relief.* South Carolina: Unknown, 1887. 14p.
http://memory.loc.gov/cgi-bin/query/r?ammem/aap:@field(SUBJ+@band(African+Methodist+Episcopal+Church--Clergy--Appointment,+call+and+election.+))

Forsyth County

Beard, Ida May. *My Own Life, or a Deserted Woman.* NC: Author, 1898. 212p.
http://metalab.unc.edu/docsouth/beard/menu.html

Greenville

Betts, Alexander Davis. *Experience of a Confederate Chaplain, 1861-1864*. Greenville, SC: Author, Date Unknown. 104p.
http://metalab.unc.edu/docsouth/betts/menu.html

Port Royal

The Negroes at Port Royal. Boston, MA: Wallcut, 1862. 36p.
http://moa.umdl.umich.edu/cgi-bin/moa/sgml/moa-idx?notisid=AFK4120

Richland County

Straker, David Augustus. *Bethel, A.M.E. Church Case, in Columbia, S.C., the State of South Carolina, Richland County, J. W. Morris et. al. Plaintiffs, against S. B. Wallace, et. al. Defendants, Action for Relief*. South Carolina: Unknown, 1887. 14p.
http://memory.loc.gov/cgi-bin/query/r?ammem/aap:@field(SUBJ+@band(African+Methodist+Episcopal+Church--Clergy--Appointment,+call+and+election.+))

Spartanburg

Colored Industrial Training School Annual Report. Spartanburg, SC: School.
1892 Report. 10p.
http://memory.loc.gov/cgi-bin/query/r?ammem/aap:@field(SUBJ+@band(Annual+reports--South+Carolina--Spartanburg--1892.+))

Young, Kenneth M. *As Some Things Appear on the Plains and among the Rockies in Mid-summer*. Spartanburg, SC: Fowler, 1890. 15p.
http://memory.loc.gov/cgi-bin/query/r?ammem/aap:@field(SUBJ+@band(Afro-Americans--Travel--United+States.+))

Summerville

Boggs, William Robertson. *Military Reminiscences of General Wm. R. Boggs, C.S.A*. Durham, NC: Seeman Printery, 1913. 115p.
http://metalab.unc.edu/docsouth/boggs/menu.html

Sumter County

Jackson, John Andrew. *The Experience of a Slave in South Carolina*. London: Passmore & Alabaster, 1862. 48p.
http://metalab.unc.edu/docsouth/jackson/menu.html

South Dakota

Andrews, Christopher Columbus. *Minnesota and Dacotah, in Letters Descriptive of a Tour through the Northwest, in the Autumn of 1856*. Washington, DC: Farnham, 1857. 215p.
http://memory.loc.gov/cgi-bin/query/r?ammem/lhbumbib:@field(SUBJ+@band(Andrews,+Christopher+Columbus,-1829-1922.+))

Dodge, Richard Irving. *The Black Hills, a Minute Description of the Routes*. New York, NY: J. Miller, 1876. 186p.
http://moa.umdl.umich.edu/cgi-bin/moa/sgml/moa-idx?notisid=AFK4433

Heard, Isaac V. D. *History of the Sioux War and Massacres of 1862 and 1863*. New York, NY: Harper, 1864. 360p.
http://moa.umdl.umich.edu/cgi-bin/moa/sgml/moa-idx?notisid=ACK0828

Parkman, Francis. *The Oregon Trail, Sketches of Prairie and Rocky Mountain Life*. Philadelphia, PA: Winston, 1831. 388p.
http://xroads.virginia.edu/~HYPER/OREGON/oregon.html

Research Outline. South Dakota. Salt Lake City, UT: Family History Library, 1997.
http://familysearch.org/sg/South_Dakota.html

Tennessee

Bokum, Hermann. *The Testimony of a Refugee from East Tennessee by Hermann Bokum, Chaplain, U.S.A.* Philadelphia, PA: Author, 1863. 24p.
http://metalab.unc.edu/docsouth/bokum/menu.html

Loguen, Jermain Wesley. *The Rev. J. W. Loguen, as a Slave and as a Freeman, a Narrative of Real Life*. Syracuse, NY: Truair, 1859. 454p.
http://moa.umdl.umich.edu/cgi-bin/moa/sgml/moa-idx?notisid=ABT6752

Research Outline. Tennessee. Salt Lake City, UT: Family History Library, 1997.
http://familysearch.org/sg/Tenness.html

Tennessee Confederate Soldiers' Home Applications Index. Nashville, TN: Tennessee State Library and Archives. 1964. 323p.
http://www.state.tn.us/sos/statelib/pubsvs/csh_intr.htm

Clarkesville
Clarkesville, 1859-60 [City Directory]. Williams, 1859.
http://www.citydirectories.psmedia.com/city/free_statesort.html

Franklin
Copley, John M. *A Sketch of the Battle of Franklin, Tennessee with Reminiscences of Camp Douglas*. Austin, TX: Eugene von Boeckmann, 1893. 206p.
http://metalab.unc.edu/docsouth/copley/menu.html

Hardeman County

Burnett, Peter Hardeman. *Recollections and Opinions of an Old Pioneer*. New York, NY: Appleton, 1880. 448p.
http://memory.loc.gov/cgi-bin/query/r?ammem/calbkbib:@field(AUTHOR+@band(Burnett,+Peter+H[ardeman],1807-1895.+))

Henderson

Carroll, John William. *Autobiography and Reminiscences of John W. Carroll, Henderson, Tenn.* Henderson, TN: Author, 1898. 66p.
http://metalab.unc.edu/docsouth/carroll/menu.html

Jefferson County

Rankin, George C. *The Story of My Life or More than a Half Century as I Have Lived It and Seen It Lived*. Nashville, TN: Smith & Lamar, 1912. 356p.
http://metalab.unc.edu/docsouth/rankin/menu.html

Jonesboro

Hoss, Elijah Embree. *Elihu Embree, Abolitionist*. Nashville, TN: University Press Co., 1897. 28p.
http://memory.loc.gov/cgi-bin/query/r?ammem/aap:@field(SUBJ+@band(Embree,+Elihu,--1782-1820.+))

Memphis

Memphis [City Directory]. Hutton & Clark, 1859.
http://www.citydirectories.psmedia.com/city/free_statesort.html

Wright, Marcus J. *Diary of Brigadier General Marcus J. Wright, C.S.A., April 23, 1861-February 26, 1863*. Author, Date Unknown. 8p.
http://metalab.unc.edu/docsouth/wrightmarcus/menu.html

Nashville

Burnett, Peter Hardeman. *Recollections and Opinions of an Old Pioneer*. New York, NY: Appleton, 1880. 448p.
http://memory.loc.gov/cgi-bin/query/r?ammem/calbkbib:@field(AUTHOR+@band(Burnett,+Peter+H[ardeman],1807-1895.+))

Morgan, Mrs. Irby. *How It Was, Four Years among the Rebels*. Nashville, TN: Methodist Episcopal Church, South, 1892. 204p.
http://metalab.unc.edu/docsouth/morgan/menu.html

Nashville [City Directory]. John P. Campbell, 1859.
http://www.citydirectories.psmedia.com/city/free_statesort.html

Springfield

Smithwick, Noah. *The Evolution of a State or Recollections of Old Texas Days*. Austin, TX: Gammel Book Co., 1900. 354p.
http://www.erols.com/hardeman/lonestar/olbooks/smithwic/otd.htm

Sullivan County

Hoss, Elijah Embree. *Elihu Embree, Abolitionist.* Nashville, TN: University Press Co., 1897. 28p.
http://memory.loc.gov/cgi-bin/query/r?ammem/aap:@field(SUBJ+@band(Embree,+Elihu,--1782-1820.+))

Texas

Braman, D. E. E. *Braman's Information about Texas.* Philadelphia, PA: Lippincott, 1858. 192p.
http://moa.umdl.umich.edu/cgi-bin/moa/sgml/moa-idx?notisid=AFK4201

Dobie, J. Frank. *Guide to Life and Literature of the Southwest.* Dallas, TX: Southern Methodist University Press, 1952. 222p.
http://www.erols.com/hardeman/lonestar/olbooks/dobie/dobie.htm
http://midcity.net/gutenberg/etext95/swest10.txt

DuVal, William Pope. *The Argument of William P. DuVal on Claim of the Citizens of Texas for Compensation for the Property Taken from Them by the Comanche Indians since the Annexation of That State to the United States.* Washington, DC: Goggin & Saunders, 1852. 12p.
http://moa.umdl.umich.edu/cgi-bin/moa/sgml/moa-idx?notisid=AJA281

Index to Texas Confederate Pension Records, 1899-1975. Austin, TX: Texas State Library and Archives Commission. N.d., n.p.
http://www.tsl.state.tx.us/lobby/cpi/cpindex.htm

Marcy, Randolph Barnes. *Exploration of the Red River of Louisiana in the Year 1852.* Washington, DC: Tucker, 1854. 390p.
http://moa.umdl.umich.edu/cgi-bin/moa/sgml/moa-idx?notisid=ABB2532

New Texas Handbook. Austin, TX: Texas State Historical Association, 1996.
http://www.tsha.utexas.edu/handbook/online/

Research Outline. Texas. Salt Lake City, UT: Family History Library, 1997. 11p.
http://familysearch.org/sg/Texas.html

Smithwick, Noah. *The Evolution of a State or Recollections of Old Texas Days.* Austin, TX: Gammel Book Co., 1900. 354p.
http://www.erols.com/hardeman/lonestar/olbooks/smithwic/otd.htm

Galveston

Galveston, 1859-60 [City Directory]. Galveston, TX: Richardson, 1859.
http://www.citydirectories.psmedia.com/city/free_statesort.html

Galveston, 1880-81 [City Directory]. Galveston, TX: Heller, 1880.
http://www.citydirectories.psmedia.com/city/free_statesort.html

Galveston [City Directory]. Galveston, TX: Morrison & Fourmy, various.
    1890-91; 1909-1910.
    http://www.citydirectories.psmedia.com/city/free_statesort.html

Marshall

Wright, Louise Wigfall. *A Southern Girl in '61, the Wartime Memories of a Confederate Senator's
    Daughter*. New York, NY: Doubleday, 1905. 258p.
    http://metalab.unc.edu/docsouth/wright/menu.html

San Antonio

United States. Congress. House Committee on Military Affairs. *Second Lieut. Henry Ossian
    Flipper*. Washington, DC: Government Printing Office, 1901. 5p.
    http://memory.loc.gov/cgi-bin/query/r?ammem/aap:@field(SUBJ+@band(Flipper,+Henry+Ossian,--1856-
    1940--Trials,+litigation,+etc.+))

Utah

Research Outline. Membership of the LDS Church, 1830-1848. Salt Lake City, UT: Family
    History Library, 1993.
    http://www.familysearch.com/sg/Membersh.html

Research Outline. Utah. Salt Lake City, UT: Family History Library, 1997.
    http://familysearch.org/sg/Utah.html

Stansbury, Howard. *An Expedition to the Valley of the Great Salt Lake of Utah: Including a
    Description of Its Geography, Natural History, and Minerals and an Analysis of Its Waters,
    with an Authentic Account of the Mormon Settlement. Also a Reconnoissance of a New
    Route through the Rocky Mountains and Two Large and Accurate Maps of That Region*.
    Philadelphia, PA: Lippincott, Grambo, 1855. 598p.
    http://moa.umdl.umich.edu/cgi-bin/moa/sgml/moa-idx?notisid=AJA3655

————. *Exploration and Survey of the Valley of the Great Salt Lake of Utah, Including a
    Reconnoissance of a New Route through the Rocky Mountains*. Philadelphia, PA: Lippincott,
    Grambo, & Co., 1852. 600p.
    http://moa.umdl.umich.edu/cgi-bin/moa/sgml/moa-idx?notisid=ABA4855

Salt Lake City (Salt Lake County)

Lapham, Macy Harvey. *Crisscross Trails, Narrative of a Soil Surveyor*. Berkeley, CA: Berg,
    1949. 258p.
    http://chla.mannlib.cornell.edu/cgi-bin/chla/viewer.cgi?docid=title2c.chla.mannlib.cornell/
    0219laph&format=1:75-GIF&section=Title+Page

Vermont

Burt, Henry M. *Burt's Illustrated Guide of the Connecticut Valley, Containing Descriptions of Mount Holyoke, Mount Mansfield, White Mountains, Lake Memphremagog, Lake Willoughby, Montreal, Quebec.* Northampton: New England Publishing Co., 1867. 294p.
http://moa.umdl.umich.edu/cgi-bin/moa/sgml/moa-idx?notisid=AAB2140

Colton, Walter. *Three Years in California.* New York, NY: A. S. Barnes, 1850. 480p.
http://moa.umdl.umich.edu/cgi-bin/moa/sgml/moa-idx?notisid=ABE2329

Research Outline. Vermont. Salt Lake City, UT: Family History Library, 1997.
http://familysearch.org/sg/Vermont.html

Talcott, S. V. *Genealogical Notes of New York and New England Families.* Albany, NY: Weed, Parsons & Co., 1883. 747p.
http://moa.cit.cornell.edu/dienst/moabrowse.fly/MOA-JOURNALS2:TALC-0006/3/1:TIFF2GIF:100

Vermont State Directory [City Directory]. Tuttle, 1859.
http://www.citydirectories.psmedia.com/city/free_statesort.html

Bennington
Barber, Edward W. *The Vermontville Colony, Its Genesis and History, with Personal Sketches of the Colonists.* Lansing, MI: Smith, 1897. 93p.
http://memory.loc.gov/cgi-bin/query/r?ammem/lhbumbib:@field(SUBJ+@band(Vermontville,+Mich.+))

Hinesburg
Perry, Belle McArthur. *Lucinda Hinsdale Stone, Her Life Story and Reminiscences.* Detroit, MI: Blinn Publishing, 1902. 369p.
http://memory.loc.gov/cgi-bin/query/r?ammem/lhbumbib:@field(SUBJ+@band(Stone,+Lucinda+Hinsdale,--1814-1900.+))

Rutland County
Inventory of the William Henry Jackson Papers. New York, NY: New York Public Library, Manuscripts and Archives Division, 1998. Unpgd.
http://digilib.nypl.org/dynaweb/ead/human/jacksonw/@Generic__BookView

Ward, David. *The Autobiography of David Ward.* New York, NY: Author, 1912. 194p.
http://memory.loc.gov/cgi-bin/query/r?ammem/lhbumbib:@field(SUBJ+@band(Michigan--Social+life+and+customs.+))

St. Albans
Manly, William Lewis. *Death Valley in '49. Important Chapter of California Pioneer History. The Autobiography of a Pioneer, Detailing His Life from a Humble Home in the Green Mountains to the Gold Mines of California and Particularly Reciting the Sufferings of the*

Band of Men, Women and Children Who Gave "Death Valley" Its Name. San Jose, CA: Pacific Tree and Vine Co., 1894. 498p.
http://memory.loc.gov/cgi-bin/query/r?ammem/calbkbib:@field(AUTHOR+@band(Manly,+William+Lewis,b.+1820.+))

Wells (Rutland County)
Ward, David. *The Autobiography of David Ward.* New York, NY: Author, 1912. 194p.
http://memory.loc.gov/cgi-bin/query/r?ammem/lhbumbib:@field(SUBJ+@band(Michigan--Social+life+and+customs.+))

Virginia

Bagby, George William. *Canal Reminiscences, Recollections of Travel in the Old Days on the James River and Kanawha Canal.* Richmond, VA: West, Johnston & Co., Publishers, 1879. 37p.
http://metalab.unc.edu/docsouth/bagby/menu.html

Bradford, Sarah H. *Harriet, the Moses of Her People.* New York, NY: Lockwood, 1886. 149p.
http://metalab.unc.edu/docsouth/harriet/menu.html

Burwell, Letitia M. *A Girl's Life in Virginia before the War.* New York, NY: Stokes, 1895. 209p.
http://metalab.unc.edu/docsouth/burwell/menu.html

Edwards, Richard. *Statistical Gazetteer of the State of Virginia, Embracing Important Topographical and Historical Information from Recent and Original Sources, together with the Results of the Last Census of Population in Most Cases to 1854.* Richmond, VA: State, 1855. 428p.
http://moa.umdl.umich.edu/cgi-bin/moa/sgml/moa-idx?notisid=AJA2520

Ferebee, London R. *A Brief History of the Slave Life of Rev. L. R. Ferebee, and the Battles of Life and Four Years of His Ministerial Life.* Raleigh, NC: Edwards, Broughton & Co., Steam Printers, Publishers and Binders,1882. 24p.
http://metalab.unc.edu/docsouth/ferebee/menu.html

Hambleton, James Pinkney. *A Biographical Sketch of Henry A. Wise, with a History of the Political Campaign in Virginia in 1855.* Richmond, VA: J. W. Randolph, 1856. 509p.
http://moa.umdl.umich.edu/cgi-bin/moa/sgml/moa-idx?notisid=AFJ9125

Johnston, David Emmons. *The Story of a Confederate Boy in the Civil War.* Portland, OR: Glass & Prudhomme, 1914. 379p.
http://metalab.unc.edu/docsouth/johnstond/menu.html

Maury, Matthew Fontaine. *Physical Survey of Virginia. Her Geographical Position; Its Commercial Advantages and National Importance.* New York, NY: Van Nostrand, 1869. 100p.
http://moa.umdl.umich.edu/cgi-bin/moa/sgml/moa-idx?notisid=AFQ0861

McKim, Randolph Harrison. *A Soldier's Recollections, Leaves from the Diary of a Young Confederate, with an Oration on the Motives and Aims of the Soldiers of the South.* New York, NY: Longmans, Green & Co., 1910. 362p.
http://metalab.unc.edu/docsouth/mckim/menu.html

Page, Thomas Nelson. *Social Life in Old Virginia before the War.* New York, NY: Scribners, 1897. 109p.
http://metalab.unc.edu/docsouth/pagesocial/menu.html

Pickett, George Edward. *The Heart of a Soldier as Revealed in the Intimate Letters of General George E. Pickett, C.S.A.* New York, NY: Moyle, 1913. 215p.
http://metalab.unc.edu/docsouth/pickett/menu.html

Plunkett, Michael. *Afro-American Sources in Virginia, a Guide to Manuscripts.* Charlottesville, VA: University of Virginia, 1994. Unpgd.
http://www.upress.virginia.edu/plunkett/mfp.html

Pollard, Edward Alfred. *The Virginia Tourist.* Philadelphia, PA: Lippincott, 1870. 277p.
http://moa.umdl.umich.edu/cgi-bin/moa/sgml/moa-idx?notisid=AFK4089

Pryor, Sara Agnes Rice. *My Day, Reminiscences of a Long Life.* New York, NY: Macmillan, 1909. 454p.
http://metalab.unc.edu/docsouth/pryor/menu.html

Research Outline. Virginia. Salt Lake City, UT: Family History Library, 1997.
http://familysearch.org/sg/Virginia.html

Robson, John S. *How a One Legged Rebel Lives, Reminiscences of the Civil War. The Story of the Campaigns of Stonewall Jackson, as Told by a High Private in the "Foot Cavalry" from Alleghany Mountain to Chancellorsville, with the Complete Regimental Rosters of both the Great Armies at Gettysburg, by John S. Robson, Late of the 52d Regiment Virginia Infantry.* Durham, NC: Author, 1898. 186p.
http://metalab.unc.edu/docsouth/robson/menu.html

Royall, William L. *Some Reminiscences.* New York, NY: Neale Publishing Co., 1909. 210p.
http://metalab.unc.edu/docsouth/royall/royall.html

Virginia. Board of Immigration. *Virginia: A Geographical and Political Summary, Embracing a Description of the State.* Richmond, VA: Walker, 1876. 319p.
http://moa.umdl.umich.edu/cgi-bin/moa/sgml/moa-idx?notisid=AFK4063

Virginia, a Guide to the Old Dominion. New York, NY: Oxford, 1940, 1992. 710p.
http://xroads.virginia.edu/~HYPER/VAGuide/frame.html

Virginia Magazine of History and Biography. Richmond, VA: Virginia Historical Society. Quarterly. Table of Contents, Vol. 140, No. 1, Winter 1996- .
http://www.vahistorical.org/publicat/vmhb.htm

Wood, James H. *The War, Stonewall Jackson, His Campaigns and Battles, the Regiment as I Saw Them.* Cumberland, MD: Eddy Press, 1910. 181p.
http://metalab.unc.edu/docsouth/wood/menu.html

Worsham, John H. *One of Jackson's Foot Cavalry, His Experience and What He Saw During the War 1861-1865, Including a History of "F Company" Richmond, Va., 21st Regiment Virginia Infantry, Second Brigade, Jackson's Division, Second Corps, A.N.Va.* New York, NY: Neale, 1912. 353p.
http://metalab.unc.edu/docsouth/worsham/menu.html

Charleston (Jefferson County)

Hughes, Louis. *Thirty Years a Slave, from Bondage to Freedom, the Institution of Slavery as Seen on the Plantation and in the Home of the Planter.* Milwaukee, WI: South Side Printing Co., 1897. 210p.
http://metalab.unc.edu/docsouth/hughes/menu.html

McIlhany, Edward Washington. *Recollections of a '49er, a Quaint and Thrilling Narrative of a Trip across the Plains, and Life in the California Gold Fields during the Stirring Days Following the Discovery of Gold in the Far West.* Kansas City, MO: Hailman Printing, 1908. 212p.
http://memory.loc.gov/cgi-bin/query/r?ammem/calbkbib:@field(AUTHOR+@band(McIlhany,+Edward+Washington,b.+1828.+))

Rollin, Frank A. *Life and Public Services of Martin R. Delany, Sub-Assistant Commissioner Bureau Relief of Refugees, Freedmen and of Abandoned Lands, and Late Major 104th U.S. Colored Troops.* Boston, MA: Lee and Shepard, 1883. 367p.
http://digilib.nypl.org/dynaweb/digs/wwm9720/

Fredericksburg

Maury, Dabney Herndon. *Recollections of a Virginian in the Mexican, Indian and Civil Wars.* New York, NY: Scribners, 1894. 279p.
http://metalab.unc.edu/docsouth/maury/menu.html

Halifax

Episcopal Church, Commission of Home Missions to Colored People. New York, NY: Church, 1875, 1876.
9th Annual Report, 1873-74. 20p.
http://memory.loc.gov/cgi-bin/query/r?ammem/murray:@field(FLD001+91898515+):@@@REF

11th Annual Report, 1875-76. 24p.
http://memory.loc.gov/cgi-bin/query/r?ammem/murray:@field(FLD001+91898514+):@@@REF

Hampden

Stanford, Peter Thomas. *Imaginary Obstructions to True Spiritual Progress, Preached during the Service at the Day Street Congregational Church, August 14, 1898.* West Somerville, MA: Davis Square Printing, Co., 1898. 12p.
http://memory.loc.gov/cgi-bin/query/r?ammem/aap:@field(SUBJ+@band(Day+Street+Congregational+Church.+))

Hanover County

Wirt, William. *Sketches of the Life and Character of Patrick Henry.* Philadelphia, PA: James Webster, 1817. 427p.
http://metalab.unc.edu/docsouth/wirt/menu.html

King and Queen County

Smedes, Susan Dabney. *Memorials of a Southern Planter.* Baltimore, MD: Cushings & Bailey, 1888. 348p.
http://moa.umdl.umich.edu/cgi-bin/moa/sgml/moa-idx?notisid=AFK4047

Loudon County

Janney, Samuel M. *Memoirs of Samuel M. Janney, Late of Lincoln, Loudon County, Virginia. A Minister in the Religious Society of Friends*. Philadelphia, PA: Friends' Book Association, 1881. 309p.
http://metalab.unc.edu/docsouth/janney/menu.html

Norfolk

Armstrong, George D. *The Summer of the Pestilence, a History of the Ravages of the Yellow Fever in Norfolk, Virginia, A.D. 1855*. 2nd ed. Philadelphia, PA: Lippincott, 1856. 192p.
http://users.visi.net/~cwt/sum-pest.html

Norfolk [City Directory]. Norfolk, VA: Vickery & Co., 1859.
http://www.citydirectories.psmedia.com/city/free_statesort.html

Page County

Veney, Bethany. *The Narrative of Bethany Veney, a Slave Woman*. Worcester, MA: Author, 1889. 47p.
http://metalab.unc.edu/docsouth/veney/menu.html
http://digilib.nypl.org/dynaweb/digs/wwm97269/

Petersburg

Episcopal Church, Commission of Home Missions to Colored People. New York, NY: Church, 1875, 1876.
9th Annual Report, 1873-74. 20p.
http://memory.loc.gov/cgi-bin/query/r?ammem/murray:@field(FLD001+91898515+):@@@REF

11th Annual Report, 1875-76. 24p.
http://memory.loc.gov/cgi-bin/query/r?ammem/murray:@field(FLD001+91898514+):@@@REF

General Military Hospital for the North Carolina Troops in Petersburg, Virginia. Raleigh, NC: Strother & Marcom Book and Job Printers, 1861. 8p.
http://metalab.unc.edu/docsouth/generalhospital/menu.html

Petersburg [City Directory]. George E. Ford, 1859.
http://www.citydirectories.psmedia.com/city/free_statesort.html

Powhatan County

Harland, Marion. *Marion Harland's Autobiography, the Story of a Long Life*. New York, NY: Harper, 1910. 498p.
http://metalab.unc.edu/docsouth/harland/menu.html

Mosby, John Singleton. *The Memoirs of Colonel John S. Mosby*. Boston, MA: Little, Brown & Co., 1917. 414p.
http://metalab.unc.edu/docsouth/mosby/menu.html

Williams, James. *Narrative of James Williams, an American Slave, Who Was for Several Years a Driver on a Cotton Plantation in Alabama*. New York, NY: American Anti-Slavery Society, 1838. 108p.
http://metalab.unc.edu/docsouth/williams/menu.html

Prince Edward County

Bruce, Henry Clay. *The New Man, Twenty-nine Years a Slave, Twenty-nine Years a Free Man, Recollections of H. C. Bruce.* York, PA: Anstadt & Sons, 1895. 176p.
http://metalab.unc.edu/docsouth/bruce/menu.html

Prince William County

Stewart, Austin. *Twenty-two Years a Slave and Forty Years a Freeman, Embracing a Correspondence of Several Years, while President of Wilberforce Colony, London, Canada West.* Rochester, NY: Alling, 1857. 360p.
http://metalab.unc.edu/docsouth/steward/menu.html

Richmond

Macon, Thomas Joseph. *Life Gleanings.* Richmond, VA: Author, 1913. 101p.
http://metalab.unc.edu/docsouth/macon/menu.html

Richmond [City Directory]. Richmond, VA: George M. West, 1859.
http://www.citydirectories.psmedia.com/city/free_statesort.html

Wise, John Sergeant. *The End of an Era.* Boston, MA: Houghton, Mifflin & Co., 1899. 474p.
http://metalab.unc.edu/docsouth/wise/menu.html

Rockbridge County

Paxton, Elisha Franklin. *Memoir and Memorials, composed of His Letters from Camp and Field while an Officer in the Confederate Army, with an Introductory and Connecting Narrative Collected and Arranged by His Son, John Gallatin Paxton.* New York, NY: Neale, 1907. 114p.
http://metalab.unc.edu/docsouth/paxton/menu.html

Shenandoah Valley

Ashby, Thomas Almond. *The Valley Campaigns, Being the Reminiscences of a Non-Combatant While between the Lines in the Shenandoah Valley during the War of the States.* New York, NY: Neale, 1914. 327p.
http://metalab.unc.edu/docsouth/ashby/menu.html

Vicksburg

Delany, Lucy A. *From the Darkness Cometh the Light, or Struggles for Freedom.* St. Louis, MO: J. T. Smith, unknown. 64p.
http://digilib.nypl.org/dynaweb/digs/wwm97254/

Waynesboro

Hamilton, James Gillespie. *Notebooks of James Gillespie Hamilton, a Merchant of Old Westport, Missouri (1844-1858).* Fresno, CA: Katharine Jones Moore, 1953. 301p.
http://memory.loc.gov/cgi-bin/query/r?ammem/calbkbib:@field(AUTHOR+@band(Hamilton,+James+Gillespie,1816-1869.+))

Westmoreland County

Lee, William Mack. *History of the Life of Rev. William Mack Lee, Body Servant of General Robert E. Lee through the Civil War, Cook from 1861 to 1865.* Norfolk, VA: Smith Printing, 1908. 10p.
http://metalab.unc.edu/docsouth/leewilliam/menu.html

Washington

Research Outline. Washington. Salt Lake City, UT: Family History Library, 1997.
http://familysearch.org/sg/Washington.html

West Virginia

Cross, Jonathan. *Five Years in the Alleghanies.* New York, NY: Amerian Tract Society, 1863.
208p.
http://moa.umdl.umich.edu/cgi-bin/moa/sgml/moa-idx?notisid=ANY9680

Debar, Joseph Hubert Diss. *The West Virginia Hand-book and Immigrant's Guide. A Sketch of the State of West Virginia.* Parkersbury, WV: Gibbens, 1870. 200p.
http://moa.umdl.umich.edu/cgi-bin/moa/sgml/moa-idx?notisid=AFJ9234

Maury, M. F. and William M. Fontaine. *Resources of West Virginia.* Wheeling, WV: Register, 1876. 442p.
http://moa.umdl.umich.edu/cgi-bin/moa/sgml/moa-idx?notisid=AAW1607

Research Outline. West Virginia. Salt Lake City, UT: Family History Library, 1997.
http://familysearch.org/sg/West_Virginia.html

Washington, Booker Talieferro. *My Larger Education, Being Chapters from My Experience.* Garden City, NY: Doubleday, Page & Co., 1911. 313p.
http://metalab.unc.edu/docsouth/washeducation/menu.html

———. *Up from Slavery, an Autobiography.* New York, NY: Doubleday, 1901. 330p.
http://metalab.unc.edu/docsouth/washington/menu.html

West Virginia. State Board of Centennial Managers. *Resources of West Virginia.* Wheeling, WV: Register Co., 1876. 442p.
http://moa.umdl.umich.edu/cgi-bin/moa/sgml/moa-idx?notisid=AAW1607

Shenandoah Valley

Ashby, Thomas Almond. *The Valley Campaigns, Being the Reminiscences of a Non-Combatant While between the Lines in the Shenandoah Valley during the War of the States.* New York, NY: Neale, 1914. 327p.
http://metalab.unc.edu/docsouth/ashby/menu.html

Wisconsin

Aikens, Andrew Jackson and Lewis A. Proctor. *Men of Progress, Wisconsin, a Selected List of Biographical Sketches and Portraits of the Leaders in Business, Professional and Official Life, together with Short Notes on the History and Character of Wisconsin.* Milwaukee, WI: Evening Wisconsin Co., 1897. 640p.
http://memory.loc.gov/ammem/mdbquery.html

Curtiss, Daniel S. *Western Portraiture, and Emigrants' Guide, a Description of Wisconsin, Illinois, and Iowa with Remarks on Minnesota and Other Territories.* New York, NY: Colton, 1852. 370p.
http://moa.umdl.umich.edu/cgi-bin/moa/sgml/moa-idx?notisid=AJA3436

Folsom, William Henry Carman. *Fifty Years in the Northwest.* St. Paul, MN: Pioneer Press Co., 1888. 763p.
http://memory.loc.gov/cgi-bin/query/r?ammem/lhbum:@field(DOCID+@lit(01070T000)):@@@REF

Henry, William Arnon. *Northern Wisconsin, a Handbook for the Homeseeker.* Madison, WI: Democrat Printing, 1896. 192p.
http://memory.loc.gov/cgi-bin/query/r?ammem/lhbumbib:@field(SUBJ+@band(Agriculture--Wisconsin.+))

Hunt, John Warren. *Wisconsin Gazetteer, Containing the Names, Location and Advantages of the Counties, Cities, Towns, Villages, Post Offices, and Settlements Together with a Description of the Lakes, Water Courses, Prairies, and Public Localities in the State of Wisconsin.* Madison, WI: Brown, 1853. 258p.
http://moa.umdl.umich.edu/cgi-bin/moa/sgml/moa-idx?notisid=AFK4346

Notable Men of Wisconsin. Milwaukee, WI: Williams Publishing Co., 1902. 259p.
http://memory.loc.gov/cgi-bin/query/r?ammem/lhbumbib:@field(SUBJ+@band(Wisconsin--Biography--Portraits.+))

Research Outline. Wisconsin. Salt Lake City, UT: Family History Library, 1997.
http://familysearch.org/sg/Wisconsin.html

Smith, William Rudolph. *The History of Wisconsin. In Three Parts, Historical, Documentary, and Descriptive.* Madison, WI: Brown, 1854. 432p.
http://moa.umdl.umich.edu/cgi-bin/moa/sgml/moa-idx?notisid=AAZ9854a

State Historical Society of Wisconsin. *Collections of the State Historical Society of Wisconsin.* Madison, WI: The Society, various.
Vol. 11 http://memory.loc.gov/cgi-bin/query/r?ammem/lhbum:@field(DOCID+@lit(7689aT000)):@@@REF
Vol. 12 http://memory.loc.gov/cgi-bin/query/r?ammem/lhbum:@field(DOCID+@lit(7689bT000)):@@@REF
Vol. 14 http://memory.loc.gov/cgi-bin/query/r?ammem/lhbum:@field(DOCID+@lit(7689cT000)):@@@REF
Vol. 15 http://memory.loc.gov/cgi-bin/query/r?ammem/lhbum:@field(DOCID+@lit(7689dT000)):@@@REF
Vol. 16 http://memory.loc.gov/cgi-bin/query/r?ammem/lhbum:@field(DOCID+@lit(7689eT000)):@@@REF
Vol. 17 http://memory.loc.gov/cgi-bin/query/r?ammem/lhbum:@field(DOCID+@lit(7689fT000)):@@@REF
Vol. 18 http://memory.loc.gov/cgi-bin/query/r?ammem/lhbum:@field(DOCID+@lit(7689gT000)):@@@REF
Vol. 19 http://memory.loc.gov/cgi-bin/query/r?ammem/lhbum:@field(DOCID+@lit(7689hT000)):@@@REF
Vol. 20 http://memory.loc.gov/cgi-bin/query/r?ammem/lhbum:@field(DOCID+@lit(7689iT000)):@@@REF
Vol. 25 http://memory.loc.gov/cgi-bin/query/r?ammem/lhbum:@field(DOCID+@lit(7689jT000)):@@@REF

The State Wisconsin, Embracing Brief Sketches of Its History, Position, Resources, and Industries and a Catalogue of Its Exhibits at the Centennial at Philadelphia. Madison, WI: Atwood & Culver, 1876. 80p.
http://moa.umdl.umich.edu/cgi-bin/moa/sgml/moa-idx?notisid=AAW4308

Tuttle, Charles R. *An Illustrated History of the State of Wisconsin.* Boston, MA: B. B. Russell, 1875. 800p.
http://moa.umdl.umich.edu/cgi-bin/moa/sgml/moa-idx?notisid=AFK4349

Appleton

Older, Fremont. *My Own Story.* San Francisco, CA: Call Publishing, 1919. 197p.
http://memory.loc.gov/cgi-bin/query/r?ammem/calbkbib:@field(AUTHOR+@band(Older,+Fremont,1856-1935+))

Chippewa Valley

Bundy, Charles Smith. *Early Days in the Chippewa Valley.* Menominie, WI: Flint Douglas Printing, 1916. 16p.
http://memory.loc.gov/cgi-bin/query/r?ammem/lhbum:@field(DOCID+@lit(16807T000)):@@@REF

Dane County

La Follette, Robert Marion. *La Follette's Autobiography, a Personal Narrative of Political Experiences.* Madison, WI: La Follette Co., 1913. 807p.
http://memory.loc.gov/cgi-bin/query/r?ammem/lhbumbib:@field(SUBJ+@band(Presidents--United+States--Election--1912.+))

Dunn County

Bundy, Charles Smith. *Early Days in the Chippewa Valley.* Menominie, WI: Flint Douglas Printing, 1916. 16p.
http://memory.loc.gov/cgi-bin/query/r?ammem/lhbum:@field(DOCID+@lit(16807T000)):@@@REF

Fayette (Lafayette County)

Parkinson, John Barber. *Memories of Early Wisconsin and the Gold Mines.* Author, 1921. 25p.
http://memory.loc.gov/cgi-bin/query/r?ammem/lhbum:@field(DOCID+@lit(M456542))

Fort Winnebago

Kinzie, Juliette Augusta Magill. *Wau-bun, the Early Day in the Northwest.* Philadelphia, PA: Lippincott, 1873. 390p.
http://memory.loc.gov/cgi-bin/query/r?ammem/lhbum:@field(DOCID+@lit(16762T000)):@@@REF

Hudson

Lenroot, Clara Clough. *Long, Long Ago.* Appleton, WI: Badger Printing, 1929. 68p.
http://memory.loc.gov/cgi-bin/query/r?ammem/lhbum:@field(DOCID+@lit(09423T000)):@@@REF

Janesville

Janesville, 1859-60 [City Directory]. Janesville, WI: Brigham, 1859.
http://www.citydirectories.psmedia.com/city/free_statesort.html

Kenosha County

Bradford, Mary Davison. *Memoirs of Mary D. Bradford, Autobiographical and Historical Reminiscences of Education in Wisconsin, through Progressive Service from Rural School Teaching to City Superintendent.* Evansville, WI: Antes Press, 1932. 542p.
http://memory.loc.gov/cgi-bin/query/r?ammem/lhbumbib:@field(SUBJ+@band(Education--Wisconsin--History.+))

Kingston

Muir, John. *The Story of My Boyhood and Youth.* Boston, MA: Houghton Mifflin, 1913. 294p.
http://memory.loc.gov/cgi-bin/query/r?ammem/lhbum:@field(DOCID+@lit(05573T000)):@@@REF

Lafayette County

Parkinson, John Barber. *Memories of Early Wisconsin and the Gold Mines.* Author, 1921. 25p.
http://memory.loc.gov/cgi-bin/query/r?ammem/lhbum:@field(DOCID+@lit(M456542))

Madison

Fairchild, Lucius. *California Letters of Lucius Fairchild.* Madison, WI: State Historical Society of Wisconsin, 1931. 212p.
http://memory.loc.gov/cgi-bin/query/r?ammem/calbkbib:@field(AUTHOR+@band(Fairchild,+Lucius,1831-1896.+))

Marinette

Stephenson, Isaac. *Recollections of a Long Life, 1829-1915.* Chicago, IL: Donnelley & Sons, 1915. 264p.
http://memory.loc.gov/ammem/mdbquery.html

Milwaukee

Holton, Edward Dwight. *Travels with Jottings. From Midland to the Pacific.* Milwaukee, WI: Trayser Brothers, 1880. 94p.
http://memory.loc.gov/cgi-bin/query/r?ammem/calbkbib:@field(AUTHOR+@band(Holton,+Edward+D.+))

Milwaukee, 1859-60 [City Directory]. Milwaukee, WI: Jermain & Brightman, 1859.
http://www.citydirectories.psmedia.com/city/free_statesort.html

Mineral Point

Mineral Point [City Directory]. Mineral Point, WI: Allen, 1859.
http://www.citydirectories.psmedia.com/city/free_statesort.html

Osceola

Lenroot, Clara Clough. *Long, Long Ago.* Appleton, WI: Badger Printing, 1929. 68p.
http://memory.loc.gov/cgi-bin/query/r?ammem/lhbum:@field(DOCID+@lit(09423T000)):@@@REF

Paris (Kenosha County)

Bradford, Mary Davison. *Memoirs of Mary D. Bradford, Autobiographical and Historical Reminiscences of Education in Wisconsin, through Progressive Service from Rural School Teaching to City Superintendent.* Evansville, WI: Antes Press, 1932. 542p.
http://memory.loc.gov/cgi-bin/query/r?ammem/lhbumbib:@field(SUBJ+@band(Education--Wisconsin--History.+))

Pierce County

Haugen, Nils Pederson. *Pioneer and Political Reminiscences*. Evansville, WI: Antes Press, 1930. 109p.
http://memory.loc.gov/cgi-bin/query/r?ammem/lhbumbib:@field(SUBJ+@band(Frontier+and+pioneer+life--Wisconsin--Pierce+Co.+))

Superior

Lenroot, Clara Clough. *Long, Long Ago*. Appleton, WI: Badger Printing, 1929. 68p.
http://memory.loc.gov/cgi-bin/query/r?ammem/lhbum:@field(DOCID+@lit(09423T000)):@@@REF

Waupun

Miller, Wesson Gage. *Thirty Years in the Itinerancy*. Milwaukee, WI: Hauser, 1875. 304p.
http://memory.loc.gov/ammem/mdbquery.html

Wyoming

Research Outline. Wyoming. Salt Lake City, UT: Family History Library, 1997.
http://familysearch.org/sg/Wyoming.html

GENERAL SUBJECTS

African Americans

Albert, Octavia V. Rogers, Mrs. *The House of Bondage, or Charlotte Brooks and Other Slaves Original and Life-like, as They Appeared in Their Old Plantation and City Slave Life, together with Pen Pictures of the Peculiar Institution, with Sights and Insights into Their Relations as Freedmen, Freemen and Citizens.* New York, NY: Hunt & Eaton, 1890. 161p.
http://digilib.nypl.org/dynaweb/digs/wwm972/

American Society for Colonizing the Free People of Color, of the United States, and the Proceedings of the Society at Their Annual Meeting in the City of Washington. Washington, DC: The Society, 1818. Various.

1st Annual Report. 1818. 49p.
http://memory.loc.gov/cgi-bin/query/r?ammem/murray:@field(FLD001+91898198+):@@@REF

2nd Annual Report. 1819. 153p.
http://memory.loc.gov/cgi-bin/query/r?ammem/murray:@field(FLD001+91898199+):@@@REF

3rd Annual Report. 1820. 146p.
http://memory.loc.gov/cgi-bin/query/r?ammem/murray:@field(FLD001+91898201+):@@@REF

4th Annual Report. 1821. 72p.
http://memory.loc.gov/cgi-bin/query/r?ammem/murray:@field(FLD001+91898252+):@@@REF

10th Annual Report. 1827. 101p.
http://memory.loc.gov/cgi-bin/query/r?ammem/murray:@field(FLD001+88880154+):@@@REF

11th Annual Report. 1828. 120p.
http://memory.loc.gov/cgi-bin/query/r?ammem/rbaapc:@field(DOCID+@lit(01800T000)):@@@REF

Arnett, Benjamin William. *An Address to Have Been Delivered before the International Sunday School Convention.* Boston, MA: Author, 1896. 15p.
http://memory.loc.gov/cgi-bin/query/r?ammem/murray:@field(FLD001+91898108+):@@@REF

————. *Centennial Address on the Mission of Methodism to the Extremes of Society (with Statistics on the A.M.E. Church).* Xenia, OH: Torchlight Printing and Publishing, 1884. 40p.
http://memory.loc.gov/cgi-bin/query/r?ammem/aap:@field(SUBJ+@band(African+Methodist+Episcopal+Church--Statistics.+))

Benjamin, Robert C. Co. *The Zion Methodist.* Tuscaloosa, AL: Warren, 1893. 12p.
http://memory.loc.gov/cgi-bin/query/r?ammem/murray:@field(FLD001+90898309+):@@@REF

Black Studies, a Select Catalog of National Archives Microfilm Publications. Washington, DC: National Archives, 1984.
http://www.nara.gov/publications/microfilm/blackstudies/blackstd.html

Brown, William Wells. *The Negro in the American Rebellion, His Heroism and His Fidelity.* Boston, MA: Lee & Shepard, 1867. 396p.
http://moa.umdl.umich.edu/cgi-bin/moa/sgml/moa-idx?notisid=ABY0202

Bruce, John Edward. *The Blood Red Record, a Review of the Horrible Lynchings and Burnings of Negroes by Civilized White Men in the United States, as Taken from the Records.* Albany, NY: Argus Co., 1901. 27p.
http://memory.loc.gov/cgi-bin/query/r?ammem/murray:@field(FLD001+91898232+):@@@REF

Clark, Rufus Wheelwright. *The African Slave Trade.* Boston, MA: American Tract Society, 1860. 100p.
http://moa.umdl.umich.edu/cgi-bin/moa/sgml/moa-idx?notisid=AHL6707

Douglass, Frederick. *Life and Times of Frederick Douglass, His Early Life as a Slave, His Escape from Bondage and His Complete History to the Present Time.* Hartford, CT: Park, 1881. 516p.
http://metalab.unc.edu/docsouth/douglasslife/menu.html

Episcopal Church, Commission of Home Missions to Colored People. New York, NY: Church, 1875, 1876.
9th Annual Report, 1873-74. 20p.
http://memory.loc.gov/cgi-bin/query/r?ammem/murray:@field(FLD001+91898515+):@@@REF

11th Annual Report, 1875-76. 24p.
http://memory.loc.gov/cgi-bin/query/r?ammem/murray:@field(FLD001+91898514+):@@@REF

Fleetwood, Christian Abraham. *The Negro as a Soldier.* Washington, DC: Howard University Press, 1895. 19p.
http://memory.loc.gov/cgi-bin/query/r?ammem/murray:@field(FLD001+12000751+):@@@REF

Gilbert, Olive. *Narrative of Sojourner Truth, a Bonds-woman of Olden Time, Emancipated by the New York Legislature in the Early Part of the Present Century, with a History of Her Labors and Correspondence, Drawn from Her Book of Life.* Battle Creek, MI: Author, 1878. 320p.
http://memory.loc.gov/cgi-bin/query/r?ammem/lhbumbib:@field(SUBJ+@band(Truth,+Sojourner,--d.+1883.+))

Gronniosaw, James Albert Ukawsaw. *A Narrative of the Most Remarkable Particulars in the Life of James Albert Ukawsaw Gronniosaw, an African Prince, Written by Himself.* Newport, RI: Solomon Southwick, 1774. 48p.
http://www.lib.virginia.edu/etext/readex/13311.html

Howell, John Bruce and Yvette Scheven. *Electronic Journal of African Bibliography.* Iowa City, IA: University of Iowa Libraries, 1996. Unpgd.
http://www.lib.uiowa.edu/proj/ejab/1/

Johnson, William Bishop. *Sermons and Addresses (Including, Eulogy on William J. Simmons, D.D., LL.D.; Religious Status of the Negro; National Perils; the Character and Work of the Apostle Paul; Robert G. Shaw; the Religious and the Secular Press Compared; the Value of Baptist Principles to the American Government; the Church as a Factor in the Race Problem; the Divinity of the Church).* Lynchburg, VA: Virginia Seminary Steam Print, 1899. 51p.
http://memory.loc.gov/cgi-bin/query/r?ammem/murray:@field(FLD001+90898305+):@@@REF

Lane, Isaac. *Autobiography of Bishop Isaac Lane, LL.D. with a Short History of the C.M.E. Church in America and of Methodism*. Nashville, TN: Publishing House of the M.E. Church, South, 1916. 192p.
http://metalab.unc.edu/docsouth/lane/menu.html

A List of the East India Company's Ships, April 18, 1766. London: East India Company, 1766. 1p. (Handwritten List of Slaves on Verso, 1784/85).
http://memory.loc.gov/cgi-bin/query/r?ammem/rbpebib:@field(TITLE+@band(London,+April+18,+1766.+A+list+of+the+East-India+Company's+ships.+[London,+1766].+))

Minutes of the Presbyterian and Congregational Convention, together with the Organization of the Evangelical Association of Presbyterian and Congregational Clergyman of Color in the United States. Brooklyn, NY: The Association.
2nd Annual Convention, 1858, 19p. Philadelphia, PA
http://memory.loc.gov/cgi-bin/query/r?ammem/murray:@field(FLD001+91898496+):@@@REF

3rd Annual Convention, 1858. 16p. Hartford, CT
http://memory.loc.gov/cgi-bin/query/r?ammem/murray:@field(FLD001+91898497+):@@@REF

Moore, George Henry. *Historical Notes on the Employment of Negroes in the American Army of the Revolution*. New York, NY: Evans, 1862. 24p.
http://memory.loc.gov/cgi-bin/query/r?ammem/murray:@field(FLD001+02003395+):@@@REF

Mossell, N. F., Mrs. *The Work of the Afro-American Woman*. Philadelphia, PA: Ferguson, 1928. 178p.
http://digilib.nypl.org/dynaweb/digs/wwm9729/

Observations on the Slaves and the Indentured Servants, Inlisted in the Army and in the Navy of the United States. Philadelphia, PA: Styner and Cist, 1777.
http://etext.lib.virginia.edu/etcbin/browse-mixed-new?id=AntSlav&tag=public&images=images/modeng&data=/texts/english/modeng/parsed

The Quarterly Almanac. Wilmington, NC
1893. 32p.
http://memory.loc.gov/cgi-bin/query/r?ammem/aap:@field(SUBJ+@band(Almanacs,+American--North+Carolina.+))

1894. 32p.
http://memory.loc.gov/cgi-bin/query/r?ammem/murray:@field(FLD001+91898155+):@@@REF

Savage, John A. *Presbyterianism and the Negro*. Franklinton, NC: Franklinton Printing Co., 1895. 8p.
http://memory.loc.gov/cgi-bin/query/r?ammem/aap:@field(SUBJ+@band(Afro-American+Presbyterians--Southern+States.+))

Washington, Booker Talieferro. *My Larger Education, Being Chapters from My Experience*. Garden City, NY: Doubleday, Page & Co., 1911. 313p.
http://metalab.unc.edu/docsouth/washeducation/menu.html

_____. *Up from Slavery, an Autobiography*. New York, NY: Doubleday, 1901. 330p.
http://metalab.unc.edu/docsouth/washington/menu.html

Washington, Reginald. "The Freedman's Savings and Trust Company and African American Genealogical Research." *Prologue*. Vol. 29, No. 2 (Summer 1997).
http://www.nara.gov/publications/prologue/freedman.html

African Americans—Alabama

Edwards, William James. *Twenty-five Years in the Black Belt*. Boston, MA: Cornhill Co., 1918. 143p.
http://metalab.unc.edu/docsouth/edwards/menu.html

Williams, James. *Narrative of James Williams, an American Slave, Who Was for Several Years a Driver on a Cotton Plantation in Alabama.* New York, NY: American Anti-Slavery Society, 1838. 108p.
http://metalab.unc.edu/docsouth/williams/menu.html

African Americans—Arkansas

Catalogue and Circular of the Branch Normal College of the Arkansas Industrial University, Located at Pine Bluff, Arkansas.
1892-93. 29p.
http://memory.loc.gov/cgi-bin/query/r?ammem/murray:@field(FLD001+91898260+):@@@REF

1893-94. 32p.
http://memory.loc.gov/cgi-bin/query/r?ammem/murray:@field(FLD001+91898259+):@@@REF

Proceedings of the Eighth Annual Convocation of the Most Excellent Royal Arch Chapter of Free Masons for the State and Jurisdiction of Arkansas and of a Meeting Preliminary to the Same, Held in the City of Little Rock, Ark., Dec. 16th and 17th Anno Inventionis 2428, A.D. 1898. Pine Bluff, AR: Courier Printing Co., 1899.14p.
http://memory.loc.gov/cgi-bin/query/r?ammem/aap:@field(SUBJ+@band(Afro-American+freemasons.+))

African Americans—Connecticut

Hammon, Jupiter. *An Address to the Negroes in the State of New York, by Jupiter Hammon, Servant of John Lloyd, Jun., Esq. of the Manor of Queen's Village, Long Island.* New York, NY: Carroll and Patterson, 1787. 20p.
http://www.lib.virginia.edu/etext/readex/20400.html

Memoir of Thomas Hamitah Patoo, a Native of the Marqueas Islands, Who Died June 19, 1823, while a Member of the Foreign Mission School in Cornwall, Connecticut. New York, NY: New York Religious Tract Society, 1823. 48p.
http://memory.loc.gov/cgi-bin/query/r?ammem/aap:@field(SUBJ+@band(Biographies--New+York++N.Y.+--1825.+))

Plato, Ann. *Essays, Including Biographies and Miscellaneous Pieces in Prose and Poetry.* Hartford, CT: Author, 1841. 122p.
http://digilib.nypl.org/dynaweb/digs/wwm97251/

Stanford, Peter Thomas. *Imaginary Obstructions to True Spiritual Progress, Preached during the Service at the Day Street Congregational Church, August 14, 1898.* West Somerville, MA: Davis Square Printing, Co., 1898. 12p.
http://memory.loc.gov/cgi-bin/query/r?ammem/aap:@field(SUBJ+@band(Day+Street+Congregational+Church.+))

African Americans—District of Columbia

Crummell, Alexander. *Charitable Institutions in Colored Churches.* Washington, DC: Pendleton, 1892. 8p.
http://memory.loc.gov/cgi-bin/query/r?ammem/aap:@field(SUBJ+@band(Afro-American+clergy--Biography.+))

———. *1844-1894, the Shades and the Lights of a Fifty Years' Ministry, Juilate, a Sermon.* Washington, DC: St. Luke's Church, 1894. 31p.
http://memory.loc.gov/cgi-bin/query/r?ammem/aap:@field(SUBJ+@band(Afro-American+clergy--Biography.+))

Keckley, Elizabeth. *Behind the Scenes, by Elizabeth Keckley, formerly a Slave, but More Recently Modiste, and Friend to Mrs. Abraham Lincoln or Thirty Years a Slave, and Four Years in the White House*. New York, NY: G. W. Carleton & Co., 1868. 371p.
http://metalab.unc.edu/docsouth/keckley/menu.html
http://digilib.nypl.org/dynaweb/digs/wwm9713/

National Association for the Relief of Destitute Colored Women and Children. Annual Report. Washington, DC: The Association, 1883, 1887, 1895, 1900.
20th Annual Report, 1883. 16p.
http://memory.loc.gov/cgi-bin/query/r?ammem/murray:@field(FLD001+91898518+):@@@REF

24th Annual Report, 1887. 16p.
http://memory.loc.gov/cgi-bin/query/r?ammem/murray:@field(FLD001+91898517+):@@@REF

32nd Annual Report, 1895. 20p.
http://memory.loc.gov/cgi-bin/query/r?ammem/murray:@field(FLD001+91898480+):@@@REF

37th Annual Report, 1900. 24p.
http://memory.loc.gov/cgi-bin/query/r?ammem/murray:@field(FLD001+91898495+):@@@REF

Northup, Solomon. *Narrative of Solomon Northup, a Citizen of New York, Kidnapped in Washington City in 1841, Rescued in 1853, from a Cotton Plantation near the Red River, in Louisiana*. Auburn, NY: Derby and Miller, 1853. 336p.
http://metalab.unc.edu/docsouth/northup/menu.html

Phillips, Henry L. *In Memoriam of the Late Rev. Alex Crummell, D.D. of Washington, D.C., an Address Delivered before the American Negro Historical Society of Philadelphia*. Philadelphia, PA: Coleman Printery, 1899. 21p.
http://memory.loc.gov/cgi-bin/query/r?ammem/murray:@field(FLD001+91898532+):@@@REF

Report of the Board of Trustees of Colored Schools of Washington and Georgetown, D.C., Made in Compliance with a Resolution of the Senate of the United States, Passed December 8, 1870. Washington, DC: McGill & Witherow, 1871. 56p.
http://memory.loc.gov/cgi-bin/query/r?ammem/murray:@field(FLD001+91898510+):@@@REF

Report of the Freedmen's Hospital to the Secretary of the Interior. Washington, DC: Government Printing Office, 1899. 21p.
http://memory.loc.gov/cgi-bin/query/r?ammem/aap:@field(SUBJ+@band(Freedmen's+Hospital++Washington,+D.C.++))

Waller, Owen Meredith. *The Episcopal Church and the Colored People, a Statement of Facts*. Washington, DC: Emmett C. Jones & Co., 1898. 14p.
http://memory.loc.gov/cgi-bin/query/r?ammem/aap:@field(SUBJ+@band(Afro-American+Episcopalians.+))

African Americans—Georgia

Andrews, Sidney. *The South since the War, as Shown by Fourteen Weeks of Travel and Observation in Georgia and the Carolinas*. Boston, MA: Ticknor & Fields, 1866. 408p.
http://moa.umdl.umich.edu/cgi-bin/moa/sgml/moa-idx?notisid=AAW0193

Branham, Levi. *My Life and Travels*. Dalton, GA: Showalter, 1929. 64p.
http://metalab.unc.edu/docsouth/branham/menu.html

Burton, Annie L. *Memories of Childhood's Slavery Days*. Boston, MA: Ross Publishing, 1909. 97p.
http://metalab.unc.edu/docsouth/burton/menu.html
http://digilib.nypl.org/dynaweb/digs/wwm97252/

Doesticks, Q. K. Philander. *What Became of the Slaves on a Georgia Plantation? Great Auction Sale of Slaves, at Savannah, Georgia, March 2d & 3d, 1859. A Sequel to Mrs. Kemble's Journal.* Author, 1863. 20p.
http://memory.loc.gov/cgi-bin/query/r?ammem/murray:@field(FLD001+11003986+):@@@REF

Episcopal Church, Commission of Home Missions to Colored People. New York, NY: Church, 1875, 1876.
9th Annual Report, 1873-74. 20p.
http://memory.loc.gov/cgi-bin/query/r?ammem/murray:@field(FLD001+91898515+):@@@REF

11th Annual Report, 1875-76. 24p.
http://memory.loc.gov/cgi-bin/query/r?ammem/murray:@field(FLD001+91898514+):@@@REF

Love, Emanuel K. *Annual Address to the Missionary Baptist Convention of Georgia (Containing History of the Church).* Nashville, TN: National Baptist Publishing Board, 1899. 44p.
http://memory.loc.gov/cgi-bin/query/r?ammem/aap:@field(SUBJ+@band(Installation+sermons--Georgia--Savannah--1885.+))

————. *Introductory Sermon of Rev. Emanuel K. Love, on Entering the Pastorate of the First African Baptist Church, Savannah, Georgia.* Augusta, GA: Sentinel Print, 1885. 11p.
http://memory.loc.gov/cgi-bin/query/r?ammem/aap:@field(SUBJ+@band(Installation+sermons--Georgia--Savannah--1885.+))

————. *Learning of Christ, the Anniversary Sermon of the First Bryan Baptist Church, West Broad Street, Savannah, Georgia.* Augusta, GA: Georgia Baptist Printing Co., 1882. 19p.
http://memory.loc.gov/cgi-bin/query/r?ammem/aap:@field(SUBJ+@band(Anniversary+sermons--Georgia--Savannah--1883.+))

The Marvelous Musical Prodigy, Blind Tom, the Negro Boy Pianist, Whose Performances at the Great St. James and Egyptian Halls, London and Salle Hertz, Paris, Have Created Such a Profound Sensation. Anecdotes, Songs, Sketches of the Life, Testimonials of Musicians and Savans, and Opinions of the American and English Press of Blind Tom (Thomas Greene Bethune). New York, NY: French & Wheat, 1868. 30p.
http://memory.loc.gov/cgi-bin/query/r?ammem/aap:@field(SUBJ+@band(Bethune,+Thomas+Greene,--1849-1908.+))

Stearns, Charles Woodward. *The Black Man of the South and the Rebels, or the Characteristics of the Former and the Recent Outrages of the Latter.* New York, NY: American News, 1872. 578p.
http://moa.umdl.umich.edu/cgi-bin/moa/sgml/moa-idx?notisid=ABL5152

Taylor, Susie King. *Reminiscences of My Life in Camp with the 33d United States Colored Troops Late 1st S.C. Volunteers.* Boston, MA: Author, 82p.
http://digilib.nypl.org/dynaweb/digs/wwm97267/

Wells Barnett, Ida B. *Lynch Law in Georgia.* Chicago, IL: Author, 1899. 18p.
http://memory.loc.gov/cgi-bin/query/r?ammem/aap:@field(SUBJ+@band(Hose,+Samuel.+))

African Americans—Kentucky
Brown, Josephine. *Biography of an American Bondsman, Written by His Daughter.* Boston, MA: Wallcut, 1856. 104p.
http://digilib.nypl.org/dynaweb/digs/wwm975/

Brown, William Wells. *Narrative of William W. Brown, an American Slave.* 3rd ed. London: Charles Gilpin, 1849. 168p.
http://metalab.unc.edu/docsouth/brownw/menu.html

Burton, Thomas William. *What Experience Has Taught Me, an Autobiography of Thomas William Burton, Doctor of Medicine, Springfield, Ohio.* Cincinnati, OH: Jennings and Graham, 1910, 126p.
http://metalab.unc.edu/docsouth/burtont/menu.html

McCray, S. J. *Life of Mary F. McCray, Born and Raised a Slave in the State of Kentucky, by Her Husband and Son.* Lima, OH: Author, 1898. 115p.
http://metalab.unc.edu/docsouth/mccray/menu.html

African Americans—Louisiana

Northup, Solomon. *Narrative of Solomon Northup, a Citizen of New York, Kidnapped in Washington City in 1841, Rescued in 1853, from a Cotton Plantation near the Red River, in Louisiana.* Auburn, NY: Derby and Miller, 1853. 336p.
http://metalab.unc.edu/docsouth/northup/menu.html

African Americans—Maryland

Ball, Charles. *Fifty Years in Chains, or the Life of an American Slave.* New York, NY: Dayton, 1859. 430p.
http://metalab.unc.edu/docsouth/ball/menu.html

Bluett, Thomas. *Some Memoirs of the Life of Job, the Son of Solomon the Highest Priest of Boonda in Africa, Who Was a Slave about Two Years in Maryland, and afterwards Being Brought to England Was Set Free and Sent to His Native Land in the Year 1734.* London: Ford, 1734. 63p.
http://metalab.unc.edu/docsouth/bluett/menu.html

Bradford, Sarah H. *Harriet, the Moses of Her People.* New York, NY: Lockwood, 1886. 149p.
http://metalab.unc.edu/docsouth/harriet/menu.html

Catalogue of Pupils of Saint Frances' Academy for Colored Girls, under the Direction of the Sisters of Providence, for the Academic Year 1867-8, Incorporated 1867. Baltimore, MD: John Murphy & Co., 1868. 24p.
http://memory.loc.gov/cgi-bin/query/r?ammem/murray:@field(FLD001+91898522+):@@@REF

Douglass, Frederick. *Life and Times of Frederick Douglass, His Early Life as a Slave, His Escape from Bondage and His Complete History to the Present Time.* Hartford, CT: Park, 1881. 516p.
http://metalab.unc.edu/docsouth/douglasslife/menu.html

Johnson, Harvey. *A Plea for Our Work as Colored Baptists, Apart from the Whites.* Baltimore, MD: Afro-American Company Printers,1897. 15p.
http://memory.loc.gov/cgi-bin/query/r?ammem/murray:@field(FLD001+91898120+):@@@REF

Mason, Isaac. *Life of Isaac Mason as a Slave.* Worcester, MA: Author, 1893. 74p.
http://metalab.unc.edu/docsouth/mason/menu.html

Lame, J. S. *Maryland Slavery and Maryland Chivalry, Containing the Letters of Junius, Originally Published in Zion's Herald, together with a Brief History of the Circumstances that Prompted the Publication of Those Letters. Also a Short Account of the Persecution Suffered by the Author at the Hands of Southern Slaveholders.* Philadelphia, PA: Collins, 1858. 60p.
http://moa.umdl.umich.edu/cgi-bin/moa/sgml/moa-idx?notisid=ABJ5141

Memoir of Old Elizabeth a Coloured Woman. Philadelphia, PA: Collins Printer, 1863. 19p.
http://digilib.nypl.org/dynaweb/digs/wwm97259/

Smith, Amanda. *An Autobiography, the Story of the Lord's Dealings with Mrs. Amanda Smith, the Colored Evangelist, Containing an Account of Her Life Work of Faith, and Her Travels in America, England, Ireland, Scotland, India and Africa, as an Independent Missionary.* Chicago, IL: Meyer and Brother, 1893. 506p.
http://digilib.nypl.org/dynaweb/digs/wwm97264/

African Americans—Massachusetts
Boston Slave Riot, and Trial of Anthony Burns, Containing the Report of the Faneuil Hall Meeting, the Murder of Batchelder, Theodore Parker's Lesson for the Day, Speeches of Counsel on Both Sides, Corrected by Themselves, a Verbatim Report of Judge Loring's Decision and Detailed Account of the Embarkation. Boston, MA: Fetridge and Co., 1854. 98p.
http://moa.umdl.umich.edu/cgi-bin/moa/sgml/moa-idx?notisid=ABT7939

Hallowell, Norwood Penrose. *The Negro as a Soldier in the War of the Rebellion.* Boston, MA: Little, Brown & Co., 1897. 29p.
http://memory.loc.gov/cgi-bin/query/r?ammem/murray:@field(FLD001+22002319+):@@@REF

Massachusetts Anti-Slavery Society Board of Managers. Boston, MA: Andrews, Prentiss & Studley, 1845.
13th Annual Report. 1845. 81p.
http://memory.loc.gov/cgi-bin/query/r?ammem/aap:@FIELD(AUTHOR+@band(+Massachusetts+Anti+Slavery+Society.++Board+of+Managers.))

Prince, Nancy. *A Narrative of the Life and Travels of Mrs. Nancy Prince.* 2nd ed. Boston, MA: Author, 1853. 89p.
http://digilib.nypl.org/dynaweb/digs/wwm97263/

Roper, Moses. *A Narrative of the Adventures and Escape of Moses Roper, from American Slavery.* Philadelphia, PA: Merrihew & Gunn, 1838. 89p.
http://metalab.unc.edu/docsouth/roper/menu.html

African Americans—Mississippi
Episcopal Church, Commission of Home Missions to Colored People. New York, NY: Church, 1875, 1876.
9th Annual Report, 1873-74. 20p.
http://memory.loc.gov/cgi-bin/query/r?ammem/murray:@field(FLD001+91898515+):@@@REF

11th Annual Report, 1875-76. 24p.
http://memory.loc.gov/cgi-bin/query/r?ammem/murray:@field(FLD001+91898514+):@@@REF

Hughes, Louis. *Thirty Years a Slave, from Bondage to Freedom, the Institution of Slavery as Seen on the Plantation and in the Home of the Planter.* Milwaukee, WI: South Side Printing Co., 1897. 210p.
http://metalab.unc.edu/docsouth/hughes/menu.html

African Americans—Missouri
Brown, Josephine. *Biography of an American Bondsman, Written by His Daughter.* Boston, MA: Wallcut, 1856. 104p.
http://digilib.nypl.org/dynaweb/digs/wwm975/

Brown, William Wells. *Narrative of William W. Brown, an American Slave.* 3rd ed. London: Charles Gilpin, 1849. 168p.
http://metalab.unc.edu/docsouth/brownw/menu.html

Bruce, Henry Clay. *The New Man, Twenty-nine Years a Slave, Twenty-nine Years a Free Man, Recollections of H. C. Bruce.* York, PA: Anstadt & Sons, 1895. 176p.
http://metalab.unc.edu/docsouth/bruce/menu.html

Delany, Lucy A. *From the Darkness Cometh the Light, or Struggles for Freedom.* St. Louis, MO: J. T. Smith, unknown. 64p.
http://digilib.nypl.org/dynaweb/digs/wwm97254/

Thompson, George. *Prison Life and Reflections or a Narrative of the Arrest, Trial, Conviction, Imprisonment, Treatment, Observations, Reflections and Deliverance of Work, Burr and Thompson Who Suffered an Unjust and Cruel Imprisonment in Missouri Penitentiary for Attempting to Aid Some Slaves to Liberty.* Hartford, CT: Alanson Work, 1850. 376p.
http://moa.umdl.umich.edu/cgi-bin/moa/sgml/moa-idx?notisid=ACK4077

African Americans—New Jersey

Lee, Jarena. *Religious Life and Experience and Journal of Mrs. Jarena Lee, Giving an Account of Her Call to Preach the Gospel.* Philadelphia, PA: Author, 1849. 97p.
http://digilib.nypl.org/dynaweb/digs/wwm9716/

African Americans—New York

Association for the Benefit of Colored Orphans. Annual Report. New York, NY: Trow's Printing and Bookbinding, 1879. 23p.
http://memory.loc.gov/cgi-bin/query/r?ammem/murray:@field(FLD001+91898249+):@@@REF

Foote, Julia A. J. *A Brand Plucked from the Fire, an Autobiographical Sketch.* Cleveland, OH: Lauer & Yost, 1879. 124p.
http://digilib.nypl.org/dynaweb/digs/wwm978/

Gilbert, Olive. *Narrative of Sojourner Truth, a Bonds-woman of Olden Time, Emancipated by the New York Legislature in the Early Part of the Present Century, with a History of Her Labors and Correspondence, Drawn from Her Book of Life.* Battle Creek, MI: Author, 1878. 320p.
http://memory.loc.gov/cgi-bin/query/r?ammem/lhbumbib:@field(SUBJ+@band(Truth,+Sojourner,--d.+1883.+))

Hammon, Jupiter. *An Address to the Negroes in the State of New York, by Jupiter Hammon, Servant of John Lloyd, Jun., Esq. of the Manor of Queen's Village, Long Island.* New York, NY: Carroll and Patterson, 1787. 20p.
http://www.lib.virginia.edu/etext/readex/20400.html

James, Thomas. *Wonderful Eventful Life of Rev. Thomas James.* Rochester, NY: Post Express Printing Co., 1887. 24p.
http://memory.loc.gov/cgi-bin/query/r?ammem/aap:@field(SUBJ+@band(Autobiographies--New+York++State+--1887.+))

New York State Archives and Records Administration. *Records Relating to African Americans in the New York State Archives.* Albany, NY: Author, 1997. Unpgd.
http://www.sara.nysed.gov/holding/fact/leaf8.htm

Northup, Solomon. *Narrative of Solomon Northup, a Citizen of New York, Kidnapped in Washington City in 1841, Rescued in 1853, from a Cotton Plantation near the Red River, in Louisiana.* Auburn, NY: Derby and Miller, 1853. 336p.
http://metalab.unc.edu/docsouth/northup/menu.html

Report of the Committee of Merchants for the Relief of Colored People, Suffering from the Late Riots in the City of New York. New York, NY: Whitehorne, 1863. 48p.
http://memory.loc.gov/cgi-bin/query/r?ammem/aap:@field(SUBJ+@band(Draft+Riot,+1863.+))

Roper, Moses. *A Narrative of the Adventures and Escape of Moses Roper, from American Slavery.* Philadelphia, PA: Merrihew & Gunn, 1838. 89p.
http://metalab.unc.edu/docsouth/roper/menu.html

Thompson, Mary W. *Broken Gloom, Sketches of the History, Character, and Dying Testimony of Beneficiaries of the Colored Home in the City of New York.* New York, NY: John F. Trow, 1851. 78p.
http://metalab.unc.edu/docsouth/thompson/menu.html

African Americans—North Carolina

Episcopal Church, Commission of Home Missions to Colored People. New York, NY: Church, 1875, 1876.
9th Annual Report, 1873-74. 20p.
http://memory.loc.gov/cgi-bin/query/r?ammem/murray:@field(FLD001+91898515+):@@@REF

11th Annual Report, 1875-76. 24p.
http://memory.loc.gov/cgi-bin/query/r?ammem/murray:@field(FLD001+91898514+):@@@REF

Grandy, Moses. *Narrative of the Life of Moses Grandy, Late a Slave in the United States of America.* London: Gilpin, 1843. 72p.
http://metalab.unc.edu/docsouth/grandy/menu.html

Horton, George Moses. *Life of George M. Horton, the Colored Bard of North Carolina.* Hillsborough, NC: Heartt, 1845. 20p.
http://metalab.unc.edu/docsouth/hortonlife/menu.html

Jones, Thomas H. *The Experience of Thomas H. Jones, Who Was a Slave for Forty-Three Years.* Boston, MA: Bazin & Chandler, 1862. 48p.
http://metalab.unc.edu/docsouth/jones/menu.html

Lane, Lunsford. *The Narrative of Lunsford Lane, formerly of Raleigh, NC. Embracing an Account of His Early Life, the Redemption by Purchase of Himself and Family from Slavery, and His Banishment from the Place of His Birth for the Crime of Wearing a Colored Skin.* 2nd ed. Boston, MA: Torrey,1842. 56p.
http://metalab.unc.edu/docsouth/lanelunsford/menu.html

Pyatt, Timothy D. *Guide to African-American Documentary Resources in North Carolina.* Charlottesville, VA: University of Virginia, 1996. Unpgd.
http://www.upress.virginia.edu/epub/pyatt/index.html

Robinson, William H. *From Log Cabin to Pulpit, or Fifteen Years in Slavery.* 3rd ed. Eau Claire, WI: Tifft, 1913. 200p.
http://metalab.unc.edu/docsouth/robinson/menu.html

Roper, Moses. *A Narrative of the Adventures and Escape of Moses Roper, from American Slavery.* Philadelphia, PA: Merrihew & Gunn, 1838. 89p.
http://metalab.unc.edu/docsouth/roper/menu.html

African Americans—Ohio

Arnett, Benjamin William. *The Black Laws.* Columbus, OH: Ohio State Journal, 1886. 40p.
http://memory.loc.gov/cgi-bin/query/r?ammem/aap:@field(SUBJ+@band(Afro-Americans--Legal+status,+laws,+etc.--Ohio--History.+))

Funeral Services in Respect to the Memory of Rev. William Paul Quinn, Late Senior Bishop of the African M.E. Church, Held at Warren Chapel, Toledo, Ohio, March 9th, 1873. Toledo, OH: Warren Chapel, 1873. 52p.
http://memory.loc.gov/cgi-bin/query/r?ammem/aap:@field(SUBJ+@band(Quinn,+William+Paul,--1799-1873.+))

Mattison, Hiram. *Louisa Picquet, the Octoroon, a Tale of Southern Slave Life.* New York, NY: Author, 1861. 60p.
http://digilib.nypl.org/dynaweb/digs/wwm97258/

McCray, S. J. *Life of Mary F. McCray, Born and Raised a Slave in the State of Kentucky, by Her Husband and Son.* Lima, OH: Author, 1898. 115p.
http://metalab.unc.edu/docsouth/mccray/menu.html

Proceedings of the Semi-centenary Celebration of the African Methodist Episcopal Church of Cincinnati, Held in Allen Temple, February 8th, 9th, and 10th, 1874, with an Account of the Rise and Progress of the Colored Schools, also a List of the Charitable and Benevolent Societies of the City. Cincinnati, OH: Watkin, 1874. 136p.
http://memory.loc.gov/cgi-bin/query/r?ammem/murray:@field(FLD001+91898101+):@@@REF

African Americans—Pennsylvania

Home for the Aged and Infirm Colored Persons. Annual Report of the Board of Managers. Philadelphia, PA: Various.
2ⁿᵈ Annual Meeting, 1866. 28p.
http://memory.loc.gov/cgi-bin/query/r?ammem/murray:@field(FLD001+91898494+):@@@REF

5ᵗʰ Annual Meeting, 1869. 20p.
http://memory.loc.gov/cgi-bin/query/r?ammem/murray:@field(FLD001+91898492+):@@@REF

6ᵗʰ Annual Meeting, 1870. 24p.
http://memory.loc.gov/cgi-bin/query/r?ammem/murray:@field(FLD001+91898491+):@@@REF

9ᵗʰ Annual Meeting, 1873. 32p.
http://memory.loc.gov/cgi-bin/query/r?ammem/murray:@field(FLD001+91898493+):@@@REF

35ᵗʰ Annual Report, 1899. 38p.
http://memory.loc.gov/cgi-bin/query/r?ammem/murray:@field(FLD001+91898490+):@@@REF

Hunt, B. P. *Why Colored People in Philadelphia Are Excluded from the Street Cars.* Philadelphia, PA: Merrihew & Son, 1866. 28p.
http://moa.umdl.umich.edu/cgi-bin/moa/sgml/moa-idx?notisid=AJA2395

Jacobs, Harriet A. *Incidents in the Life of a Slave Girl.* Boston, MA: Author, 1861. 306p.
http://digilib.nypl.org/dynaweb/digs/wwm97255/

Lee, Jarena. *Religious Life and Experience and Journal of Mrs. Jarena Lee, Giving an Account of Her Call to Preach the Gospel.* Philadelphia, PA: Author, 1849. 97p.
http://digilib.nypl.org/dynaweb/digs/wwm9716/

Narrative of Facts in the Case of Passmore Williamson. Philadelphia, PA: Pennsylvania Anti-Slavery Society, 1855. 24p.
http://moa.umdl.umich.edu/cgi-bin/moa/sgml/moa-idx?notisid=ABJ1564

Palmer, John M. *Was Richard Allen Great?* Philadelphia, PA: Weekly Astonisher Print, 1898. 9p.
http://memory.loc.gov/cgi-bin/query/r?ammem/aap:@field(SUBJ+@band(Allen,+Richard,-1760-1831.+))

A Statistical Inquiry into the Condition of the People of Colour of the City and Districts of Philadelphia. Philadelphia, PA: Kite & Walton, 1849. 44p.
http://memory.loc.gov/cgi-bin/query/r?ammem/murray:@field(FLD001+12014690+):@@@REF

Promoting the Abolition of Slavery, Board of Education, 1859. 24p.
http://memory.loc.gov/ammem/mdbquery.html

African Americans—South Carolina

Colored Industrial Training School Annual Report. Spartanburg, SC: School. 1892 Report. 10p.
http://memory.loc.gov/cgi-bin/query/r?ammem/aap:@field(SUBJ+@band(Annual+reports--South+Carolina--Spartanburg--1892.+))

Edwards, William James. *Twenty-five Years in the Black Belt*. Boston, MA: Cornhill Co., 1918. 143p.
http://metalab.unc.edu/docsouth/edwards/menu.html

Episcopal Church, Commission of Home Missions to Colored People. New York, NY: Church, 1875, 1876.
9th Annual Report, 1873-74. 20p.
http://memory.loc.gov/cgi-bin/query/r?ammem/murray:@field(FLD001+91898515+):@@@REF

11th Annual Report, 1875-76. 24p.
http://memory.loc.gov/cgi-bin/query/r?ammem/murray:@field(FLD001+91898514+):@@@REF

Jackson, John Andrew. *The Experience of a Slave in South Carolina*. London: Passmore & Alabaster, 1862. 48p.
http://metalab.unc.edu/docsouth/jackson/menu.html

Mattison, Hiram. *Louisa Picquet, the Octoroon, a Tale of Southern Slave Life*. New York, NY: Author, 1861. 60p.
http://digilib.nypl.org/dynaweb/digs/wwm97258/

A Memorial Souvenir of Rev. J. Wofford White, Pastor of Wesley, M.E. Church, Charleston, S.C. Who Fell Asleep, January 7th, 1890, Aged 33 Years. Charleston, SC: Walker, Evans & Cogswell, 1890. 8p.
http://memory.loc.gov/cgi-bin/query/r?ammem/aap:@field(SUBJ+@band(Wesley+Methodist+Episcopal+Church++Charleston,+S.C.++))

The Negroes at Port Royal. Boston, MA: Wallcut, 1862. 36p.
http://moa.umdl.umich.edu/cgi-bin/moa/sgml/moa-idx?notisid=AFK4120

Pickens, William. *The Heir of Slaves, an Autobiography*. Boston, MA: Pilgrim Press, 1911. 138p.
http://metalab.unc.edu/docsouth/pickens/menu.html

Straker, David Augustus. *Bethel, A.M.E. Church Case, in Columbia, S.C., the State of South Carolina, Richland County, J. W. Morris et. al. Plaintiffs, against S. B. Wallace, et. al. Defendants, Action for Relief*. South Carolina: Unknown, 1887. 14p.
http://memory.loc.gov/cgi-bin/query/r?ammem/aap:@field(SUBJ+@band(African+Methodist+Episcopal+Church--Clergy--Appointment,+call+and+election.+))

Taylor, Susie King. *Reminiscences of My Life in Camp with the 33d United States Colored Troops Late 1st S.C. Volunteers*. Boston, MA: Author, 82p.
http://digilib.nypl.org/dynaweb/digs/wwm97267/

Young, Kenneth M. *As Some Things Appear on the Plains and among the Rockies in Mid-summer*. Spartanburg, SC: Fowler, 1890. 15p.
http://memory.loc.gov/cgi-bin/query/r?ammem/aap:@field(SUBJ+@band(Afro-Americans--Travel--United+States.+))

African Americans—Tennessee

Broughton, V. W. *Twenty Years Experience of a Missionary*. Chicago, IL: Pony Press, 1907. 140p.
http://digilib.nypl.org/dynaweb/digs/wwm974/

Hoss, Elijah Embree. *Elihu Embree, Abolitionist*. Nashville, TN: University Press Co., 1897. 28p.
http://memory.loc.gov/cgi-bin/query/r?ammem/aap:@field(SUBJ+@band(Embree,+Elihu,--1782-1820.+))

Loguen, Jermain Wesley. *The Rev. J. W. Loguen, as a Slave and as a Freeman, a Narrative of Real Life*. Syracuse, NY: Truair, 1859. 454p.
http://moa.umdl.umich.edu/cgi-bin/moa/sgml/moa-idx?notisid=ABT6752

African Americans—Virginia

Albert, Octavia V. Rogers, Mrs. *The House of Bondage, or Charlotte Brooks and Other Slaves Original and Life-like, as They Appeared in Their Old Plantation and City Slave Life, together with Pen Pictures of the Peculiar Institution, with Sights and Insights into Their Relations as Freedmen, Freemen and Citizens*. New York, NY: Hunt & Eaton, 1890. 161p.
http://digilib.nypl.org/dynaweb/digs/wwm972/

Bradford, Sarah H. *Harriet, the Moses of Her People*. New York, NY: Lockwood, 1886. 149p.
http://metalab.unc.edu/docsouth/harriet/menu.html

Broughton, V. W. *Twenty Years Experience of a Missionary*. Chicago, IL: Pony Press, 1907. 140p.
http://digilib.nypl.org/dynaweb/digs/wwm974/

Bruce, Henry Clay. *The New Man, Twenty-nine Years a Slave, Twenty-nine Years a Free Man, Recollections of H. C. Bruce*. York, PA: Anstadt & Sons, 1895. 176p.
http://metalab.unc.edu/docsouth/bruce/menu.html

Delany, Lucy A. *From the Darkness Cometh the Light, or Struggles for Freedom*. St. Louis, MO: J. T. Smith, unknown. 64p.
http://digilib.nypl.org/dynaweb/digs/wwm97254/

Episcopal Church, Commission of Home Missions to Colored People. New York, NY: Church, 1875, 1876.
9th Annual Report, 1873-74. 20p.
http://memory.loc.gov/cgi-bin/query/r?ammem/murray:@field(FLD001+91898515+):@@@REF

11th Annual Report, 1875-76. 24p.
http://memory.loc.gov/cgi-bin/query/r?ammem/murray:@field(FLD001+91898514+):@@@REF

Ferebee, London R. *A Brief History of the Slave Life of Rev. L. R. Ferebee, and the Battles of Life and Four Years of His Ministerial Life*. Raleigh, NC: Edwards, Broughton & Co., Steam Printers, Publishers and Binders, 1882. 24p.
http://metalab.unc.edu/docsouth/ferebee/menu.html

Hughes, Louis. *Thirty Years a Slave, from Bondage to Freedom, the Institution of Slavery as Seen on the Plantation and in the Home of the Planter.* Milwaukee, WI: South Side Printing Co., 1897. 210p.
http://metalab.unc.edu/docsouth/hughes/menu.html

Keckley, Elizabeth. *Behind the Scenes, by Elizabeth Keckley, formerly a Slave, but More Recently Modiste, and Friend to Mrs. Abraham Lincoln or Thirty Years a Slave, and Four Years in the White House.* New York, NY: G. W. Carleton & Co., 1868. 371p.
http://metalab.unc.edu/docsouth/keckley/menu.html
http://digilib.nypl.org/dynaweb/digs/wwm9713/

Lee, William Mack. *History of the Life of Rev. William Mack Lee, Body Servant of General Robert E. Lee through the Civil War, Cook from 1861 to 1865.* Norfolk, VA: Smith Printing, 1908. 10p.
http://metalab.unc.edu/docsouth/leewilliam/menu.html

Plunkett, Michael. *Afro-American Sources in Virginia, a Guide to Manuscripts.* Charlottesville, VA: University of Virginia, 1994. Unpgd.
http://www.upress.virginia.edu/plunkett/mfp.html

Rollin, Frank A. *Life and Public Services of Martin R. Delany, Sub-Assistant Commissioner Bureau Relief of Refugees, Freedmen and of Abandoned Lands, and Late Major 104th U.S. Colored Troops.* Boston, MA: Lee and Shepard, 1883. 367p.
http://digilib.nypl.org/dynaweb/digs/wwm9720/

Smedes, Susan Dabney. *Memorials of a Southern Planter.* Baltimore, MD: Cushings & Bailey, 1888. 348p.
http://moa.umdl.umich.edu/cgi-bin/moa/sgml/moa-idx?notisid=AFK4047

Stanford, Peter Thomas. *Imaginary Obstructions to True Spiritual Progress, Preached during the Service at the Day Street Congregational Church, August 14, 1898.* West Somerville, MA: Davis Square Printing, Co., 1898. 12p.
http://memory.loc.gov/cgi-bin/query/r?ammem/aap:@field(SUBJ+@band(Day+Street+Congregational+Church.+))

Stewart, Austin. *Twenty-two Years a Slave and Forty Years a Freeman, Embracing a Correspondence of Several Years, while President of Wilberforce Colony, London, Canada West.* Rochester, NY: Alling, 1857. 360p.
http://metalab.unc.edu/docsouth/steward/menu.html

Veney, Bethany. *The Narrative of Bethany Veney, a Slave Woman.* Worcester, MA: Author, 1889. 47p.
http://metalab.unc.edu/docsouth/veney/menu.html
http://digilib.nypl.org/dynaweb/digs/wwm97269/

Williams, James. *Narrative of James Williams, an American Slave, Who Was for Several Years a Driver on a Cotton Plantation in Alabama.* New York, NY: American Anti-Slavery Society, 1838. 108p.
http://metalab.unc.edu/docsouth/williams/menu.html

African Americans—West Virginia
Washington, Booker Taliaferro. *My Larger Education, Being Chapters from My Experience.* Garden City, NY: Doubleday, Page & Co., 1911. 313p.
http://metalab.unc.edu/docsouth/washeducation/menu.html

———. *Up from Slavery, an Autobiography.* New York, NY: Doubleday, 1901. 330p.
http://metalab.unc.edu/docsouth/washington/menu.html

Albania

Zickel, Raymond and Walter R. Iwaskiw. *Albania, a Country Study.* Washington, DC: Library of Congress, Federal Research Division, 1992.
http://lcweb2.loc.gov/frd/cs/altoc.html

Algeria

Genealogical Word List. French. Salt Lake City, UT: Family History Library, 1997.
http://www.familysearch.com/sg/WLFrench.html

Letter Writing Guide. French. Salt Lake City, UT: Family History Library, 1997.
http://www.familysearch.com/sg/LGFrench.html

Metz, Helen Chapan. *Algeria, a Country Study.* Washington, DC: Library of Congress, Federal Research Division, 1993.
http://lcweb2.loc.gov/frd/cs/dztoc.html

Angola

Collelo, Thomas. *Angola, a Country Study.* Washington, DC: Library of Congress, Federal Research Division, 1989.
http://lcweb2.loc.gov/frd/cs/aotoc.html

Genealogical Word List. Portuguese. Salt Lake City, UT: Family History Library, 1993.
http://familysearch.org/sg/WLPortug.html

Archives

International Council on Archives. *Directory.* Paris, France: ICA, 1997.
http://data1.archives.ca/ica/cgi-bin/ica?0104_e

Matchette, Robert B. *Guide to Federal Records in the National Archives of the United States.* Washington, DC: National Archives, 1995.
http://www.nara.gov/guide/

Armenia

Curtis, Glen E. *Armenia, a Country Study.* Washington, DC: Library of Congress, Federal Research Division, 1994.
http://lcweb2.loc.gov/frd/cs/amtoc.html

Associations

McCabe, James Dabney. *History of the Grange Movement; or, the Farmer's War Against Monopolies, Being a Full and Authentic Account of the Struggles of the American Farmers against the Extortions of the Railroad Companies. With a History of the Rise and Progress of the Order of Patrons of Husbandry, its Objects, Present Condition and Prospects. To Which is Added Sketches of the Leading Grangers.* Chicago, IL: National Publishing Co., 1874. 558p.
http://moa.umdl.umich.edu/cgi-bin/moa/sgml/moa-idx?notisid=AJC3502

Austria

Genealogical Word List. German. Salt Lake City, UT: Family History Library, 1997.
http://www.familysearch.com/sg/WLGerman.html

Letter Writing Guide. German. Salt Lake City, UT: Family History Library, 1997.
http://www.familysearch.com/sg/LGGerman.html

Solsten, Eric. *Austria, a Country Study.* Washington, DC: Library of Congress, Federal Research Division, 1993.
http://lcweb2.loc.gov/frd/cs/attoc.html

Azerbaijan
Curtis, Glenn E. *Azerbaijan, a Country Study.* Washington, DC: Library of Congress, Federal Research Division, 1994.
http://lcweb2.loc.gov/frd/cs/aztoc.html

Bahrain
Metz, Helen Chapin. *Bahrain, a Country Study.* Washington, DC: Library of Congress, Federal Research Division, 1993.
http://lcweb2.loc.gov/frd/cs/bhtoc.html

Bangladesh
Heitzman, James and Robert Worden. *Bangladesh, a Country Study.* Washington, DC: Library of Congress, Federal Research Division, 1988.
http://lcweb2.loc.gov/frd/cs/bdtoc.html

Baptists
Baptist Magazine. Washington, DC: National Baptist Magazine Publishing Co., 1897.
http://memory.loc.gov/cgi-bin/query/r?ammem/murray:@field(FLD001+91898270+):@@@REF

Benedict, David. *Fifty Years among the Baptists.* New York, NY: Sheldon & Co., 1860. 444p.
http://moa.umdl.umich.edu/cgi-bin/moa/sgml/moa-idx?notisid=AJK2010

Broughton, V. W. *Twenty Years Experience of a Missionary.* Chicago, IL: Pony Press, 1907. 140p.
http://digilib.nypl.org/dynaweb/digs/wwm974/

Compton, Lucius Bunyan. *Life of Lucius B. Compton, the Mountain Evangelist, or from the Depths of Sin to the Heights of Holiness.* Cincinnati, OH: Author, 1903. 102p.
http://metalab.unc.edu/docsouth/compton/menu.html

Johnson, Harvey. *A Plea for Our Work as Colored Baptists, Apart from the Whites.* Baltimore, MD: Afro-American Company Printers,1897. 15p.
http://memory.loc.gov/cgi-bin/query/r?ammem/murray:@field(FLD001+91898120+):@@@REF

Johnson, William Bishop. *Sermons and Addresses. (including, Eulogy on William J. Simmons, D.D., LL.D.; Religious Status of the Negro; National Perils; the Character and Work of the Apostle Paul; Robert G. Shaw; the Religious and the Secular Press Compared; the Value of Baptist Principles to the American Government; the Church as a Factor in the Race Problem; the Divinity of the Church).* Lynchburg, VA: Virginia Seminary Steam Print, 1899. 51p.
http://memory.loc.gov/cgi-bin/query/r?ammem/murray:@field(FLD001+90898305+):@@@REF

National Baptist Magazine. Nashville, TN: National Baptist Publishing Board, 1899.
http://memory.loc.gov/cgi-bin/query/r?ammem/murray:@field(FLD001+91898268+):@@@REF

National Baptist Statistics and Sunday School Text Book, 1900. Nashville, TN: National Baptist Publishing Board, 1899. 32p.
http://memory.loc.gov/cgi-bin/query/r?ammem/aap:@field(SUBJ+@band(National+Baptist+Convention+of+the+United+States+of+America--Statistics.+))

Baptists—Georgia

Love, Emanuel K. *Annual Address to the Missionary Baptist Convention of Georgia (Containing History of the Church)*. Nashville, TN: National Baptist Publishing Board, 1899. 44p.
http://memory.loc.gov/cgi-bin/query/r?ammem/aap:@field(SUBJ+@band(Afro-American+Baptists--Georgia.+))

————. *Introductory Sermon of Rev. Emanuel K. Love, on Entering the Pastorate of the First African Baptist Church, Savannah, Georgia*. Augusta, GA: Sentinel Print, 1885. 11p.
http://memory.loc.gov/cgi-bin/query/r?ammem/aap:@field(SUBJ+@band(Installation+sermons--Georgia--Savannah--1885.+))

————. *Learning of Christ, the Anniversary Sermon of the First Bryan Baptist Church, West Broad Street, Savannah, Georgia*. Augusta, GA: Georgia Baptist Printing Co., 1882. 19p.
http://memory.loc.gov/cgi-bin/query/r?ammem/aap:@field(SUBJ+@band(Anniversary+sermons--Georgia--Savannah--1883.+))

Baptists—Kansas

Stimson, Hiram K. *From the Stage Coach to the Pulpit, Being an Autobiographical Sketch, with Incidents and Anecdotes of Elder H. K. Stimson, the Veteran Pioneer of Western New York, Now of Kansas*. Saint Louis, MO: Campbell, 1874. 430p.
http://moa.umdl.umich.edu/cgi-bin/moa/sgml/moa-idx?notisid=AJK2081

Baptists—New Jersey

Levy, Edgar Mortimer. *History of the Newark Baptist City Mission from Its Origin in 1851 to Its Seventeenth Anniversary in 1868*. New York, NY: Hurd and Houghton, 1869. 144p.
http://moa.umdl.umich.edu/cgi-bin/moa/sgml/moa-idx?notisid=AJG8034

Baptists—New York

Stimson, Hiram K. *From the Stage Coach to the Pulpit, Being an Autobiographical Sketch, with Incidents and Anecdotes of Elder H. K. Stimson, the Veteran Pioneer of Western New York, Now of Kansas*. Saint Louis, MO: Campbell, 1874. 430p.
http://moa.umdl.umich.edu/cgi-bin/moa/sgml/moa-idx?notisid=AJK2081

Belarus

Fedor, Helen. *Bahrain, a Country Study*. Washington, DC: Library of Congress, Federal Research Division, 1995.
http://lcweb2.loc.gov/frd/cs/bytoc.html

Belize

HLAS Online. Handbook of Latin American Studies. Washington, DC: Library of Congress, 1995. 49 vols.
http://lcweb2.loc.gov/hlas/hlashome.html

Merrill, Tim. *Belize, a Country Study*. Washington, DC: Library of Congress, Federal Research Division, 1992.
http://lcweb2.loc.gov/frd/cs/bztoc.html

Research Outline. Latin America. Salt Lake City, UT: Family History Library, 1992.
http://www.familysearch.com/sg/Latin_America.html

Bermuda

Prince, Mary. *The History of Mary Prince, a West Indian Slave, Related by Herself with a Supplement by the Editor to which is Added the Narrative of Asa Asa, a Captured African.* London: Westley and Davis, 1831. 44p.
http://digilib.nypl.org/dynaweb/digs/wwm97262/

Bhutan

Savada, Andrea Matles. *Bhutan, a Country Study.* Washington, DC: Library of Congress, Federal Research Division, 1991.
http://lcweb2.loc.gov/frd/cs/bttoc.html

Bolivia

Genealogical Word List, Spanish. Salt Lake City, UT: Family History Library, 1997.
http://familysearch.org/sg/WLSpanis.html

HLAS Online. Handbook of Latin American Studies. Washington, DC: Library of Congress, 1995. 49 vols.
http://lcweb2.loc.gov/hlas/hlashome.html

Hudson, Rex A. and Dennis M. Hanratty. *Bolivia, a Country Study.* Washington, DC: Library of Congress, Federal Research Division, 1989.
http://lcweb2.loc.gov/frd/cs/botoc.html

Research Outline. Latin America. Salt Lake City, UT: Family History Library, 1992.
http://www.familysearch.com/sg/Latin_America.html

Bulgaria

Curtis, Glenn E. *Bulgaria, a Country Study.* Washington, DC: Library of Congress, Federal Research Division, 1992.
http://lcweb2.loc.gov/frd/cs/bgtoc.html

Cambodia

Ross, Russell R. *Cambodia, a Country Study.* Washington, DC: Library of Congress, Federal Research Division, 1987.
http://lcweb2.loc.gov/frd/cs/khtoc.html

Canada

National Capital Region Library Directory. Ottawa, Ontario: National Library of Canada, 1999.
http://www.nlc-bnc.ca/ncr-rcn/encrintr.htm

Research Outline. Canada. Salt Lake City, UT: Family History Library, 1993.
http://www.familysearch.com/sg/Canada.html

Traill, Catherine Parr. *The Backwoods of Canada, Being Letters from the Wife of an Emigrant Officer, Illustrative of the Domestic Economy of British America.* London: Knight, 1836. 361p.
http://www.canadiana.org/cgi-bin/ECO/mtq?id=04ee01375f&doc=41930

Canada—Alberta

Research Outline. Alberta. Salt Lake City, UT: Family History Library, 1997.
http://www.familysearch.com/sg/Alberta.html

Canada—British Columbia

Research Outline. British Columbia. Salt Lake City, UT: Family History Library, 1997.
http://www.familysearch.com/sg/British_Columbia.html

Canada—Manitoba

Research Outline. Manitoba. Salt Lake City, UT: Family History Library, 1997.
http://www.familysearch.com/sg/Manitoba.htm

Canada—New Brunswick

Research Outline. New Brunswick. Salt Lake City, UT: Family History Library, 1997.
http://www.familysearch.com/sg/New_Brunswick.html

Stephenson, Isaac. *Recollections of a Long Life, 1829-1915.* Chicago, IL: Donnelley & Sons, 1915. 264p.
http://memory.loc.gov/cgi-bin/query/r?ammem/lhbum:@field(DOCID+@lit(26800T000)):@@@REF

Canada—Newfoundland

Research Outline. Newfoundland. Salt Lake City, UT: Family History Library, 1997.
http://www.familysearch.com/sg/Newfoundland.html

Rollmann, Hans. *Anglicans, Puritans and Quakers in Sixteenth and Seventeenth Century Newfoundland.* Unknown.
http://www.mun.ca/rels/ang/texts/ang1.html

Thoresby, William. *A Narrative of God's Love to William Thoresby.*
http://www.mun.ca/rels/meth/thoresby.html

Canada—Nova Scotia

Haliburton, Thomas Chandler and Walter Bromley. *A General Description of Nova Scotia, Illustrated by a New and Correct Map.* Halifax, NS: Author, 1823. 217p.
http://www.canadiana.org/cgi-bin/ECO/mtq?id=04ee01375f&doc=35672

Research Outline. Nova Scotia. Salt Lake City, UT: Family History Library, 1997.
http://www.familysearch.com/sg/Nova_Scotia.html

Canada—Ontario

Haviland, Laura Smith. *A Woman's Life-work, Labors and Experiences of Laura S. Haviland.* Cincinnati, OH: Walden & Stowe, 1882. 531p.
http://memory.loc.gov/cgi-bin/query/r?ammem/lhbumbib:@field(SUBJ+@band(Freedmen.+))

Research Outline. Ontario. Salt Lake City, UT: Family History Library, 1997.
http://www.familysearch.com/sg/Ontario.html

Canada—Ontario, London

Norton, Lewis Adelbert. *Life and Adventures of Col. L. A. Norton.* Oakland, CA: Pacific Press, 1887. 492p.
http://memory.loc.gov/cgi-bin/query/r?ammem/calbkbib:@field(AUTHOR+@band(Norton,+Lewis+Adelbert,b.+1819.+))

Stewart, Austin. *Twenty-two Years a Slave and Forty Years a Freeman, Embracing a Correspondence of Several Years, while President of Wilberforce Colony, London, Canada West.* Rochester, NY: Alling, 1857. 360p.
http://metalab.unc.edu/docsouth/steward/menu.html

Canada—Prince Edward Island

Research Outline. Prince Edward Island. Salt Lake City, UT: Family History Library, 1997.
http://www.familysearch.com/sg/Prince_Edward_Island.html

Canada—Quebec

Research Outline. Quebec. Salt Lake City, UT: Family History Library, 1997.
http://www.familysearch.com/sg/Quebec.html

Canada—Saskatchewan

Research Outline. Saskatchewan. Salt Lake City, UT: Family History Library, 1997.
http://www.familysearch.com/sg/Saskwan.html

Census Records

"Clues in Census Records, 1850-1920." National Archives, Record. Vol. 4, No. 3 (January 1998).
http://www.nara.gov/genealogy/cenclues.html

"How to Use NARA's Census Microfilm Catalogs." Washington, DC: National Archives.
http://www.nara.gov/genealogy/microcen.html

"Using the Census Soundex." General Information Leaflet 55. Washington, DC: National Archives, 1995.
http://www.nara.gov/genealogy/coding.html

Census Records—Federal Census 1790—1890

The 1790-1890 Federal Population Censuses: A Catalog of Microfilm Copies of the Schedules. Washington, DC: National Archives, 1997.
http://www.nara.gov/publications/microfilm/census/1790-1890/17901890.html

Census Records—Federal Census 1900

The 1900 Federal Population Census: A Catalog of Microfilm Copies of the Schedules. Washington, DC: National Archives, 1997.
http://www.nara.gov/publications/microfilm/census/1900/1900.html

Census Records—Federal Census 1910

Blake, Kellee. "First in the Path of the Firemen, the Fate of the 1890 Population Census." *Prologue.* Vol. 28, No. 1 (Spring 1996).
http://www.nara.gov/publications/prologue/1890cen1.html

The 1910 Federal Population Census: A Catalog of Microfilm Copies of the Schedules. Washington, DC: National Archives, 1997.
http://www.nara.gov/publications/microfilm/census/1910/1910.html

Census Records—Federal Census 1920

The 1920 Federal Population Census: A Catalog of Microfilm Copies of the Schedules. Washington, DC: National Archives, 1991.
http://www.nara.gov/publications/microfilm/census/1920/1920.html

Chad

Collelo, Thomas. *Chad, a Country Study.* Washington, DC: Library of Congress, Federal Research Division, 1988.
http://lcweb2.loc.gov/frd/cs/tdtoc.html

Chile

Chile, a Country Study. Washington, DC: Library of Congress, Federal Research Division, 1994.
http://lcweb2.loc.gov/frd/cs/cltoc.html

Genealogical Word List, Spanish. Salt Lake City, UT: Family History Library, 1997.
http://familysearch.org/sg/WLSpanis.html

HLAS Online. Handbook of Latin American Studies. Washington, DC: Library of Congress, 1995. 49 vols.
http://lcweb2.loc.gov/hlas/hlashome.html

Research Outline. Latin America. Salt Lake City, UT: Family History Library, 1992.
http://www.familysearch.com/sg/Latin_America.html

China

Chinese Immigration. The Social, Moral, and Political Effect of Chinese Immigration. Testimony Taken before a Committee of the Senate of the State of California, Appointed April 3d, 1876. Sacramento, CA: State Printing Office, 1876. 182p.
http://moa.umdl.umich.edu/cgi-bin/moa/sgml/moa-idx?notisid=AEX5872

Natale, Valerie. "Angel Island, Guardian of the Western Gate." *Prologue*. Vol. 30, No. 2 (Summer 1998).
http://www.nara.gov/publications/prologue/angel1.html

Worden, Robert L.; Andrea Matles Savada and Ronald E. Dolan. *China, a Country Study*. Washington, DC: Library of Congress, Federal Research Division, 1987.
http://lcweb2.loc.gov/frd/cs/cntoc.html

The Church of Jesus Christ of Latter-day Saints

Carson, James H. *Early Recollections of the Mines and a Description of the Great Tulare Valley*. Tarrytown, NY: Abbatt, 1931. 82p.
http://memory.loc.gov/cgi-bin/query/r?ammem/calbkbib:@field(AUTHOR+@band(Carson,+James+H.,d.+1853.+))

Research Outline. Early Church Information File. Salt Lake City, UT: Family History Library, 1993.
http://www.familysearch.com/sg/ECIF.html

Research Outline. Membership of the LDS Church, 1830-1848. Salt Lake City, UT: Family History Library, 1993.
http://www.familysearch.com/sg/Membersh.html

City Directories — New York

Boyd, Andrew. *Boyd's Business Directory of the One Hundred Cities and Villages in New York State, together with Post Offices, Postmasters' Names, Money Order Post Offices and Telegraph and Express Stations throughout the States, History of the States and Territories, and Brief Sketches of the Places Contained in the Directory, Incorporated and Manufacturing Companies, Railroads, Newspapers, etc. United States, New York State, County, City Officers. 1869-1870*. Albany, NY: Van Benthuysen, 1869. 864p.
http://moa.cit.cornell.edu/dienst/moabrowse.fly/MOA-JOURNALS2:BOYD-0001/3/1:TIFF2GIF:100

————. *New York State Business Directory and Gazetteer*. Albany, NY: Boyds, 1,410p.
http://moa.cit.cornell.edu/dienst/moabrowse.fly/MOA-JOURNALS2:BOYD-0002/3/1:TIFF2GIF:100

Child, Hamilton. *Gazetteer and Business Directory of Cortland County, New York, for 1869.* Syracuse, NY: Journal Office, 1869. 204p.
http://moa.cit.cornell.edu/dienst/moabrowse.fly/MOA-JOURNALS2:CHIL-0078/9/1:TIFF2GIF:100?,,

————. *Gazetteer and Business Directory of Madison County, New York, for 1868-9.* Syracuse, NY: Journal Office, 1868. 234p.
http://moa.cit.cornell.edu/dienst/moabrowse.fly/MOA-JOURNALS2:CHIL-0021/7/1:TIFF2GIF:100?,,

————. *Gazetteer and Business Directory of Monroe County, New York, for 1869-70.* Syracuse, NY: Journal Office, 1869. 420p.
http://moa.cit.cornell.edu/dienst/moabrowse.fly/MOA-JOURNALS2:CHIL-0104/9/1:TIFF2GIF:100?,,

Franks, David. *The New York Directory, 1786.* New York, NY: Patterson, 1786, 1874.
http://moa.cit.cornell.edu/dienst/moabrowse.fly/MOA-JOURNALS2:NEWY-0053/3/1:TIFF2GIF:100

Stetson, G. Emmet. *New Gazetteer and Business Directory for Livingston County, N.Y. for 1868.* Geneva, NY: Adams, 1868. 246p.
http://moa.cit.cornell.edu/dienst/moabrowse.fly/MOA-JOURNALS2:STET-0047/3/1:TIFF2GIF:100

City Directories—Pennsylvania

Whitehead, William. *Directory of the Borough of Chester, for the years 1859-60, Containing a Concise History of the Borough from its First Settlement to the Present Time, the Names of all the Inhabitants Alphabetically Arranged, Their Occupations, Places of Business, and Dwelling Houses: A List of the Streets of the Borough, Statistics of Public and Private Schools.* West Chester, PA: James, 1859. 128p.
http://moa.umdl.umich.edu/cgi-bin/moa/sgml/moa-idx?notisid=AFJ8568

Colombia

Genealogical Word List, Spanish. Salt Lake City, UT: Family History Library, 1997.
http://familysearch.org/sg/WLSpanis.html

HLAS Online. Handbook of Latin American Studies. Washington, DC: Library of Congress, 1995. 49 vols.
http://lcweb2.loc.gov/hlas/hlashome.html

Hanratty, Dennis M. and Sandra W. Meditz. *Colombia, a Country Study.* Washington, DC: Library of Congress, Federal Research Division, 1988.
http://lcweb2.loc.gov/frd/cs/cotoc.html

Research Outline. Latin America. Salt Lake City, UT: Family History Library, 1992.
http://www.familysearch.com/sg/Latin_America.html

Solsten, Eric. *Colombia, a Country Study.* Washington, DC: Library of Congress, Federal Research Division, 1995.
http://lcweb2.loc.gov/frd/cs/detoc.html

Congregationalists. *See* United Church of Christ

Court Records

Federal Court Records, a Select Catalog of NARA Microfilm Publications. Washington, DC: National Archives.
http://www.nara.gov/publications/microfilm/courts/fedcourt.html

Cyprus

Solsten, Eric. *Cyprus, a Country Study*. Washington, DC: Library of Congress, Federal Research Division, 1991.
http://lcweb2.loc.gov/frd/cs/cytoc.html

Denmark

Douglas, Lee V. *Danish Immigration to America, an Annotated Bibliography of Resources at the Library of Congress*. Research Guide No. 28. Washington, DC: Library of Congress, Local History and Genealogy Reading Room, 1998.
http://lcweb.loc.gov/rr/genealogy/bib_guid/danish.html

Genealogical Word List. Danish. Salt Lake City, UT: Family History Library, 1993.
http://www.familysearch.com/sg/WLDanish.html

Research Outline. Denmark. Salt Lake City, UT: Family History Library, 1993.
http://www.familysearch.com/sg/Denmark.html

Dominican Republic

Genealogical Word List, Spanish. Salt Lake City, UT: Family History Library, 1997.
http://familysearch.org/sg/WLSpanis.html

HLAS Online. Handbook of Latin American Studies. Washington, DC: Library of Congress, 1995. 49 vols.
http://lcweb2.loc.gov/hlas/hlashome.html

Haggerty, Richard A. *Dominican Republic, a Country Study*. Washington, DC: Library of Congress, Federal Research Division, 1989.
http://lcweb2.loc.gov/frd/cs/dotoc.html

Research Outline. Latin America. Salt Lake City, UT: Family History Library, 1992.
http://www.familysearch.com/sg/Latin_America.html

Ecuador

Genealogical Word List, Spanish. Salt Lake City, UT: Family History Library, 1997.
http://familysearch.org/sg/WLSpanis.html

HLAS Online. Handbook of Latin American Studies. Washington, DC: Library of Congress, 1995. 49 vols.
http://lcweb2.loc.gov/hlas/hlashome.html

Haggerty, Richard A. *Ecuador, a Country Study*. Washington, DC: Library of Congress, Federal Research Division, 1989.
http://lcweb2.loc.gov/frd/cs/ectoc.html

Research Outline. Latin America. Salt Lake City, UT: Family History Library, 1992.
http://www.familysearch.com/sg/Latin_America.html

Egypt

Metz, Helen Chapin. *Egypt, a Country Study*. Washington, DC: Library of Congress, Federal Research Division, 1990.
http://lcweb2.loc.gov/frd/cs/egtoc.html

England, United Kingdom
Denton, Jeffrey and Sarah Davnall, Dorothy Ross and Beryl Taylor. *Taxation Database (1291-1292)*. Manchester, England: University of Manchester.
http://www.mimas.ac.uk/taxatio/

Research Outline. England. Salt Lake City, UT: Family History Library, 1997.
http://www.familysearch.com/sg/England.html

Research Outline. 1881 British Census Indexes. Salt Lake City, UT: Family History Library, 1996.
http://www.familysearch.com/sg/1881_British_Census_Indexes.html

Research Outline. Using the 1881 British Census Indexes (For England, Wales, Channel Islands, Isle of Man, and Scotland). Salt Lake City, UT: Family History Library, 1996.
http://www.familysearch.com/sg/USING_1881_Brit_Cen_Ind.html

Southall, H.R., and D. R. Gilbert and I. Gregory. *Great Britain Historical Database, 1841-1939*. Colchester, Essex: History Data Service, The Data Archive.
http://hds.essex.ac.uk/gbh.stm

England, United Kingdom—Channel Islands
Garcelon, Pierre. *Mon Adieu a Mes Chers Enfans, Rev. Pierre Garcelon, Rector of St. Pierre du Bois, Island of Guernsey, 1739-1772*. Unknown.
http://www.lib.usf.edu/spccoll/guide/g/garcelon/page1.html

England, United Kingdom—Manchester
Denton, Jeffrey and Sarah Davnall, Dorothy Ross and Beryl Taylor. *Taxation Database (1291-1292)*. Manchester, England: University of Manchester.
http://cs6400.mcc.ac.uk/taxatio/

Gregson, Eliza Marshall. *The Gregson Memoirs, Containing Mrs. Eliza Gregson's Memory and the Statement of James Gregson*. San Francisco, CA: Kennedy, 1940. 31p.
http://memory.loc.gov/cgi-bin/query/r?ammem/calbkbib:@field(AUTHOR+@band(Gregson,+Eliza+Marshall,1824-+))

England, United Kingdom—Wales
Denton, Jeffrey and Sarah Davnall, Dorothy Ross and Beryl Taylor. *Taxation Database (1291-1292)*. Manchester, England: University of Manchester.
http://www.mimas.ac.uk/taxatio/

Research Outline. Wales. Salt Lake City, UT: Family History Library, 1995.
http://familysearch.org/sg/Wales.html

Episcopalians
Rollmann, Hans. *Anglicans, Puritans and Quakers in Sixteenth and Seventeenth Century Newfoundland*. Unknown.
http://www.mun.ca/rels/ang/texts/ang1.html

Episcopalians—California
Kip, William Ingraham. *The Early Days of My Episcopate*. New York, NY: Whittaker, 1892. 263p.
http://memory.loc.gov/cgi-bin/query/r?ammem/calbkbib:@field(AUTHOR+@band(Kip,+William+Ingraham,bp.,1811-1893.+))

Episcopalians—District of Columbia

Episcopal Church, Commission of Home Missions to Colored People. New York, NY: Church, 1875, 1876.
9th Annual Report, 1873-74. 20p.
http://memory.loc.gov/cgi-bin/query/r?ammem/murray:@field(FLD001+91898515+):@@@REF

11th Annual Report, 1875-76. 24p.
http://memory.loc.gov/cgi-bin/query/r?ammem/murray:@field(FLD001+91898514+):@@@REF

Waller, Owen Meredith. *The Episcopal Church and the Colored People, a Statement of Facts.* Washington, DC: Emmett C. Jones & Co., 1898. 14p.
http://memory.loc.gov/cgi-bin/query/r?ammem/aap:@field(SUBJ+@band(Afro-American+Episcopalians .+))

Episcopalians—Georgia

Episcopal Church, Commission of Home Missions to Colored People. New York, NY: Church, 1875, 1876.
9th Annual Report, 1873-74. 20p.
http://memory.loc.gov/cgi-bin/query/r?ammem/murray:@field(FLD001+91898515+):@@@REF

11th Annual Report, 1875-76. 24p.
http://memory.loc.gov/cgi-bin/query/r?ammem/murray:@field(FLD001+91898514+):@@@REF

Episcopalians—Kansas

In Perils by Mine Own Countrymen, Three Years on the Kansas Border, by a Clergyman of the Episcopal Church. New York, NY: Auburn, Miller, Orton & Mulligan, 1856. 242p.
http://moa.umdl.umich.edu/cgi-bin/moa/sgml/moa-idx?notisid=ABA0775

Episcopalians—Louisiana

Episcopal Church, Commission of Home Missions to Colored People. New York, NY: Church, 1875, 1876.
9th Annual Report, 1873-74. 20p.
http://memory.loc.gov/cgi-bin/query/r?ammem/murray:@field(FLD001+91898515+):@@@REF

11th Annual Report, 1875-76. 24p.
http://memory.loc.gov/cgi-bin/query/r?ammem/murray:@field(FLD001+91898514+):@@@REF

Episcopalians—Massachusetts

Adams, Brooks. *The Emancipation of Massachusetts.* Boston, MA: Houghton Mifflin, 1887. 388p.
http://moa.cit.cornell.edu/dienst/moabrowse.fly/MOA-JOURNALS2:ADAM-0033/3/1:TIFF2GIF:100?,,

Bacon, Leonard. *The Genesis of the New England Churches.* New York, NY: Harper, 1874.
http://moa.cit.cornell.edu/dienst/moabrowse.fly/MOA-JOURNALS2:BACO-0030/5/1:TIFF2GIF:100

Episcopalians—Mississippi

Episcopal Church, Commission of Home Missions to Colored People. New York, NY: Church, 1875, 1876.
9th Annual Report, 1873-74. 20p.
http://memory.loc.gov/cgi-bin/query/r?ammem/murray:@field(FLD001+91898515+):@@@REF

11th Annual Report, 1875-76. 24p.
http://memory.loc.gov/cgi-bin/query/r?ammem/murray:@field(FLD001+91898514+):@@@REF

Episcopalians—North Carolina

Episcopal Church, Commission of Home Missions to Colored People. New York, NY: Church, 1875, 1876.

9th Annual Report, 1873-74. 20p.
http://memory.loc.gov/cgi-bin/query/r?ammem/murray:@field(FLD001+91898515+):@@@REF

11th Annual Report, 1875-76. 24p.
http://memory.loc.gov/cgi-bin/query/r?ammem/murray:@field(FLD001+91898514+):@@@REF

Episcopalians—South Carolina

Episcopal Church, Commission of Home Missions to Colored People. New York, NY: Church, 1875, 1876.

9th Annual Report, 1873-74. 20p.
http://memory.loc.gov/cgi-bin/query/r?ammem/murray:@field(FLD001+91898515+):@@@REF

11th Annual Report, 1875-76. 24p.
http://memory.loc.gov/cgi-bin/query/r?ammem/murray:@field(FLD001+91898514+):@@@REF

Episcopalians—Virginia

Episcopal Church, Commission of Home Missions to Colored People. New York, NY: Church, 1875, 1876.

9th Annual Report, 1873-74. 20p.
http://memory.loc.gov/cgi-bin/query/r?ammem/murray:@field(FLD001+91898515+):@@@REF

11th Annual Report, 1875-76. 24p.
http://memory.loc.gov/cgi-bin/query/r?ammem/murray:@field(FLD001+91898514+):@@@REF

Ethiopia

Ofcansky, Thomas P. and LaVerle Berry. *Ethiopia, a Country Study.* Washington, DC: Library of Congress, Federal Research Division, 1991.
http://lcweb2.loc.gov/frd/cs/ettoc.html

Federal Records

Matchette, Robert B. *Guide to Federal Records in the National Archives of the United States.* Washington, DC: National Archives, 1995.
http://www.nara.gov/guide/

Finland

Genealogical Word List. Finnish. Salt Lake City, UT: Family History Library, 1997.
http://www.familysearch.com/sg/WLFinnis.html

Solsten, Eric and Sandra W. Meditz. *Finland, a Country Study.* Washington, DC: Library of Congress, Federal Research Division, 1988.
http://lcweb2.loc.gov/frd/cs/fitoc.html

France

Genealogical Word List. French. Salt Lake City, UT: Family History Library, 1997.
http://www.familysearch.com/sg/WLFrench.html

Letter Writing Guide. French. Salt Lake City, UT: Family History Library, 1997.
http://www.familysearch.com/sg/LGFrench.html

Research Outline. France. Salt Lake City, UT: Family History Library, 1995.
http://www.familysearch.com/sg/France.html

Research Outline. French Republican Calendar. Salt Lake City, UT: Family History Library, 1990.
http://www.familysearch.com/sg/FrRepCal.html

Germany

Bokum, Hermann. *The Testimony of a Refugee from East Tennessee by Hermann Bokum, Chaplain, U.S.A.* Philadelphia, PA: Author, 1863. 24p.
http://metalab.unc.edu/docsouth/bokum/menu.html

Genealogical Word List. German. Salt Lake City, UT: Family History Library, 1997.
http://www.familysearch.com/sg/WLGerman.html

Lecouvreur, Frank. *From East Prussia to the Golden Gate. Letters and Diary of the California Pioneer.* New York, NY: Angelina Book, 1906. 355p.
http://memory.loc.gov/cgi-bin/query/r?ammem/calbkbib:@field(AUTHOR+@band(Lecouvreur,+Frank, 1829-1901.+))

Letter Writing Guide. German. Salt Lake City, UT: Family History Library, 1997.
http://www.familysearch.com/sg/LGGerman.html

Newmark, Harris. *Sixty Years in Southern California, 1853-1913, containing the Reminiscences of Harris Newmark.* New York, NY: Knickerbocker Press, 1916. 732p.
http://memory.loc.gov/cgi-bin/query/r?ammem/calbkbib:@field(AUTHOR+@band(Newmark,+Harris, 1834-1916.+))

Nordhoff, Charles. *California for Health, Pleasure and Residence. A Book for Travelers and Settlers.* New York, NY: Harper, 1873. 255p.
http://memory.loc.gov/cgi-bin/query/r?ammem/calbkbib:@field(AUTHOR+@band(Nordhoff,+Charles, 1830-1901.+))

————. *Northern California, Oregon, and the Sandwich Islands.* New York, NY: Harper, 1875. 256p.
http://moa.umdl.umich.edu/cgi-bin/moa/sgml/moa-idx?notisid=AJL3484

Reimann, Lewis Charles. *Between the Iron and the Pine, a Biography of a Pioneer Family and a Pioneer Town.* Ann Arbor, MI: Edwards Brothers, 1951. 225p.
http://memory.loc.gov/cgi-bin/query/r?ammem/lhbumbib:@field(SUBJ+@band(Frontier+and+pioneer+ life--Michigan,+Upper+Peninsula.+))

Research Outline. Germany. Salt Lake City, UT: Family History Library, 1997.
http://www.familysearch.com/sg/Germany.html

Research Outline. The Hamburg Passenger Lists, 1850-1934. Salt Lake City, UT: Family History Library, 1992.
http://www.familysearch.com/sg/Hamburg_Pass_List.html

Scharmann, Hermann B. *Scharmann's Journey to California, from the Pages of a Pioneer's Diary from the German of H. B. Scharmann by Margaret Hoff Zimmermann, A.B. and Erich W. Zimmermann, Ph.D.* New York, NY: New Yorker Stats Zeitung, 1852, 1918. 114p.
http://memory.loc.gov/cgi-bin/query/r?ammem/calbkbib:@field(AUTHOR+@band(Scharmann,+ Hermann+B.,b.+1838.+))

Germany—Hamburg

Gerstacker, Friedrich Wilhelm Christian. *Gerstacker's Travels.* London: Nelson, 1854. 290p.
http://memory.loc.gov/cgi-bin/query/r?ammem/calbk:@field(DOCID+@lit(C110T00)):@@@REF

————. *Scenes of Life in California.* San Francisco, CA: Howell, 1942. 188p.
http://memory.loc.gov/cgi-bin/query/r?ammem/calbk:@field(DOCID+@lit(C017T00)):@@@REF

Ghana

Berry, La Verle. *Ghana, a Country Study.* Washington, DC: Library of Congress, Federal Research Division, 1994.
http://lcweb2.loc.gov/frd/cs/ghtoc.html

Guyana

Merrill, Tim. *Ghana, a Country Study.* Washington, DC: Library of Congress, Federal Research Division, 1992.
http://lcweb2.loc.gov/frd/cs/gytoc.html

Haiti

Genealogical Word List. French. Salt Lake City, UT: Family History Library, 1997.
http://www.familysearch.com/sg/WLFrench.html

Haggerty, Richard A. *Haiti, a Country Study.* Washington, DC: Library of Congress, Federal Research Division, 1989.
http://lcweb2.loc.gov/frd/cs/httoc.html

Letter Writing Guide. French. Salt Lake City, UT: Family History Library, 1997.
http://www.familysearch.com/sg/LGFrench.html

Hispanic Americans

Genealogical Word List, Spanish. Salt Lake City, UT: Family History Library, 1997.
http://familysearch.org/sg/WLSpanis.html

HLAS Online. Handbook of Latin American Studies. Washington, DC: Library of Congress, 1995. 49 vols.
http://lcweb2.loc.gov/hlas/hlashome.html

Research Outline. Latin America. Salt Lake City, UT: Family History Library, 1992.
http://www.familysearch.com/sg/Latin_America.html

Solsten, Eric and Sandra W. Meditz. *Spain, a Country Study.* Washington, DC: Library of Congress, Federal Research Division, 1988.
http://lcweb2.loc.gov/frd/cs/estoc.html

Honduras

Genealogical Word List, Spanish. Salt Lake City, UT: Family History Library, 1997.
http://familysearch.org/sg/WLSpanis.html

HLAS Online. Handbook of Latin American Studies. Washington, DC: Library of Congress, 1995. 49 vols.
http://lcweb2.loc.gov/hlas/hlashome.html

Merrill, Tim. *Honduras, a Country Study.* Washington, DC: Library of Congress, Federal Research Division, 1993.
http://lcweb2.loc.gov/frd/cs/hntoc.html

Research Outline. Latin America. Salt Lake City, UT: Family History Library, 1992.
http://www.familysearch.com/sg/Latin_America.html

How-to, handbooks, and guidebooks
Genealogical and Biographical Research, a Select Catalog of NARA Microfilm Publications. Washington, DC: National Archives.
http://www.nara.gov/publications/microfilm/biographical/genbio.html

Turner, Frederick Jackson. *The Frontier in American History.* New York, NY: Holt, 1921.
http://xroads.virginia.edu/~HYPER/TURNER/

Research Outline. Genealogical Word List, Latin. Salt Lake City, UT: Family History Library, 1997.
http://www.familysearch.com/sg/WLLatin.html

Huguenots
Waldron, William Watson. *Huguenots of Westchester and Parish of Fordham.* New York, NY: Kelley & Brother, Publishers, 1864.126p.
http://moa.cit.cornell.edu/dienst/moabrowse.fly/MOA-JOURNALS2:WALD-0050/5/1:TIFF2GIF:100

Hungary
Burant, Stephen R. *Hungary, a Country Study.* Washington, DC: Library of Congress, Federal Research Division, 1989.
http://lcweb2.loc.gov/frd/cs/hutoc.html

Indexes
Research Outline. PERiodical Source Index on Microfiche (PERSI). Salt Lake City, UT: Family History Library, 1996.
http://www.familysearch.com/sg/Periodical_Source_Index.html

Indonesia
Frederick, William H. and Robert L. Worden. *Indonesia, a Country Study.* Washington, DC: Library of Congress, Federal Research Division, 1992.
http://lcweb2.loc.gov/frd/cs/idtoc.html

Internet
Bailey, Charles W., Jr. *Scholarly Electronic Publishing Bibliography.* Version 25. 1999.
http://info.lib.uh.edu/sepb/sepb.html

Besser, Howard and Robert Yamashita. *The Cost of Digital Image Distribution, the Social and Economic Implications of the Production, Distribution and Usage of Image Data. Final Report.* 1998.
http://sunsite.berkeley.edu/Imaging/Databases/1998mellon/

Computers in Libraries. Medford, NJ: Information Today. Vol. 18, No. 7 (July/August 1998- .)
http://www.infotoday.com/cilmag/ciltop.htm

D-lib Magazine, the Magazine of Digital Library Research. (Serial) ISSN: 1082-9873. Vol. 1, No. 1 (July 1995- .).
http://www.dlib.org/

Guide for Managing Electronic Records from an Archival Perspective. Paris, France: International Council on Archives.
http://data1.archives.ca/ica/cgi-bin/ica?0508_e

Howells, Cyndi. "Tracking Your Family through Time and Technology." *American Heritage.* (March 1999)
http://www.americanheritage.com/99/feb/005.htm

Information Today. Medford, NJ: Information Today. Vol. 15, No. 3, March 1998- .
http://www.infotoday.com/it/itnew.htm

Link-Up, The Newsmagazine for Users of Online Services, CD-ROM, and the Internet. Medford, NJ: Information Today. Vol.15, No. 2 (March/April 1998- .)
http://www.infotoday.com/lu/lunew.htm

Townsend, Sean and Cressida Chappell and Oscar Struijve. *Digitising History, a Guide to Creating Digital Resources from Historical Documents.* Colchester, Essex: History Data Service, Arts and Humanities Data Service, 1999.
http://hds.essex.ac.uk/g2gp/digitising_history/index.html

Iran

Metz, Helen Chapin. *Iran, a Country Study.* Washington, DC: Library of Congress, Federal Research Division, 1987.
http://lcweb2.loc.gov/frd/cs/irtoc.html

Iraq

Metz, Helen Chapin. *Iraq, a Country Study.* Washington, DC: Library of Congress, Federal Research Division, 1988.
http://lcweb2.loc.gov/frd/cs/iqtoc.html

Ireland

Biography of James Patton. Asheville, NC: Patton Family, 1850. 34p.
http://metalab.unc.edu/docsouth/patton/menu.html

Byrne, Stephen. *Irish Emigration to the United States, What It Has Been and What It Is.* New York, NY: Catholic Publication Society, 1873. 168p.
http://moa.umdl.umich.edu/cgi-bin/moa/sgml/moa-idx?notisid=AJJ9240

Maguire, John Francis. *The Irish in America.* New York, NY: D. & J. Sadlier & Co., 1868. 668p.
http://moa.umdl.umich.edu/cgi-bin/moa/sgml/moa-idx?notisid=ABL3952

Research Outline. Ireland. Salt Lake City, UT: Family History Library, 1993.
http://www.familysearch.com/sg/Ireland.html

Research Outline. Ireland Householder's Index. Salt Lake City, UT: Family History Library, 1992.
http://www.familysearch.com/sg/Ireland_Householders_Index.html

Italy

Genealogical Word List. Italian. Salt Lake City, UT: Family History Library, 1997.
http://www.familysearch.com/sg/WLItalia.html

Mazzuchelli, Samuel Charles. *Memoirs, Historical and Edifying of a Missionary Apostolic of the Order of Saint Dominic among Various Indian Tribes and among the Catholics and Protestants in the United States of America.* Chicago, IL: Hall Printing Co., 1915. 375p.
http://memory.loc.gov/cgi-bin/query/r?ammem/lhbumbib:@field(SUBJ+@band(Catholic+church+in+the+United+States.+))

Ivory Coast

Genealogical Word List. French. Salt Lake City, UT: Family History Library, 1997.
http://www.familysearch.com/sg/WLFrench.html

Handloff, Robet E. *Ivory Coast, a Country Study.* Washington, DC: Library of Congress, Federal Research Division, 1988.
http://lcweb2.loc.gov/frd/cs/citoc.html

Letter Writing Guide. French. Salt Lake City, UT: Family History Library, 1997.
http://www.familysearch.com/sg/LGFrench.html

Jamaica

Williams, James. *A Narrative of Events Since the First of August, 1834, by James Williams an Apprenticed Labourer in Jamaica.* London: J. Rider, 1837. 26p.
http://metalab.unc.edu/docsouth/williamsjames/menu.html

Japan

Dolan, Ronald E. and Robert L. Worden. *Japan, a Country Study.* Washington, DC: Library of Congress, Federal Research Division, 1994.
http://lcweb2.loc.gov/frd/cs/jptoc.html

Heco, Joseph. *The Narrative of a Japanese, What He Has Seen and the People He Has Met in the Course of the Last Forty Years.* Tokyo, Japan: Maruzen, 1895. 2 vols.
http://memory.loc.gov/cgi-bin/query/r?ammem/calbkbib:@field(AUTHOR+@band(Heco,+Joseph,1837-1897.+))

Jewish Americans

Between the Lines. New York, NY: Jewish Theological Seminary of America. Vol. 8, Spring 1995.
http://www.jtsa.edu/library/news/

Metz, Helen Chapin. *Israel, a Country Study.* Washington, DC: Library of Congress, Federal Research Division, 1988.
http://lcweb2.loc.gov/frd/cs/iltoc.html

Newmark, Harris. *Sixty Years in Southern California, 1853-1913, Containing the Reminiscences of Harris Newmark.* New York, NY: Knickerbocker Press, 1916. 732p.
http://memory.loc.gov/cgi-bin/query/r?ammem/calbkbib:@field(AUTHOR+@band(Newmark,+Harris,1834-1916.+))

Jordan

Metz, Helen Chapin. *Jordan, a Country Study.* Washington, DC: Library of Congress, Federal Research Division, 1989.
http://lcweb2.loc.gov/frd/cs/jotoc.html

Kazakstan

Curtis, Glenn E. *Kazakstan, a Country Study.* Washington, DC: Library of Congress, Federal Research Division, 1996.
http://lcweb2.loc.gov/frd/cs/kztoc.html

Korea

Savada, Andrea Matles. *North Korea, a Country Study.* Washington, DC: Library of Congress, Federal Research Division, 1993.
http://lcweb2.loc.gov/frd/cs/kptoc.html

————, and William Shaw. *South Korea, a Country Study*. Washington, DC: Library of Congress, Federal Research Division, 1990.
http://lcweb2.loc.gov/frd/cs/krtoc.html

Laos
Savada, Andrea Matles. *Laos, a Country Study*. Washington, DC: Library of Congress, Federal Research Division, 1994.
http://lcweb2.loc.gov/frd/cs/latoc.html

Lebanon
Collelo, Thomas. *Lebanon, a Country Study*. Washington, DC: Library of Congress, Federal Research Division, 1987.
http://lcweb2.loc.gov/frd/cs/lbtoc.html

Libya
Metz, Helen Chapin. *Libya, a Country Study*. Washington, DC: Library of Congress, Federal Research Division, 1987.
http://lcweb2.loc.gov/frd/cs/lytoc.html

Lutherans
Grose, Ingebrikt F. *Fifty Memorable Years at St. Olaf, Marking the History of the College on the Hill from Its Founding in 1874 to Its Golden Jubilee Celebration in 1925*. Northfield, MN: Northfield News, 1925. 46p.
http://memory.loc.gov/cgi-bin/query/r?ammem/lhbumbib:@field(SUBJ+@band(St.+Olaf+college,+Northfield,+Minn.+))

Ronning, Nils Nilsen. *Fifty Years in America*. Minneapolis, MN: Friend Publishing Co., 1938. 243p.
http://memory.loc.gov/cgi-bin/query/r?ammem/lhbum:@field(DOCID+@lit(08330T000)):@@@REF

Schmucker, S. S. *The American Lutheran Church, Historically, Doctrinally and Practically Delineated in Several Occasional Discourses*. Philadelphia, PA: Miller, 1852. 288p.
http://moa.umdl.umich.edu/cgi-bin/moa/sgml/moa-idx?notisid=AJK2506

Maps, Gazetteers
Post Office Directory. List of Post Offices in the United States, Arranged Alphabetically and Giving the Salaries of the Postmasters also an Appendix Containing the Names of the Post Offices Arranged by States and Counties, with Money Order Offices and other Postal Information. Washington, DC: Government Printing Office, 1870. 400p.
http://moa.umdl.umich.edu/cgi-bin/moa/sgml/moa-idx?notisid=AHJ3101b

Marqueas Islands
Memoir of Thomas Hamitah Patoo, a Native of the Marqueas Islands, Who Died June 19, 1823, while a Member of the Foreign Mission School in Cornwall, Connecticut. New York, NY: New York Religious Tract Society, 1823. 48p.
http://memory.loc.gov/cgi-bin/query/r?ammem/aap:@field(SUBJ+@band(Biographies--New+York++N.Y.+--1825.+))

Mauritania

Handloff, Robert E. *Mauritania, a Country Study.* Washington, DC: Library of Congress, Federal Research Division, 1987.
http://lcweb2.loc.gov/frd/cs/mrtoc.html

Mayflower

Bradford, William. *Of Plymouth Plantation, 1620-1647.* New York, NY: Knopf, 1952. 448p.
http://members.aol.com/calebj/bradford_journal.html

Methodists

Balch, Thomas Bloomer. *My Manse during the War, a Decade of Letters to the Rev. J. (Joshua) Thomas Murray, Editor of the Methodist Protestant.* Baltimore, MD: Sherwood, 1866. 42p.
http://metalab.unc.edu/docsouth/balch/menu.html

Methodists—African Methodist Episcopal Church

Arnett, Benjamin William. *Centennial Address on the Mission of Methodism to the Extremes of Society (with Statistics on the A.M.E. Church).* Xenia, OH: Torchlight Printing and Publishing, 1884. 40p.
http://memory.loc.gov/cgi-bin/query/r?ammem/aap:@field(SUBJ+@band(African+Methodist+Episcopal+Church--Statistics.+))

Benjamin, Robert C. Co. *The Zion Methodist.* Tuscaloosa, AL: Warren, 1893. 12p.
http://memory.loc.gov/cgi-bin/query/r?ammem/murray:@field(FLD001+90898309+):@@@REF

Funeral Services in Respect to the Memory of Rev. William Paul Quinn, Late Senior Bishop of the African M.E. Church, Held at Warren Chapel, Toledo, Ohio, March 9th, 1873. Toledo, OH: Warren Chapel, 1873. 52p.
http://memory.loc.gov/cgi-bin/query/r?ammem/aap:@field(SUBJ+@band(Quinn,+William+Paul,--1799-1873.+))

Lane, Isaac. *Autobiography of Bishop Isaac Lan, LL.D. with a Short History of the C.M.E. Church in America and of Methodism.* Nashville, TN: Publishing House of the M.E. Church, South, 1916. 192p.
http://metalab.unc.edu/docsouth/lane/menu.html

Lee, Jarena. *Religious Life and Experience and Journal of Mrs. Jarena Lee, Giving an Account of Her Call to Preach the Gospel.* Philadelphia, PA: Author, 1849. 97p.
http://digilib.nypl.org/dynaweb/digs/wwm9716/

A Memorial Souvenir of Rev. J. Wofford White, Pastor of Wesley, M.E. Church, Charleston, S.C. Who Fell Asleep, January 7th, 1890, Aged 33 Years. Charleston, SC: Walker, Evans & Cogswell, 1890. 8p.
http://memory.loc.gov/cgi-bin/query/r?ammem/aap:@field(SUBJ+@band(Wesley+Methodist+Episcopal+Church++Charleston,+S.C.++))

Proceedings of the Semi-centenary Celebration of the African Methodist Episcopal Church of Cincinnati, Held in Allen Temple, Februrary 8th, 9th, and 10th, 1874, with an Account of the Rise and Progress of the Colored Schools, also a List of the Charitable and Benevolent Societies of the City. Cincinnati, OH: Watkin, 1874. 136p.
http://memory.loc.gov/cgi-bin/query/r?ammem/murray:@field(FLD001+91898101+):@@@REF

Straker, David Augustus. *Bethel, A.M.E. Church Case, in Columbia, S.C., the State of South Carolina, Richland County, J. W. Morris et. al. Plaintiffs, against S. B. Wallace, et. al. Defendants, Action for Relief*. South Carolina: Unknown, 1887. 14p.
http://memory.loc.gov/cgi-bin/query/r?ammem/aap:@field(SUBJ+@band(African+Methodist+Episcopal+
Church--Clergy--Appointment,+call+and+election.+))

Methodists—California
Hines, Joseph Wilkinson. *Touching Incidents in the Life and Labors of a Pioneer on the Pacific Coast since 1853*. San Jose, CA: Eaton & Co., 1911. 198p.
http://memory.loc.gov/cgi-bin/query/r?ammem/calbkbib:@field(AUTHOR+@band(Hines,+Joseph+
Wilkinson+))

Methodists—Indiana
Holliday, Fernandez C. *Indiana Methodism being an Account of the Introduction, Progress, and Present Position of Methodism in the State; and also a History of the Literary Institutions under the Care of the Church, with Sketches of the Principal Methodist Educators in the State down to 1872*. Cincinnati, OH: Hitchcock and Walden, 1873. 378p.
http://moa.umdl.umich.edu/cgi-bin/moa/sgml/moa-idx?notisid=AGV9056

Methodists—Missouri
Leftwich, William M. *Martyrdom in Missouri, a History of Religious Proscription, the Seizure of Churches and the Persecution of Ministers of the Gospel in the State of Missouri during the Late Civil War and under the Test Oath of the New Constitution*. St. Louis, MO: Author, 1870. 438p.
http://moa.umdl.umich.edu/cgi-bin/moa/sgml/moa-idx?notisid=AGU9422b

Methodists—Ohio
Funeral Services in Respect to the Memory of Rev. William Paul Quinn, Late Senior Bishop of the African M.E. Church, Held at Warren Chapel, Toledo, Ohio, March 9th, 1873. Toledo, OH: Warren Chapel, 1873. 52p.
http://memory.loc.gov/cgi-bin/query/r?ammem/aap:@field(SUBJ+@band(Quinn,+William+Paul,--1799-
1873.+))

Proceedings of the Semi-centenary Celebration of the African Methodist Episcopal Church of Cincinnati, Held in Allen Temple, Februrary 8th, 9th, and 10th, 1874, with an Account of the Rise and Progress of the Colored Schools, also a List of the Charitable and Benevolent Societies of the City. Cincinnati, OH: Watkin, 1874. 136p.
http://memory.loc.gov/cgi-bin/query/r?ammem/murray:@field(FLD001+91898101+):@@@REF

Methodists—Pennsylvania
Manship, Andrew. *Thirteen Years' Experience in the Itinerancy*. Philadelphia, PA: Higgins and Perkinpine, 1856. 412p.
http://moa.umdl.umich.edu/cgi-bin/moa/sgml/moa-idx?notisid=AJK2747

Methodists—South Carolina
A Memorial Souvenir of Rev. J. Wofford White, Pastor of Wesley, M.E. Church, Charleston, S.C. Who Fell Asleep, January 7th, 1890, Aged 33 Years. Charleston, SC: Walker, Evans & Cogswell, 1890. 8p.
http://memory.loc.gov/cgi-bin/query/r?ammem/aap:@field(SUBJ+@band(Wesley+Methodist+Episcopal+
Church++Charleston,+S.C.++))

Straker, David Augustus. *Bethel, A.M.E. Church Case, in Columbia, S.C., the State of South Carolina, Richland County, J. W. Morris et. al. Plaintiffs, against S. B. Wallace, et. al. Defendants, Action for Relief*. South Carolina: Unknown, 1887. 14p.
http://memory.loc.gov/cgi-bin/query/r?ammem/aap:@field(SUBJ+@band(African+Methodist+Episcopal+Church--Clergy--Appointment,+call+and+election.+))

Methodists—Wisconsin

Miller, Wesson Gage. *Thirty Years in the Itinerancy*. Milwaukee, WI: Hauser, 1875. 304p.
http://memory.loc.gov/cgi-bin/query/r?ammem/lhbum:@field(DOCID+@lit(27351T000)):@@@REF

Mexico

Genealogical Word List, Spanish. Salt Lake City, UT: Family History Library, 1997.
http://familysearch.org/sg/WLSpanis.html

HLAS Online. Handbook of Latin American Studies. Washington, DC: Library of Congress, 1995. 49 vols.
http://lcweb2.loc.gov/hlas/hlashome.html

Janssens, Victor Eugene August. *The Life and Adventures in California of Don Agustin Janssens, 1834-1856*. San Marino, CA: Huntington, 1953. 165p.
http://memory.loc.gov/cgi-bin/query/r?ammem/calbkbib:@field(AUTHOR+@band(Janssens,+Victor+Eugene+August,1817-1894.+))

Research Outline. Latin America. Salt Lake City, UT: Family History Library, 1992.
http://www.familysearch.com/sg/Latin_America.html

Military Records

Crawford, Michael J. and Christine F. Hughes. *The Reestablishment of the Navy, 1787-1801, Historical Overview and Select Bibliography*. Naval History Bibliogrpahies, No. 4. Washington, DC: Naval Historical Center, 1997.
http://www.history.navy.mil/biblio/biblio4/biblio4.htm

Emery, George W. *Historical Manuscripts in the Navy Department Library, a Catalog. Naval History Bibliographies No. 3*. Washington, DC: Naval Historical Center, 1994.
http://www.history.navy.mil/biblio/biblio3/biblio3.htm

Lynch, Barbara A. and John E. Vajda. *United States Naval History, a Bibliography. Naval History Bibliographies No. 1*. 7th ed. Washington, DC: Naval Historical Center, 1993.
http://www.history.navy.mil/biblio/biblio1/biblio1.htm

Means, Dennis R. *A Heavy Sea Running, the Formation of the U.S. Life Saving Service, 1846-1878. Prologue*. Vol. 19, No. 4 (Winter 1987).
http://www.nara.gov/publications/prologue/saving.html

Military Service Records, a Select Catalog of NARA Microfilm Publications. Washington, DC: National Archives.
http://www.nara.gov/publications/microfilm/military/service.html

New York State Archives and Records Administration. *War Service Records and Searches*. Albany, NY: Author, 1997. Unpgd.
http://www.sara.nysed.gov/holding/aids/rev/content.htm

Records About Impressed Seamen, 1793-1814. Washington, DC: National Archives.
http://www.nara.gov/genealogy/impsea.html

Unit History Bibliographies. Carlisle, PA: US Army Military History Institute, Historical Reference Branch, 1999.
http://carlisle-www.army.mil/usamhi/UnitHistories.html

Military Records—Revolutionary War

Fleetwood, Christian Abraham. *The Negro as a Soldier.* Washington, DC: Howard University Press, 1895. 19p.
http://memory.loc.gov/cgi-bin/query/r?ammem/murray:@field(FLD001+12000751+):@@@REF

Moore, George Henry. *Historical Notes on the Employment of Negroes in the American Army of the Revolution.* New York, NY: Evans, 1862. 24p.
http://memory.loc.gov/cgi-bin/query/r?ammem/murray:@field(FLD001+02003395+):@@@REF

Raymond, Samuel. *The Record of Andover in the Revolution.* Andover, MA: R. W. Draper, 1875. 240p.
http://moa.umdl.umich.edu/cgi-bin/moa/sgml/moa-idx?notisid=AFJ7552

Wirt, William. *Sketches of the Life and Character of Patrick Henry.* Philadelphia, PA: James Webster, 1817. 427p.
http://metalab.unc.edu/docsouth/wirt/menu.html

Military Records—War of 1812

Fleetwood, Christian Abraham. *The Negro as a Soldier.* Washington, DC: Howard University Press, 1895. 19p.
http://memory.loc.gov/cgi-bin/query/r?ammem/murray:@field(FLD001+12000751+):@@@REF

Records About Impressed Seamen, 1793-1814. Washington, DC: National Archives.
http://www.nara.gov/genealogy/impsea.html

Military Records—Mexican-American War

Buffum, Edward Gould. *Six Months in the Gold Mines from a Journal of Three Years' Residence in Upper and Lower California, 1847-8-9.* Philadelphia, PA: Lea & Blanchard, 1850. 172p.
http://memory.loc.gov/cgi-bin/query/r?ammem/calbkbib:@field(AUTHOR+@band(Buffum,+Edward+Gould,1820-1867.+))

Maury, Dabney Herndon. *Recollections of a Virginian in the Mexican, Indian and Civil Wars.* New York, NY: Scribners, 1894. 279p.
http://metalab.unc.edu/docsouth/maury/menu.html

Military Records—Civil War

American Civil War Biographical Bibliographies. Carlisle, PA: US Army Military History Institute, Historial Reference Branch, 1999.
http://carlisle-www.army.mil/usamhi/ACWBiogs.html

American Civil War Unit Bibliographies. Carlisle, PA: US Army Military History Institute, Historial Reference Branch, 1999.
http://carlisle-www.army.mil/usamhi/ACWUnits.html

Brown, William Wells. *The Negro in the American Rebellion, His Heroism and His Fidelity.* Boston, MA: Lee & Shepard, 1867. 396p.
http://moa.umdl.umich.edu/cgi-bin/moa/sgml/moa-idx?notisid=ABY0202

Civil War Records. Washington, DC: National Archives.
http://www.nara.gov/genealogy/civilwar.html

Confederate Pension Records. Washington, DC: National Archives.
http://www.nara.gov/genealogy/confed.html

Fleetwood, Christian Abraham. *The Negro as a Soldier.* Washington, DC: Howard University Press, 1895. 19p.
http://memory.loc.gov/cgi-bin/query/r?ammem/murray:@field(FLD001+12000751+):@@@REF

Plante, Trevor K. "The Shady Side of the Family Tree, Civil War Union Court Martial Case Files." *Prologue.* Vol. 30, No. 4 (Winter 1998).
http://www.nara.gov/publications/prologue/crtmar.html

Worthington, C. J. *The Woman in Battle, a Narrative of the Exploits, Adventures, and Travels of Madame Loreta Janeta Velazquez, otherwise Known as Lieutenant Harry T. Buford, Confederate States Army in which is Given Full Descriptions of the Numerous Battles in Which She Participated as a Confederate Officer.* Richmond, VA: Dustin, Gilman, 1876. 606p.
http://metalab.unc.edu/docsouth/velazquez/menu.html

Military Records—Civil War—Alabama
Gordon, John Brown. *Reminiscences of the Civil War.* New York, NY: Scribners, 1904. 474p.
http://metalab.unc.edu/docsouth/gordon/menu.html

Wyeth, John Allan. *With Sabre and Scalpel, the Autobiography of a Soldier and Surgeon.* New York, NY: Harper, 1914. 535p.
http://metalab.unc.edu/docsouth/wyeth/menu.html

Military Records—Civil War—District of Columbia
Lomax, Virginia. *The Old Capitol (Prison) and Its Inmates. By a Lady Who Enjoyed the Hospitalities of the Government for a Season.* New York, NY: Hale, 1867. 226p.
http://metalab.unc.edu/docsouth/lomax/menu.html

Military Records—Civil War—Florida
Eppes, Susan Bradford. *Through Some Eventful Years.* Macon, GA: Burke, 1926. 382p.
http://moa.umdl.umich.edu/cgi-bin/moa/sgml/moa-idx?notisid=AFJ8883

Mitchel, Cora. *Reminiscences of the Civil War.* Providence, RI: Snow & Farnham, 1916. 43p.
http://metalab.unc.edu/docsouth/mitchel/menu.html

Military Records—Civil War—Georgia
Andrews, Eliza Frances. *The Wartime Journal of a Georgia Girl, 1865-1865.* New York, NY: Appleton, 1908. 387p.
http://metalab.unc.edu/docsouth/andrews/menu.html

Andrews, Sidney. *The South since the War, as Shown by Fourteen Weeks of Travel and Observation in Georgia and the Carolinas.* Boston, MA: Ticknor & Fields, 1866. 408p.
http://moa.umdl.umich.edu/cgi-bin/moa/sgml/moa-idx?notisid=AAW0193

Burge, Dolly Sumner Lunt. *A Woman's Wartime Journal, an Account of the Passage over Georgia's Plantation of Sherman's Army on the March to the Sea, as Recorded in the Diary of Dolly Sumner Lunt (Mrs. Thomas Burge).* New York, NY: Century Co., 1918. 54p.
http://metalab.unc.edu/docsouth/burge/menu.html

Howard, Wiley C. *Sketch of Cobb Legion Cavalry and Some Incidents and Scenes Remembered*. Author, 1901. 20p.
http://metalab.unc.edu/docsouth/howard/menu.html

Jones, Charles Colcock. *The Siege of Savannah in December, 1864, and the Confederate Operations in Georgia, and the Third Military District of South Carolina during General Sherman's March from Atlanta to the Sea*. Albany, NY: Munsell, 1874. 184p.
http://metalab.unc.edu/docsouth/jonescharles/menu.html

Kell, John McIntosh. *Recollections of a Naval Life, Including the Cruises of the Confederate States Steamers, Sumter and Alabama*. Washington, DC: Neale, 1900. 307p.
http://metalab.unc.edu/docsouth/kell/menu.html

Radical Rule, Military Outrage in Georgia. Arrest of Columbus Prisoners, with Facts Connected with Their Imprisonment and Release. Louisville, KY: Morton, 1868. 200p.
http://moa.umdl.umich.edu/cgi-bin/moa/sgml/moa-idx?notisid=AFJ9489

Stearns, Charles Woodward. *The Black Man of the South and the Rebels, or the Characteristics of the Former and the Recent Outrages of the Latter*. New York, NY: American News, 1872. 578p.
http://moa.umdl.umich.edu/cgi-bin/moa/sgml/moa-idx?notisid=ABL5152

Military Records—Civil War—Kansas
Cordley, R. *The Lawrence Massacre by a Band of Missouri Ruffians under Quantrell, August 21, 1863, 150 Men Killed, Eighty Women Made Widows and 250 Children Made Orphans*. Lawrence, KS: Broughton Publisher, 1865.
http://www.ukans.edu/carrie/kancoll/books/cordley_massacre/quantrel.raid.html

Military Records—Civil War—Kentucky
Stone, Henry Lane. *Morgan's Men, a Narrative of Personal Experience*. Louisville, KY: Westerfield Bonte Co., 1919. 36p.
http://metalab.unc.edu/docsouth/stone/menu.html

Young, Lot D. *Reminiscences of a Soldier of the Orphan Brigade, by Lieut. L. D. Young, Paris, Kentucky*. Louisville, KY: Courier Journal Print Job, 1918. 99p.
http://metalab.unc.edu/docsouth/young/menu.html

Military Records—Civil War—Louisiana
Bacon, Edward. *Among the Cotton Thieves*. Detroit, MI: Free Press Steam Book, 1867. 300p.
http://moa.umdl.umich.edu/cgi-bin/moa/sgml/moa-idx?notisid=ACK4755

Morgan, James Morris. *Recollections of a Rebel Reefer*. Boston, MA: Houghton, Mifflin, 1917. 492p.
http://metalab.unc.edu/docsouth/morganjames/menu.html

Military Records—Civil War—Massachusetts
Hallowell, Norwood Penrose. *The Negro as a Soldier in the War of the Rebellion*. Boston, MA: Little, Brown & Co., 1897. 29p.
http://memory.loc.gov/cgi-bin/query/r?ammem/murray:@field(FLD001+22002319+):@@@REF

Military Records—Civil War—Michigan
Bacon, Edward. *Among the Cotton Thieves*. Detroit, MI: Free Press Steam Book, 1867. 300p.
http://moa.umdl.umich.edu/cgi-bin/moa/sgml/moa-idx?notisid=ACK4755

Military Records—Civil War—Mississippi
Montgomery, Frank Alexander. *Reminiscences of a Mississippian in Peace and War*. Cincinnati, OH: Robert Clarke Press, 1901. 305p.
http://metalab.unc.edu/docsouth/montgomery/menu.html

Military Records—Civil War—Missouri
Cordley, R. *The Lawrence Massacre by a Band of Missouri Ruffians under Quantrell, August 21, 1863, 150 Men Killed, Eighty Women Made Widows and 250 Children Made Orphans*. Lawrence, KS: Broughton Publisher, 1865.
http://www.ukans.edu/carrie/kancoll/books/cordley_massacre/quantrel.raid.html

Leftwich, William M. *Martyrdom in Missouri, a History of Religious Proscription, the Seizure of Churches and the Persecution of Ministers of the Gospel in the State of Missouri during the Late Civil War and under the Test Oath of the New Constitution*. St. Louis, MO: Author, 1870. 438p.
http://moa.umdl.umich.edu/cgi-bin/moa/sgml/moa-idx?notisid=AGU9422b

Military Records—Civil War—New York
Clark, L. H. *Military History of Wayne County, N.Y., the County in the Civil War*. Syracuse, NY: Truair, Smith & Bruce, 1883. 936p.
http://moa.cit.cornell.edu/dienst/moabrowse.fly/MOA-JOURNALS2:CLAR-0048/3/1:TIFF2GIF:100

Doty, Lockwood Lyon. *A History of Livingston County, New York, from Its Earliest Traditions to Its Part in the War for Our Union, with an Account of the Seneca Nation of Indians and Biographical Sketches of Earliest Settlers and Prominent Public Men*. Geneseo, NY: Edward E. Doty, 1876. 686p.
http://moa.cit.cornell.edu/dienst/moabrowse.fly/MOA-JOURNALS2:DOTY-0102/5/1:TIFF2GIF:100

Graham, Robert H. *Yates County's Boys in Blue, 1861-1865, Who They Were and What They Did*. Penn Yan, NY: Author, 1926. 204p.
http://moa.cit.cornell.edu/dienst/moabrowse.fly/MOA-JOURNALS2:GRAH-0051/3/1:TIFF2GIF:100

Military Records—Civil War—North Carolina
General Military Hospital for the North Carolina Troops in Petersburg, Virginia. Raleigh, NC: Strother & Marcom Book and Job Printers, 1861. 8p.
http://metalab.unc.edu/docsouth/generalhospital/menu.html

Green, Wharton Jackson. *Recollections and Reflections, an Auto of Half a Century and More*. Raleigh, NC: Edwards & Broughton Printing, 1906. 349p.
http://metalab.unc.edu/docsouth/green/menu.html

United Daughters of the Confederacy, J. E. B. Stuart Chapter. *War Days in Fayetteville, North Carolina, Reminiscences of 1861-1865*. Fayetteville, NC: Judge Print Co., 1910. 60p.
http://metalab.unc.edu/docsouth/chapter/menu.html

Ward, Dallas T. *The Last Flag of Truce*. Franklinton, NC: Author, 1915. 16p.
http://metalab.unc.edu/docsouth/ward/menu.html

Military Records—Civil War—Ohio
Ohio Boys in Dixie, the Adventures of Twenty-two Scouts Sent by Gen. O.M. Mitchell to Destroy a Railroad, with a Narrative of Their Barbarous Treatment by the Rebels and Judge Holt's Report. New York, NY: Miller & Mathews, 1863. 48p.
http://moa.umdl.umich.edu/cgi-bin/moa/sgml/moa-idx?notisid=ACR4661

Military Records—Civil War—Pennsylvania

Shepherd, Henry Elliot. *Narrative of Prison Life at Baltimore and Johnson's Island, Ohio.* Baltimore, MD: Commercial Printing, 1917. 22p.
http://metalab.unc.edu/docsouth/shepherd/menu.html

Military Records—Civil War—Prisons

Lomax, Virginia. *The Old Capitol (Prison) and Its Inmates. By a Lady Who Enjoyed the Hospitalities of the Government for a Season.* New York, NY: Hale, 1867. 226p.
http://metalab.unc.edu/docsouth/lomax/menu.html

Sherrill, Miles O. *A Soldier's Story, Prison Life and Other Incidents in the War of 1861-65.* Author, 1904. 20p.
http://metalab.unc.edu/docsouth/sherrill/menu.html

Military Records—Civil War—South Carolina

Boggs, William Robertson. *Military Reminiscences of General Wm. R. Boggs, C.S.A.* Durham, NC: Seeman Printery, 1913. 115p.
http://metalab.unc.edu/docsouth/boggs/menu.html

Ford, Arthur Peronneau. *Life in the Confederate Army, Being Personal Experience of a Private Soldier in the Confederate Army and Some Experiences and Sketches of Southern Life and Marion Johnstone Ford.* New York, NY: Neale, 1905. 136p.
http://metalab.unc.edu/docsouth/ford/menu.html

Jones, Charles Colcock. *The Siege of Savannah in December, 1864, and the Confederate Operations in Georgia, and the Third Military District of South Carolina during General Sherman's March from Atlanta to the Sea.* Albany, NY: Munsell, 1874. 184p.
http://metalab.unc.edu/docsouth/jonescharles/menu.html

Military Records—Civil War—Tennessee

Copley, John M. *A Sketch of the Battle of Franklin, Tennessee with Reminiscences of Camp Douglas.* Austin, TX: Eugene von Boeckmann, 1893. 206p.
http://metalab.unc.edu/docsouth/copley/menu.html

Morgan, Mrs. Irby. *How It Was, Four Years among the Rebels.* Nashville, TN: Methodist Episcopal Church, South, 1892. 204p.
http://metalab.unc.edu/docsouth/morgan/menu.html

Tennessee Confederate Soldiers' Home Applications Index. Nashville, TN: Tennessee State Library and Archives.
http://www.state.tn.us/sos/statelib/pubsvs/csh_intr.htm

Military Records—Civil War—Texas

Index to Texas Confederate Pension Records, 1899-1975. Austin, TX: Texas State Library and Archives Commission.
http://www.tsl.state.tx.us/lobby/cpi/cpindex.htm

Military Records—Civil War—Virginia

Ashby, Thomas Almond. *The Valley Campaigns, Being the Reminiscences of a Non-Combatant While between the Lines in the Shenandoah Valley during the War of the States.* New York, NY: Neale, 1914. 327p.
http://metalab.unc.edu/docsouth/ashby/menu.html

General Military Hospital for the North Carolina Troops in Petersburg, Virginia. Raleigh, NC: Strother & Marcom Book and Job Printers, 1861. 8p.
http://metalab.unc.edu/docsouth/generalhospital/menu.html

Maury, Dabney Herndon. *Recollections of a Virginian in the Mexican, Indian and Civil Wars.* New York, NY: Scribners, 1894. 279p.
http://metalab.unc.edu/docsouth/maury/menu.html

McKin, Randolph Harrison. *A Soldier's Recollections, Leaves from the Diary of a Young Confederate, with an Oration on the Motives and Aims of the Soldiers of the South.* New York, NY: Longmans, Green & Co., 1910. 362p.
http://metalab.unc.edu/docsouth/mckim/menu.html

Mosby, John Singleton. *The Memoirs of Colonel John S. Mosby.* Boston, MA: Little, Brown & Co., 1917. 414p.
http://metalab.unc.edu/docsouth/mosby/menu.html

Paxton, Elisha Franklin. *Memoir and Memorials, composed of His Letters from Camp and Field While an Officer in the Confederate Army, with an Introductory and Connecting Narrative Collected and Arranged by His Son, John Gallatin Paxton.* New York, NY: Neale, 1907. 114p.
http://metalab.unc.edu/docsouth/paxton/menu.html

Pickett, George Edward. *The Heart of a Soldier as Revealed in the Intimate Letters of General George E. Pickett, C.S.A.* New York, NY: Moyle, 1913. 215p.
http://metalab.unc.edu/docsouth/pickett/menu.html

Robson, John S. *How a One Legged Rebel Lives, Reminiscences of the Civil War. The Story of the Campaigns of Stonewall Jackson, as Told by a High Private in the "Foot Cavalry" from Alleghany Mountain to Chancellorsville, with the Complete Regimental Rosters of both the Great Armies at Gettysburg, by John S. Robson, Late of the 52d Regiment Virginia Infantry.* Durham, NC: Author, 1898. 186p.
http://metalab.unc.edu/docsouth/robson/menu.html

Wood, James H. *The War, Stonewall Jackson, His Campaigns and Battles, the Regiment as I Saw Them.* Cumberland, MD: Eddy Press, 1910. 181p.
http://metalab.unc.edu/docsouth/wood/menu.html

Worsham, John H. *One of Jackson's Foot Cavalry, His Experience and What He Saw During the War 1861-1865, Including a History of "F Company" Richmond, Va., 21st Regiment Virginia Infantry, Second Brigade, Jackson's Division, Second Corps, A.N.Va.* New York, NY: Neale, 1912. 353p.
http://metalab.unc.edu/docsouth/worsham/menu.html

Military Records—Civil War—West Virginia

Ashby, Thomas Almond. *The Valley Campaigns, Being the Reminiscences of a Non-Combatant While between the Lines in the Shenandoah Valley during the War of the States.* New York, NY: Neale, 1914. 327p.
http://metalab.unc.edu/docsouth/ashby/menu.html

Military Records—Civil War—Wisconsin

Bundy, Charles Smith. *Early Days in the Chippewa Valley.* Menominie, WI: Flint Douglas Printing, 1916. 16p.
http://memory.loc.gov/cgi-bin/query/r?ammem/lhbum:@field(DOCID+@lit(16807T000)):@@@REF

Fairchild, Lucius. *California Letters of Lucius Fairchild*. Madison, WI: State Historical Society of Wisconsin, 1931. 212p.
http://memory.loc.gov/cgi-bin/query/r?ammem/calbkbib:@field(AUTHOR+@band(Fairchild,+Lucius, 1831-1896.+))

Military Records—Spanish American War
Livingston, Rebecca. "Sailors, Soldiers and Marines of the Spanish American War, the Legacy of USS Maine." *Prologue*. Vol. 30, No. 1 (Spring 1998).
http://www.nara.gov/publications/prologue/1898gen1.html

Military Records—World War I
Yockelson, Mitchell. "They Answered the Call, Military Service in the United States Army during World War I, 1917-1919." *Prologue*. Vol. 30, No. 3 (Fall 1998).
http://www.nara.gov/publications/prologue/ww1serv.html

Military Records—World War II
B-24 Airscoop. (Serial). Pueblo, CO: Pueblo Historical Aircraft Society. Vol. 6, No. 1 (1st Quarter, 1998- .).
http://www.co.pueblo.co.us/pwam/newsletter_idx.html

Mawdsley, Dean L. *Cruise Books of the United States Navy in World War II, a Bibliography*. Naval History Bibliographies, No. 2. Washington, DC: Naval Historical Center, 1992.
http://www.history.navy.mil/biblio/biblio2/biblio2.htm

Military Records—Korean War
State-level Lists of Casualties from the Korean Conflict (1951-1957). Washington, DC: National Archives, Center for Electronic Records.
http://www.nara.gov/nara/electronic/korvnsta.html

Military Records—Vietnam War
State-level Lists of Casualties from the Vietnam Conflict (1957-). Washington, DC: National Archives, Center for Electronic Records.
http://www.nara.gov/nara/electronic/korvnsta.html

Military Records—Desert Shield/Desert Storm
Borwn, R. A. and Robert J. Schneller. *United States Naval Forces in Desert Shield and Desert Storm, a Select Bibliography*. Washington, DC: Naval Historical Center, 1993.
http://www.history.navy.mil/biblio/biblio5/biblio5.htm

Mongolia
Worden, Robert L. and Andrea Matles Savada. *Mongolia, a Country Study*. Washington, DC: Library of Congress, Federal Research Division, 1989.
http://lcweb2.loc.gov/frd/cs/mntoc.html

Moravians
Henry, James. *Sketches of Moravian Life and Character. Comprising a General View of the History, Life, Character, and Religious and Educational Institutions of the Unitas Fratrum*. Philadelphia, PA: Lippincott, 1859. 318p.
http://moa.umdl.umich.edu/cgi/sgml/moa=idx?notisid=AJK2796

Native Americans

American Indians, a Select Catalog of NARA Microfilm Publications. Washington, DC: National Archives, 1995.

http://www.nara.gov/publications/microfilm/amerindians/indians.html

Brownell, Charles De Wolf. *The Indian Races of North and South America, Comprising an Account on the Principal Aboriginal Races, a Description of Their National Customs, Mythology and Religious Ceremonies, the History of Their Most Powerful Tribes, and of Their Most Celebrated Chiefs and Warriors, Their Intercourse and Wars with the European Settlers and a Great Variety of Anecdote and Description, Illustrative of Personal an National Character.* Hartford, CT: Hurlbut, Scranton & Co., 1864. 766p.

http://moa.umdl.umich.edu/cgi-bin/moa/sgml/moa-idx?notisid=ACP2103

Kane, Paul. *Wanderings of an Artist among the Indians of North America from Canada to Vancouver's Island and Oregon through the Hudson's Bay Company's Territory and Back Again.* London: Longman, Brown, Green, Longmans and Roberts, 1859. 515p.

http://www.canadiana.org/cgi-bin/ECO/mtq?id=985701065f&doc=35931

Painter, Charles Cornelius Coffin. *The Condition of Affairs in Indian Territory and California.* Philadelphia, PA: Indian Rights Association, 1888. 114p.

http://memory.loc.gov/cgi-bin/query/r?ammem/calbkbib:@field(AUTHOR+@band(Painter,+Charles+Cornelius+Coffin.+))

Native Americans—Apache

Cozzens, Samuel Woodworth. *The Marvellous Country, or, Three Years in Arizona and New Mexico. Containing an Authentic History of This Wonderful Country and Its Ancient Civilization . . . Together with a Full and Complete History of the Apache Tribe of Indians.* Boston, MA: Lee & Shepard, 1876. 606p.

http://moa.umdl.umich.edu/cgi-bin/moa/sgml/moa-idx?notisid=AJA3616

Stratton, Royal B. *Captivity of the Oatman Girls, Being an Interesting Narrative of Life among the Apache and Mohave Indians, Containing an Interesting Account of the Massacre of the Oatman Family by the Apache Indians in 1851, the Narrow Escape of Lorenze D. Oatman, the Capture of Olive A. and Mary A. Oatman, as Given by Lorenzo D. and Olive A. Oatman.* New York, NY: Carlton & Porter, 1858. 312p.

http://moa.umdl.umich.edu/cgi-bin/moa/sgml/moa-idx?notisid=ABB5623

Native Americans—California

Painter, Charles Cornelius Coffin. *The Condition of Affairs in Indian Territory and California.* Philadelphia, PA: Indian Rights Association, 1888. 114p.

http://memory.loc.gov/cgi-bin/query/r?ammem/calbkbib:@field(AUTHOR+@band(Painter,+Charles+Cornelius+Coffin.+))

Reid, Hugo. *The Indians of Los Angeles County, Hugh Reid's Letters of 1852.* Los Angeles, CA: Soutwest Museum, 1968. 142p.

http://memory.loc.gov/cgi-bin/query/r?ammem/calbkbib:@field(AUTHOR+@band(Reid,+Hugo,1811?-1853.+))

Wilson, Benjamin Davis. *The Indians of Southern California in 1852.* San Marino, CA: Huntington Library, 1952. 154p.

http://memory.loc.gov/cgi-bin/query/r?ammem/calbkbib:@field(AUTHOR+@band(Wilson,+Benjamin+Davis,1811-1878.+))

Native Americans—Cayuga

Hawley, Charles and John Gilmary Shea. *Early Chapters of Cayuga History, Jesuit Missions in Goi-o-gouen, 1656-1684, also an Account of the Sulpitian Mission among the Emigrant Cayugas about Quinte Bay, in 1668.* Auburn, NY: Author, 1879. 114p.
http://www.canadiana.org/cgi-bin/ECO/mtq?id=04ee01375f&doc=05519

Native Americans—Cherokee

Featherstonhaugh, George William. *A Canoe Voyage up the Minnay Sotor, with an Account of the Lead and Copper Deposits in Wisconsin, of the Gold Region in the Cherokee Country and Sketches of Popular Manners.* London: Bentley, 1847. 2 vols.
http://memory.loc.gov/cgi-bin/query/r?ammem/lhbum:@field(DOCID+@lit(6643aT000)):@@@REF
http://memory.loc.gov/cgi-bin/query/r?ammem/lhbum:@field(DOCID+@lit(6643bT000)):@@@REF

Native Americans—Chippewa

Blackbird, Andrew J. *History of the Ottawa and Chippewa Indians of Michigan, a Grammar of Their Language and Personal and Family History of the Author.* Ypsilanti, MI: Ypsilantian Job Printing House, 1887. 128p.
http://memory.loc.gov/cgi-bin/query/r?ammem/lhbum:@field(DOCID+@lit(16465T000)):@@@REF

Schoolcraft, Henry Rowe. *Narrative Journal of Travels through the Northwestern Regions of the United States, extending from Detroit through the Great Chain of American Lakes to the Sources of the Mississippi River, Performed as a Member of the Expedition under Governor Cass in the Year 1820.* Albany, NY: Hosford, 1821. 423p.
http://memory.loc.gov/cgi-bin/query/r?ammem/lhbum:@field(DOCID+@lit(01453T000)):@@@REF

————. *Narrative of an Expedition through the Upper Mississippi to Itasca Lake, the Actual Source of This River Embracing an Exploratory Trip through the St. Croix and Burntwood (or Broule) Rivers in 1832.* New York, NY: Harper, 1834. 308p.
http://memory.loc.gov/cgi-bin/query/r?ammem/lhbum:@field(DOCID+@lit(08794T000)):@@@REF

——————. *Personal Memoirs of a Residence of Thirty Years with the Indian Tribes on the American Frontiers with Brief Notices of Passing Events, Facts, and Opinions, A.D. 1812 to A.D. 1842.* Philadelphia, PA: Lippincott, 1851. 703p.
http://memory.loc.gov/cgi-bin/query/r?ammem/lhbum:@field(DOCID+@lit(15006T000)):@@@REF

Native Americans—Comanche

DuVal, William Pope. *The Argument of William P. DuVal on Claim of the Citizens of Texas for Compensation for the Property Taken from Them by the Comanche Indians since the Annexation of That State to the United States.* Washington, DC: Goggin & Saunders, 1852. 12p.
http://moa.umdl.umich.edu/cgi-bin/moa/sgml/moa-idx?notisid=AJA281

Eastman, Edwin. *Seven and Nine Years among the Comanches and Apaches, an Autobiograpy.* Jersey City, NJ: Johnson, 1874. 326p.
http://moa.umdl.umich.edu/cgi-bin/moa/sgml/moa-idx?notisid=ABB5201

Native Americans—Cree

Sevareid, Arnold Eric. *Canoeing with the Cree.* New York, NY: Macmillan, 1935. 201p.
http://memory.loc.gov/cgi-bin/query/r?ammem/lhbumbib:@field(SUBJ+@band(Canoes+and+canoeing.+))

Native Americans—Dakota

Belden, George P. *Belden, the White Chief, or Twelve Years among the Wild Indians of the Plains, from the Diaries and Manuscripts of George P. Belden.* New York, NY: Vent, 1870. 522p.
http://moa.umdl.umich.edu/cgi-bin/moa/sgml/moa-idx?notisid=ABJ1451

Native Americans—Minnesota

Schoolcraft, Henry Rowe. *Narrative Journal of Travels through the Northwestern Regions of the United States, Extending from Detroit through the Great Chain of American Lakes to the Sources of the Mississippi River, Performed as a Member of the Expedition under Governor Cass in the Year 1820.* Albany, NY: Hosford, 1821. 423p.
http://memory.loc.gov/cgi-bin/query/r?ammem/lhbum:@field(DOCID+@lit(01453T000)):@@@REF

————. *Narrative of an Expedition through the Upper Mississippi to Itasca Lake, the Actual Source of This River Embracing an Exploratory Trip through the St. Croix and Burntwood (or Broule) Rivers in 1832.* New York, :NY: Harper, 1834. 308p.
http://memory.loc.gov/cgi-bin/query/r?ammem/lhbum:@field(DOCID+@lit(08794T000)):@@@REF

————. *Personal Memoirs of a Residence of Thirty Years with the Indian Tribes on the American Frontiers with Brief Notices of Passing Events, Facts, and Opinions, A.D. 1812 to A.D. 1842.* Philadelphia, PA: Lippincott, 1851. 703p.
http://memory.loc.gov/cgi-bin/query/r?ammem/lhbum:@field(DOCID+@lit(15006T000)):@@@REF

Native Americans—Mohave

Stratton, Royal B. *Captivity of the Oatman Girls, Being an Interesting Narrative of Life among the Apache and Mohave Indians, Containing an Interesting Account of the Massacre of the Oatman Family by the Apache Indians in 1851, the Narrow Escape of Lorenze D. Oatman, the Capture of Olive A. and Mary A. Oatman, as Given by Lorenzo D. and Olive A. Oatman.* New York, NY: Carlton & Porter, 1858. 312p.
http://moa.umdl.umich.edu/cgi-bin/moa/sgml/moa-idx?notisid=ABB5623

Native Americans—Ojibwa

Kohl, Johann Georg. *Kitchi-gami, Wanderings around Lake Superior.* London: Chapman and Hall, 1860. 442p.
http://www.canadiana.org/cgi-bin/ECO/mtq?id=985701065f&doc=36182

Native Americans—Okemos

Mevis, Daniel Stafford. *Pioneer Recollections, Semi-historic Side Lights on the Early Days of Lansing.* Lansing, MI: Robert Smith Printing, 1911. 129p.
http://memory.loc.gov/cgi-bin/query/r?ammem/lhbum:@field(DOCID+@lit(10313T000)):@@@REF

Native Americans—Ottawa

Blackbird, Andrew J. *History of the Ottawa and Chippewa Indians of Michigan, a Grammar of Their Language and Personal and Family History of the Author.* Ypsilanti, MI: Ypsilantian Job Printing House, 1887. 128p.
http://memory.loc.gov/cgi-bin/query/r?ammem/lhbum:@field(DOCID+@lit(16465T000)):@@@REF

Native Americans—Sagamore

Rowlandson, Mary. *Narrative of the Captivity and Restoration of Mrs. Mary Rowlandson.* Unknown. 1862. 316p.
ftp://uiarchive.cso.uiuc.edu/pub/etext/gutenberg/etext97/crmmr10.txt
http://tom.cs.cmu.edu/cgi-bin/book/lookup?num=851

Native Americans—Seneca

Doty, Lockwood Lyon. *A History of Livingston County, New York, from Its Earliest Traditions to Its Part in the War for Our Union, with an Account of the Seneca Nation of Indians and*

Biographical Sketches of Earliest Settlers and Prominent Public Men. Geneseo, NY: Edward E. Doty, 1876. 686p.
http://moa.cit.cornell.edu/dienst/moabrowse.fly/MOA-JOURNALS2:DOTY-0102/5/1:TIFF2GIF:100

Native Americans—Sioux

Belden, George P. *Belden, the White Chief, or Twelve Years among the Wild Indians of the Plains, from the Diaries and Manuscripts of George P. Belden.* New York, NY: Vent, 1870. 522p.
http://moa.umdl.umich.edu/cgi-bin/moa/sgml/moa-idx?notisid=ABJ1451

Carriagan, Wilhelmina Bruce. *Captured by the Indians, Reminiscences of Pioneer Life in Minnesota.* Buffalo Lake, MN: News Print, 1912. 68p.
http://memory.loc.gov/cgi-bin/query/r?ammem/lhbumbib:@field(SUBJ+@band(Carrigan,+Wilhelmina+Buce.+))

Eastman, Mary Henderson. *Dahcotah or Life and Legends of the Sioux around Fort Snelling.* New York, NY: Wiley, 1849. 293p.
http://www.canadiana.org/cgi-bin/ECO/mtq?id=04ee01375f&doc=35037

Heard, Isaac V. D. *History of the Sioux War and Massacres of 1862 and 1863.* New York, NY: Harper, 1864. 360p.
http://moa.umdl.umich.edu/cgi-bin/moa/sgml/moa-idx?notisid=ACK0828

Kelly, Fanny Wiggins. *Narrative of My Captivity among the Sioux Indians, with a Brief Account of General Sully's Indian Expedition in 1864, Bearing upon Events Occuring in My Captivity.* Hartford, CT: Mutual Publishing Co., 1871. 310p.
http://moa.umdl.umich.edu/cgi-bin/moa/sgml/moa-idx?notisid=ABB5283

Native Americans—Wampanoag

Peirce, Ebenezer Weaver. *Indian History, Biography and Genealogy, Pertaining to the Good Sachem Massasoit of the Wampanoag Tribe and His Descendants, with an Appendix.* North Abington, MA: Zerviah Gould Mitchell, 1878. 261p.
http://www.genweb.net/~massasoit/book01.htm

Naturalization Records

Naturalization Records. Washington, DC: National Archives.
http://www.nara.gov/genealogy/natural.html

Passport Records. Washington, DC: National Archives.
http://www.nara.gov/genealogy/passport.html

Smith, Marian L. "Any Woman Who Is Now or May Hereafter be Married, Women and Naturalization, ca. 1802-1940." *Prologue.* Vol. 30, No. 2 (Summer 1998).
http://www.nara.gov/publications/prologue/natural1.html

Netherlands

Davis, Ashable. *History of New Amsterdam or New York as It Was in the Days of the Dutch Governors, together with Papers on Events Connected with the American Revolution and on Philadelphia in the Times of William Penn.* New York, NY: Young, 1854. 240p.
http://moa.cit.cornell.edu/dienst/moabrowse.fly/MOA-JOURNALS2:DAVI-0057/5/1:TIFF2GIF:100

Genealogical Word List. Dutch. Salt Lake City, UT: Family History Library, 1997.
http://familysearch.org/sg/WLDutch.html

McManus, Blanche. *How the Dutch Came to Manhattan*. New York, NY: Herrick, 1897. 82p.
http://moa.cit.cornell.edu/dienst/moabrowse.fly/MOA-JOURNALS2:MCMA-0058/5/1:TIFF2GIF:100

O'Callaghan, E. B. *Laws and Ordinances of New Netherland, 1638-1674*. Albany, NY: Weed, Parsons and Co., 1868. 602p.
http://moa.cit.cornell.edu/dienst/moabrowse.fly/MOA-JOURNALS2:NEWY-0010/3/1:TIFF2GIF:100

Riker, James. *Harlem, Its Origin and Early Annals, Prefaced by Home Scenes in the Fatherlands, or Notices of Its Founders before Emigration also, Sketches of Numerous Families and the Recovered History of the Land Titles*. New York, NY: Author, 1881. 636p.
http://moa.cit.cornell.edu/dienst/moabrowse.fly/MOA-JOURNALS2:RIKE-0161/3/1:TIFF2GIF:100

Rogers, E. P. *A Historical Discourse on the Reformed Protestant Dutch Church of Albany*. New York, NY: Church, 1858. 120p.
http://moa.cit.cornell.edu/dienst/moabrowse.fly/MOA-JOURNALS2:ROGE-0062/5/1:TIFF2GIF:100

Tuckerman, Bayard. *Peter Stuyvesant, Director General for the West India Company in New Netherland*. New York, NY: Dodd, Mead & Co., 1893.
http://moa.cit.cornell.edu/dienst/moabrowse.fly/MOA-JOURNALS2:TUCK-0011/5/1:TIFF2GIF:100

Vandergon, Gertrude Braat. *Our Pioneer Days in Minnesota*. Author, 1949. 138p.
http://memory.loc.gov/cgi-bin/query/r?ammem/lhbum:@field(DOCID+@lit(03667T000)):@@@REF

Van Hoosen, Bertha. *Petticoat Surgeon*. Chicago, IL: Pellegrini & Cudahy, 1947. 324p.
http://memory.loc.gov/cgi-bin/query/r?ammem/lhbumbib:@field(SUBJ+@band(Gynecologists--Illinois--Biography.+))

Newspapers

Atwood, Millard Van Marter. *The Country Newspaper*. Chicago, IL: McClurg, 1923. 158p.
http://chla.mannlib.cornell.edu/cgi-bin/chla/viewer.cgi?docid=title2c.chla.mannlib.cornell/0575atwo&format=1:75-GIF&section=Title+Page

Nicaragua

Genealogical Word List, Spanish. Salt Lake City, UT: Family History Library, 1997.
http://familysearch.org/sg/WLSpanis.html

HLAS Online. Handbook of Latin American Studies. Washington, DC: Library of Congress, 1995. 49 vols.
http://lcweb2.loc.gov/hlas/hlashome.html

Merrill, Tim. *Nicaragua, a Country Study*. Washington, DC: Library of Congress, Federal Research Division, 1993.
http://lcweb2.loc.gov/frd/cs/nitoc.html

Nigeria

Metz, Helen Chapin. *Nigeria, a Country Study*. Washington, DC: Library of Congress, Federal Research Division, 1991.
http://lcweb2.loc.gov/frd/cs/ngtoc.html

Norway

Douglas, Lee V. *A Select Bibliography of Works Norwegian-American Immigration and Local History*. Research Guide No. 6. Washington, DC: Library of Congress, Local History and Genealogy Reading Room, 1998.
http://lcweb.loc.gov/rr/genealogy/bib_guid/norway.html

Genealogical Word List. Norwegian. Salt Lake City, UT: Family History Library, 1997.
http://familysearch.org/sg/WLNorway.html

Grose, Ingebrikt F. *Fifty Memorable Years at St. Olaf, Marking the History of the College on the Hill from Its Founding in 1874 to Its Golden Jubilee Celebration in 1925.* Northfield, MN: Northfield News, 1925. 46p.
http://memory.loc.gov/cgi-bin/query/r?ammem/lhbumbib:@field(SUBJ+@band(St.+Olaf+college,+Northfield,+Minn.+))

Haugen, Nils Pederson. *Pioneer and Political Reminiscences.* Evansville, WI: Antes Press, 1930. 109p.
http://memory.loc.gov/cgi-bin/query/r?ammem/lhbumbib:@field(SUBJ+@band(Frontier+and+pioneer+life--Wisconsin--Pierce+Co.+))

Research Outline. Norway. Salt Lake City, UT: Family History Library, 1992.
http://familysearch.org/sg/Norway.html

Ronning, Nils Nilsen. *Fifty Years in America.* Minneapolis, MN: Friend Publishing Co., 1938. 243p.
http://memory.loc.gov/cgi-bin/query/r?ammem/lhbum:@field(DOCID+@lit(08330T000)):@@@REF

Pakistan

Blood, Peter. *Pakistan, a Country Study.* Washington, DC: Library of Congress, Federal Research Division, 1994.
http://lcweb2.loc.gov/frd/cs/pktoc.html

Panama

Genealogical Word List, Spanish. Salt Lake City, UT: Family History Library, 1997.
http://familysearch.org/sg/WLSpanis.html

HLAS Online. Handbook of Latin American Studies. Washington, DC: Library of Congress, 1995. 49 vols.
http://lcweb2.loc.gov/hlas/hlashome.html

Meditz, Sandra W. and Dennis M. Hanratty. *Panama, a Country Study.* Washington, DC: Library of Congress, Federal Research Division, 1987.
http://lcweb2.loc.gov/frd/cs/patoc.html

Research Outline. Latin America. Salt Lake City, UT: Family History Library, 1992.
http://www.familysearch.com/sg/Latin_America.html

Paraguay

Genealogical Word List, Spanish. Salt Lake City, UT: Family History Library, 1997.
http://familysearch.org/sg/WLSpanis.html

HLAS Online. Handbook of Latin American Studies. Washington, DC: Library of Congress, 1995. 49 vols.
http://lcweb2.loc.gov/hlas/hlashome.html

Hanratty, Dennis M. and Sandra W. Meditz. *Paraguay, a Country Study.* Washington, DC: Library of Congress, Federal Research Division, 1988.
http://lcweb2.loc.gov/frd/cs/pytoc.html

Research Outline. Latin America. Salt Lake City, UT: Family History Library, 1992.
http://www.familysearch.com/sg/Latin_America.html

Passenger Lists

American Society for Colonizing the Free People of Color, of the United States, and the Proceedings of the Society at Their Annual Meeting in the City of Washington. Washington, DC: The Society, 1818. Various.

1ˢᵗ Annual Report. 1818. 49p.
http://memory.loc.gov/cgi-bin/query/r?ammem/murray:@field(FLD001+91898198+):@@@REF

2ⁿᵈ Annual Report. 1819. 153p.
http://memory.loc.gov/cgi-bin/query/r?ammem/murray:@field(FLD001+91898199+):@@@REF

3ʳᵈ Annual Report. 1820. 146p.
http://memory.loc.gov/cgi-bin/query/r?ammem/murray:@field(FLD001+91898201+):@@@REF

4ᵗʰ Annual Report. 1821. 72p.
http://memory.loc.gov/cgi-bin/query/r?ammem/murray:@field(FLD001+91898252+):@@@REF

10ᵗʰ Annual Report. 1827. 101p.
http://memory.loc.gov/cgi-bin/query/r?ammem/murray:@field(FLD001+88880154+):@@@REF

11ᵗʰ Annual Report. 1828. 120p.
http://memory.loc.gov/cgi-bin/query/r?ammem/rbaapc:@field(DOCID+@lit(01800T000)):@@@REF

Hall, Linville John and George Gideon Webster. *Around the Horn in '49, Journal of the Hartford Union Mining and Trading Company. Containing the Name, Residence and Occupation of Each Member, with Incidents of the Voyage*. Wethersfield, CT: L. J. Hall, 1898. 252p.
http://memory.loc.gov/cgi-bin/query/r?ammem/calbkbib:@field(AUTHOR+@band(Hartford+Union+Mining+and+Trading+Company.+))

Immigrant and Passenger Arrivals, Select Catalog of NARA Microfilm Publications. Washington, DC: National Archives.
http://www.nara.gov/publications/microfilm/immigrant/immpass.html

Immigration Records. Washington, DC: National Archives, 1998.
http://www.nara.gov/genealogy/immigration/immigrat.html

A List of the East India Company's Ships, April 18, 1766. London: East India Company, 1766. 1p. (Handwritten List of Slaves on Verso, 1784/85).
http://memory.loc.gov/cgi-bin/query/r?ammem/rbpebib:@field(TITLE+@band(London,+April+18,+1766.+A+list+of+the+East-India+Company's+ships.+[London,+1766].+))

Natale, Valerie. "Angel Island, Guardian of the Western Gate." *Prologue*. Vol. 30, No. 2 (Summer 1998).
http://www.nara.gov/publications/prologue/angel1.html

Partial List of Survivors of the Titanic Who Were Taken Aboard the Carpathia, which Arrived at the Port of New York, NY, April 18, 1912. Washington, DC: National Archives.
http://www.nara.gov/genealogy/immigration/titanic.html

Passport Records. Washington, DC: National Archives.
http://www.nara.gov/genealogy/passport.html

Passport Records

Passport Records. Washington, DC: National Archives.
http://www.nara.gov/genealogy/passport.html

Peru

Genealogical Word List, Spanish. Salt Lake City, UT: Family History Library, 1997.
http://familysearch.org/sg/WLSpanis.html

HLAS Online. Handbook of Latin American Studies. Washington, DC: Library of Congress, 1995. 49 vols.
http://lcweb2.loc.gov/hlas/hlashome.html

Hudson, Rex A. *Paraguay, a Country Study.* Washington, DC: Library of Congress, Federal Research Division, 1992.
http://lcweb2.loc.gov/frd/cs/petoc.html

Research Outline. Latin America. Salt Lake City, UT: Family History Library, 1992.
http://www.familysearch.com/sg/Latin_America.html

Philippines
Dolan, Ronald E. *Philippines, a Country Study.* Washington, DC: Library of Congress, Federal Research Division, 1991.
http://lcweb2.loc.gov/frd/cs/phtoc.html

Research Outline Philippines. Salt Lake City, UT: Family History Library, 1992.
http://familysearch.org/sg/Philippines.html

Polish Americans
Curtis, Glenn E. *Poland, a Country Study.* Washington, DC: Library of Congress, Federal Research Division, 1992.
http://lcweb2.loc.gov/frd/cs/pltoc.html

Genealogical Word List. Polish. Salt Lake City, UT: Family History Library, 1993.
http://familysearch.org/sg/WLPolish.html

Wierzbicki, Felix Paul. *California as It Is and as It May Be, or a Guide to the Gold Region.* San Francisco, CA: Grabhorn Press, 1933. 100p.
http://memory.loc.gov/cgi-bin/query/r?ammem/calbkbib:@field(AUTHOR+@band(Wierzbicki,+Felix+Paul,1815-1860.+))

Portuguese Americans
Genealogical Word List. Portugese. Salt Lake City, UT: Family History Library, 1993.
http://familysearch.org/sg/WLPortug.html

Peters, Charles. *The Autobiography of Charles Peters in 1915 the Oldest Pioneer Living in California, Who Mined in the Days of '49. Also Historical Happenings, Interesting Incidents and Illustrations of the Old Mining Towns in the Good Luck Era, the Placer Mining Days of the '50s.* Sacramento, CA: LaGrave, 1915. 231p.
http://memory.loc.gov/cgi-bin/query/r?ammem/calbkbib:@field(AUTHOR+@band(Peters,+Charles,b.+1825.+))

Solsten, Eric. *Portugal, a Country Study.* Washington, DC: Library of Congress, Federal Research Division, 1993.
http://lcweb2.loc.gov/frd/cs/pttoc.html

Post Office Records
Post Office Records. Washington, DC: National Archives.
http://www.nara.gov/genealogy/postal.html

Presbyterians
Balch, Thomas Bloomer. *My Manse during the War, a Decade of Letters to the Rev. J. (Joshua) Thomas Murray, Editor of the Methodist Protestant.* Baltimore, MD: Sherwood, 1866. 42p.
http://metalab.unc.edu/docsouth/balch/menu.html

Lowrie, John Cameron. *A Manual of Missions, or Sketches of the Foreign Missions of the Presbyterian Church, with Maps Showing the Stations and Statistics of Protestant Missions among Unevangelized Nations.* New York, NY: Randolph, 1854. 86p.
http://moa.umdl.umich.edu/cgi-bin/moa/sgml/moa-idx?notisid=AGA4121

Minutes of the Presbyterian and Congregational Convention, together with the Organization of the Evangelical Association of Presbyterian and Congregational Clergyman of Color in the United States. Brooklyn, NY: The Association.
2nd Annual Convention, 1858, 19p. Philadelphia, PA.
http://memory.loc.gov/cgi-bin/query/r?ammem/murray:@field(FLD001+91898496+):@@@REF

3rd Annual Convention, 1858. 16p. Hartford, Connecticut, CT.
http://memory.loc.gov/cgi-bin/query/r?ammem/murray:@field(FLD001+91898497+):@@@REF

Presbyterian Church in the USA. Executive Committee on Colored Evangelization.
1st *Annual Report*, 1892. 39p.
http://memory.loc.gov/cgi-bin/query/r?ammem/aap:@field(SUBJ+@band(Annual+reports--Alabama--1892.+))

Savage, John A. *Presbyterianism and the Negro.* Franklinton, NC: Franklinton Printing Co., 1895. 8p.
http://memory.loc.gov/cgi-bin/query/r?ammem/aap:@field(SUBJ+@band(Afro-American+Presbyterians--Southern+States.+))

Presbyterians—California
Taylor, William. *California Life Illustrated.* New York, NY: Carlton & Porter, 1858. 348p.
http://memory.loc.gov/cgi-bin/query/r?ammem/calbk:@field(DOCID+@lit(C063T00)):@@@REF

————. *Seven Year's Street Preaching in San Francisco, California, Embracing Incidents, Triumphant Death Scenes, etc.* New York, NY: Author, 1857. 394p.
http://memory.loc.gov/cgi-bin/query/r?ammem/calbk:@field(DOCID+@lit(C109T00)):@@@REF

————. 1859 Edition. 418p.
http://moa.umdl.umich.edu/cgi-bin/moa/sgml/moa-idx?notisid=AJG9120

Willey, Samuel Hopkins. *Thirty Years in California, a Contribution to the History of the State from 1849 to 1879.* San Francisco, CA: Bancroft, 1879. 76p.
http://memory.loc.gov/cgi-bin/query/r?ammem/calbkbib:@field(AUTHOR+@band(Willey,+Samuel+Hopkins.+))

Williams, Albert. *A Pioneer Pastorate and Times Embodying Contemporary Local Transactions and Events by the Rev. Albert Williams, Founder and First Pastor of the First Presbyterian Church, San Francisco.* San Francisco, CA: Wallace & Hassett Printers, 1879. 240p.
http://memory.loc.gov/cgi-bin/query/r?ammem/calbkbib:@field(AUTHOR+@band(Williams,+Albert,1809-1893.+))

Woods, James. *Recollections of Pioneer Work in California.* San Francisco, CA: Winterburn, 1878. 260p.
http://memory.loc.gov/cgi-bin/query/r?ammem/calbkbib:@field(AUTHOR+@band(Woods,+James,1814+or+5-1886.+))

Presbyterians—Michigan
Duffield, Samuel Willoughby. *A Farewell Sermon Delivered in the First Presbyterian Church, Ann Arbor, Michigan.* Ann Arbor, MI: Courier Steam Printing, 1874. 20p.
http://moa.umdl.umich.edu/cgi-bin/moa/sgml/moa-idx?notisid=AAM7378

In Memoriam William S. Huggins, Three Sermons to Young Men, Preached by Rev. William S. Huggins of Kalamazoo, Michigan, and a Funeral Discourse by Rev. Samuel Haskell, with an Account of the Funeral and Memorial Meeting. Philadelphia, PA: Presbyterian Publication Committee, 1862. 150p.
http://moa.umdl.umich.edu/cgi-bin/moa/sgml/moa-idx?notisid=AJK3161

Presbyterians—Minnesota
Neill, Edward D. *A Hand Book for the Presbyterian Church in Minnesota, Designed to Promote Order in and Love for the Sanctuary.* Philadelphia, PA: Ashmead, 1856. 72p.
http://moa.umdl.umich.edu/cgi-bin/moa/sgml/moa-idx?notisid=AJK3012

Presbyterians—Mississippi
Aughey, John Hill. *Tupelo.* Chicago, IL: Rhodes & McLure Publishing, 1905. Unpgd.
http://metalab.unc.edu/docsouth/aughey/menu.html

Presbyterians—New York
Clarke, Walter. *Half Century Discourse, the First Church in Buffalo.* Buffalo, NY: Theodore Butler, 1862. 92p.
http://moa.cit.cornell.edu/dienst/moabrowse.fly/MOA-JOURNALS2:CLAR-0067/3/1:TIFF2GIF:100

Quakers
George, Alice Mendenhall. *The Story of My Childhood, Written for My Children.* Whittier, CA: Smith, 1923. 87p.
http://memory.loc.gov/cgi-bin/query/r?ammem/lhbum:@field(DOCID+@lit(04681T000)):@@@REF

Haviland, Laura Smith. *A Woman's Life-work, Labors and Experiences of Laura S. Haviland.* Cincinnati, OH: Walden & Stowe, 1882. 531p.
http://memory.loc.gov/cgi-bin/query/r?ammem/lhbumbib:@field(SUBJ+@band(Freedmen.+))

Hoss, Elijah Embree. *Elihu Embree, Abolitionist.* Nashville, TN: University Press Co., 1897. 28p.
http://memory.loc.gov/cgi-bin/query/r?ammem/aap:@field(SUBJ+@band(Embree,+Elihu,--1782-1820.+))

Lurting, Thomas. *The Fighting Sailor Turn'd Peaceable Christian, Manifested in the Convincement and Conversion of Thomas Lurting with a Short Relation of Many Great Dangers and Wonderful Deliverances He Met Withal.* London: Sowle, 1711.
http://www.voicenet.com/~kuenning/qhp/lurting.html

Quakers—Canada
Rollmann, Hans. *Anglicans, Puritans and Quakers in Sixteenth and Seventeenth Century Newfoundland.* Unknown.
http://www.mun.ca/rels/ang/texts/ang1.html

Quakers—Massachusetts
Adams, Brooks. *The Emancipation of Massachusetts.* Boston, MA: Houghton Mifflin, 1887. 388p.
http://moa.cit.cornell.edu/dienst/moabrowse.fly/MOA-JOURNALS2:ADAM-0033/3/1:TIFF2GIF:100?,,

Hallowell, Richard Price. *The Quaker Invasion of Massachusetts.* 2nd ed. Boston, MA: Houghton Mifflin, 1883. 227p.
http://moa.cit.cornell.edu/dienst/moabrowse.fly/MOA-JOURNALS2:HALL-0037/3/1:TIFF2GIF:100

Rogers, Horatio, *Mary Dyer of Rhode Island, the Quaker Martyr That Was Hanged on Boston Common, June 1, 1660.* Providence, RI: Preston and Rounds, 1896. 115p.
http://moa.cit.cornell.edu/dienst/moabrowse.fly/MOA-JOURNALS2:ROGE-0035/5/1:TIFF2GIF:100

Quakers—New Jersey

Woolman, John. *A Journal of the Life, Gospel Labours and Christian Experiences of That Faithful Minister of Jesus Christ, John Woolman, Late of Mount Holly in the Province of New Jersey.* Philadelphia, PA: Crukshank, 1774. 436p.
http://darkwing.uoregon.edu/~rbear/woolman.html

Quakers—Pennsylvania

Hoag, Joseph. *The Transformation of Joseph Hoag.* Philadelphia, PA: Tract Association of Friends. N.d., n.p.
http://people.delphi.com/pdsippel/hoag.htm

Wetherill, Charles. *History of the Religious Society of Friends Called by Some the Free Quakers in the City of Philadelphia.* Philadelphia, PA: Society of Friends, 1894. 10p.
http://people.delphi.com/pdsippel/fq-a1.htm

Quakers—Rhode Island

Rogers, Horatio. *Mary Dyer of Rhode Island, the Quaker Martyr That Was Hanged on Boston Common, June 1, 1660.* Providence, RI: Preston and Rounds, 1896. 115p.
http://moa.cit.cornell.edu/dienst/moabrowse.fly/MOA-JOURNALS2:ROGE-0035/5/1:TIFF2GIF:100

Quakers—Virginia

Janney, Samuel M. *Memoirs of Samuel M. Janney, Late of Lincoln, Loudon County, Virginia. A Minister in the Religious Society of Friends.* Philadelphia, PA: Friends' Book Association, 1881. 309p.
http://metalab.unc.edu/docsouth/janney/menu.html

Reformed Church

Rogers, E. P. *A Historical Discourse on the Reformed Protestant Dutch Church of Albany.* New York, NY: The Church, 1858. 120p.
http://moa.cit.cornell.edu/dienst/moabrowse.fly/MOA-JOURNALS2:ROGE-0062/5/1:TIFF2GIF:100

Roman Catholics

Bunkley, Josephine M. *The Testimony of an Escaped Novice from the Sisterhood of St. Joseph, Emmittsburg, Maryland, the Mother House of the Sisters of Charity in the United States.* New York, NY: Harper, 1855. 348p.
http://moa.umdl.umich.edu/cgi-bin/moa/sgml/moa-idx?notisid=AGU6805

Catholic Encyclopedia. 1917.
http://www.knight.org/advent/cathen/cathen.htm

Guyon, Jean Marie Bouvier de la Motte. *Autobiography of Madame Guyon.*
http://ccel.wheaton.edu/guyon/auto/autobi.htm

Mazzuchelli, Samuel Charles. *Memoirs, Historical and Edifying of a Missionary Apostolic of the Order of Saint Dominic among Various Indian Tribes and among the Catholics and Protestants in the United States of America.* Chicago, IL: Hall Printing Co., 1915. 375p.
http://memory.loc.gov/cgi-bin/query/r?ammem/lhbumbib:@field(SUBJ+@band(Catholic+church+in+the+United+States.+))

Roman Catholics—Hawaii

Ellis, William. *The American Mission in the Sandwich Islands, a Vindication and an Appeal in Relation to the Proceedings of the Reformed Catholic Mission at Honolulu.* Honolulu, HI: Whitney, 1866. 78p.
http://moa.umdl.umich.edu/cgi-bin/moa/sgml/moa-idx?notisid=AGA4516

Roman Catholics—Maryland

Catalogue of Pupils of Saint Frances' Academy for Colored Girls, under the Direction of the Sisters of Providence, for the Academic Year 1867-8, Incorporated 1867. Baltimore, MD: John Murphy & Co., 1868. 24p.
http://memory.loc.gov/cgi-bin/query/r?ammem/murray:@field(FLD001+91898522+):@@@REF

Romania

Bachman, Ronald D. *Portugal, a Country Study.* Washington, DC: Library of Congress, Federal Research Division, 1989.
http://lcweb2.loc.gov/frd/cs/rotoc.html

Saudi Arabia

Bachman, Ronald D. *Saudi Arabia, a Country Study.* Washington, DC: Library of Congress, Federal Research Division, 1992.
http://lcweb2.loc.gov/frd/cs/satoc.html

Scottish Americans

Muir, John. *The Story of My Boyhood and Youth.* Boston, MA: Houghton Mifflin, 1913. 294p.
http://memory.loc.gov/cgi-bin/query/r?ammem/lhbum:@field(DOCID+@lit(05573T000)):@@@REF

Reid, Hugo. *The Indians of Los Angeles County, Hugh Reid's Letters of 1852.* Los Angeles, CA: Soutwest Museum, 1968. 142p.
http://memory.loc.gov/cgi-bin/query/r?ammem/calbkbib:@field(AUTHOR+@band(Reid,+Hugo,1811?-1853.+))

Research Outline. Old Parochial Registers (OPR) Index for Scotland. Salt Lake City, UT: Family History Library, 1994.
http://familysearch.org/sg/OlParReg.html

Research Outline. Scotland. Salt Lake City, UT: Family History Library, 1997.
http://familysearch.org/sg/Scotland.html

Scottish Church Records. Salt Lake City, UT: Family History Library, 1995.
http://familysearch.org/sg/Scottish.html

Smith, Harry. *The Autobiography of Harry Smith.* 1901. 2 vols.
http://homepages.ihug.co.nz/~awoodley/harry/harryintro.html

Serials

American Heritage. Vol. , No. , August 1997-.
http://www.americanheritage.com/

American Historical Review (1895-) ISSN: 0002-8762.
http://www.indiana.edu/~ahr/

American Library Association. *American Libraries.* ISSN: 0002-9769.
http://www.ala.org/alonline/index.html

American Library Association. *RUSA Update*. ISSN: 1095-2624.
http://www.ala.org/rusa/rusq/

American Missionary (1878-1901).
http://moa.cit.cornell.edu/MOA/MOA-JOURNALS2/AMIS.html

American Quarterly. Index, 1975-1995.
http://www.georgetown.edu/crossroads/aq/

American Whig Review (1845-1852).
http://moa.cit.cornell.edu/MOA/MOA-JOURNALS2/AMWH.html

Atlantic Monthly (1857-1901).
http://moa.cit.cornell.edu/MOA/MOA-JOURNALS2/ATLA.html

B-24 Airscoop. Pueblo, CO: Pueblo Historical Aircraft Society. Vol. 6, No. 1.
(1st Quarter, 1998-).
http://www.co.pueblo.co.us/pwam/newsletter_idx.html

Baptist Magazine. Washington, DC: National Baptist Magazine Publishing Co., 1897.
http://memory.loc.gov/cgi-bin/query/r?ammem/murray:@field(FLD001+91898270+):@@@REF

Bay State Monthly (1884-1886).
http://moa.cit.cornell.edu/MOA/MOA-JOURNALS2/BAY.html

Between the Lines. New York, NY: Jewish Theological Seminary of America. Vol. 8, Spring
1995-.
http://www.jtsa.edu/library/news/

Catalog of U.S. Government Publications. Washington, DC: Government Printing Office.
http://www.access.gpo.gov/su_docs/dpos/adpos400.html

Century (1881-1899).
http://moa.cit.cornell.edu/MOA/MOA-JOURNALS2/CENT.html

Collections of the Minnesota Historical Society. St. Paul, MN: Society, varies.
Vol. 1   http://memory.loc.gov/cgi-bin/query/r?ammem/lhbum:@field(DOCID+@lit(0866aT000)):@@@REF
Vol. 5   http://memory.loc.gov/cgi-bin/query/r?ammem/lhbum:@field(DOCID+@lit(0866bT000)):@@@REF
Vol. 7   http://memory.loc.gov/cgi-bin/query/r?ammem/lhbum:@field(DOCID+@lit(0866cT000)):@@@REF
Vol. 9   http://memory.loc.gov/cgi-bin/query/r?ammem/lhbum:@field(DOCID+@lit(0866dT000)):@@@REF
Vol. 10 http://memory.loc.gov/cgi-bin/query/r?ammem/lhbum:@field(DOCID+@lit(0866eT000)):@@@REF
         http://memory.loc.gov/cgi-bin/query/r?ammem/lhbum:@field(DOCID+@lit(0866fT000)):@@@REF
Vol. 12 http://memory.loc.gov/cgi-bin/query/r?ammem/lhbum:@field(DOCID+@lit(0866gT000)):@@@REF
Vol. 15 http://memory.loc.gov/cgi-bin/query/r?ammem/lhbum:@field(DOCID+@lit(0866hT000)):@@@REF

State Historical Society of Wisconsin. *Collections of the State Historical Society of Wisconsin*.
Madison, WI: The Society, various.
Vol. 11 http://memory.loc.gov/cgi-bin/query/r?ammem/lhbum:@field(DOCID+@lit(7689aT000)):@@@REF
Vol. 12 http://memory.loc.gov/cgi-bin/query/r?ammem/lhbum:@field(DOCID+@lit(7689bT000)):@@@REF
Vol. 14 http://memory.loc.gov/cgi-bin/query/r?ammem/lhbum:@field(DOCID+@lit(7689cT000)):@@@REF
Vol. 15 http://memory.loc.gov/cgi-bin/query/r?ammem/lhbum:@field(DOCID+@lit(7689dT000)):@@@REF
Vol. 16 http://memory.loc.gov/cgi-bin/query/r?ammem/lhbum:@field(DOCID+@lit(7689eT000)):@@@REF
Vol. 17 http://memory.loc.gov/cgi-bin/query/r?ammem/lhbum:@field(DOCID+@lit(7689fT000)):@@@REF
Vol. 18 http://memory.loc.gov/cgi-bin/query/r?ammem/lhbum:@field(DOCID+@lit(7689gT000)):@@@REF
Vol. 19 http://memory.loc.gov/cgi-bin/query/r?ammem/lhbum:@field(DOCID+@lit(7689hT000)):@@@REF
Vol. 20 http://memory.loc.gov/cgi-bin/query/r?ammem/lhbum:@field(DOCID+@lit(7689iT000)):@@@REF
Vol. 25 http://memory.loc.gov/cgi-bin/query/r?ammem/lhbum:@field(DOCID+@lit(7689jT000)):@@@REF

Computers in Libraries. Medford, NJ: *Information Today*. Vol. 18, No. 7 (July/August 1998-).
http://www.infotoday.com/cilmag/ciltop.htm

The Continental Monthly (1862-1864).
http://moa.cit.cornell.edu/MOA/MOA-JOURNALS2/CONT.html

D-lib Magazine, the Magazine of Digital Library Research. ISSN: 1082-9873. Vol. 1, No. 1 (July 1995-).
http://www.dlib.org/

Eastman's Online Genealogy Newsletter.
http://www.ancestry.com/columns/eastman/eastnew.htm

Florida Libraries. Vol. 40, No. 1, (January-February 1997-).
http://www.flalib.org/library/fla/florlibs/florlibs.htm

Galaxy (May, 1866-January, 1878).
http://moa.cit.cornell.edu/MOA/MOA-JOURNALS2/GALA.html

Harpers New Monthly Magazine (December, 1889-November, 1896).
http://moa.cit.cornell.edu/MOA/MOA-JOURNALS2/HARP.html

Historical Collections. Lansing, MI: The Michigan State Historical Society, various.
Vol. 8 http://memory.loc.gov/cgi-bin/query/r?ammem/lhbum:@field(DOCID+@lit(5298aT000)):@@@REF
Vol. 9 http://memory.loc.gov/cgi-bin/query/r?ammem/lhbum:@field(DOCID+@lit(5298bT000)):@@@REF
Vol. 10 http://memory.loc.gov/cgi-bin/query/r?ammem/lhbum:@field(DOCID+@lit(5298cT000)):@@@REF
Vol. 11 http://memory.loc.gov/cgi-bin/query/r?ammem/lhbum:@field(DOCID+@lit(5298dT000)):@@@REF
Vol. 12 http://memory.loc.gov/cgi-bin/query/r?ammem/lhbum:@field(DOCID+@lit(5298eT000)):@@@REF
Vol. 15 http://memory.loc.gov/cgi-bin/query/r?ammem/lhbum:@field(DOCID+@lit(5298fT000)):@@@REF
Vol. 16 http://memory.loc.gov/cgi-bin/query/r?ammem/lhbum:@field(DOCID+@lit(5298gT000)):@@@REF
Vol. 19 http://memory.loc.gov/cgi-bin/query/r?ammem/lhbum:@field(DOCID+@lit(5298hT000)):@@@REF
Vol. 20 http://memory.loc.gov/cgi-bin/query/r?ammem/lhbum:@field(DOCID+@lit(5298iT000)):@@@REF

Historical Methods, a Journal of Quantitative and Interdisciplinary History. Table of Contents, Vol. 12, No. 1, Winter 1979-.
http://www.ucr.edu/methods/

Information Today. Medford, NJ: *Information Today.* Vol. 15, No. 3, March 1998-.
http://www.infotoday.com/it/itnew.htm

International Monthly Magazine (July, 1850-April, 1852).
http://moa.cit.cornell.edu/MOA/MOA-JOURNALS2/INTR.html

Journal of Electronic Publishing. Vol. 1, No. 1, January 1995-.
http://www.press.umich.edu/jep/

Journal of Online Genealogy.
http://www.onlinegenealogy.com

Journal of Southern History. Table of Contents, Vol. LXI, No. 1, February 1995-.
http://www.ruf.rice.edu/~jsh/index.html

Library Journal
http://www.bookwire.com/ljdigital/

Library of Congress Information Bulletin. Vol. 52, No. 1, January 11, 1993-.
http://lcweb.loc.gov/loc/lcib/

Link-Up, The Newsmagazine for Users of Online Services, CD-ROM, and the Internet. Medford, NJ: *Information Today.* Vol.15, No. 2 (March/April 1998-).
http://www.infotoday.com/lu/lunew.htm

Littell's Living Age (1844-1900).
http://moa.cit.cornell.edu/MOA/MOA-JOURNALS2/LIVN.html

Manufacturer and Builder (January, 1869-December, 1894).
http://moa.cit.cornell.edu/MOA/MOA-JOURNALS2/MANU.html

NAGARA Clearinghouse (Vol. 13, 1997-).
http://www.nagara.org/clearinghouse/clearinghousehome.html

Narragansett Historical Register, a Magazine Devoted to the Antiquities, Genealogy and Historical Matter Illustrating the History of the State of Rhode Island and Providence Plantation. Providence, RI: Narragansett Historical Pubishing Co., various.
Vol. 6, 1888.
http://members.xoom.com/daveblql/

National Baptist Magazine. Nashville, TN: National Baptist Publishing Board, 1899.
http://memory.loc.gov/cgi-bin/query/r?ammem/murray:@field(FLD001+91898268+):@@@REF

New England Magazine (1831-1835).
http://moa.cit.cornell.edu/MOA/MOA-JOURNALS2/NWEN.html

New England Magazine (1887-1900).
http://moa.cit.cornell.edu/MOA/MOA-JOURNALS2/NEWE.html

New Englander (1843-1892).
http://moa.cit.cornell.edu/MOA/MOA-JOURNALS2/NWNG.html

North American Review (1815-1900).
http://moa.cit.cornell.edu/MOA/MOA-JOURNALS2/NORA.html

The Official Records of the Union and Confederate Navies (1861-1865).
http://moa.cit.cornell.edu/MOA/MOA-JOURNALS2/OFRE.html

The Old Guard (1863-1865).
http://moa.cit.cornell.edu/MOA/MOA-JOURNALS2/OLDG.html

Prologue, the Journal of the National Archives. ISSN: 0033-1031.
http://www.nara.gov/publications/prologue/prologue.html

Punchinello (July, 1870-December, 1870).
http://moa.cit.cornell.edu/MOA/MOA-JOURNALS2/PUNC.html

Putnam's Monthly (1853-1870).
http://moa.cit.cornell.edu/MOA/MOA-JOURNALS2/PUTN.html

Scientific American (September, 1846-September, 1850).
http://moa.cit.cornell.edu/MOA/MOA-JOURNALS2/SCIA.html

Scribner's Magazine (January, 1887-June, 1896).
http://moa.cit.cornell.edu/MOA/MOA-JOURNALS2/SCRI.html

Scribner's Monthly (November, 1870-October, 1881).
http://moa.cit.cornell.edu/MOA/MOA-JOURNALS2/SCMO.html

Searcher: The Magazine for Database Professionals.
http://www.infotoday.com/searcher/default.htm

Today's Librarian
http://www.todayslibrarian.com

The United States Magazine, and Democratic Review (October, 1837-October, 1859).
http://moa.cit.cornell.edu/MOA/MOA-JOURNALS2/USDE.html

Virginia Magazine of History and Biography. Richmond, VA: Virginia Historical Society. Quarterly. Table of Conents, Vol. 140, No. 1, Winter 1996-.
http://www.vahistorical.org/publicat/vmhb.htm

The War of the Rebellion (1880-1901).
http://moa.cit.cornell.edu/MOA/MOA-JOURNALS2/WARO.html

Western Historical Quarterly. Table of Contents for Current Issue Only.
http://www.usu.edu/~history/whq/index.html

Singapore
Lepoer, Barbara Leitch. *Singapore, a Country Study.* Washington, DC: Library of Congress, Federal Research Division, 1989.
http://lcweb2.loc.gov/frd/cs/sgtoc.html

Social Security Records
Social Security Records. Washington, DC: National Archives.
http://www.nara.gov/genealogy/socsec.html

Somalia
Metz, Helen Chapin. *Somolia, a Country Study.* Washington, DC: Library of Congress, Federal Research Division, 1992.
http://lcweb2.loc.gov/frd/cs/sotoc.html

Spain
Genealogical Word List, Spanish. Salt Lake City, UT: Family History Library, 1997.
http://familysearch.org/sg/WLSpanis.html

HLAS Online. Handbook of Latin American Studies. Washington, DC: Library of Congress, 1995. 49 vols.
http://lcweb2.loc.gov/hlas/hlashome.html

Research Outline. Latin America. Salt Lake City, UT: Family History Library, 1992.
http://www.familysearch.com/sg/Latin_America.html

Solsten, Eric and Sandra W. Meditz. *Spain, a Country Study.* Washington, DC: Library of Congress, Federal Research Division, 1988.
http://lcweb2.loc.gov/frd/cs/estoc.html

Sri Lanka
Ross, Russell R. and Andrea Matles Savada. *Sri Lanka, a Country Study.* Washington, DC: Library of Congress, Federal Research Division, 1988.
http://lcweb2.loc.gov/frd/cs/lktoc.html

Sudan
Metz, Helen Chapin. *Sri Lanka, a Country Study.* Washington, DC: Library of Congress, Federal Research Division, 1991.
http://lcweb2.loc.gov/frd/cs/sdtoc.html

Switzerland

Lienhard, Heinrich. *A Pioneer at Sutter's Fort, 1846-1850, the Adventures of Heinrich Lienhard, Translated, Edited and Annotated by Marguerite Eyer Wilbur from the Original German Script.* Los Angeles, CA: Calafia Society, 1941. 291p.
http://memory.loc.gov/cgi-bin/query/r?ammem/calbkbib:@field(AUTHOR+@band(Lienhard,+Heinrich,1822-1903.+))

Meyer, Carl. *Bound for Sacramento, Travel Pictures of a Returned Wanderer, Translated from the German by Ruth Frey Axe.* Claremont, CA: Saunders Studio Press, 1938. 282p.
http://memory.loc.gov/cgi-bin/query/r?ammem/calbkbib:@field(AUTHOR+@band(Meyer,+Carl,of+Basel.+))

Sutter, John Augustus. *The Diary of Johann August Sutter.* San Francisco, CA: Grabhorn Press, 1932. 56p.
http://memory.loc.gov/cgi-bin/query/r?ammem/calbkbib:@field(AUTHOR+@band(Sutter,+John+Augustus,1803-1880.+))

Syria

Collelo, Thomas. *Sri Lanka, a Country Study.* Washington, DC: Library of Congress, Federal Research Division, 1987.
http://lcweb2.loc.gov/frd/cs/sytoc.html

Thailand

LePoer, Barbara Leitch. *Sri Lanka, a Country Study.* Washington, DC: Library of Congress, Federal Research Division, 1987.
http://lcweb2.loc.gov/frd/cs/thtoc.html

Uganda

Byrnes, Rita M. *Uganda, a Country Study.* Washington, DC: Library of Congress, Federal Research Division, 1990.
http://lcweb2.loc.gov/frd/cs/ugtoc.html

United Church of Christ—California

Pond, William Chauncey. *Gospel Pioneering, Reminiscences of Early Congregationalism in California, 1833-1920.* Oberlin, OH: New Printing Co., 1921. 191p.
http://memory.loc.gov/cgi-bin/query/r?ammem/calbkbib:@field(AUTHOR+@band(Pond,+William+Chauncey,1830-1925.+))

Todd, John. *The Sunset Land or the Great Pacific Slope.* Boston, MA: Lee & Shepard, 1870. 322p.
http://memory.loc.gov/cgi-bin/query/r?ammem/calbkbib:@field(AUTHOR+@band(Todd,+John,1800-1873.+))

United Church of Christ—Hawaii

Damon, Samuel Chenery. *Puritan Missions in the Pacific, a Discourse Delivered at Honolulu, on the Anniversary of the Hawaiian Evangelical Association, Sabbath Evening, June 17, 1866.* New Haven, CT: Hunnewell, 1868. 52p.
http://moa.umdl.umich.edu/cgi-bin/moa/sgml/moa-idx?notisid=AJG8991

United Church of Christ—Massachusetts

Adams, Brooks. *The Emancipation of Massachusetts.* Boston, MA: Houghton Mifflin, 1887. 388p.
http://moa.cit.cornell.edu/dienst/moabrowse.fly/MOA-JOURNALS2:ADAM-0033/3/1:TIFF2GIF:100?,,

Bacon, Leonard. *The Genesis of the New England Churches*. New York, NY: Harper, 1874. 485p.
http://moa.cit.cornell.edu/dienst/moabrowse.fly/MOA-JOURNALS2:BACO-0030/5/1:TIFF2GIF:100

Emery, Samuel Hopkins. *The History of the Church of North Middleborough, Massachusetts in Six Discourses*. Middleborough, MA: Harlow & Thatcher, Steam Book and Job Printers, 1876. 106p.
http://genweb.net/~blackwell/ma/middleborochurch/

Goodwin, John Abbot. *The Pilgrim Republic, an Historical Review of the Colony of New Plymouth, with Sketches of the Rise of Other New England Settlements, the History of Congregationalism and the Creeds of the Period*. Boston, MA: Ticknor, 1888. 662p.
http://moa.cit.cornell.edu/dienst/moabrowse.fly/MOA-JOURNALS2:GOOD-0032/7/1:TIFF2GIF:100

Minutes of the Presbyterian and Congregational Convention, together with the Organization of the Evangelical Association of Presbyterian and Congregational Clergyman of Color in the United States. Brooklyn, NY: The Association.
2nd Annual Convention, 1858, 19p. Philadelphia, PA
http://memory.loc.gov/cgi-bin/query/r?ammem/murray:@field(FLD001+91898496+):@@@REF

3rd Annual Convention, 1858. 16p. Hartford, Connecticut, CT.
http://memory.loc.gov/cgi-bin/query/r?ammem/murray:@field(FLD001+91898497+):@@@REF

United Church of Christ—New York
A Narrative of Some Recent Occurrences in the Church of the Puritans, New York with Documents Relating Thereto. New York, NY: Dorr, 1857. 50p.
http://moa.umdl.umich.edu/cgi-bin/moa/sgml/moa-idx?notisid=AJK2271

Proceedings of a Council of Congregational Churches, Relative to the Privileges of Members of the Church of the Puritans, New York. New York, NY: Jennkins, 1859. 92p.
http://moa.umdl.umich.edu/cgi-bin/moa/sgml/moa-idx?notisid=AJK2272

Proceedings of a Council of Congregational Churches, Relative to the Church of the Puritans, New York, and to the Privileges of Members Thereof, May, 1861. New York, NY: Gray, 1861. 132p.
http://moa.umdl.umich.edu/cgi-bin/moa/sgml/moa-idx?notisid=AJK2273

Uruguay
Hudson, Rex A. and Sandra W. Meditz. *Uruguay, a Country Study*. Washington, DC: Library of Congress, Federal Research Division, 1990.
http://lcweb2.loc.gov/frd/cs/uytoc.html

Research Outline. Latin America. Salt Lake City, UT: Family History Library, 1992.
http://www.familysearch.com/sg/Latin_America.html

Venezuela
Haggerty, Richard A. *Venezuela, a Country Study*. Washington, DC: Library of Congress, Federal Research Division, 1990.
http://lcweb2.loc.gov/frd/cs/vetoc.html

Research Outline. Latin America. Salt Lake City, UT: Family History Library, 1992.
http://www.familysearch.com/sg/Latin_America.html

Vietnam

Cima, Ronald J. *Viet Nam, a Country Study.* Washington, DC: Library of Congress, Federal
Research Division, 1987.
http://lcweb2.loc.gov/frd/cs/vntoc.html

Women

Farnham, Eliza Woodson Burhans. *California, Indoors and Out, or How We Farm, Mine and
Live Generally in the Golden State.* New York, NY: Dix, Edwards, 1856. 508p.
http://memory.loc.gov/cgi-bin/query/r?ammem/calbkbib:@field(AUTHOR+@band(Farnham,+Eliza+
Woodson+Burhans,1815-1864.+))

Fowler, William Worthington. *Woman on the American Frontier, a Valuable and Authentic History of the Heroism, Adventures, Privations, Captivities, Trials and Noble Lives and Deaths
of the Pioneer Mothers of the Republic.* Hartford, CT: Scranton, 1877. 562p.
http://moa.umdl.umich.edu/cgi-bin/moa/sgml/moa-idx?notisid=ABK8507

Lee, Jarena. *Religious Life and Experience and Journal of Mrs. Jarena Lee, Giving an Account
of Her Call to Preach the Gospel.* Philadelphia, PA: Author, 1849. 97p.
http://digilib.nypl.org/dynaweb/digs/wwm9716/

McCray, S. J. *Life of Mary F. McCray, Born and Raised a Slave in the State of Kentucky, By Her
Husband and Son.* Lima, OH: Author, 1898. 115p.
http://metalab.unc.edu/docsouth/mccray/menu.html

Mossell, N. F., Mrs. *The Work of the Afro-American Woman.* Philadelphia, PA: Ferguson, 1928.
178p.
http://digilib.nypl.org/dynaweb/digs/wwm9729/

Ripley, Eliza Moore Chinn McHatton. *From Flag to Flag, a Woman's Adventures and Experiences in the South during the War, in Mexico and in Cuba.* New York, NY: Appleton, 1889.
296p.
http://metalab.unc.edu/docsouth/ripleyflag/menu.html

Shaw, Anna Howard. *The Story of a Pioneer.* New York, NY: Harper, 1915. 337p.
http://memory.loc.gov/cgi-bin/query/r?ammem/lhbumbib:@field(SUBJ+@band(Woman--Suffrage--United
+States.+))

Smtih, Marian L. "Any Woman Who Is Now or May Hereafter be Married, Women and Naturalization, ca. 1802-1940." *Prologue.* Vol. 30, No. 2 (Summer 1998).
http://www.nara.gov/publications/prologue/natural1.html

Van Hoosen, Bertha. *Petticoat Surgeon.* Chicago, IL: Pellegrini & Cudahy, 1947. 324p.
http://memory.loc.gov/cgi-bin/query/r?ammem/lhbumbib:@field(SUBJ+@band(Gynecologists--Illinois--
Biography.+))

Veney, Bethany. The Narrative of Bethany Veney, a Slave Woman. Worcester, MA: Author,
1889. 47p.
http://metalab.unc.edu/docsouth/veney/menu.html
http://digilib.nypl.org/dynaweb/digs/wwm97269/

Worthington, C. J. *The Woman in Battle, a Narrative of the Exploits, Adventures, and Travels of
Madame Loreta Janeta Velazquez, otherwise Known as Lieutenant Harry T. Buford, Confederate States Army in which is Given Full Descriptions of the Numerous Battles in Which
She Participated as a Confederate Officer.* Richmond, VA: Dustin, Gilman, 1876. 606p.
http://metalab.unc.edu/docsouth/velazquez/menu.html

Yugoslavia

Curtis, Glenn E. *Yugoslavia, a Country Study.* Washington, DC: Library of Congress, Federal
    Research Division, 1990.
http://lcweb2.loc.gov/frd/cs/yutoc.html

Zaire

Meditz, Sandra W. and Tim Merrill. *Zaire, a Country Study.* Washington, DC: Library of Con-
    gress, Federal Research Division, 1993.
http://lcweb2.loc.gov/frd/cs/zrtoc.html

Notes

Notes

Notes

Notes

Notes

NOTE: BEFORE OPENING THE DISC PACKAGE, CAREFULLY READ THE TERMS AND CONDITIONS OF THE FOLLOWING COPYRIGHT STATEMENT AND LIMITED CD-ROM WARRANTY.

Copyright Statement

This software is protected by both United States copyright law and international copyright treaty provision. Except as noted in the contents of the CD-ROM, you must treat this software just like a book. Just as a book cannot be read by two different people in two different places at the same time, neither can the software be used by two different people in two different places at the same time. However, you may copy it into a computer to be used, and you may make archival copies of the software for the sole purpose of backing up the software and protecting your investment from loss.

Limited Warranty

SR BOOKS warrants the physical compact disc enclosed herein to be free of defects in materials and workmanship for a period of sixty days from the purchase date. If the CD included in your book has defects in materials or workmanship, please call SR BOOKS at 1-800-772-8937, 9am to 5pm, Monday through Friday, Eastern Standard Time, and SR BOOKS will replace the defective disc.

The entire and exclusive liability and remedy for breach of this Limited Warranty shall be limited to replacement of the defective disc, and shall not include or extend to any claim for or right to cover any other damages, including but not limited to, loss of profit, data, or use of the software, or special incidental, or consequential damages or other similar claims. In no event will SR's liability for any damages to you or any other person ever exceed the lower of the suggested list price or actual price paid for the license to use the software, regardless of any form of the claim.

SR BOOKS SPECIFICALLY DISCLAIMS ALL OTHER WARRANTIES, EXPRESS OR IMPLIED, INCLUDING BUT NOT LIMITED TO, ANY IMPLIED WARRANTY OF MERCHANTABILITY OR FITNESS FOR A PARTICULAR PURPOSE.

This agreement constitutes the entire agreement between the parties relating to the use of the Product. The terms of any purchase order shall have no effect on the terms of this Agreement. Failure of SR BOOKS to insist at any time on strict compliance with this Agreement shall not constitute a waiver of any rights under this Agreement. This Agreement shall be construed and governed in accordance with the laws of the State of Delaware.

NO TECHNICAL SUPPORT IS PROVIDED WITH THIS CD-ROM.

NOTE: BEFORE OPENING THE DISC PACKAGE, CAREFULLY READ THE TERMS AND CONDITIONS OF THE FOLLOWING COPYRIGHT STATEMENT AND LIMITED CD-ROM WARRANTY.

Copyright Statement

This software is protected by both United States copyright law and international copyright treaty provision. Except as noted in the contents of the CD-ROM, you must treat this software just like a book. Just as a book cannot be read by two different people in two different places at the same time, neither can the software be used by two different people in two different places at the same time. However, you may copy it into a computer to be used, and you may make archival copies of the software for the sole purpose of backing up the software and protecting your investment from loss.

Limited Warranty

SR BOOKS warrants the physical compact disc enclosed herein to be free of defects in materials and workmanship for a period of sixty days from the purchase date. If the CD included in your book has defects in materials or workmanship, please call SR BOOKS at 1-800-772-8937, 9am to 5pm, Monday through Friday, Eastern Standard Time, and SR BOOKS will replace the defective disc.

The entire and exclusive liability and remedy for breach of this Limited Warranty shall be limited to replacement of the defective disc, and shall not include or extend to any claim for or right to cover any other damages, including but not limited to, loss of profit, data, or use of the software, or special incidental, or consequential damages or other similar claims. In no event will SR's liability for any damages to you or any other person ever exceed the lower of the suggested list price or actual price paid for the license to use the software, regardless of any form of the claim.

SR BOOKS SPECIFICALLY DISCLAIMS ALL OTHER WARRANTIES, EXPRESS OR IMPLIED, INCLUDING BUT NOT LIMITED TO, ANY IMPLIED WARRANTY OF MERCHANTABILITY OR FITNESS FOR A PARTICULAR PURPOSE.

This agreement constitutes the entire agreement between the parties relating to the use of the Product. The terms of any purchase order shall have no effect on the terms of this Agreement. Failure of SR BOOKS to insist at any time on strict compliance with this Agreement shall not constitute a waiver of any rights under this Agreement. This Agreement shall be construed and governed in accordance with the laws of the State of Delaware.

NO TECHNICAL SUPPORT IS PROVIDED WITH THIS CD-ROM.

ISBN 0-8420-2864-1

9 780842 028646

90000 >